Literary Optics

Middle East Studies Beyond Dominant Paradigms
Peter Gran, *Series Editor*

Select Titles in Middle East Studies Beyond Dominant Paradigms

Artisan Entrepreneurs in Cairo and Early-Modern Capitalism (1600–1800)
    Nelly Hanna

The Large Landowning Class and the Peasantry in Egypt, 1837–1952
    Raouf Abbas and Assem El-Dessouky; Peter Gran, ed.;
    Amer Mohsen with Mona Zikri, trans.

Minorities and the Modern Arab World: New Perspectives
    Laura Robson, ed.

Native Tongue, Stranger Talk: The Arabic and French Literary Landscapes of Lebanon
    Michelle Hartman

The Persistence of Orientalism: Anglo-American Historians and Modern Egypt
    Peter Gran

Pragmatism in Islamic Law: A Social and Intellectual History
    Ahmed Fekry Ibrahim

The Shi'ites of Lebanon: Modernism, Communism, and Hizbullah's Islamists
    Rula Jurdi Abisaab and Malek Abisaab

Unveiling the Harem: Elite Women and the Paradox of Seclusion in Eighteenth-Century Cairo
    Mary Ann Fay

For a full list of titles in this series,
visit https://press.syr.edu/supressbook-series
/middle-east-studies-beyond-dominant-paradigms.

Literary Optics

Staging the Collective in the Nahda

Maha AbdelMegeed

Syracuse University Press

This book will be made open access within three years of publication thanks to Path to Open, a program developed in partnership between JSTOR, the American Council of Learned Societies (ACLS), University of Michigan Press, and The University of North Carolina Press to bring about equitable access and impact for the entire scholarly community, including authors, researchers, libraries, and university presses around the world. Learn more at https://about.jstor.org/path-to-open/

Copyright © 2024 by Syracuse University Press
Syracuse, New York 13244-5290

All Rights Reserved

First Edition 2024

24 25 26 27 28 29   6 5 4 3 2 1

For a listing of books published and distributed by Syracuse University Press, visit https://press.syr.edu.

ISBN: 978-0-8156-3827-8 (hardcover)
      978-0-8156-3828-5 (paperback)
      978-0-8156-5701-9 (e-book)

Library of Congress Cataloging-in-Publication Data

Names: AbdelMegeed, Maha, author.
Title: Literary optics : staging the collective in the nahda / Maha AbdelMegeed.
Description: First edition. | Syracuse, NY : Syracuse University Press, 2024. |
    Series: Middle East studies beyond dominant paradigms | Includes
    bibliographical references and index.
Identifiers: LCCN 2023034681 (print) | LCCN 2023034682 (ebook) |
    ISBN 9780815638278 (hardcover) | ISBN 9780815638285 (paperback) |
    ISBN 9780815657019 (ebook)
Subjects: LCSH: Arabic literature—19th century—History and criticism. |
    European literature—Influence.
Classification: LCC PJ7538 .A23 2024 (print) | LCC PJ7538 (ebook) |
    DDC 892.709009/034—dc23/eng/20231206
LC record available at https://lccn.loc.gov/2023034681
LC ebook record available at https://lccn.loc.gov/2023034682

The authorized representative in the EU for product safety and compliance is Mare Nostrum Group B.V.
Mauritskade 21D, 1091 GC Amsterdam, The Netherlands
gpsr@mare-nostrum.co.uk

To Radwa Ashour
&
To Wa3oodi

Contents

Preface *ix*

Acknowledgments *xi*

Note on Translation and Transliteration *xiii*

Introduction
Setting the Stage 1

1. The Literary Optic 20

2. *Khayal*
   Literature as a Theater of History 73

3. Excavating *Athar*
   History through Objects, Traces, and Stage Props 104

4. History's Actors and the Collective Sovereignty of *al-Nas* 139

5. Literature as a Political Problem 181

   Epilogue 203

   Notes 209

   Bibliography 255

   Index 271

Preface

In the spring of 2010, I summoned up all of my courage and made a phone call to Radwa Ashour asking for graduate school advice. It was the suggestion of Hend Ashour, her niece and my close friend. "Send me something in writing. It'd be better, don't you think?" Sweet, to the point, the call took about two minutes. In less than twenty-four hours, we were speaking again. The conversation was long, intense, and enjoyable—we discussed everything! As we were hanging up, I was scrambling to write down the names of an author and his book—names that felt really slippery and difficult to remember at the time. Radwa insisted that they were crucial for my questions. These were the only times I ever spoke with Radwa, but they were enough to set off a decade-long journey with Muhammad al-Muwaylihi and his *hadith 'isa ibn hisham,* and enough for me to always think of Radwa as a mentor, partner, and friend.

The project started as an effort to rethink the rise of modern Arabic literature, capitalizing on social history's and world literature's critical revisionist energies. My interest did not lie necessarily in the production of an alternative historical narrative. Rather, I was moved by a vague sense that the potential for radical change and intervention in the present was arrested by varieties of melancholic nostalgia and defeated anger at inheriting an incomplete, failed, or defective modernity. These visions overcrowd contemporary discourse in Arabic. As if a birth defect, seemingly specific to Arab modernity, has marked it since its inception during *al-nahda*—or perhaps it was a curse that destines it to cyclical repetitions of a failed or betrayed moment of origin. In the process, the present is usurped as just another performance of an already known cycle—a repetition of a failed moment of origin.

2011 heightened the stakes. These questions were no longer just at the core of a deep intellectual interest, but they seemed to me to be part of a pressing need to *turn* to face the present. This research, then, is an attempt to respond to a call to learn *how* to read: both through watching collectives venture to rip open a horizon foreclosed by an arrested present, and through realizing how our failures to read, name, and trace intellectually the social form of collective action could contribute to *new* defeats. As a result, questions of reading and literary form have taken on added urgency and dimensions for this work.

How would one read this ostensible moment of origin (i.e., *al-nahda*) without reproducing its cyclical temporality? Asked otherwise, what mode of reading could be carved out of a different engagement with the present? What are the conditions of possibility of such an engagement, and how might one name it? These are some of the questions I grapple with in this book. Consequently, my primary aim is not to shed light on a little-known historical fact, or to bring to attention the singularity of a text that would shatter long held claims. The focus is on confronting the methodological and theoretical assumptions forging an impasse in the present. Yet what is offered here is not a move beside history toward methodology, but an attempt to show how a critical methodology of reading could *become* history. The thought punctuates the structure of the book.

Acknowledgments

Nineteenth-century authors writing in Arabic, like many before them, often begin their books with an appeal to an unnamed group of friends who urged them to publish their work—which had hitherto existed either in manuscript form or as a series dispersed in journals of the day. Faced with this incessant demand, authors claim that they, somewhat reluctantly, had to accede. Unlike them, there is no unnamed collective propelling me to hesitantly share this work, but, every bit like them, my voice is woven through with the voices of others; some of them will be encountered in the body of the text or in the footnotes, and others I want to take a moment to name and thank.

From my time at the American University of Cairo: Mona Ibrahim, Wafaa Wali, Nathaniel Bowditch, William Melaney, and Nelly Hanna were profoundly generous mentors. I continue to draw inspiration from my encounters with each one of them.

In London, I was incredibly lucky to meet so many amazing teachers-friends: Tareq al-Rubei, Faisal Hamadah, Chanokporn Chutikamoltham (a.k.a. Nok), Angela Becher, Priyanka Basu, Peter Hill, and the numerous veterans of Room 301. Leyla Azizova's and Clare Fickling's friendship, and our tradition of five-minute updates, were a source of immense joy. Rachel Harrison's incredible sharpness coupled with her radical kindness continue to inspire me. Stephen Quirke's brilliance and effortless modesty taught me more than he knows.

EUME (Forum Transregionale Studien) was the home for the first attempts to think these ideas as a book, and I am indebted to the warmth and space I was given there and to Georges Khalil for his readiness to welcome diverse projects and people.

Nada Ramadan, Hend Ashour, Shaimaa Moustafa, Yassmin Atef, Hesham Ashour, Hanine Omari, Yomna Ali, Amira Mhadabi, and Betty Rosen, my close friends, have all patiently listened to me as I tried to disentangle, and weave anew, the early threads of the ideas of this book. In listening patiently and sharply and in being who you are, you have deeply contributed to my thinking.

Michael Allan and Zeina Halabi, each in their own way, have been a force of good in my life; they appear deus ex machina and, just like that, my problems disappear.

Meeting the *indubitable* Rasha Chatta and Alexandria Milton ("Darmok"; the one who speaks in metaphors) is one of the best things that have happened to me; I am profoundly grateful that you are just *here*.

My family, my parents: Bahaa and Karima, my brother: Muhammad, Sarah Doebbert-Epstein, Aunt Gwyn and Uncle Rich, B&B (a.k.a. Mahmoud al-Batal and Kristen Brustad), and Ayman el-Desouky are my home.

Waad Ramadan, I miss you dearly, but I am grateful that I still feel your presence, and, like you, I will always feel fortunate to have witnessed 2011 and its complex and painful aftershocks, which we still inhabit. My sincerest thanks go to people I do not know . . . though I am still struggling to figure out how that appreciation may be lived . . .

Note on Translation and Transliteration

I have opted for using extant English translations of Arabic texts whenever possible. However, since many of the nineteenth-century texts I read are yet to be translated in full, I offer my own translations. In transliterating words from Arabic, I have opted for a simplified form of the IJMES system. I do not use diacritics for long vowels, but I do maintain the (') for *'ayn* and (') for hamza.

Literary Optics

Introduction

Setting the Stage

To study nineteenth-century Arabic literature is to come into direct confrontation with the problem of historicizing both modern Arabic literature specifically and Arab modernity more broadly. Previous scholarship has not unriddled this problem, either in the form of first-generation literary histories tinged by shades of modernization paradigm, or second-generation approaches inflected by poststructuralism. Despite the vast differences in their aims and approaches, both of these theoretical positions have engaged with—and, in the process, transformed without thoroughly undoing—the already existing challenge posed by "the trope of the encounter."[1]

The trope of the encounter does not solely present itself as an outcome of the centralization of the so-called encounter between Europe and its others in particularized analytic instances, and, by extension, it does not disappear by virtue of deemphasizing it either via analytic maneuvers or through selecting an earlier historical moment from where to begin the analysis. Rather, it is often firmly established as an inner constituent of the object of knowledge itself, since the latter is arguably forged through the encounter. In the case of modern Arabic literature, this is most palpable in the persistence of the long-standing conviction that nineteenth-century Arabic literature can be studied through the meticulous scrutinization of the encounter between traditional Arabic narrative forms and incoming modern European ones, which is not only assumed to condition the emergence of the rise of modern Arabic literature but also to take place inside the texts themselves—that is, *inside nineteenth-century*

Arabic literature as an object of knowledge.[2] This condition is what I describe as the challenge of the trope of encounter: it cuts at the core of the possibility of historicizing, frustrating it while demanding that literary analysis respond to a reticent historical enquiry that probes into the "origins" that are, then, organized in a narrative of perpetual though often unfulfilled rise or excavate for in search of the present's obscured infrastructure.

To make the point more forcefully: I understand the problem posed by the trope of the encounter to be not the result of some peculiar specificity of the historical trajectory of Arabic literature or modernity—in this case, the actual occurrence of the encounter and, later, of direct colonialism—but the product of a specific history of, and approach to, knowledge production.

The challenge is further amplified by the implication of nineteenth-century literature with *nahda* as the intellectual movement through which modern Arabic literature arises, as well as the period in which the foundations of Arab modernity are laid down. *Nahda* (which is predominantly rendered in English translation as "renaissance," "awakening," and, to a lesser extent, "enlightenment") names a broad movement for reinvigorating Arab culture—either as part, however distinct, of the Ottoman sphere, or in opposition to it. Simultaneously, it names the period in which this movement takes place. *Nahda* is conventionally periodized as beginning in 1798—the date of the Napoleonic invasion of Egypt and Syria (1798–1801), echoing the trope of the encounter mentioned above. Alternative schemas loosely locate its beginning in the second half of the nineteenth century. Its end date is equally contentious, hovering between the beginning of World War II and the present, particularly as the challenges the *nahda* posed and the specific forms in which they were encoded are presumed to persist.[3]

The entwinement between *nahda* and nineteenth-century Arabic literature has granted the latter a foundational status as the early beginning of (literary) modernity in Arabic. In the process, these perceived early examples of modern literature came to be construed as manifestations of the encounter on the level of form. The move reproduces the trope of the encounter not as a historical narrative, but as an inner constituent of the form of these texts, and, by extension, of *nahda*, and of (literary) modernity in Arabic. Consequently, the trope of the encounter has been simultaneously critiqued to the point of near annihilation as a narrative while the centrality of the ideas of the formal encounter have been maintained as a "fact" that needs to be addressed and explained, which ultimately implicitly reproduces the trope not in its triumphalist overtones, but as a tragedy of separation between "traditional Arabic" and "modern European" that beleaguers Arab modernity.

This tension between critique and reproduction is not exclusively owed to dominant trends within the field of literary studies, but is equally susceptible to the mechanisms for producing hegemony. The latter process does not take place either simply "inside" (be that the scholarly field or the Arabic-speaking world) or outside, but through their complex articulation. Put differently, there is no location—be it disciplinary or geographic—where the effects of the trope of the encounter could be assumed to simply desist on their own. There is, however, the possibility for carving out positionalities from where it could be confronted. Let's pause to unpack this thought.

At least two mercurial difficulties lie at the heart of the study of nineteenth-century Arabic literature. The first pertains to naming, in the wake of accurately conceptualizing, the objects and phenomena we study, while the second seeks to capture and describe rhythms of historical processes enframed and experienced by the named objects and phenomena. These latter rhythms include both the motions through which what exists is reproduced as well as transformed, often through the very same process. Furthermore, the second difficulty also deals with radical transformation to the point of utter eradication or to the extent of the emergence of the "new": what is in need of a name. Clearly, these two difficulties are inseparable. To name something in contradistinction to other things is to give it not only its identity but also the potentiality of a history, and vice versa.[4]

For the study of nineteenth-century Arabic literature, names and rhythms have, to date, been subtended by uneven comparisons that grapple with the history of modern Arabic literature (its rhythms and names) through thinking them with and against other cases—predominantly modern English and French literatures. To these (often implicit) comparisons, we owe some of the broad generalizations about the distinctions between traditional Arabic forms and modern European ones. For example: Arabic is predominantly episodic, whereas European is teleological, with the latter focusing on individual subjects and their interiorities while the former has a more social and collective emphasis. These generalizations periodically resurge in heated apologia for Arabic literature and its alternative modernity, or in debates concerning world literature and distinctions between first and third world literatures—with Arabic being part of third world literature.[5]

It might be helpful to flesh out this dual challenge, and its underpinning comparative move, by surveying the ways in which it manifests within the study of nineteenth-century Arabic literature itself. I do not aim at exhaustiveness here, nor do I propound to offer a genealogy of the field. Rather, my goal is to give a sense of how these broad issues that have been described rather abstractly are instantiated across different approaches to Arabic literature and scales of its study and to show how, in so doing, we can see the persistence of the challenges facing us. While there are numerous examples to focus on, we will direct our attention to two seminal names-rhythms: the novel, and the *nahda*. These allow us to better see the triangulation between the form of nineteenth-century Arabic literature, *nahda*, and (literary) modernity in Arabic alluded to earlier.

The question of what a novel is—and, by extension, when novels began to be written in Arabic—is foundational to the field. Both Samah Selim and Mohamad-Salah Omri have contributed comprehensive critiques of what Omri describes as an "over-valorization" of the novel, which, in this instance, does not solely name a genre of literary practice but stands as an emblem of a host of other transformations associated with the achievement of modernity, which is here construed as a status.[6] In other words, to ask what a novel is and whether there are novels in Arabic was, for a long time, to enquire if Arab societies are modern or not before it later transformed into an exploration into the specificity, usually shortcomings or failures, of that modernity. The role played by the intersection of nationalist and Orientalist historiographies in both overemphasizing the importance of the novel and obstructing its study is both well documented and well analyzed and was, in fact, a crucial benchmark for solidifying the turn away from the old genealogical approaches. Yet, in revisiting the questions surrounding the novel, the following discussion does not directly engage the influential critiques directed at first-generation literary histories. Instead, it sketches the ways in which these questions around the novel in Arabic are particularized renditions of what I have referred to as a methodological challenge facing historical thinking in the wake of the reproduced trope of the encounter.

The labyrinthine debate on the Arabic novel—whose history is coextensive with, and has often been rendered the same as, the history of modern Arabic literature as a field of knowledge production—can be schematized in this manner: it offers a continual replay of the interpermeation between the formation of the object of knowledge (modern Arabic literature) and the thinking of the history through which this object comes to emerge as an object of knowledge (the history of modern Arabic literature). In other words, modern Arabic literature is the name that enframes a series of movements through which this name (i.e., modern Arabic literature) came to exist and in the process "exorcised" some of these rhythms out of itself and kept others—either as traces or as discursive performances. This dynamic is exclusive neither to Arabic literature nor to literature at large.[7] Even the concentration on the novel and the marginalization of other genres is a trait shared with the study of other modern national literatures. The comparative tendencies, despite their overpowering geopolitical overtones, are also part of an uneven process of abstracting Literature, across and through its varied historical instances, as a singular object of knowledge.[8]

To put it differently, the debates on the Arabic novel constitute one specific site for grappling with the relationship between the object of knowledge and its temporality. Yet what is confounding about this site—the Arabic novel and the study of the history of modern Arabic literature more broadly—is the proclivity of this methodological challenge at the heart of historical thinking to be perpetually masked as *a problem of the historical context* itself. As a result, the question of historical method is overwritten precisely at the moment when it seems to emerge—that is, when a historical explanation is demanded. Consequently, the possibility for historicizing is precluded by the elision of questions of method while the demand for a response to an unposed historical inquiry is sustained.

6 Literary Optics

The tragedy of separation seemingly at the heart of Arab modernity may be less of a "fact" that needs to be addressed than a particular dominant vision produced and reproduced through radical dehistoricization. This point can be further explained by turning to our second name-rhythm: *nahda*, revisiting Samah Selim's significant engagement with the history of the field in her latest work.

To begin at the end, I argue that this tension between the demand for a historically specific analysis and the collapse of its necessary ground is the most durable and profound effect of the trope of the encounter, through which this transference from method to historical context is shrouded in facticity, unceasingly presenting us with "context" as a precritical fact that may thereupon be confronted critically. In the process, the directions and limits of critique are curtailed because the trope of the encounter is both overwritten as a narrative and its facticity is reproduced and enshrined as an inner constituent of the object of knowledge.

Selim's book opens by registering the persistent challenges in defining *nahda* as a historical period, traditionally coinciding with the long nineteenth century:

> In Western and Arab accounts throughout most of the last century, the term was often defined by analogy: the modern Arab "renaissance" or "awakening" instigated by the "dramatic encounter" with Europe in the nineteenth century and left at that. In the Arab world, the 1970s and 1980s witnessed an intense interest in revisiting this historical moment on the part of critical theorists from North Africa to Syria, propelled by the Arab military defeat of 1967. More recently, in the wake of postcolonial studies, an entire field that can loosely be described as *"nahda studies"* has emerged, primarily in American academia, a vibrant interdisciplinary field which includes important scholarship in intellectual and cultural history, urban studies, literary studies, gender studies and translation studies. *Throughout these shifting engagements, there is a striking continuity in the way in which the term nahda marks a foundational cultural problem, in the sense of a difficulty, a puzzle or predicament.* This is the problem of Arab modernity as simulacrum or failure or trauma, a problem where the terms of engagement between a tragically renascent Arab subject and Europe are staged in a kind of melodrama

of domination and affliction, and where mimicry, ambivalence, anxiety and defeat (and I might add a certain *innocence* in the face of domination) are alternatively or concurrently proposed as analytical keys with which to unlock the problem of *nahda*.[9]

In this quote, Selim notices that despite the dramatic shifts in the approaches to *nahda* and the theoretical language through which it is spoken, the term consistently delineates a "foundational cultural problem." To draw more explicit conclusions, we can say that *nahda* does not primarily refer to a period of time, nor is it merely the name of an intellectual movement. Rather, *nahda* is a position in contemporary thought itself, one that enables the emplotment of the historical trajectory of the present in vocally melodramatic terms, as Selim herself points out. At its core—and with no small risk of presenting an overly schematic view—the ostensible cultural problem lies in the apparent incommensurability between name and object; therefore, we have novels that are not really novels and modern literature that is not really modern, and not entirely literary. As such, the task is to explain the process through which the name and object were severed. Therefore, to study *nahda* is to *explain* this severing in a historical overtone.

Different studies demarcate divergent sites as the "origins" of this problem, locating its source in the imposition of a conceptual language, its attendant metaphysics never fully in sync with local practice, in the wake of capitalist modernity; alternatively, they trace the origins to the incomplete or failed transformation to capitalist modernity.[10] While these interpretations have pronouncedly different stakes, we are concerned here with the fact that the question being responded to is not just shared but is already institutionalized as *the* question. As a result, critique is largely restricted to *the stance* one takes vis-à-vis the unearthed historical processes explaining the dissonance between name and object. In other words, one could take one of several stances vis-à-vis the *nahda*. Yet these stances follow from approaching *nahda* either as a moment of dissonance, or as the name of a foundational cultural problem.[11] Looked at through our lens, we can say that *nahda* names a position in contemporary thought that enfolds the history of Arab modernity into the trope of the encounter.

In the process, the history of *nahda* becomes equated with the drama (or, in Selim's words, melodrama), that unfolds in the wake of the encounter. The implications of subsuming the *nahda* within the trope of the encounter typically encompass the entirety of Arab modernity, since the *nahda*—and the nineteenth century more broadly—is marked as "at once the moment of origin and origins of Arab modernity."[12] This historical imaginary propels a mode of engaging the present by returning to its foundational origins: the *nahda* (which explains the intensification of revisiting this moment in the wake of the 1967 defeat mentioned by Selim and using different terms in the aftermath of the Iranian revolution in 1979).

The rise of modern Arabic literature is both the product of this process, of the drama that unfolds in the wake of the encounter, and a lens through which to view the drama that grows out of the encounter. Per this perspective, nineteenth-century Arabic literature occupies a foundational position in determining the specific literary, discursive, and ideological forms for registering this drama from the vantage point of literature. The persistence of the long-standing conviction that nineteenth-century Arabic literature can be studied through the meticulous scrutinization of the encounter between traditional Arabic narrative forms and incoming modern European is, then, a result of the assumption that this split or separation is how the drama of the encounter is registered by the form of Arabic literature.

The view is far from unique to modern Arabic literature. The debates on world literature theory, in particular the strands that loosely base their discussions and methods on world-system theory, have elevated this separation to the status of the law of world literature. World literature—here, primarily the novel as the quintessentially modern genre—is argued to be born in the throes of the encounter between local and foreign form (with local context added into the mix). The result is a fracture in form that is, then, mitigated through narrative voice. The English and French novels are deemed the sole exceptions to this law. In light of our discussion, what these debates discover is less the law of world literature than evidence that the effects of the trope of the encounter seep across the different national literatures and how we think their history as well as across units and scales of literary analysis.[13]

What I am proposing in this book is to turn our critique to this very idea that there is in fact a severance or a split that needs an explanation—specifically, a historical explanation. This apparent split, I argue, is the product of the transference of the methodological challenge of historical thinking (how to historicize) into a problem of the historical context itself (be that how the conditions of the rise of world literature shape literature as an object of knowledge, or the supposed split between name and object ostensibly *specific to* Arabic). The result of this transfer is complicated: on the one hand, it obstructs historicization while incessantly demanding a historical explanation, and, on the other, it furnishes the "historical context" itself, the map from where we start and upon which we position our objects, by way of forging an ostensibly historical explanation. To put it simply, the trope of the encounter produces profoundly ahistorical histories that narrate the severance between name and object—which is the result of a problem in method and a particular form of ideological hegemony—as history itself. We can now go back to nineteenth-century Arabic literature, taking a closer look at how the trope of the encounter results in a challenge specific to literary analysis and to historicizing literature.

In assuming that one could study nineteenth-century Arabic literature through a careful dissection of the mixing between traditional Arabic forms and incoming modern European ones, what remains missing from this picture is the form of nineteenth-century Arabic literature itself. This obvious elision of the object one is supposedly historicizing (nineteenth-century Arabic literature) that stubbornly presents itself as the history of the excluded object (history of nineteenth-century Arabic literature as the history of the rise of modern Arabic literature) is a pithy example of what I have referred to as profoundly ahistorical histories produced by the trope of the encounter. Yet my argument that the form of nineteenth-century Arabic literature is eradicated at the moment of its supposed historicization might seem like an exaggeration, particularly since its form does in fact mix different narrative forms, genres, and techniques. Consequently, to study this mixture would appear to be to study the form itself—or, at the very least, parts of it. Moreover, key literary texts from the period seem to be themselves preoccupied with the encounter with Europe; their pages are filled with comparisons between the "East" and the "West."

Nonetheless, these points further support the argument of eradication rather than disprove it.

While, like many other literary texts, nineteenth-century Arabic literature draws on various forms, genres, and techniques—an issue that this book will study in detail over the coming chapters—dividing them between traditional Arabic versus modern European does not follow from this point. In fact, upon a closer look, one realizes that this dyad derives its explanatory power from the trope of the encounter itself, since neither traditional Arabic nor modern European have clear formal literary referents to which they point in these scholarly debates. Rather, this is a schema that allows for turning the form of nineteenth-century Arabic literature into a taxonomy of elements that can be categorized via this dyad and, in the process, gives the illusion of narrating the history of the rise of modern Arabic literature as the history of either the broadening or the supplanting of traditional Arabic narrative forms to include modern European ones. I cannot stress enough that the problem with this vision is not in its claim of influence or effect, but in its profound ahistoricity. To view this more clearly, I suggest that we reverse the direction in which we have been reading these assertions.

Thus far, we have (1) the form of nineteenth-century Arabic literature that is forged out of a mixture between (2) traditional Arabic forms and (3) modern European ones. These are our three nodes in thinking the history of this literary form. Another way of reading the matter is to say that the form of nineteenth-century Arabic literature is the position through which traditional Arabic narrative forms and modern European ones are postulated as opposed categories that are then mobilized to tell the "history" of the rise of modern Arabic literature as the history of their encounter. In this way, the form of nineteenth-century Arabic literature, much like the *nahda* in which it is written, is a position that enables enfolding history into the encounter. This is confirmed by the dissonance between the insistence on viewing these texts as "in-between" the modern and the premodern, connecting the two, and the continued lack in studies that connect nineteenth-century Arabic literature to what lies before it or after it. As the latter gap is methodological, it cannot be redressed just by expanding our corpus or enlarging our scale of analysis; instead, it necessitates confronting the trope of the encounter as a problem within literary studies, one that does not just shape our understanding of what is often described as "context," but that shapes our perception of literature (here, nineteenth-century Arabic literature) as an object of knowledge. In other words, it makes our texts appear to be riven between two different stable "forms"—though the latter are not so much forms as they are stand ins for self-enclosed opposed (cultural) identities.

The issue is most palpable in the fact that despite the insistence that these texts usher in modern Arabic literature, studies rarely divulge what they mean by this statement—or how they define modern Arabic literature—except that these texts "mix" both traditional Arabic and modern European. Furthermore, both elements of the dyad do not refer to specific features traced back to examples culled out from "traditional Arabic" or "modern European" literatures. Rather, they both refer to elements *within* the form of nineteenth-century texts, presenting what is ultimately a taxonomy as a chronology. If one were to analyze a similar "mixing" in a contemporary text, using this same taxonomical approach, the claim that this directly communicates something about chronological transformation, or transition, would seem far fetched. The seeming explanatory power of these literary taxonomies has its source in the trope of the encounter and the ensuing supposition of the analytic purchase of the notion of the formal encounter (though it could also include discourse and genre) within literary texts from the nineteenth century.

This substitution, presenting the taxonomical as chronology-cum-history, necessitates overwriting hundreds of years of literary practice in Arabic (specifically the so-called postclassical period, or otherwise the post-'Abbasid). In this way, any appearance of "classical" tropes is read as a sign of historical continuity with traditional Arabic forms that have been restricted to the examples drawn out of the classical period), rather than be seriously approached as a participation in a process of defining and canonizing traditional forms, unfolding within nineteenth-century texts.[14]

Put simply, while most scholarly engagements point to the historical significance of these works, which are in fact primarily studied from a historical lens, these engagements did not result in a thorough synchronic or diachronic analysis of this significance that can *tell history* or contribute a thoroughgoing literary reading. Thus, there is a claim to history and an elision of it through the same gesture.

This book is an experiment in confronting the trope of the encounter from the position of literary studies. *Literary Optics* returns to the usual suspects in the story of rise of modern Arabic literature, i.e., the canon of nineteenth-century Arabic literature. It accompanies its readers on a journey *inside* this canon's form, exploring not the provenance of its elements but *how* and *why* they are drawn together into a form. The decision to focus on the delimited canon of nineteenth-century Arabic literature, rather than expand it to include the more "marginal" texts, is deliberate. In engaging with the same body of works that has been central for our field, and that has therefore been heavily analyzed by the scholarship, I focalize the dramatic transformation that is brought about by simply desisting from using the trope of the encounter as an explanatory framework.

In relinquishing the trope of the encounter, readers will notice additional crucial shifts in both the questions *Literary Optics* brings to this canon as well as in its presentation of its reading of it. To begin with the questions, we desert the preoccupation with where these texts "fit" on a predrawn map of circulation of ideas, forms, and genres, and with that we let go of the assumption that these texts hold *the key* to the totality of modern Arabic literature, or that they explain the entirety of Arab modernity and its history—let alone that they hold the answers to the impasses in our present. In short, we forsake the explanatory framework provided by the trope of the encounter that already positions nineteenth-century literary texts in Arabic as the moment of origin of modern Arabic literature at the intersection of the dramatic encounter between Europe and its others. Instead, we turn to a fundamental, but often eluded, question, throwing it into sharp relief: What does literary practice in these texts tell us about how literature is conceptualized? With this, we turn away from the encounter, and the exchange, between Europe and its others as the predominant entryway into the literary world of this canon and turn toward the relationship between conception and practice. This move is a methodological maneuver that enables us to begin with a much simpler question about what literature is and does in this period, as it is perceived from the position of literary form itself.[15] In the process, we sidestep the entrenched assumption that this canon is riven between uneven dichotomies of name and object, or traditional Arabic forms and modern European ones.

Foregrounding the relationship between conception and practice, as it is viewed from the position of literary form, the arguments of this book unfold like a play in medias res. Readers are invited to envision themselves as inside the world of this canon, grappling with how and why its parts are drawn together and exploring the world that is created out of this process of weaving together. As a result, they will observe that the book does not try to position them vis-à-vis the canon by annexing genealogies, offering definitions of the period (the nineteenth-century *nahda*), or providing biographies of the authors and their assumed social or ideological positions. Whenever possible, I will provide readers with some of the extant information on these subjects in the footnotes and refer them to additional sources. However, I ask them to patiently resist the urge for more "context," assuming that in positioning this canon on an already drawn map we gain better knowledge of it or of our position in relation to it. I have already argued that this approach has in fact eradicated the form of the canon of nineteenth-century Arabic literature at its supposed moment of historicization. In bringing this canon to stand in front of us, as if on a stage, but without its long attendant explanatory framework, it might at first seem disorienting to be asked to enter the world of this canon without being told more about its "context." Yet this potential "disorientation" is not a lack that could be remedied by saying more, but an integral step in confronting that we do not actually know the form of this canon. This, then, is a precondition for asking questions that take steps toward discovering an alternative explanatory framework—a larger project of which *Literary Optics* is but one step.

Similarly, while I return to the usual suspects, I am not invested in arguing for these texts' foundational status from a new perspective. The preceding pages should have already made it clear that, even if one were interested in narratives of founding and canonicity, we do not know enough about the form of these texts to make assessments rooted in an actual study of form. While "canon" in this study refers to the position these texts have occupied in our field, I am not staking a claim for their place for literary practice in Arabic—a different undertaking than the one with which the arguments of this book engage, requiring a broader scope, necessitating the work here as a stepping stone, and, most importantly, requiring the relinquishment of the idea of "founding" and the entire temporal rhythm that comes with it.

The Canon, Its Authors, and the Coming Chapters

In the coming chapters, we will meet the following texts and their authors: Hassan Husni al-Tuwayrani's (1850–1897) "The Floral Publishing of the Eternal Eagle's Letters" (*al-nashr al-zahri fi rasa'il al-nisr al-dahri*, 1889); Muhammad al-Muwaylihi's (1858–1930) *hadith 'isa ibn hisham* (1898–1902, 1907, *A Period of Time*); Ali Mubarak's (1823–1893) *'alam al-din* (1881/2); Francis al-Marrash's (1835–1873) "The Forest of Truth" (*ghabat al-haqq*, 1865), and a couple of 'Abdallah al-Nadim's (d. 1896) sketches, with a particular focus on his 1881 "A Medical Council for a Person Infected by the Alien" (*majlis tibbi 'ala musab bil ifranji*).[16] Other characters from the nineteenth century will also feature, often bringing with them books and their authors that were written long before the nineteenth century. Yet the key canon is comprised of the texts just mentioned. I will present a brief synopsis.

Tuwayrani's "Floral Publishing" follows its protagonist, the Eternal Eagle (*al-Nisr al-Dahri*), on his journey back to his home, a fictive planet known as Kiwan. The Eternal Eagle, who appears to be an astronomer, has left his planet eons ago after his mentor decided to withdraw in the wake of the assassination of the second Rightly Guided Caliph, Omar ibn al-Khattab (d. 644, r. 634–44). In returning to his planet, he explores the changes it had undergone since he saw it last and engages in a series of conversations and debates with other characters, who are often the personifications of abstract virtues and whose form is sometimes human and at other times, like the Eagle, a celestial "bird." "Floral Publishing" first appeared serially in the pages of *al-insan* ("The Human") newspaper (1884–85), edited by Tuwayrani himself.[17] When the narrative was later collected in book form (1889), it did not include all of the episodes. While the text is prefaced with a promise to collect the rest later, the promise is never kept.

Muwaylihi's *hadith*, like Tuwayrani's "Floral Publishing," was also first published serially in *misbah al-sharq* ("Lantern of the East"), between 1898 and 1902 before being collected in book form (1907). The journal was founded by the Muwaylihis, father and son, and they also assumed the position of editor in chief, the father Ibrahim (1844–1906) first and later Muhammad, the author of *hadith*. The story follows two main characters who are also exploring history—this time, however, not the history of Kiwan, but of Cairo and, to a lesser extent, Paris: 'Isa Ibn Hisham, a modern-style writer by vocation, and Ahmed al-Manikli Pasha (1796–1862), a military leader in the army of Muhammad 'Ali Pasha (1769–1849, r. 1805–48), who, in *hadith*, is supposed to have come back from the dead. Returning half a century later, the Pasha goes on a journey to explore the history of the city he once knew, accompanied by 'Isa Ibn Hisham. Throughout the episodes, they spy on some characters and engage others in conversation.

Mubarak's *'alam al-din* is the journey of its eponymous character, who is a religious scholar at the famous mosque and educational institution Al-Azhar with his son Burhan al-Din. Together, the two accompany an unnamed English Orientalist on a trip through France, on the way to England, though the book concludes while they are still on the outskirts of Paris. The father and the English Orientalist are collaborating on a project to edit a book edition of Ibn Manzur's (1233-1312) momentous dictionary *lisan al-'arab* (The Language of the Arabs). Mubarak's *'alam al-din* is made up of a series of "Colloquies" (*musamarat*) in which the characters discuss what they see in Egypt and France on their way from one to the other. As in the other texts, they also encounter more characters with whom they converse.

Marrash's "Forest" uses the news of the unfurling civil war in America to stage a battle between a Kingdom of Light, Civilization, and Freedom against a Kingdom of Darkness, Barbarity, and Slavery. The narrative is framed as the daydream of its narrator, who dreams up a trial that follows from the victory of the Kingdom of Light during which the latter decides what to do with its captured enemies from the Kingdom of Darkness. The main characters are mainly the personifications of abstract virtues who are brought together to discuss how to better civilization and push it toward progress.

Finally, Nadim's "Medical Council" tells the story of a beautiful youth who flourished under the care of his people until strangers interfered, distracting his people away from him so that they may better control him. Stranded and left to the care of these strangers, the youth collapses in ruin, surrendering to a terrible illness that ravishes his body, until one of his people passes by, sees his horrible state, and calls on others for help.

My selection of texts closely mirrors this book's methodological maneuver in approaching nineteenth-century literary texts in Arabic: it is less dependent on the "contextual" links tying them together in the nineteenth century than it is on the accidental canonicity bestowed upon them by our field. To clarify, the arguments of this book do not begin from the foundational status of these texts, nor do they depart from the series of textual, filial, or institutional links bringing the writers together. Rather, we begin with a much simpler, and more peculiar, point that I have referred to as these texts' "accidental canonicity."

Each of these texts occupies a seminal position in the history of the rise of modern Arabic literature, and they are granted a similarly prominent role in the histories of journalism, education, and social and political thought.[18] The reading of Arab modernity has changed—from the modernization paradigm to the poststructuralist approaches—and, therefore, the assessment of the specific roles played by these texts has also shifted. Yet they have consistently maintained their seminal status for the project of Arab modernity, however the latter may be understood across the long history of scholarship in the field. Throughout this history, while each text has been approached as an example of the shared story of modernity, the texts themselves have remained isolated, as discreet examples that are contextually connected, but whose form is not looked at together. In this way, they offer us a ready corpus, an archive of sorts, that allows us to understand the history of our field (Arabic literature as one specific site of literary studies more broadly) and its underpinning assumptions. In beginning to undo the assumptions pertaining to the trope of the encounter, *Literary Optics* starts from this corpus without subscribing to the contextual and historical indices used to position it—not as a rejection of history, but of the dehistoricized history mapped out by the trope of the encounter, or what we can describe as the cartographic imaginary of modernity. This is most obvious in the way this book shifts from approaching each text as one instance of a broader, often largely already known, context toward experimenting with what it might mean to look at these texts together. We ask what the form of these texts can tell us about how literature is conceptualized.

In beginning with this question and methodological maneuver, I did not know if there were multiple concepts, one concept, or even something else entirely. What I did know is that without undertaking this experiment, whatever it may beget, the necessary ground for literary analysis and literary historicizing will continue to elude us. Grappling with the relationship between conception and practice, the coming chapters take off from what may at first appear to be a minor detail. Our canon is studded with passing references to optical devices: microscopes, telescopes, and spectacles. These often appear in conjunction with an appeal to theater or elements intimately related to it (stage, curtains, or actors) as well as to dreams and visions. The term *khayal* tends to make an appearance at these moments. While in our contemporary use *khayal* is the imagination—with a strong emphasis on its relationship to fictionality—the coming chapters show that, from the position of this corpus, it is perhaps best understood as capturing a "spectral" quality of the imagination. The spectral describes both a visual quality as well as a kind of motion of object, images, or thought.

Beginning by paying attention to this repeated association between optical devices, theater, dreams, and *khayal*, the chapters discover the key for reading the form of these texts, moving on an arc that reveals how literature is conceptualized as an optic for *making* history *visible*. Uncovering the literary optic, we come to see the seminal features of this canon's form—ones that have often been dismissed as vestiges of the encounter between traditional Arabic and modern European forms—to be deliberate literary techniques for making history visible. Thus, *Literary Optics* offers a literary explanation for why these texts are "episodic": they are comprised of self-enclosed scenes that could be reshuffled with minimal impact to their "loose" plot; characters seem to appear and disappear suddenly, and they "lack" a discernible psychological interiority; the texts read like direct social commentaries or pedagogic texts with a weak literary narrative. The following chapters trace why these features are actually necessary to the notion of making history visible that comes to define literature in this canon.[19]

In so doing, the book begins from a concern with "formal cohesion," asking how the common features of these texts constitute a particular literary form and literary ideology. The literary optic allows us to understand the way in which these texts are organized via a visual logic of unfolding whose ultimate object of visuality is history and whose narrative techniques are deeply inspired by theatrical ones. We, then, turn to face history, excavating its conceptualization in an intimate connection to ideas of civilizational progress. This takes us to the book's conclusion, with history's dual meaning as both a concept in its own right and an anonym for a political problem.

Thus, although, as a whole, *Literary Optics* seems to move on an arc from narrative to concept to politics, this arc exists within each single chapter. We draw out the concepts (the literary optic, history, and politics) through an engagement with narrative features. On the other hand, the concepts—and, by extension, the formal decisions—are undergirded by politics at every step. These connections (between narrative form, concept, and politics) are drawn out through the close reading of the aesthetic vocabulary deployed by and in these texts. I have already briefly mentioned *khayal*; we will also encounter *athar* ("visible trace"), and *al-nas* (the collective). I see these concepts as nodes in the language we need to learn in order to inhabit the world of these texts.

Consequently, I do not explain these terms as either traditional Arabic concepts or as translational equivalents. Rather, I disclose them as the language through which certain conceptual—and sociopolitical—problems could be rendered intelligible and therefore potentially solvable, or at least manageable. In other words, I approach these concepts as parts of a double relationality: on the one level they exist in relationship to a host of other concepts, and it is this connection that gives them their meaning. While some chapters focus on a key concept, we read it as part of a broader conceptual world and approach it as part of a continuum that we can access through this specific position. On the other level, this first conceptual relationality is also imbricated with a social continuum through which the seemingly "inner" conceptual logic is worked out. This is key not only in how concepts are treated here but also in connection with projecting an interiority to our canon that we step inside. As the chapters unfold, we will see this to be a methodological maneuver necessitated by confronting the trope of the encounter, but not rooted in the assumption of a solipsistic literary object.

Yet I wish to clarify here once again that by moving away from foregrounding the search for a translational equivalent, I am not assuming that the circulation of ideas did not take place. Instead, I claim that circulation needs to be analytically understood within the above double relationality instead of being placed as its prior ground—or as a preanalytic fact.[20]

The first chapter introduces the literary optic, delineating its relationship to history and alluding to its connection with empiricism and the avalanche of debates on cognition and epistemology in its wake. Each of the following chapters examines this relationship between the literary optic and history from a different angle, until we not only reveal what the conception of literature is and why the so-called episodic form is necessary but also uncover history and the specters it both summons and dispels, bringing us face to face with the sociopolitical core undergirding the conception of literature as making history visible.

Chapter 2 takes us further inside this canon, exploring how the literary optic is forged via narrative structure while chapter 3 remains within narrative structure, probing into what it tells us about the conception of history, the object of literary visualization. Chapter 4 confronts the specters of history, which brings us to concluding in chapter 5 with the sociopolitical "contradiction" that gives rise to this canon as simultaneously a resolution and intensified dramatization of it.

1

The Literary Optic

This chapter lays the groundwork for the argument that the form of nineteenth-century Arabic literature is organized via a visual logic of unfolding. The narrative form coheres predominantly not via a chain of causality (i.e., plot), nor through a chain of narration, where the different characters partake in telling tales or debating certain topics. Two wildly famous examples of "chain of narration" are *One Thousand and One Nights* and Geoffrey Chaucer's (d. 1400) *The Canterbury Tales*. The latter uses a pilgrimage as a loose frame for drawing different characters together, each of whom tells a story, whereas *Nights* employs a frame narrative that opens the paths for a series of stories by a host of storytellers who are all being "quoted" by the frame narrative's main storyteller. To these, we could also add al-Tawhidi's (d. 1032) *al-imta' wa al-mu'anasa* (The Book of Enjoyment and Bonhomie), where the characters meet for thirty-seven consecutive nights in the palace of the Vizier and converse on a topic or theme. Formal cohesion, in these cases, depends on the exchange of stories that is given within a loose frame such as travel and night gatherings. In contradistinction, chain of causality is taken to be symptomatic of modernity and its attendant novelization, through which external frames increasingly dissolve and are replaced by an inner structure of causation emanating from events and their effects.[1] While nineteenth-century Arabic texts appear to use combinations of the latter two approaches—hence their long-standing "transitional" status—the latter two, among other techniques, are ultimately subsumed by a visual logic that specifically aims at the visualization of history. The move is underpinned by the crystallization of literary truth around a concern with history. This chapter elucidates the triangulation of literature, history, and visuality that coheres the form of nineteenth-century Arabic literary texts.

"History," in this context, does not refer to the chronological emplotment of past events, nor does it engage in debating standards of veracity (e.g., how do we confirm that an event in the past took place, and what are the reliable sources for reporting about the past). Rather, history is primarily constituted by the narrative structure of this literary canon as the link between seemingly disparate events—be they contemporary or in the remote past—and the abstract universal principles governing civilizational progress. Consequently, the concept of history hovers between historicity as the recognition that all phenomena can be studied from within the prism of history because they are constituted through its dynamic and determining principles, and history as a diagnostic tool for discerning the degree to which the universal abstract principles are applied in specific instances—a view with grave hierarchal implications.[2]

Scientific empiricism is central for the above conceptualization of history as one that is split between event and principle. In fact, "history" and "science" consistently appear as two interlinked pivotal categories in our texts; therefore, they are critical for reconsidering truth from the position of literature, or what we can call literary truth.[3]

Science does not just encapsulate a set of discursive claims on rationality, impartiality, and certitude. More importantly, it indexes the increasing splitting of the world, on new grounds, since these splits were also common to metaphysical and idealistic visions, between the sensory and the cognitive, object and subject, in the wake of empiricism and the storm of debates it ushered in on evidence and truth. Science and the scientific method are entrusted with bridging these splits, between objects in the world and in our minds, and therefore between object and subject, to arrive at the universal principles underpinning natural phenomena. Similarly, history, as it appears from within this canon, navigates seemingly disparate events to reveal the laws of history, specifically the laws of civilizational progress, that govern "historical" phenomena. We will later discover that historical phenomena refer primarily to social phenomena. Thus, science and history are analogical: the first reveals the laws governing the natural world while the second uncovers those controlling the social one. The complex parallelism drawn between nature and society is a major theme that runs throughout the canon of nineteenth-century Arabic literature and will therefore peek through the chapters of this book, especially as we turn our attention to human nature, the site for the convergence of sociohistorical and scientific concerns.[4]

Yet, in engaging with "history" and "science," our focus remains on the way the narrative structure of this canon weaves them together to articulate a notion of literary truth, which interlaces science's concern with objects as they appear in the world versus how they appear in the mind, with history's preoccupation with the relationship between events and laws (of civilizational progress). The result is an ambitious project of embodying the abstract laws of history in the visible objects of sensory perception, rendering the abstract seemingly directly visible because it is written into every object and event. In this way, literature is implicated in the project of civilizational progress by rendering the latter's law(s) visible.

At the core of these debates on history, science, and literary truth lie a series of seismic shifts whose multifaceted genesis precludes the existence of a definitive moment, or location, of inception. Nonetheless, the canon of nineteenth-century Arabic literature offers us a position from which we can observe not the origins of these shifts, but their convergence from the perspective of literature with a concern with truth.

I see *khayal*, a term that flickers throughout this canon (much as it does throughout the history of Arabic literature and thought) as crucial for grappling with the quest for visualizing what lies between sensory embodiment and nonsensory abstract renditions. The term comes to acquire further layers in the nineteenth century, since the sensory and the abstract are now mapped onto the historical event and the abstract civilizational principles respectively (i.e., onto the quest for literary truth).

At its lexical core, *khayal* signifies an incorporeal, shadow-like form, a tricky "image" that is neither entirely embodied and sensory nor disembodied and abstract but rather lies somewhere between the two. As such, it has the potential to be implicated in a series of seamless cognitive processes that mediate—though they appear to be immediate—the relationship between the sensory and the abstract and words and image. This neither-nor status, between the sensory and its other with its powerful potential, is at the crux of the term's complex history across different knowledge-producing discourses in Arabic (to which we will turn shortly). Across these sites, *khayal* has oscillated between being the threshold of a highly affective and aesthetic mode of experiencing the world that could motivate actions in accordance with ethical dispositions on the one hand, and a risky distraction from truth on the other. The canon of nineteenth-century Arabic literature emplaces *khayal*'s neither-nor within a new set of epistemological concerns, experimenting with the ways in which the concept's combination of the sensory and the nonsensory can bridge their increasing disconnect (into sensory experiences and historical events, and into their driving abstract principles or laws) by making history visible in language. Put differently, the embodied visualization of the abstract law in objects and events takes place through an experience of language as it is organized into a narrative structure. Both the "sensory" and "nonsensory," "objects" and "law," are in this case created through an experience in language, via *khayal*. Consequently, making history visible is not restricted to a passive visualization; it is equally concerned with moving people into action in accordance with the truth made visible to them. Thus, the conception of literature in this canon is tightly entwined with a pedagogic or "reformist" agenda—the latter not reducible to what the texts say about a certain subject, but rooted in the conception of literature itself.

Consequently, this chapter begins with an exploration of the flickers of *khayal* in the canon of nineteenth-century Arabic literature, exploring their association with other gestures of visualization culled from science, theater, and literature. In deliberately deploying *khayal* to tackle questions of visualization, our canon taps into the long history of the term, reworking its contours and stakes. In so doing, it also creates a position from which a coherent conceptual history of *khayal* could retrospectively emerge.

I understand the connection between these flickers of *khayal*, both in the nineteenth century and before it, not through the prism of intellectual filiation (a concern with who read what) as much as through the lens of conceptual history, focusing on the series of concerns that have become encoded in *khayal* and that, as our discussion will go on to show, are not restricted to a specific intellectual or field, but have come to suffuse a variety of literary genres and practices in different ways. In this sense, whenever the term is called on and mobilized, it brings with it this history of possibilities that could be—and in fact is—rearticulated and reshaped, regardless of whether each writer/intellectual read the entire corpus of debates or not.

The preceding distinction between intellectual filiation and conceptual history is not absolute. In fact, every figure or genre I refer to throughout this book is one that we know was engaged in the nineteenth century—even though we do not always know which specific works or which particular versions of those works. Instead, the distinction is meant to draw our attention to the central point of this chapter and of this book more broadly: that the appearance of names, genres, or terms from other positions (temporal or geographic) does not in itself offer us sufficient clues to determine our form as a map of a series of influences or shifts from an originating point (whether we understand that analytically, chronologically, or even geographically). Instead, they allow us to further highlight the ground (i.e., the form) as a whole that holds these "clues" within a particular relationality that draws them together as parts of a whole. This will be most apparent in the fact that while I will present my reading of the conceptual history of *khayal* first, that reading is anchored in my analysis of how the term is mobilized by nineteenth-century texts, which we cannot fully grasp without sketching out the history of the concept. I present the latter neither chronologically nor through a series of filiations, but through a careful organization of the problems of the image hovering between the sensory and the abstract with which the term has come to be encoded throughout its long history.

Flickers in the Canon

In this canon, Marrash's "Forest" contributes the most distilled example of deploying *khayal*, because, throughout the narrative, it weaves an explicit, full web of relationalities connecting *khayal* to visualization, history, and literature. It specifically focuses on the term's relationship to theater, dreams, and history, an emphasis that we will uncover in other texts, too, though often with slight shifts in their configuration. Consequently, "Forest" offers us a portal into the world of *khayal*, providing us with a comprehensive background against which we can read the activation of specific threads of this web in the other texts studied here.

The narrative begins with the half-asleep narrator drifting into the world of what he describes as "*khayal* dreams" (*ahlam takhayyuliyya*). On the cusp of a dream vision, a "scene" (*mashhad*) is opened up, appearing to the mind's eye (*'ayun khawatiri*) of this unnamed narrator. In it, he witnesses the parade of great civilizations, one after the other, beginning with the Egyptians and Assyrians and culminating in the Roman Empire, which is further divided into the East and the West, which ostensibly linger until the narrator's present. Each new incoming civilization supersedes its predecessor in a great chronological march toward attaining ever more progress; this is history's great march.

In this scene, the "ghosts of the past eras play/perform" (*tal'ab fihi ashbah al-a'sar al-salifa*), coming into view from behind the "veils of the immortal histories" (*hujub al-tawarikh al-khalida*). Wanting to better see the scene that has opened up to his mind's eye, the narrator-protagonist dons his *nazzarat al-ikhtibar*, "spectacles of experimentation," the term suggesting not exactly a corrective device, but something more like a set of microscopes or magnifying glasses. Having put them on, two statements suddenly appear to him: "The intellect rules" (*al-'aql yahkum*), followed shortly by "Science/knowledge triumphs" (*al-'ilm yaghlib*). Overcome by these effervescent thoughts and emotions, the narrator finally gives in to sleep, and the "theater of dreams" emerges in front of his eyes (*infatah lada a'yuni marsah al-ahlam*). He views the performance of what is described in the text as a *khayal* dream. In fact, the first chapter is titled "The Dream," and it sketches a dream vision of history that will continue throughout the text.[5]

In the dream, the narrator sees himself hiding behind a tree, peeping, and eavesdropping on a debate, followed by a long trial that he watches like a performance on a stage. It is the trial that ensues in the wake of the Kingdom of Light's triumph in its war against the Kingdom of Darkness. The debate aims to decide on the best way to deal with the Kingdom of Darkness once and for all; its procedures follow a pattern that is similar to the great march of history, whereby one character after another expounds their vision for how to best deal with the Kingdom of Darkness. The central stage is given to the Philosopher, and it is in fact his long speech and the ensuing debate of it that take up most of the text. These series of discussions aim at delineating the harmonious balance through which civilizational progress could be attained.

In suggesting that this text reads like a play, I am not solely referring to the incessant appeal to theater, actors, stage, and curtains, but also to the narrative techniques themselves, which we will explore at length in the following chapter. For now, it suffices to mention just one example. When the leaders of the Kingdom of Darkness, now imprisoned by the Kingdom of Light, are made to stand trial, they come on stage, one by one, holding a placard that reveals their identity. This is one of the classic theatrical techniques through which characters disclose their identity; others include dialogue, where the characters reveal their relationships to one another via their mode of address, or a variety of stage props (icons, emblems, placards, or the reading aloud of letters in certain ways). These techniques are widely used in theater in general and are repurposed by this canon. Marrash activates varieties of these techniques in order to maintain the narrator's absolute externality to the narrative events by positioning him as a member of the audience, a spectator; at times, this is done quite literally.[6] This position robs the narrator of knowledge privileges that are often ascribed to narrators, a gap which is in turn redressed by relying on theatrical modes of sharing knowledge with the audience.

The text clearly does not elucidate what it means by *khayal* or how it uses the term. Rather, it allows us to see how the term is placed within a network whose other nodes are dreams, theater, and history. More explicitly, "Forest" positions *khayal* within the convergence of three central and overlapping gestures of visualization. The first is inspired by the long literary tradition of dream visions, often realized as a highly allegorical narrative wherein a poet recounts a dream. The dream vision enables the poet to give concrete form to abstract notions—hence the association of this literary device with allegory. For Marrash, the dream vision is used specifically to bring abstract notions, which are all connected to history and the abstract universal principles governing historical progress, to stand in front of the mind's eye. This gesture is sharpened by a second, scientific one that entails putting objects under spectacles (which here also seem to refer to optical devices in general that are meant to enhance one's perception of an object). This second gesture, then, allows the narrator to see the abstract principles (intellect rules, and science triumphs) undergirding the great march of history. *Khayal*, therefore, is associated with a dual gesture of bringing objects to stand in front of the mind's eye and placing them under optic devices to better see the nature of the object. In this case, what we perceive through the optic is not a concrete sensory object, but abstract principles that underpin myriad instantiations. The two gestures together bring forth a connection between the universal principles governing the great march of history and the particular examples (the Egyptians, the Assyrians, and the Romans) that embody those principles. There is a third, and final, gesture of visualization that is encapsulated in the appeal to theater: objects are put onstage and come to stand in front of an audience, the stage here being the forest itself. In "Forest," it is history—here as both the set of principles and their particular manifestations brought into equilibrium through debate—that is put onstage. These three gestures ultimately all converge as a frame that gives form to the narrator's tempestuous thoughts and emotions, turning them into objects that he can grapple with as if they are external objects that come to face him from the outside.

It is vital to note that I use "history" here as a placeholder for an even more elusive object of visualization that we cannot perceive now, but that will emerge gradually in the chapters to follow. For now, it is enough to think of history as the connection between particularized instances and abstract principle that literature seeks to visualize. We can map out the network woven through Marrash's mobilization of *khayal* in "Forest," noting history's criticality without assigning a precise connotation to it yet. *Khayal* is a rubric for three intersecting gestures of visualization that make objects appear to the mind's eye, places them under an optical device, and puts them onstage.

In "Forest," these three gestures have a single object; what appears to the narrator's mind's eye, what he puts his spectacles on to better see, and what he views on stage are all one and the same object—history. While each gesture clearly entails a slightly different relationship between the subject and the object and, as such, offers a different perspective through which the object appears, they are all necessary to enable seeing history.

Khayal encompasses the layering of these three gestures of visualization and marks them as precisely what is meant by the literary. In the opening scene of this text, we encounter *khayal* as a combination of three distinct but entwined gestures of visualization through which history is made visible, appearing in front of the mind's eye, placed under optical devices, and made to stand onstage all at once.

This network is not exclusive to Marrash's "Forest." It is similarly present in other key texts from this canon, although its evocation is not always as explicit nor as condensed into a single framing episode as it is here. This network is evoked in two more texts, Tuwayrani's "Floral Publishing" and Muwaylihi's *hadith*. Through these examples, we can discover the consistent link between *khayal*, these three gestures of visualization, and the task of making history visible that I argue comes to define what the literary is for this canon.

"Floral Publishing" begins with a poetic contemplation of time and history, drawing on tropes from the classical ode, particularly the iconic opening lines of the *muʿallaqa* of Imruʾ al-Qays, whose name is often synonymous with the origins of poetry in Arabic. Imruʾ al-Qays' poem memorably starts in medias res with the narratorial "I" of the poem pausing to lament over the ruins. The verses are quintessential founding examples of the lamentation of ruins as a central trope in Arabic poetry.[7] In Tuwayrani's text, the narrator, an astronomer, starts with a similar mourning of the passing of time before focusing his telescope on several celestial bodies, planets, and "birds" that he will encounter again during his journey to explore the history of the world.[8] Two of the main characters are an old sheikh who has deserted life and humans, residing in a cave since the assassination of the second Rightly Guided Caliph, Omar ibn al-Khattab (AD 586–644). The other is the Eternal Eagle, who has been traveling around different planets. Together, these characters embark on a journey, tracing historical changes starting from the present and going back in time. Ultimately, their attention is directed at the present, whose meaning is understood by resurrecting a temporal nexus.[9]

We can already discern crucial similarities with Marrash's opening scene. In "Floral Publishing," the lamentation of ruins, a literary trope with a long history, is evoked to give form to the affective turbulations the narrator-character feels. Much like dream visions, it becomes the literary vehicle through which these ineffable emotions can be externalized, made to face the narrator-protagonist as if they constitute an external object. In the process, they are given literary form that creates a narrative space within which the following events can unfold. In Marrash's text, this is both the narrator's mind as a space that we can access via the dream vision, and the Forest as a concretized version of the narrator's mind—the theater of his mind, so to speak. In "Floral Publishing," the narrator's mind is always already concretized in the ruins of Kiwan: the fictive idyllic planet whose current crisis, and its history, are the subject of the narrative. "Floral Publishing" excavates the history of the present of Kiwan.

As in "Forest," an optical device, a telescope, appears early on in "Floral Publishing"; unlike "Forest," theater is completely absent. However, *khayal* is present. The early pages of the text declare that the Eternal Eagle reports his encounters in letters, which he sends via the mail of *khayal* to whoever chooses to read them.[10] Even though the text is not framed as a play, there is a parallel emphasis on the visual, manifest in the use of pivotal terms such as telescope/glasses (*al-nazzara*), sight (*nazar*), and *khayal*.[11] They are parallel to the terms used by Marrash, and they exhibit a similar preoccupation with history (i.e., of Kiwan and its crisis). Consequently, from Marrash's comprehensive network, Tuwayrani focalizes both the externalization of what the narrator-protagonist experiences as placing things in front of the mind's eye (here through the mail of *khayal*, through Kiwan, and through the ode form) and the scientific gesture. The theatrical gesture, however, appears to be absent. Tuwayrani does not overtly mention it, but an assessment of whether it is maintained in his narrative structure requires analyzing narrative structure through this network, a task that we will take up in the following chapters. With the apparent elision of theater, dreams are similarly sidelined, though; as the above description suggests, their function is maintained through other literary devices, primarily the ode.

The entire narrative of Muwaylihi's *hadith*, like Marrash's "Forest," is framed as a dream had by the narrator-protagonist 'Isa Ibn Hisham. He told this dream to an anonymous group, and they are, in turn, recounting it to an unknown audience (this latter position is meant to be occupied by the readers of the text). The recourse to a chain of fictive narrators, or transmitters, through which the audience's direct access to the narrative is deferred is a stable feature of the *maqama*, a renowned classical narrative genre in Arabic whose invention is attributed to a single tenth-century author, Badi' al-Zaman al-Hamadhani (969–1008). The *maqama* is a short narrative characterized by its lavish, rhymed prose style (*saj'*) and burlesque themes and plots—particularly in its early phases. It enjoyed an enduring importance and continued to occupy a significant position among other narrative genres for more than ten centuries after its originator's death.[12] Hamadhani's original version is a series of autonomous episodes that generally feature two main recurring characters: the narrator, 'Isa Ibn Hisham, who is reincarnated by Muwaylihi to fulfill the same function in his nineteenth-century text, and Abu-l Fath al-Iskandari an ingenious, eloquent trickster. Muwaylihi's allusion to the first iteration of the *maqama* is explicit in that he adopts the name 'Isa Ibn Hisham for *hadith*'s main character and narrator, except that 'Isa of the nineteenth century is a writer by vocation, and his dream encompasses the entire narrative: it never ends, no one ever wakes up, and we seem to not exit the dream even with the abrupt conclusion of the book.

In his dream vision, 'Isa Ibn Hisham is walking in the cemetery, contemplating life and death, when he is struck by the resurrection of Ahmed al-Manikli Pasha (1796–1862).[13] The latter is an actual historical character and important figure in the military of Muhammad 'Ali (1796–1849, r. 1805–48). The uneasy exchange between 'Isa Ibn Hisham and the Pasha is followed by the latter's brush with modern legal institutions. As a result, Ibn Hisham feels responsible for showing the Pasha "the history of the present era." Consequently, their sojourn in Cairo, and, later, in Paris, is an investigation into "the history of the present era."[14]

The dream sets up the text as an exploration of the history of the present through traversing vignettes of the then-contemporary Cairo and Paris. In this opening scene, *khayal* is nowhere to be found, but it appears twice later. The first time is in the French capital, and this is the only time it is featured within the text.[15] The second is found in al-Muwaylihi's introduction to the first book version in 1907 in which the serialized episodes of 'Isa Ibn Hisham and the Pasha, which were originally published between 1898 and 1902, are bound into a single book.¹⁶ Since its Parisian manifestation is the sole reference to the term inside the text, it is also the older one, because the introduction was written for the book version, five years after the conclusion of the narrative's serialization. We shall begin with the more recent example before going to Paris.

To celebrate the publication of the first edition of the book, Muwaylihi dedicates it to all its readers, before specifying five people: his father, the writer and journalist Ibrahim al-Muwaylihi (1844–1906), who started his life as a silk trader (which was the family's business in Hijaz before they moved to Egypt); the mercurial reformist writer and political dissenter Jamal al-Din al-Afghani (1838–1897); the luminary religious scholar (Azharite) Muhammad Abduh (1849–1906), who left an indelible mark on modern thought in Arabic; Muhammad Mahmoud Amin Al-Shanqiti (d. 1904/5?), one of the leading masters of classical Arabic language sciences at the time and a close associate of Abduh and his younger contemporary Rashid Rida (1865–1935); and, finally, the famous poet and politician Mahmud Sami al-Barudi (1839–1904).¹⁷ He also includes an old letter that al-Afghani had written to him in which he praises the then-young Muwaylihi. Most significantly, *hadith*'s author pens what was to become a seminal landmark for the early critical reception of the text, and for the interpretations of the canon of nineteenth-century Arabic literature more broadly, and it is here that he evokes *khayal*.

In the introduction, Muwaylihi makes an emphatic yet cryptic assertion: his text is a truthful narrative, and, therefore, it corresponds to the actuality of things (*haqiqa*), even though it is presented in the form of the imaginary (*takhyil*) and the figurative (*taswir*). Muwaylihi insists that the text should not be read as engaged in the inverse movement—that is, it is not an imaginary (*khayal*) and figurative narrative made to appear as if it is an actual one. While this statement does not offer us a definition of *khayal* or what it is, it does tell us three things. The first is that *hadith* tells its story and, by extension, the history of the present, through *khayal*; the second is that *khayal* is intimately associated with the figurative; and, third, that there is a good and a bad way for telling history through *khayal*.¹⁸ Muwaylihi wants his readers to believe that his work definitely belongs to the "good" way for achieving this. Judging by this excerpt alone, it is of course difficult to ascertain if *khayal* moves within the same network we saw fully in Marrash, or in a more delimited way in Tuwayrani. It does, however, maintain a connection with the visual through the term's association with "*taswir*"—which clearly evokes a visual dimension—and it also upholds the pronounced preoccupation with history.

The second, earlier use of *khayal* tells us more. In Paris, the Pasha and 'Isa Ibn Hisham are introduced to the French political system by a French wise man whom they befriend, also referred to as "the Philosopher." In a crucial passage the Pasha turns his attention to "the president" as a manifestation of what strikes him to be a perplexing anomaly that he cannot explain except by resorting to *khayal*. The only way he can make sense of the role of the president is by drawing a complex link between striving for self-rule on the one hand, and the contradictions produced by representational politics as the tool for self-rule on the other. The Pasha ultimately criticizes the latter, arguing that it can only function through instituting the president, despite his political marginality from the Pasha's perspective. He dubs the process as "takhyil hukm al-malik." A rough literal translation of the phrase would render it as "the figuration/evocation of the image of the rule of the king."[19] But a more apt translation, one that wrestles with the conceptual stakes of the argument, could be phrased in this way: "The evocation of the specter of the rule of the king."

On the surface, this example seems to stand at a distance from the term's association with a trio of visualization gestures defining literature as the attempt to make history visible because it has a more palpable political concern rather than an obviously visual one. Upon a closer look, however, it can be seen as one of the most poignant examples of what it means to think of *khayal* as the core of the multifaceted gestures of visualization that help make history visible. The statement suggests that the president is actually nothing but the phantom of the king whose necessity emerges from the contradictions of politics that beget the present in both France and, in a different way, Egypt. In other words, the president is a visualization—or, better yet, simulacra—of the rule of the king. Bracketing the "content" of the criticism of, if not disdain for, this political system, what matters for us here is that *takhyil hukm al-malik* also ties *khayal* to a concern with visualization; specifically, it enables us to see the core of the processes governing the history of the present.

In evoking these processes, *khayal* clearly functions not as a simple image-for-image substitution that we might expect when we think of the debates on cognition and epistemology in the wake of empiricism (e.g., how we ensure the correspondence between the image in mind/image in world). Rather, *khayal* names a complex process of linking particular instantiations to their underpinning laws whereby the two are fused into a single "image." This fusion broadens the stakes of *khayal* beyond the cognitive, in the typical empiricist sense. Literary truth is not restricted to the correspondence between the portrayal within the text, and the world outside the text. Instead, it curates a visual experience that makes history visible, and, in the process, it injects affective and active dimensions—or, in one word, interventionist designs that hinge on aligning action with abstract principles. Consequently, *khayal*'s movement on an arc of cognitive, affective, and active is key to the conception of literature here and its ability to entwine the literary and the pedagogic (or social reform) through an arc of visualization, truth (as history), and action (in accordance with the abstract principles of civilizational progress).

Thus far, we have encountered *khayal* and dreams in Muwaylihi's narrative, though not always in the form of a neat frame for the beginning of the narrative, as it was in Marrash's "Forest." The same can be said of optical devices and micrographs that play a crucial role in the inversion of the text's plot but are not used in the framing of the text. Theater is also mentioned, as one of the contemporary entertainments surveyed by the Pasha and Ibn Hisham, and it seems to play a less crucial role than either *khayal* or optical devices.

What we know so far is that across these three texts *khayal* seems tied to a question of visualization that is characterized by unevenness in its discursive associations. While its connection with dreams, theater, and optical devices is clear in Marrash, the connections are not always played out in full in the discourse of the other texts. What we also know is that these texts always express an explicit concern for showing history. While what is entailed in showing history is not always explained to us from the outset, I want to suggest that on the level of narratological practice it is continuously linked with the convergence of these three gestures of visualization (making an object appear to the mind's eye, placing it under optical devices, and putting it onstage) that find their most explicit articulation in Marrash, but whose narratological practice is equally strongly present, though in different ways, across this canon. What we cannot yet perceive is what, if anything, links these various deployments of *khayal*. In order to look at this, we must turn to what the texts do with *khayal*, and how they intervene in its long conceptual history and imbue it with new stakes. The first step in this journey is to look back at this history. Toward this end, the next section offers a large brushstroke exploration of *khayal* that sets the stage for recognizing the far-reaching changes involved in aligning *khayal* and history as the definers of literary truth in this canon.

Working Out a Core Meaning

While *khayal* is a considerably well-studied concept in many of the fields in which it deploys, its full conceptual history remains elusive. The sheer richness of its semantic field, its expansiveness, and its constantly evolving nature tend to thwart attempts at fully grasping that history. Wolfhart Heinrichs contributes some of the most comprehensive work to date in exploring *khayal* across discourses of knowledge production. He contends that the iterations of the term are too distinct within each field in which it is mobilized, as well as within any one given field, to justify grappling with these myriad instantiations as related—a point that continues to be debated by scholars of premodern Arabic literary theory. In looking at *khayal*, from the position of our nineteenth-century canon, we are not in pursuit of an original meaning that anchors the different debates as their origin that the later discussions supposedly either reproduce or incrementally change. Rather, the aim is to look at some of the ways the term appears to function in diverse conceptual networks. We are confronted with the question of whether these appearances in diverse sites are related both in the nineteenth century and before it: I argue that they are, that the ways that *khayal* functions in these fields share certain potentialities that follow from the basic definition that I presented above (a shadow-like image that hovers between the sensory and the nonsensory).[20]

In my encounter with *khayal*, I am including its adjectival and verbal derivatives: *khayali, mukhayyila, takhyil, takhyiliyya, takhayyuliyya, khayyala, takhayyal,* and *takhayyul*. Looking back at the three short examples from the previous section, we can see that Marrash uses *khayal* and *takhayyuliyya,* Tuwayrani relies on *khayal* exclusively, and al-Muwaylihi moves comfortably between *takhyil* and *khayal* in the space of a couple of sentences. Later in the chapter, we will encounter Tahtawi's use of *khayali,* Mubarak's discussion of *khayal* and *takhayyul,* and Shidyaq's ruminations on *al-mukhayyila wal takhayyul*.

In addressing the question of whether there is a coherent force at play animating the flickers of *khayal,* we fortunately cannot simply fall back on an already established definition of *khayal* that can be culled out of "tradition." On the contrary, there is a shared challenge in approaching *khayal* that extends between both its nineteenth-century and its earlier incarnations, and it is in fact the tight grip of this challenge that presents us with a way to approach it. The absence of a founding definition, or an origin, propels us to explore not an obscure origin, but an economy of meaning, mapping out *khayal*'s indexical field, in which multifarious accrued meanings do not represent an obstacle as much as a path to its elucidation.[21] In this way, we are neither in pursuit of an origin that can be discovered in tradition, nor are we treating the term as a translational equivalent that can be uncovered through a series of direct intellectual influences and filiations.[22] Rather, in unpacking the economy of meaning, we are looking at the series of questions and problematics encoded in this concept through its long history.

To understand the connection between these seemingly different iterations necessitates pointing out to how these varied articulations of *khayal* inhabit the same universe defined at its broadest via the relationship of the transcendental divine to humans and the role of language within it. It is in this latter universe that *khayal* accrues cognitive, affective, and active dimensions that are positioned along the axes of presence/absence, inside/outside, and the exchanges between the sensory/sensory and sensory/nonsensory.

Looking at *khayal* outside of a concern with pinpointing an original fixed meaning, we can see that, at its core, it names an image or visual object that stands at a distance from its original object that it evokes. Yet it can continue to evoke that object. This core meaning amassed radically different connotations as *khayal* traversed diverse discursive sites, participating in debates on issues such as the nature of the poetic (with a strong focus on its affective dimension) the interpretation of the anthropomorphic verses in the Quran, and music. Again, this core meaning does not furnish us with *khayal*'s "original" meaning in the sense of one that chronologically precedes the others, standing outside the "later" debates and functioning as their anchor. Consequently, while, in presenting *khayal* here, we begin with the core meaning, the move should be seen as part of analytically constructing an anchor for tracing the complexity of the debates rather than an actual historical or semantic point located prior to, and therefore outside of, these debates. This point is crucial, because in this book I will have occasion to present a definition that has grown out of my analysis but that I must present prior to it, so that the definition can function as an anchor for the analysis. Thus, it is important for me to emphasize that this mode of presentation is not to be confused with a claim about genealogical origins or a singular meaning.

The core meaning can be worked out by reading across three different basic, well-known examples: the vision of the beloved in the Arabic ode (poetry), the shadow play (theater), and a human or animal decoy (lexicography). These examples exist within the complex universe of the debates (both before and during the nineteenth century) that we will turn to shortly; therefore their profound meaning must be grappled with against the backdrop of the debates. For now, however, it is heuristically useful to treat them as isolatable instances which will facilitate our turn to the debates.

Tayf al-khayal, or the vision of the beloved that appears by night, either in a dream or as an actual apparition, is a central motif in the Arabic ode (*qasida*)—in particular the *nasib*, the initial thematic unit in which the poet reminisces about a departed beloved whose memory is conjured by the remains of the encampment where the beloved once resided.[23] This is the famous lamentation-of-ruins trope with which Tuwayrani begins his narrative, and that Muwaylihi summons in his dedication of the book version via the appeal to the vision of the beloved. The terms *tayf* and *khayal* can each be used on its own to refer to the same thing—that is, to *tayf al-khayal*.

The sighting of *tayf al-khayal* induces dizzying emotions in the "I" of the poem: he expresses his longing and yearning for the beloved as well as his doubts about this potentially menacing spirit. He worries whether this image can be truthfully identified as the beloved, and he compares his experiences with the two (the beloved and their specter or dream vision). What we see here is reversed in Tuwayrani and Marrash, whose dream visions follow from being overcome by emotions, unlike in the ode, where it is the vision that produces the overwhelming emotions. In the case of the ode, *tayf al-khayal*, the image—whether we take it to be a directly perceived apparition that stands outside the poet, or as a dream vision that appears to the poet's mind's eye—cannot be simply equated with the beloved. Rather, *khayal* is an image that evokes the original object (the beloved), but there are no guarantees that the two (evoked original object and image) can ever be seamlessly equated. In fact, this equation is often called into question.

The tension between the image and the original is often thematized by the *qasida*, and the "I" of the poem tends to draw comparisons between the two.[24] We can therefore see how what we have identified as *khayal*'s core meaning operates within the ode, and we can similarly extrapolate that this core meaning must be constantly reworked within the ode as this motif is redeployed and reinvented. Furthermore, we can begin to see that *khayal* is a lexeme that is actively used, encoded, and reencoded in literary genres, not just in critical debates.

Khayal can also denote a shadow. The latter meaning is clearly activated in shadow theater (*khayal al-dhill*), although it is also referred to as *al-la'ib al-khayali*, and *karakooz* in other Arabic-speaking provinces of the Ottoman Empire, with the exception of Egypt, where *karakooz* refers specifically to puppet theater as a form distinct from shadow theater.[25] These synonyms broaden our comprehension of *khayal* from being a concept whose presence is not restricted to critical debates, but is also embedded in literary forms that evoke *khayal* both directly and indirectly (i.e., *khayal* still matters even when shadow plays are grouped with puppet theater as karakooz, and it is also relevant whether the specter of the beloved is referred to as *tayf, khayal,* or *tayf al-khayal*). The shadow, like *tayf al-khayal*, is an image that stands at a remove from its original object while continuing to evoke it. This is true both in the case of the shadow of any object as well as the shadows appearing on a screen in a shadow play. Li-Guo describes shadow plays as "a type of optical mime," referring to Ibn al-Haytham's (d. 1039, the renowned Cairo-based optician who was born in Basra) documentation of the form, which is generally believed to be its earliest extant accurate documentation. Ibn al-Haytham describes the way in which a *khayal* play appears from behind a screen; as we know from other sources, this effect was often created by spreading a large white piece of cloth. It consists of figures that the puppeteer (*mukhayyil* or *muharrik*) moves in a certain way so that their shadows appear both on the screen as well as on the wall behind it.[26] In this case, unlike other situations involving the shadow of an object, there is a potential doubling. Not only do we see two shadows of the original object but the original itself could also have dual referents, if not more. It could simply be the leather puppets whose shadows the audience view, or it could be persons or virtues summoned through the puppets' shadows. This doubling is heavily thematized in the plot of one of the most famous shadow plays we know of: Muhammad Shams al-Din ibn Daniyal's (d. 1310) *tayf al-khayal*.

Ibn Daniyal, one of the most prominent figures in the history of Arabic shadow plays, was born in Mosul and is widely believed to have moved to Cairo at the age of fourteen in the wake of the Mongol invasion. He started his career as an eye doctor before finding his path as a playwright, poet, and court entertainer. He is credited with the only extant pre-Ottoman shadow plays in Arabic, whose numerous copies testify to their popularity: *tayf al-khayal* (The Phantom), *'ajib wa-gharib* (The Amazing [Preacher] and the Stranger), and al-*mutayyam wa al-da'i' al-yutayyim* (The Charmed and the Wayward Charmer).[27] The title of *tayf al-khayal* clearly alludes to the famous poetic trope we surveyed earlier, a trope Ibn Daniyal engaged in his own poetic production. The play is a farcical story of a salacious soldier, Amir Wisal, and his sidekick, Tayf al-khayal (the Phantom). Although Amir Wisal is planning to finally settle down and get married, the Phantom urges him to ruminate on his hedonistic past (in a parodic play off of the poetic trope of the lamentation of ruins and its typical expression of nostalgia). Consequently, while the play supposedly moves along an arc of repentance, it unfolds as a lecherous story, peppered with ribaldries. In this short synopsis, doubling exists on the level of characters and of visual experience; a main character and his phantom appear to the audience once on the screen and another on the wall, but there is also a literary doubling and inversion of *tayf al-khayal* as an iconic poetic motif. More explicitly, Ibn Daniyal's play ends with a direct appeal to the relationship between the shadow play performance and the potential that it refers to "its original object," translated as the relationship of *majaz* to *haqiqa* (truth or actuality): "I have determined to go to Hijaz, *having attained the Truth (haqiqa) beyond metaphors*" (*wa kharajt bil haqiqa 'an al-majaz*).[28] In an earlier passage, one of the characters insists that behind every shadow (*khayal*) lies an actual object/truth (*taht kul khayal haqiqa*)—two terms juxtaposed by Muwaylihi in his epilogue. This move recurs, in a different way, at the end of Ibn Daniyal's play "The Charmed and the Wayward Charmer." When a respected man walks in and asks everyone to wake up from their past, that entering the world of the shadow play entails a crossing into a dreamlike or allegorical world is a point that will be reinterpreted in the nineteenth century as a crossing into a "theatrical" world—specifically into a theater of history. Like the comparison between the beloved and her specter, these shadow plays thematize—though in a more parodic tone—the absurdity of the original object being simply a leather dummy while pointing to the potential that the performance may be thought of allegorically. In other words, the original object may be even further removed than we had originally assumed and is merely invoked in the puppet and its shadow.

We can now begin to see why shadow plays serve as an appealing symbol for arguments about transcendence, where this world and life are but the shadow of reality, a removed "reflection," to use a loaded term, but not reality itself.[29] It is enough to mention that shadow plays came to stand in as a symbol for metaphysical debates, highlighting the relationship between this transient world and another transcendental one, between humans (the puppets) and their divine prime mover (the puppeteer), and for the relationship between shadowy images and transcendental truth. These connections are palpable in hermeneutic treatises as well as in poetic production. In fact, shadow plays seem to flirt with these interpretations, too, not only through their choice of stories but also by taking playful jabs at this discourse itself, as we see in the epilogues of two out of only three surviving plays by Ibn Daniyal. This discursive interchange shows clearly that *khayal* moves within genres and is reworked through their own embeddedness as well as their participation in broader debates. This insight will prove vital when we return to our canon, particularly because these genres are mobilized by our nineteenth-century texts: we have already seen the use of the ode, and we will later see Rifa'a al-Tahtawi (1801–1873) drawing on shadow plays, where, I argue, he reads doubling as bearing a potential for convergence between particular event and abstract law.

The final heuristic example comes from *khayal* as a decoy made in the semblance of animals or humans to scare off predators or lure and lull prey. This meaning of the term appears primarily in works of lexicography, where it is often followed by examples of this use, which is still maintained in Egypt and Iraq, often as *khayal al-ma'ata*.[30] The transaction of images via the decoy is particularly relevant for Muwaylihi's *takhyil hukm al-malik*, or the exchange between the specter of the king and the president. Here, we can once again see that the success of the decoy hinges on its ability to seamlessly evoke an original that is clearly not there, thus becoming the image that can replace the original.

While these three examples share the same core meaning (an image standing at a remove from its original object while continuing to evoke it), the image referred to as *khayal* occupies different sites. It could be an external object perceived through the senses, or an internal one that is made to appear to the mind's eye or fancy; it could also be a combination of the two. *Tayf al-khayal* hovers between specter and fancy, the first being an object that lies before us and the other within us (the phantasma is an apt translation for both possibilities). *Khayal* in *khayal al-dhill* (shadow plays) can refer to the shadow, to the live performance as a whole, or to a mode of seeing allegorically. In the latter case, what is shown is not merely the shadows of discrete puppets. Rather, the latter evoke something in the collective fancy of the audience. Thus, the *khayal* in shadow theater is both direct and external, coming from without (on the screen and the wall)—though this direct *khayal* is an indirect perception of the puppets— but *khayal* could also be the resultant image that appears to the collective fancy of the audience, calling through allegory associations that are further removed. Finally, *khayal* as decoy refers to an object that evokes the image of another. The image, then, is not exactly of a directly present sensory object (the mannequin), because in this case one would be able to tell that it is, in fact, just a decoy. Instead, another image is evoked and superimposed on what should have been directly sensorially perceived. In this sense, the image is of something neither inside the observer nor outside them in any exact sense. At the same time, the object is not entirely directly present, nor completely absent. Instead, *khayal* as decoy lies at the convergence of these possibilities.

We can extend this relationship to the other original objects from the previous examples, such as the beloved or the puppets. In so doing, we can nuance the core meaning of *khayal* presented earlier, for it is not so much that the image continues to evoke its original object as much as it evokes an object *as if* it is the original—hence the possibility that image and object might not fully correspond. The vision of the beloved might not actually coincide with them, the shadow on the wall doubles the puppet and may not actually evoke the puppet itself but something further away, and the decoy image does not correspond exactly with the decoy but with another removed object that it evokes as the original.

In its iterations analyzed above, *khayal* is interpreted via the axes of inside/outside the observer, presence/absence, and exchanges between sensory/sensory or sensory/nonsensory. To these, we will now add the cognitive, the affective, and the active as the three aspects that enable us to capture *khayal*'s indexical field, or constellation of related meanings. Each potential arrangement of *khayal* on the axes of inside/outside, presence/absence and exchanges between sensory/sensory or sensory/nonsensory has cognitive, affective, and active dimensions. For example, when *tayf al-khayal* is understood to be a specter, standing outside the "I" of the poem, and haunting him, it elicits a series of emotional reactions (fear and dread) and actions (attempts at escape) that differ from when it is grappled with as a memory appearing in the mind's eye, rousing feelings of nostalgia and prompting the poet to reproach the imaginary beloved while continuing to think of their memory. Similarly, depending on how *khayal* in the shadow play is located on these axes, it will evoke different affective and active reactions. Consequently, there are differences both within each one of the preceding three examples as well as between them. We will turn shortly to why these affective and active dimensions are part of a broader cognitive process, often discussed in relation to language specifically.

In understanding *khayal* to be defined by this indexical field, I do not approach the varied connotations of the term as either totally separate, or as curious overlaps that require establishing direct filiations between their proponents. Instead, I grapple with how this field has been constituted and reconstituted through these different activations of *khayal* that ultimately give it its meaning as an image (in the mind, in the world, in language) that functions through the interplay of cognitive, affective, and active dimensions.

My approach to *khayal* here is justified by the book's focus on the nineteenth century. We are after the possible range of meanings that authors in this period encounter as already encapsulated in the concept, and that they could activate as they engage their world; for example, Muwaylihi couples it with *haqiqa* in a manner reminiscent of Ibn Daniyal's play on *haqiqa/khayal, majaz*, and dreams—the latter being important also for Marrash—while Tuwayrani activates its connotations in the ode, and Marrash hearkens back to the phantoms we see in dreams, which is part of the world of *tayf al-khayal* in poetry as well as the meaning of *khayal* as "dream." The core of the matter pivots on breaking with the insistence on writing the history of premodern concepts in Arabic via empirical taxonomies and genealogies.[31] I believe these to be imperative projects, but they are not in themselves historicizing acts that replace the intellectual labor of offering a conceptual history. I explain this point here because it underpins my treatment not only of *khayal* but also of the two other central concepts in this study: *athar* (the visible trace), and *al-nas* (the collective).

The Hermeneutics of *Khayal*

To figure out what these late nineteenth-century texts are doing with *khayal*, we have to nuance its core meaning by turning to its cognitive, affective, and active dimensions. The latter are vital for grasping why *khayal* as an image that can evoke an object *as if* it is the original was an important focus of debates across various fields and knowledge-producing discourses in Arabic. The latter debates, like *khayal* itself, cannot be traced back to a single point of origin. Yet, in turning to how *khayal* is mobilized across these debates, we can also discern their links.

I approach *khayal* as a concept that can give form to a problematic, and since this problematic is envisioned differently and intervened in from different positions and with different aims, the concept itself will be articulated differently. If we look at the interventions alone, from within each distinct debate, we will have to conclude that these are discrete instances of *khayal*, but if we look at them against the backdrop of their problematic, we will come to see them as related in their struggle to offer opposing visions of what the problematic is, and not simply as answers to it.

What is the problematic that *khayal* as a concept has the potential to give form to? I answer this by painting a broad—and highly abstract—picture of the tension between ontology and epistemology (the adjudication of cognitive processes that necessarily include affective and active dimensions) forging the conceptual world within which *khayal* moves. To anticipate what will be discussed in more detail shortly, *khayal* is not an ontologically grounded image—neither via sensory experience nor through abstract thought. It belongs neither to the world of the sensible nor to that of the intelligible. While *khayal* does not correspond to either of those levels, it bears an indispensable epistemological potential of mediating the two. Consequently, its conceptual world is shaped out of the tension between being ontologically ungrounded but epistemologically necessary for crossing into the world of intelligibles—or, alternatively, to the world of the poetic. The crossing occurs on multiple levels: within language itself, between mind and world via language, and between the sensory and the intelligible via language.[32] These crossings, however, are not direct replicas of one another, and they therefore complicate the tension encoded in *khayal* between an ungrounded image and meaning that exists on different levels.

Khayal is at its core an image (that exists in the world, in our minds, or in language) standing at a remove from an object that it evokes *as if* it is its original object—with the possibility that it may or may not in fact be (i.e., the image is ontologically ungrounded). This rudimentary meaning is only a core, however, and it necessarily acquires various dimensions and connotations as it moves through different questions and objects of knowledge (language, music, painting), scales (poetry in general, or a specific poetic trait), and units of analysis (utterance/meaning, syntactic structure, musical composition). Yet it enables us to grapple with the question of the place of images in a conceptual universe structured around a series of dyads born out of the task of mediating the presence of the transcendental divine, for it is against the backdrop of this task that we can grapple with the tension in *khayal*, anticipating why the shift toward a new task in the canon of nineteenth-century Arabic literature—the making visible of history—introduces dramatic transformations.

The divine/human dyad is critical in working out the other dyads that spring out of conceptions of human nature and the limits of knowledge available to humans, and hierarchies therein. The tension between *khayal* as ontologically ungrounded but necessary is related to the limits of human knowledge in the face of the daunting task of knowing the transcendental. Language is central as the mediator in this relationship (divine/human); most of the debates on *khayal* are related to language.[33]

My point is not that every instance of *khayal* deals directly, or even indirectly, with questions of transcendence. Rather, the universe within which *khayal* emerges as one concept (among a cluster of others) that informs thinking about image is a universe suffused with the effects of this transcendental cosmology, even when these concerns are not directly confronted. This is evident in competing opinions about the senses and their potential hierarchal organization, in contending ideas about what an image is, and in conceptions of language itself.[34] Thus, these debates were at once the result and renewed sites of explosive intellectual and political struggles that forged, reproduced, and reworked the overarching tendencies of this fraught cosmology as well as the detailed articulated positions within it. The variation in *khayal*, then, has to be read against the backdrop of this conceptual universe and its underpinning cosmology.

The above schema contains within it a series of interconnecting and interdependent mirroring levels that the different schools will come to grapple with differently. For our purposes, however, we can describe them in this rather abstract way: we have the divine and the human (a dyad) and they are bridged via the Quranic text, which itself represents a hermeneutic for engaging the world (and which is not itself a stable object, not only in light of debates about the createdness of the Quran (*khalq al-Quran*) but also in light of the many tools needed to interpret it, many of which are themselves texts). Language, then, is the bridge through which the human could cross to approach the divine. This central crossing is crisscrossed through other crossings that language enables. While language is the bridge between objects in the world and objects in the mind, through which cognitive functions are performed, it is also the path linking objects in the minds of one person and those in the minds of others. Finally, language itself functions through a perpetual crossing between utterance as a vocal form (*lafz*) and its meaning, or "conceptual content," according to Alexander Key (*ma'na*).[35] The initial dyad of divine/human suffuses the conceptual universe around it with other dyads—while being reformulated via them—that cannot be simply approached as reproductions of it on another level, but that remain nonetheless connected as parts of a transcendental cosmology.

This is a conceptual world in which crossings within and through language constitute the process through which meaning is produced: from crossing between the utterance and meaning within language, to crossing between objects in the world and objects in our mind through language, to finally crossing between the human and the divine. Language is the nexus for seeing the rifts and attempting the crossings. This is what I have in mind when I speak of the conceptual universe or the transcendental cosmology that suffuses every element in this network going as deeply as the relationship between *lafz* and *ma'na*. This cosmology underpins each distinct discourse or field (e.g., lexicography, poetics, exegesis) because it has a different object of knowledge (each with its own scale and units of analysis), it will intervene in it differently, and it will also encounter disparate problems that are specific to the challenges posed to it by the encounter between the network/cosmology and their specific object of knowledge. Yet, in as much as they all deal with different facets of language, they are also interconnected, regardless of how self-enclosed each field might appear to be.

Now, where does this leave us with regards to *khayal*? *Khayal*, as an image or a visual object whose idiosyncrasies have been explained, is defined conceptually in relationship to its role in the crossing, both within language and through language to the other side. In other words, when emplaced within language, *khayal*'s "sensory dimension" (the ghost or the shadow, what lies between the certainty of sensory perception and the doubt often associated with more complex intellectual endeavors) becomes mired in debates on how this image/visual object maps out on the series of crossings in language and through language to the other side. In the process, *khayal* becomes the site for nuancing the interrelationship between the cognitive, the affective, and the active in experiencing imagery in language (whether that is defined as poetry in total, or as a particular kind of poetry, or even as aspects of the Quranic text). Yet this is only one dimension of what I mean when I said earlier that *khayal* gives form to a problem. There is another crucial dimension.

While we can look at this conceptual universe from the "inside"—which is what I have done above, aligning our perception of it with its "internal logic," whereby one step leads to the other (e.g., the circle I have drawn between God and humans via language), and the pieces fit together into a whole—this "internal logic" is not self-begetting. Rather, it is forged through sociopolitical struggle. We merely need to think about defining what language is in Arabic, where the definition of the normative corpus is also a delimiting of "speaking" in some sense, and it is one that is never completely settled. The feud over the divine or human origins of language; the postulation of an archetypal Quran in some (other) language or no language of which the Quranic text is arguably derived; definitions of human nature, of the limits of human knowledge—all of these are also palpably sociopolitical debates on the nature of power and its division. In other words, while this conceptual world starts with certain givens (inherited from pre-Islamic, late antiquity world views), these "origins" are reconfigured in the encounter with new sociopolitical problems through which the conceptual world/cosmology is forged, and in so doing the debates also participate in the struggle, giving it its language. Rather ironically, this explains some of the different uses of *khayal* that are discrete as much as they are related interventions: they are not the result of a genealogy of the concept, but of accrued meanings through the roles with which *khayal* was entrusted. In some sense, we are always in medias res when it comes to the relationship of thought and sociopolitical struggle; we can annex genealogies, retrospective rhythms, or something else, but these are not history itself, which is itself always in medias res. In so doing, I depart from the empiricist approach of modern philology while drawing greatly on this scholarship and, equally, move away from assuming that we can understand concepts and terms primarily through taxonomies.

Instead, I do something that is both similar to and different from what the classical grammarians and linguists do: I postulate a "core definition" of *khayal* (an image that evokes the object *as if* it is the original) that I realize is not an actually existing empirical object but the product of intellectual labor and a step in a hermeneutic exercise.[36] This is how I approach defining *khayal*, drawing on rich studies of the concept while breaking with many of their key central assumptions. With this map in the back of our minds, and my approach clearly articulated, we can briefly sketch out the four concerns: figuration, truth, politics, and memory. In selecting my examples, I chose to focus on the well-known texts, targeting in particular crucial usages of *khayal* that have been argued to be unrelated. My aim is to show that, because we have moved from the preoccupation with genealogies and taxonomies, we will be able to see the connections between these discrete debates, which will greatly help us in reading how they are drawn together in the nineteenth century.

By the "figurative," I specifically refer to the labyrinthine arguments and disputes concerned with imagery in language that is part of a broader debate on "figurative" or tropological speech. While *majaz* came to be the term used to encompass the different kinds of figurative speech such as *isti'ara* (metaphor) and *kinaya* (metonymy/periphrasis), its early history seems to have been concerned with periphrastic exegesis: teasing out different ways of saying the same thing, particularly when faced by a potentially tricky articulation.[37] The mobilization of the term as a tool with which to tackle the question of the anthropomorphic verses in the Quran has imbued it with a strong—but in no way exclusive—focus on imagery in language. While imagery came to hold an increasingly important position in thinking about *majaz*, the term continued to refer in general to "departures from the established" ways of saying things. Clearly, this required establishing what the "original" (unchanged, usual, customary, or older) way of saying things is in order to work out the changes and classify them. *Khayal* enters the scene as one such term that falls on the side of "figurative" language, with a strong affinity with debates on imagery, closely associated with the poetic.

Khayal (often as *takhyil* in this case) is generally assumed to exist in these debates via two main streams; the first is literary criticism, and particularly the work of 'Abd al-Qahir al-Jurjani (d. 1078 or 1081), and the second is the work of the philosophers on *Poetics*.[38] There have been intense—and as yet inconclusive— arguments about the possible relationship between these two renditions of *khayal*. The differences are numerous. The first springs out of the Arabic debates that use lexicography and grammar as criteria for appreciating poetry while the second centralizes logic; the first is autochthonous while the second is ostensibly foreign; the first defines *takhyil* as one very specific trope used primarily by the "modernist" poets (*muhdathun*) while for the second it captures the very definition of what the poetic is. The term *muhdathun* poets is key to the historicization of premodern Arabic poetry, and it is typically used to refer to the poetry of the early 'Abbasid period, whose propensity toward artifice is juxtaposed with the "ancients" (*al-qudama'* as the pre-Islamic and early Islamic poets), whose style is taken to be more natural. Lara Harb carefully demonstrates the overlaps between these two branches of grappling with *khayal* while acknowledging their discrepancies.

Harb demonstrates the difference between two kinds of *khayal* in 'Abd al-Qahir al-Jurjani, a towering figure of poetics in Arabic who has enjoyed a continuous history of critical acclaim since then. While both are associated with the evocation of images in language, the first offers unrealistic imagined representations whose imaginary status remains clear beyond any doubt. The second, which Jurjani refers to as *takhyil*, is quite specific to "modernist" poetry, and it does not stop at unrealistic imagined representations, but tricks the audience into believing that they are true—Harb translates this as "make believe." In other words, their imaginary status is obfuscated, resulting in what Harb describes as an emotive response. The mystification of the imaginary status of these representations is entwined with poetic innovation attributed to "modernist" poetry, for it is the latter's break with poetic norms that muddles the status of the representations they use.[39] Put differently, the status of representations is not determined by their accordance to what is true, in terms of that which has already happened, to relating prior sensory experiences, or to expounding on abstract truths, but in accordance with poetic norms: "Poetry as a medium of expression was in general acknowledged as fictional in medieval Arabic culture in the sense that it was understood that the information it conveyed did not necessarily exist or happen in real life. As a poetic quality, however, falsehood had to do more with linguistic deviation from literal accuracy in the employment of metaphorical language and hyperbole (*ghuluww*)." The adjudication of what constituted deviation from literal accuracy was determined through appealing to the poetic canon, and its use of language and imagery that come to define, at least in part, the accurate usage of language.[40] We might then say that the difference between these two kinds of *khayal*, described by Jurjani, hinges on their respective relationship to the poetic canon itself, which results in different assessments of their effects—this argument was actually made by Ibn al-Mu'taz, who defended modernist poetry by arguing that its use of figurative and rhetorical tropes is not as radically new as some claim.[41] For our purposes here, what is of great import is that this image (*khayal*) that poetry brings to stand in the mind produces an affective response of wonder and bewilderment that is in turn produced in response to the strangeness of the image—the image that had so far seemed impossible to see, but that suddenly stands in the audience's minds. The affective response is itself the result of the cognitive processes the audience needs to perform in order to dissect this sudden bewildering image, figuring out the steps and leaps through which it was composed. Viewed in this way, the philosophers' conception of poetry does not seem too far removed from Jurjani's understanding of this "unique" feature of modernist poetry.

For the philosophers, *khayal* (i.e., *takhyil*) defines not a particular feature of a poetic corpus, but the poetic as a universal. Nonetheless, it also refers to poetry's ability to evoke images in the minds of the audience, driving the latter into accepting them and their connotations while bypassing typical procedures of verification. In other words, *khayal* (the image) is anchored by the poetic utterance itself, and the workings of language therein, but is not necessarily supported by prior sensory images or abstract thought—and, in the case of Jurjani's notion of it, not even by prior poetic norms. Consequently, *khayal* names an image that is grounded exclusively by the workings of language, specifically poetic language, not through typical verification processes. That said, the poetic still requires a "cognitive" process whose result is affective, the response to the image that appears in the mind is emotional and, for the philosophers, also active, driving people into action in accordance with or discordance to the embodiment of virtues into poetic images. Harb then carefully demonstrates the way in which the concept in both instances registers a paradigmatic shift from upholding the conventions of the poetic canon as the measure of good poetry toward a focus on the ability to elicit an experience of wonder in the audience. As such, the two streams activate *khayal* to carve out an intrinsic path for thinking of the poetic experience from within the structures of its own language rather than in accordance with its faithfulness to or departure from the established poetic canon (pre-Islamic with a few early Islamic poets). Key in this is poetry's ability to evoke images in a way that moves the soul of the audience—something that both streams agree upon. However, the philosophers ascribe this ability to all poetic language, while Jurjani identifies it as a specific trope in "modernist" poetry. There are some differences in the way contemporary scholars understand what Jurjani defines as the crux of *takhyil*.[42] Part of the difficulty stems from the way in which Jurjani identifies the characteristic style of *badi'* poetry, but, in so doing, he captures something about the poetic in general. In other words, while *takhyil* for Jurjani centers on the ability to extrapolate further imagery from initial imagery, because the latter is used as if it is literal, there is a metapoetic quality here that stems from the canonization of the earlier poetic production.

For our purposes, in both of these instances we can think of the affective as the central characteristic of *khayal*: as an image capable of moving its audience, stirring in them affective and active responses. The point is crucial for grasping the generalized pedagogic function of literature in the nineteenth century and its assumed imbrication with a project of social reform. The issue is not reducible to the popularization of modern knowledge by implanting it within a narrative form; rather, it pivots on a way through which *khayal* sets off a series of specifically poetic "cognitive" procedures that move on an arc of the cognitive, the affective, and the active. To anticipate what we will explore in more detail later, by making history visible through *khayal*, literature conjures affective responses that drive people into action in accordance with the principles of civilizational progress.

Consequently, literature's role in achieving civilizational progress is premised on the idea that literature's "making visible" via *khayal* has serious affective and active repercussions that could change history itself. One thing to note, however, is that the introduction of history—which is itself reworked in the wake of empiricism—as literature's object of visibility changes the dynamics through which *khayal* operates. While *khayal* remains an experience that unfolds through the inner workings of language itself (i.e., in the poetic utterance), the latter is now subtended by history and science. The attempt to align *khayal* with science and history changes the network surrounding it and the rifts it should enable seeing and crossing, and, in the process, it produces two seemingly distinct narrative techniques: "hyperrealist" and "allegorical." In the next chapter, we will see that while these two offer different ways for crossing toward history, they are more closely linked than what has been assumed by previous scholarship.

One thing to keep in mind, however, is that, in addition to setting off a movement on a cognitive-affective-active arc, *khayal* also brings forth an image that would have otherwise been impossible to see, either because it is far away, fantastical, or denotes an abstract quality—these are three reasons why the image (*khayal*) is ontologically ungrounded, because it is not directly present to sensory perception at the moment, because it is fantastical, or because it is something abstract. In our case this refers to the ability to render the totality of history (both the events and their underpinning abstract universal principles governing civilizational progress) into a visual object. With this in mind, we can explore some final points in these pre-nineteenth-century debates that will help us recognize the transformations brought forth by the demarcation of history as the object of visualization.

To recap, the explanations of *khayal*'s imbrication with the poetic are rooted in the cognitive processes involved in working out the image—the series of crossings and leaps the audience undertakes within the sea of language. We need to pause here briefly, because, while both Jurjani and the philosophers agree that the affective dimension is born out of this cognitive process, they explain it rather differently, not just because they are rooted in different disciplines—although that is an important part—but because their starting point regarding the Arabic poetic canon is different.[43] The naturalization of certain poetic tropes due to their canonization defines the thinking of *khayal* as being *a distinction within* poetry itself for al-Jurjani rather than a distinction of the poetic *from* its others for the philosophers. And so it is not all poetry that requires these cognitive processes and that produces this affect, but for the philosophers it is the definition of any poetry worthy of the name.

One final debate to be discussed here under figurative speech involves whether the image engages in transactions between sensory/sensory or sensory/nonsensory. Renowned Mu'tazalite (a branch of "rationalist" theology) thinker Al-Zamakhshari (d. 1144), who is generally understood to deploy Jurjani's sense of *khayal*, tends to focus on the ability of *khayal* to bring into the realm of perceptibility what is otherwise hidden from the senses (that is it ushers in a transaction between the sensory/nonsensory). The fact that he activates the concept in direct relationship with the anthropomorphic verses in the Quran plays a key role in this.

This brings us to the second concern, which is truth. We might already infer that there will be different positions on *khayal*'s truth. As an ontologically ungrounded image, *khayal* hovers between being necessarily untrue and between naming a particular kind of truth: poetic truth. In fact, Harb's argument regarding the shift, encompassing both literary theorists and philosophers, toward what she dubs "aesthetics of wonder" bespeaks an increasing ascription of an autonomous type of "truth" specific to poetry: one that cannot be squared with the procedures of verifying sensory or intelligible phenomena, but that requires a uniquely poetic one. In carving out this distinctively poetic brand of truth, the concerns with sensory and metaphysical truth did not simply evaporate, and the issue continued to be heavily debated through attempts to map out a hierarchy of these levels of truth, placing them into harmony or at least avoiding their discordance.

To give one quick example, we can think of al-Zamakhshari, who upholds that *khayal*'s truth is not measurable via its correspondence, or lack thereof, to our sensory world. Rather, it is weighed via its ability to communicate its meaning effectively (meaning, here, often being an abstract transcendent quality). In other words, the truth is defined from within the dynamic of the utterance (*qawl*) itself and primarily judged via its overall effect. For him, truth is not "irrelevant" but is defined as an effect in the soul. Yet, Zamakshari's attempt to use *khayal* (i.e., *takhyil*) in Quranic exegesis did not go without backlash, often not with regard to the specifics of his interpretation. Instead, the issue centered on whether the concept could be used in reference to the Quran, a text that has direct access to metaphysical and not poetic truth. Thus, the emergence of *khayal* as a marker of poetic truth does not necessarily dissolve the hierarchies within which it moved through a conceptual universe, and its underpinning cosmology, that are forged through a move toward transcendence. However, one thinker in particular—who makes an appearance in Muwaylihi's *hadith*—overturns the different iterations of *khayal*'s relationship to truth.[44]

The work of Ibn al-'Arabi is mentioned passingly in Muwaylihi's *hadith*. In the early episodes of the text, we meet a young unnamed inspector who has two books next to him: the first by famous Sufi philosopher and mystic Ibn al-'Arabi (1165–1240), and the second by the renowned French writer Voltaire (1694–1778). In the same episode, seminal works on positive law by Victor Dalloz (1795–1869) and René Garraud (1849–1930) are also mentioned.[45] The juxtaposition of the great Sufi figure with works from French literature and treatises on positive law is noteworthy but does not concern us here; what does is that Ibn al-'Arabi has an important intervention in the debates on *khayal*.

Ibn al-'Arabi turns the vision of *khayal* as an ontologically ungrounded image whose claim to truth can be made exclusively in relation to the poetic on its head, arguing that *khayal* defines the realm of truth accessible to humans.[46] To explain the issue from within the debates we presented earlier, we can say that Ibn al-'Arabi reveals poetic truth not as a move beside the sensory or the metaphysical but as the very definition of the truth knowable to humans, who do not have direct access to the transcendental divine either through the senses or the intellect. In other words, the philosophers' assumption that they can achieve transcendence as a divorcing, or intellectual overcoming, of this world and a relinquishing of all ties with the sensorial is the illusion.

Ironically, for Ibn al-'Arabi, the philosophers are imprisoned in one image given to them via *khayal* that they mark as the truth, rendering all the other images illusions. For him, transcendent truth is tied with *khayal*, with an ability to navigate—or perhaps swim through and with—all of these disembodied images, rather than an impossible overcoming of them towards the abstract. Learning to navigate (through) these images is what truth is. In this way, truth is not about "overcoming" *khayal* and exiting it, nor is *khayal* a move beside truth, but it's about learning to weather these storming disembodied images and *experience* truth through them. To put it simply, the poetic (in the way explained above via *khayal*) is precisely the lens through which to read the world and be in it. This brings us full circle, for if *khayal* has carved out a space for an intrinsic mode of judging (which includes appreciating, enjoying, tasting) poetry, it has, in this case, become externalized; the series of crossings and leaps involved in the experience of *khayal* are precisely the rubric for being with or in truth in the world, and not just in the poetic utterance, achievable by humans.

While Ibn al-'Arabi offers a dramatically transformed conception of *khayal* in relation to truth, it shares key central premises with the work of the philosophers that he heavily criticizes. He preliminarily accepts the basic definition of *khayal* that we have explored above in the works of both philosophers and literary theorists that *khayal* is responsible for the evocation of images. The agreement ends here, however, as he foregrounds the nature of humans and the "limits" to their knowledge. In so doing, he taps into a particular kind of truth that the philosophers—al-Farabi in particular—have often ascribed to the commoners. The point is worth further unpacking, since it enables glimpsing the political tenor of the discussions on figuration and truth.

One crucial observation with which to begin is that the philosophic discussions of *khayal* spanned works not only on poetry/rhetoric but also those dealing with the soul, ethics, and the polis. Across them, *khayal* plays a mediatory function either as a faculty that lies in between sensory perception and abstract intellection or as a mode of seeing the world that allows the commoners—those who are barred from philosophic intellection by the limits of their "natural" abilities—to take a step beyond their imprisonment in fleeting sensory experiences. Those who cannot get far enough to reach the transcendental and for whom a simulation of abstract truth needs to be made visible can rely on poetry (and, for Abu Nasr al-Farabi, on religion) to access a mediated version of the abstract via *khayal*. Politics, consequently, as the set of relationalities connecting the inhabitants of the polis, is not lost on the commoners in the fleetingness of the sensory, but it can continue to be mediated to them.

This mediatory notion of *khayal* exists, but without this hierarchy (of commoners vs. elites), in the work of al-Zamakhshari, for whom *khayal* can render the abstract and transcendental visible. Ibn al-'Arabi, then, taps into this vision, twinning it with an understanding of *khayal* as a level of knowledge through which the abstract and nonsensory may be *seen*. The concept is thought in tandem with central Quranic verses, those pertaining in particular to the creation of humans (*al-insan*) in the "image" of God, and the command to worship God as if He is *seen*. These transactions cannot assume an equivalence between the two sides of the dyad, and for Ibn al-'Arabi's *khayal* is key to navigating these transactions through which truth knowable to humans can be realized. In other words, his conception hinges on turning toward what may tentatively be called the truth of the commonality (*al-'amma*), which refers to the previously mentioned lurking line of thought—particularly in al-Farabi's reflections on the connection between the poetic and the political in the polis. Ibn al-'Arabi radicalizes the insight, transforming *khayal* from the level of *al-amma*'s knowledge of political existence (*al-wujud al-madini*), in al-Farabi, to the mode of *al-insan*'s knowledge (as *seeing*) of Existence (*al-wujud*) in general.[47]

Khayal is revealed, not as a diluted mediated path to abstract truth, but as *the* truth knowable to human beings according to their nature.[48] *Khayal* is repositioned as the threshold enabling knowledge as *seeing*, through multiple acts of crossing between images-in-flux and meaning.[49] According to Ibn al-'Arabi, there are multiple levels to the crossings; some are graspable by both the commonality (*al-'amma*) and the elite (*al-khassa*), while others form a less trodden path that can only be crossed by a select few. The repositioning of *khayal*, its reconceptualization and the ensuing rethinking of truth, is enabled through highlighting the "human" *al-insan* as a pivotal conceptual category in thinking *khayal* in general. This point will prove crucial as we continue to explore the reconceptualization of *khayal* and truth in the nineteenth century—or what we referred to at the beginning of this chapter as literary truth—in the coming chapters, discovering their entwinement not only with history and science but also with human nature.

Continuing with this thought, we come to virtue-ethics/politics in their relation to *khayal*. This discussion often emphasizes the active dimension of *khayal*—that is, how its ability to move us with or contra something can result in the embodiment of ethical dispositions that may not be rooted in an abstract examination of these virtues themselves so much as an involuntary reaction to *khayal* that results in their embodiment. This question is fleshed out in the works of philosophers, in Sufi discourse, and, in different ways, in poetry itself, through eulogy (*madih*) and lampoon (*hija'*) of virtues. This is an angle that will be particularly developed in the nineteenth century through the twining of virtue ethics with principles of civilizational progress.

My aim here has been to point out to how these varied articulations of *khayal* inhabit the same universe. That universe is defined at its broadest via the relationship of the transcendental divine to humans and the role of language within it, as *khayal* moves along an arc of cognitive, affective, and active, and within that via the axes of presence/absence, inside/outside, and the exchanges between the sensory/sensory and sensory/nonsensory.

Memory seems far removed from this world, but is actually subsumed within this universe, both through some ideas about cognitive functions and how the latter inform the production of pleasure in aesthetic experiences. This will prove key as we move to our nineteenth-century texts, where *khayal* is imagined as a site of convergence whereby all is present.[50] In his book about music, Ibn Sina deploys numerous terms often closely associated with language sciences and poetics, including "imitation"/comparison (*muhakah*) and the "figurative" (*majaz*), *'ibara*—along with *'ibra* and *'ubur*—(the first is often translated as "phrase" though the root *'abar* means "to cross", from which comes *'ibra* as "moral," and *'ubur* as "crossing"), alteration (*taghyyir*), "drawing" (*rasm*), and *khayal*.⁵¹ He argues that the pleasure of music is experienced not through sense perception (*al-hiss*), but in *al-khayal*.⁵² The explanation is simple. Music is defined as a proportion between notes. The senses are always caught with the fleeting "present"—as we have already seen in a different way in relation to the commoners in the polis. It is impossible to hear more than one note at a time. What one actually hears through the senses is a series of notes, but not music, since the latter is defined as the relationship among notes. The meeting up (*ijtima'*) of notes, of which music is formed, can only be experienced through *khayal*. This passing thought will prove critical when we turn to the episodic structure of our nineteenth-toward canon as a replaying and overcoming of sensory fragmentation towards a "meeting up" that can make history visible.

We now arrive at the end of this brief sketch of *khayal*'s indexical field, its conceptual world, and its cosmology. What I suggest in what follows is that while the indexical field of *khayal* appears to be relatively unchanged in the nineteenth century, its underpinning conceptual world and cosmology undergo dramatic change that can be summarized in the introduction of "history"—a move that will shift the crossings of *khayal* even as they seem to be simply reproduced. Specifically, we explore how *khayal* is activated to give form to a *new* problematic in this canon, drawing the contour of literary truth as a separate "crossing"—one that this book will continue to explore.

In what follows, I take up three main instances from Rifa'a al-Tahtawi, Ali Mubarak, and Ahmed Faris al-Shidyaq (1805/6–87). The analysis is not organized chronologically, but conceptually, delineating two main sites of engagement: theater (for Tahtawi and Mubarak), and language (for Shidyaq). While both cases activate elements of *khayal*'s indexical field, they also insert "history" into its conceptual infrastructure. We will continue to use history as a placeholder for what is yet to come. Yet we will also begin to explore dimensions of history, ones that center on learning to capture the abstract principle underpinning particular events (usually *waqa'i'*).⁵³

History: The Stage, the Scene, the *Horama*

The advent of *khayal* on the horizon of Arabic critical thought is repeatedly entangled with translation. We have already mentioned how the philosophers deploy it as a translation for an elusive original. In this second case, *khayal* is offered as a translation for theater. While the suggestion fails—and the Arabized forms of French (*tiyatr*) and Italian (*tiyatro*) continue to be used in addition to *marsah*; this is the term used by Marrash—the term (*khayal*) continues to circulate throughout the nineteenth century, delineating similar concerns with visuality and history across debates on theater, language, and literature.

In a famous passage from Rifaʻa al-Tahtawi's documentation of his journey to Paris (first published in 1834, but his time in Paris was between 1826 and 1831), he deliberates on the best way to capture, in Arabic, "théâtre" as a social institution and practice.[54] The entry is tacitly premised upon an understanding of the division of time, in French society, between work and leisure, and the demarcation of a public sphere. In fact, theater is one of the many entertainments in which the French engage for leisure. It is in their free time and as private individuals that the French gather, not to perform religious duty, but to form the public sphere. Tahtawi's impressions are worth quoting at length:

> You should know that when these people finish their usual activities to ensure their livelihood, they do not get involved in matters of devotion; rather, they spend their time indulging in worldly matters, entertainments and games, in which they display a truly amazing versatility. Among the entertainments, we find amusement gatherings in places they call *théâtre* and *spectacles*. Here, they re-enact everything that has happened (*taqlid saʼir ma waqaʻ*). In truth, these games deal with serious (*jidd*) things through jest (*hazl*). . . . I do not know of an Arabic word that renders the meaning spectacle or "theatre". The basic meaning of the word *spectacle* is "view", "place of recreation", or some such, whereas "theatre" originally also meant "game", "entertainment", or the venue where this takes place. And so it may be compared with those actors called "shadow players" (*arbab al-laʻib al-khayali*). More appropriately, shadow play is a form of theatre, as both are known by the Turks as *Komedya*. However, this

denomination is too restrictive, except if it is used in a broader sense. There is no objection to translating "theatre" or "spectacle" as *khayali* ["imaginary"] if you enlarge the meaning of this word (*tawassu'*), as a result of which it comes close to the idea of *spectacle*.⁵⁵

Crucially, Tahtawi's entry is not the first description of theater in Arabic. Yet it contributes one of the earliest attempts to carve out an appropriate Arabic translation for it.⁵⁶ Tahtawi surveys various registers of Arabic, and, to a lesser degree, Ottoman Turkish, in search for a potential translation. He finally settles on the adjectival form of *khayal* (i.e., *khayali*), culled from shadow plays (*al-la'ib al-khayali*). We have encountered shadow plays earlier in this chapter; now they return once again as a rubric for translating modern theater into Arabic. To go back to the translation, Tahtawi is acutely aware that *khayali* (as shadow plays) is not an evidently literal or self-explanatory translation. Nonetheless, they have enough in common to enable viewing both of them as specific forms of *khayali* through a process of conceptual *expansion* to which he refers to as *tawassu'*.⁵⁷

In the Arabic critical tradition, *tawassu'* is defined as a primarily semantic expansion. The meaning denoted by the utterance becomes wider. As the pool of referents enlarges, the utterance remains brief and, as such, becomes more condensed. The issue is often analyzed as a rhetorical trope that contributes to the inimitability of the Quran and that helps to explain the critical need for interpretation.⁵⁸ Nonetheless, the relationship between theater-*khayali* is not simply semantic, but conceptual. As such, it calls for reading *tawassu'* as a process of conceptual, rather than semantic, expansion. For if shadow plays are to be seen as one *form* of a broader category, one needs to wrench out a shared dimension that grounds both shadow plays and the French plays that Tahtawi saw into a broader category known as "theater" and captured through the adjectival form of *khayal* (*khayali*).⁵⁹

It is obviously impossible to reconstruct what Tahtawi had in mind, but we can tease out four crucial elements in Tahtawi's terse description of theater. The first is that theater has a strong visual dimension that Tahtawi focuses on in his meticulous descriptions of stage settings, which will be discussed in chapter 2. Furthermore—and this is the second element—it is equally evident in his proposal that theater, spectacle, and varieties of "*horama*" (e.g., diorama, panorama) could all be rendered as *khayal*, which must mean that *khayal* can capture something pertaining to view, scene, or spectacle. Thirdly, *khayal* assumes a relationship between actors and audience—in other words, it is a performance, and its visual aspects are understood to be something present outside the audience. For Tahtawi, this cannot be dissociated from theater's effect on virtue ethics, where it is imagined as a school for the public, and one site where the public *emerges as the public*.[60] These two points will play out differently for Mubarak, as we will see. Finally, *khayal* (theater) is an enactment of everything that has happened. It is precisely at this point that *khayal* and "history" are placed on the same level: through *khayal* we come to see that which has already happened. In arguing that the reenactment of everything that has happened is suggestive of history, I am drawing both on the examples Tahtawi gives of the plays he had seen as well as on a careful reading that compares what he says about theater to what he says about history. The connections Tahtawi makes here continue to underpin Mubarak's explanation of theater despite the fact that *khayal* does not become the accepted translation.

Of history, Tahtawi contributes a pithy discussion in his journey to Paris. It takes off by falsifying what he refers to as the commonly held perception by the Arabs that they are the pioneers of history writing.[61] He rectifies this misconception, showing that, in fact, the Greeks preceded the Arabs. The first book of history is none other than Homer's *Iliad*, which he calls *The Waqa'i' of the Trojan War*.[62] Consequently, in defining theater, he renders it as the reenactment of that which has already happened (*waqa'*), and, when identifying the first book of history, he chooses a literary text. The key term is the verb *waqa'* (to fall/befall/happen); the root for *waqa'i'* (happenings/occurrences/events).[63] In expounding on theater in his *'alam al-din*, Mubarak similarly appeals to *waqa'i'* and *khayal*. Here, however, *khayal* is not the name just of the visual experience of something that lies outside the audience; it captures a transaction between what lay inside the mind of the writer, what is present on stage, and what is internalized by the audience. This connection between *khayal* and history is central for Tahtawi's and Mubarak's ascription of a pedagogic function to theater.

Ali Mubarak's *'alam al-din* was first published in 1881 in Alexandria. The narrative follows the two main characters, 'Alam al-Din, a religious scholar who teaches at the renowned mosque and religious institution al-Azhar, and his son Burhan al-Din, as they journey to Europe accompanied by an unnamed English Orientalist. The latter is collaborating with 'Alam al-Din on the project of preparing a book edition of the monumental lexicon *lisan al-'arab* (The Language of the Arabs, the main source of Lane's famous lexicon) which had thus far circulated in manuscript form. Incidentally, the first book edition of the lexicon was released starting in 1882/3, though the publication of its twenty volumes continued until 1891. England was supposed to be the travelers' final destination; however, the book concludes before they ever arrive. The events of the book are divided between their journey to France and the time they spend there, and they unfold over several chapters described in the book as *musamara* (colloquy). Theater is the subject of a lengthy discussion in colloquy 27, in which *khayal* flashes throughout, evoking perhaps that the term *khayal* was one of the earliest suggested Arabic translations for "theater." *Khayal*, here, is explicitly linked to making something sensorially present, to history, and to a pedagogic dimension—like Tahtawi—which is in this case explicitly envisioned as a training of the senses.

In attempting to explain what theater is, the English Orientalist in Ali Mubarak says that "[theater] depicts all of these images and forms for the eyes to see; clarifies them so they may be directly perceived; externalizes them; from the power of *khayal* into the sensorial perceptible realm."[64] He goes on to add that "theatre, here, cannot be compared to the plays of *Abo Rabya* and the like. Rather, it is—as we have said before—*scientific examples in accordance with historical occurrences and the turbulence of the times. Consequently, it aids in advancing the civilization of the nation.*"[65] Thus, we see the link between theater, *khayal*, history, and "schooling" that we saw in Tahtawi, though *khayal* here is not the name of the form itself, but of the process that encompasses the form as an externalization of ideas and images (the author) into sensory experiences on stage that can, in turn, be internalized (by the audience).

The English Orientalist focuses on three main applications of this process of externalization, of turning images and ideas in the mind into a sensorial experience on stage: 1) theatrical staging of the afterlife; 2) theatrical staging of abstract personal virtues; and 3) theatrical staging of past historical events.[66] In a curious example of this third variety, it is elaborated as unearthing the history of the past nations to put them on trial. The Englishman likens this to wrenching these nations out of their graves for a premature judgement day.[67] The idea Mubarak expresses here, likening theater to a trial, is one that we saw in Marrash. In the same vein, Mubarak's point about theater being deployed to put history on trial via resurrection is central in Muwaylihi's text. I do not mean to suggest that there is any direct influence; rather, that these relationalities between theater, trials (i.e., judgment that follows scientific and historical criteria), history, and *khayal* are actually more diffuse, and it is precisely the way they suffuse discourses that enables their active fusion into a literary form born out of these relationalities. We are beginning to see that *khayal* here moves within a conceptual universe whose lexicon is formed out of history, science, and civilizational progress—to name but just a few—and it is the task of this book to unearth this conceptual universe of *khayal* from the position of this canon. This task will necessitate sharpening our literary optic to include two more central concepts that we encounter in chapters 3 and 4, and that actually appear in Mubarak's aforementioned statement (*athar* and *al-nas*).

This notion of putting the actual actions of people on trial is part of what *waqa'i'* seems to capture. Yet instead of just reenacting events, it enables seeing them and their meanings in new lights, as part of a broader temporal continuum, and it is precisely their new position that enables "judgment." The discussions of Tahtawi and Mubarak point in this direction, in their approach to theater *khayal* as a technology of visualization, which, through the arraying of objects and images on stage, produces an experience that makes history visible and, in so doing, teaches lessons that enable civilizational progress (judgments about history and actions?). Furthermore, the preceding contentions regarding theater-*khayal* evoke questions of presence/absence—this is the crux of enabling experiencing history once again as if it is a direct experience—inside/outside (mind/stage), and exchanges between the sensory/sensory (stage settings / settings of the historical event), and sensory/nonsensory (the play or scenes of the play / history as a continuum forged out of events and principles of civilizational progress). Consequently, it is worth recalling the hermeneutic of *khayal* to figure out how Tahtawi and Mubarak fit into it, which, for our purposes, is also figuring out how they reconfigure it.

The hermeneutic of *khayal* presented three intersecting layers for grappling with *khayal* as a concept. Our ground is the indexical field of *khayal*, its different meanings (e.g., shadow, ghost, decoy, as well as a poetic figure, a mediatory threshold, a visual memory). I have argued that these meanings grapple with questions of presence/absence, inside/outside, and exchanges between the sensory/sensory and the sensory/nonsensory. We can organize our indexical field by registering how each variation encodes a different relationship between the cognitive, the affective, and the active. These two layers—the indexical field, and its structuring principle—are undergirded by a conceptual universe/cosmology through which we can come to understand the variations in the field as interventions in conceptualizing the place of the "image" within the latter conceptual universe/cosmology. It is actually against the background of this nexus that I could draw out the core meaning of *khayal* as an abstraction that allows us to better grapple with its specific renditions, none of which, as I have explained before, embody the abstraction as is.

Now, where would we place Tahtawi and Mubarak's theater-*khayal* within this nexus? Framed more specifically, how does the association of *khayal* and history reconfigure the nexus I have presented earlier? To answer this question is to turn to the conceptual universe within which *khayal* is emplaced, and through which it gives form to a problematic. In this study, this conceptual universe is explored from within the canon of nineteenth-century Arabic literature, for it is within this canon that *khayal* is activated. Consequently, answering the question is to enter the world of this canon—an undertaking that will occupy us for the rest of this book. Therefore, we can think of the journey of this book as the remapping of the hermeneutic of *khayal* from within the canon of nineteenth-century Arabic literature.

Yet it is still useful to suggest that we have already encountered general trends. We have discussed three dimensions in our nineteenth-century corpus: the affective (we referred to this in Tuwayrani and Marrash, and in a different way in Tahtawi and Mubarak's arguments that direct sensory experience is more effective), the cognitive (we saw this in the appeal to history and science in literary texts as well as in the association between theater and *khayal*), and the active (this is evident in the call for civilizational progress through a change in habits and dispositions). In other words, the structuring principle of our indexical field still holds so far—the axes we have delineated (presence/absence, inside/outside, and the exchanges between the sensory/sensory and sensory/nonsensory are also evident). Finally, *khayal* did not suddenly stop having its semantic range; the crossings within which it is placed, its undergirding conceptual universe, is where the most dramatic transformation occurs. We can already see this in the introduction of history and science, or what I have referred to in the introduction of this chapter as the (re)splitting of the world between the sensory and the cognitive, and object and subject, in the wake of empiricism and the storm of debates that followed it on evidence and truth. Shidyaq's ruminations on language-*khayal* contributes a pithy example of these connections that the rest of the book will continue to explore. More importantly, it returns us to the heart of the conceptual world undergirding the hermeneutic of *khayal*: language.

Language and the Utterance: "Image"

"One could say that *al-mukhayyila* alone is the tool that allows for the composition of ideas."[68] With these words, al-Shidyaq equates *khayal* and thinking, a move that we will come to see is rooted in his understanding of language itself.[69] His first example is geometrical.[70] Yet it is linked to concerns with the relationship between utterance/vocal form (*lafz*) and meaning/conceptual content (*ma'na*), and the "figurative" (*majaz*) / the veridical (*haqiqa*). These terms were crucial in the conceptual universe/cosmology we explored in the hermeneutic of *khayal*.[71] Shidyaq's deliberation revolves around the intertwinement of the abstract and its particular embodied instantiation. Abstract thought is always implicated with images derived from sensory experience: "If you say, for example, 'triangular angle' and do not picture (*tusawwir*) an image (*sura*) of a particular (*makhsusa*) angle then it [what you said] is nothing but sound, and if you had not seen or touched a triangular angle before, you would not be able to picture/conceptualize (*tatasawwar*) what one would be {like . . . if} you calculate, you have to picture ones being added to one another, otherwise your mind won't grasp anything that your hand does [is calculating or counting]."[72] The first example in this quote is strikingly reminiscent of the ones used by Aristotle to probe the role played by the phantasma in bridging the abstract and the concrete and ensuring the correspondence between "thought" and "world."[73]

Deborah Modrak deploys these threads in Aristotle to analyze the connection between resemblance and the arrival at the universals.[74] Al-Shidyaq explicitly mentions ancient Greeks—specifically Aristotle (Aristu) and Homer (Umirus). He also engages the thought of Joseph Addison (1672–1719), whose essays on the imagination in the *Spectator* are well known.[75] In them, Addison argues that sight is the most perfect of the senses, and that it is primarily responsible for the power of the imagination because it furnishes the imagination with its objects. For Addison, primary pleasures of the imagination are immediate sensory (read visual) experiences of visible, present objects; secondary pleasures pertain to our ability to retain the imprint of those visible objects after they are no longer present for direct perception. To return to Shidyaq, his entry engages doubly with the Arabic Aristotelian commentaries as well as with Romantic thought. It also deals with the contribution of *khayal* in technical and scientific inventions. Carpentry, for example, along with other more recent scientific inventions, are dependent upon *khayal* for their creation.[76] The decision to analyze abstract mathematical thought in tandem with technical scientific production and the function of language is worth further exploration, though, at first glance, it seems to suggest that by "image" Shidyaq is thinking of a conceptual content that needs to be made to stand in front of our mind's eye for thinking to be possible at all.[77] However, this conceptual content is here given an empiricist tinge; it needs to result from prior direct personal sensory experience, as we will see shortly.[78] The following discussion focuses on the relationship between abstract virtues, language, and *khayal*, precisely because abstract virtues offer an apposite angle for grappling with Shidyaq's empiricist tendencies.

Language is meaningless if it does not conjure up images (which we can conjecture means "conceptual content"). Al-Shidyaq presses the point, creating an analogy between the relationship of language to meaning and his earlier geometrical example. If uttering words such as greatness (*'azama*), actuality (*haqq*), and justice (*'adl*) did not call forth images, they would be mere sounds, which evaporate into the air.[79] It is possible that by image he means conceptual content, though his insistence on direct experience will complicate the matter. The examples he uses resonate with both the classical debates on *khayal* and virtues that we have discussed, and with concepts shaping the political field in the nineteenth century.[80] The connection between these abstract notions and images abstracted from direct sensory experience is elusive; the analogy to the geometrical example is less clear than Shidyaq claims.

For, if the image of the "triangular angle"—appearing in *khayal*—could be attributed to an earlier actual sensory experience, how could the "images" of greatness, truth, and justice emanate from a direct sensory experience? The latter are not immediately sensory. Consequently, the abstraction of their "image" cannot be approached as resembling the process of abstracting an image of a triangle. While Shidyaq does not pick up on the tension—between his geometric and other examples—there are crucial clues in the entry.

Abstract notions are based upon extrapolations from particular personal experiences. The meaning of *haqq* (actuality), for example, is construed through hearing that something is actual and then finding it; as such, the notion of actuality or *haqq* is created. On the other hand, if it were not found, the concept of *batil*—*haqq*'s antonym—would be formulated.[81] The notion of justice is formed in a parallel manner. For al-Shidyaq, these particular personal experiences are like the letters used to write and read a book. In interpreting the world, particular personal experiences are the founding letters of thinking the most abstract concepts, and, in turn, particular incidents come to be understood vis-à-vis abstract concepts, which have themselves been formed through particular encounters. Immediate sensory experiences shape the abstract concepts at the base of all knowledge: they are the letters that give form to both abstract through the concrete and *then* vice versa. The experiences are understood through abstract concepts, which are formulated through the experiences after they have been internalized and organized. In thinking of greatness, truth, justice, or actuality, one is necessarily thinking of particular incidents that have shaped the understanding of the concepts. Al-Shidyaq's "resolution" raises more questions than answers, ranging from his definition of the abstract/noncorporeal (ma'nawiyya) to the possibility of communication through language, whose founding blocks have been formed through different particular personal experiences—in other words, what coheres the utterly individuated cognitive process with the possibility of communicating with others, and not just thinking. This is important, because Shidyaq claims that (social) conflict arises because of confusion and illusion, the latter of which occurs due to the erroneous attachment of an image (of a particular personal encounter) to an abstract concept. What are the criteria through which we gauge the difference between illusion and confusion on the one hand, and truth on the other? How are the different interpretations of justice, greatness, and actuality—all formed through the association between a particular experience and the concept—arbitrated to distinguish truth from falsehood? A potential response resides in the subdivisions of the faculty responsible for khayal (al-mukhayyila), and the position of the "magic" of language (sihr al-kalam).[82]

Khayal, for Shidyaq, is divided into two parts. The first is inert/barren ('aqima) and functions like a memory for images.[83] The second is productive (muntija), where there is no place for error, illusion, or falsehood. In the barren subdivision, falsehood and truth, illusion and reality, are confused, and the link created between the abstract and the particular is partial. The barren mukhayyila does not create a harmonious order linking the various image-notions to each other; the connection is involuntary and does not include a process of "understanding" (fahm). "Ignorant" (jahala) people only rely upon the barren mukhayyila and, consequently, are prone to error and confusion. For others, there is the generative mukhayyila, which is not associated with illusion or error.[84] The reason is not explained.

One can perhaps assume that the associations, in the generative part of this faculty between the abstract notions and the particular experiences, are rooted in a process of "understanding," which Shidyaq describes as composition (*ta'lif*) and careful thinking (*rawiyya*). Similarly, the nature of "understanding" is not elucidated. However, "understanding" is an exclusive aspect of the productive *mukhayyila*, which has an additional subpart devoted to the production of the magic of language (*sihr al-kalam*).[85]

The description of *sihr al-kalam* powerfully stresses the question of visuality, and it explicitly compares language to "*taswir*" (the same term Muwaylihi uses in his introduction). *Sihr al-kalam* draws vividly what others could merely sketch.[86] These illustrations captivate their beholders, forcing them to accept and internalize the colorfully drawn associations. The description is reminiscent of the rendition of *khayal* in the classical debates investigated earlier, where it was argued to function through an affective response (*infi'al nafsi*). Crucially, Ibn Sina relies upon the term *rawiyya* in his definition of the poetic as functioning through eliciting emotional responses, bypassing *rawiyya*.[87] For Shidyaq, the magic of "language" and poetic discourse combine the imaginal with the composition of ideas after careful thinking (*rawiyya*). He claims that *sihr al-kalam* is more predominant in poetry than any other kind of "discourse" (*kalam*).[88] The entry ends soon afterward, leaving readers in the grip of unresolved questions. Nonetheless, connecting the abrupt comment on drawing effective images to the rest of the entry potentially offers some answers.

In the inert *mukhayyila*, the actions are not willful or voluntary. Utterances evoke jumbled images (potentially understood as conceptual content) through a process of recollection, which renders the subpart closer in function to memory. *Sihr al-kalam* is part of the generative subdivision of *al-mukhayyila*. As such, its links between abstract notions and particular prior sensory experiences—maintained as images—are willful. In addition, its associations have an effect on others—that is to say, the second faculty actively creates the associations through which language may be inertly understood. Consequently, it literally creates the magic of words, giving it the ability to invoke an image, to create associations, and to have meaning, with an effect on others. The conclusion brings forth a tension in the initial claim that all meaning is formed through a particular personal process of association; it would either mean that the experience of poetry—or *sihr al-kalam* more generally—is understood as a particular personal sensory experience, or that the initial claim pertains to a "first" conception of language rather than its perpetual and continuous production. While the latter possibility is not indicated in the entry, perhaps these two aspects coexist. People ascribe meaning to words through their personal experiences, but the magic of discourse, found particularly in poetry, can play a role in changing these meanings, instilling clearer and more accurate meanings. Here, clarity and accuracy are judged in relation to experiences of the outside world, and not just through the inner logic of the poetic discourse. Shidyaq's example about the erroneously striking workers is a case in point about the real-life social implications of these terms, and of his association of poetry not only with an affective and active dimension in its reception but also with an accurate empirical judgement in its formulation. This rendition of previous sensory experience is not too far off from what we saw through *waqa'i'*: they both demonstrate an increasing focus on everything that happens in the world of perceptions either as an always already sensory experience or as something that could be rendered sensory.[89]

With these clues in our minds—or perhaps in our *khayal*—we can return to where this chapter began: with the visualization of history in the canon of nineteenth-century Arabic literature. Here, we can begin to unpack what we dubbed as a visual logic of unfolding, in which the literary form coheres as an optic that can make history visible, revealing the world within and without the texts as a theater of history. In this theater, the specific events and their underpinning law appear to be immediate "sensory" experiences capable of moving people (affectively and actively).

New Crossings: The Literary Optic and the Theater of History

Let us examine the opening scenes of three texts as a crossing to the literary. Muwaylihi's *hadith*, Marrash's "Forest," and Tuwayrani's "Floral Publishing" all resort to framing episodes that drive the events and connect the otherwise distinct vignettes or scenes together. Furthermore, all three texts exhibit a fascinating tension: as much as they seem keen on connecting abstract principles to their particular manifestations, they resort in the process to interesting fantastical ploys. For example, the dead are roaming the city, abstract principles are embodied in characters that converse with each other, and eternal birds bestow their wisdom on ghosts from the past. Crucially, in all of these texts, though in various ways, the characters are busy trying to decipher the universal principles governing civilizational progress and what it might mean to particularize and apply them (the diagnostic dimension of history); additionally, the term *khayal* appears in the framing of these texts. The frame episodes signal that one is crossing into the realm of the literary, preparing one for a visual experience whereby the world (within and without the text) is opened up as a theater of history. Nowhere is this clearer than in Marrash's "Forest."

"Forest" is framed as an attempt to bring history in front of the mind's eye, to place it under an optical device, and to put it on stage. From the very beginning, the text replays the march of consecutive civilizations and debates the principles of civilizational progress underpinning the rise and fall of each consecutive civilization. We can begin to see that these three gestures are not only gestures of visualization but also of "judgment"—a link that we focused on in discussing Tahtawi and Mubarak's theater-*khayal*. The appeal to theater and the visual is explicit, preparing the readers to witness a play. The half-asleep narrator drifts into the world of "*khayal* dreams" and finally gives in to sleep, and the "theater of dreams" opens up in front of his eyes. He witnesses the performance of what is described in the text as a *khayali* dream. As readers, browsing through the book, we are interlopers in the dream, where the narrator is hiding behind a tree, peeping and eavesdropping on a long debate/trial that he watches like a performance. In a sense, the narrator dreams up a play, a theatrical trial, in which he plays the role of the audience. As readers, we read the dream-play, which should ultimately equip us with an optic for seeing the world inside the text as well as outside of it as a theater of history.

Similarly, Muwaylihi's *hadith* deploys the familiar narrative framing of *maqama*, where an unknown narrator recounts the story he heard told by 'Isa Ibn Hisham. Here, however, the narrator has a dream in which he sees 'Isa Ibn Hisham telling a story about meeting a resurrected dead Pasha. The ghosts of the past, which were mentioned by the narrator in "Forest," are actualized and literalized in Muwaylihi's text. Mubarak had also mentioned the importance of staging great men from the past; in *hadith*, Ahmad Pasha al-Manikli, a historical figure from the era of Muhammad

'Ali, is staged as a ghost returning from the dead. Yet Muwaylihi does not make an explicit reference to *khayal* here; he just tells us that we are about to read a dream without referring to it as a *khayali* dream. While he does mention *khayal* in the short introduction to the book, the initial episodes published in *misbah al-sharq* (Lantern of the East) would not have been framed in connection to *khayal*, but solely as a dream.

There is another significant point of comparison between the framing of these two texts. While in "Forest" the narrator falls asleep as he reflects upon the ghosts of time, his reflection is focused on the rise and fall of civilizations. Muwaylihi's text opens with 'Isa in the cemetery, reflecting on time as a natural drive to death and annihilation. In other words, at the beginning of the text, time denotes nature as a ruinous force marching toward death. It is only with the resurrection of the Pasha that time takes on an added dimension: history, or what 'Isa explicitly names as the need to know "the history of the present era."

This appeal to time as a force of nature appears in other works as well. Tuwayrani's "Floral Publishing" begins with contemplations on time and history, drawing on classical poetic tropes, particularly the iconic opening lines of Umru' al-Qays's pre-Islamic ode.[90] In Tuwayrani's text, the narrator, an astronomer, focuses his telescope and sees several celestial characters, with whom he sets out on a journey to explore the history of the world, particularly Kiwan, as a foil for the Ottoman Empire. While the text is not framed as a play, there is a parallel emphasis on the visual.

Thus far, these three texts seem to be presented as dreams or visions that are anchored in a contemplation of time or history. In "Forest," the contemplation is of the rise and fall of empires; *hadith* evokes the form of the *maqama* as a vehicle for a contemplation of time as a natural destructive force, which later gives way to the attempt to perceive the history of the present. "Floral Publishing" deploys ruins, via the mediation of the Arabic ode, to excavate the history of the present in Kiwan. The three texts anticipate a visual experience, the enframing of the following scenes as the way in which history is made visible. The next chapter analyzes the relationship between the making visible of history, and the episodic structure of the texts, arguing that while we have three interlocked gestures of visualization/and modes of judgement discursively, narratologically theatrical techniques are dominant. They pivot on the deliberate, purposeful summoning of fragments from other literary genres (from odes, *maqamas*, and dream visions, among many others), creating an "episodic" structure both on the level of plot and form. Chapter 2 argues that this fragmentation is key for making history visible.

2
Khayal
Literature as a Theater of History

Chapter 1 concluded with a survey of the opening scenes, or framing narratives, of key texts from the canon of nineteenth-century Arabic literature. Focusing on seminal examples from that canon, I argued that these scenes initiate a crossing into literature as the world of *khayal*, intertwining three gestures of visualization and judgment by making objects stand in front of the mind's eye, placing them under an optic device, and putting them onstage.

Thus far, our argument stands at the threshold of these texts, drawing links between disparate debates on *khayal*/theater, theater/history, history/the literary framing narratives. But, then, what happens to these sets of relationalities surrounding *khayal*—which give it its very definition—when we actually step *inside* the literary texts? In other words, how is this conception of *khayal*, as an optic and a stage for historical truth, practiced in these texts beyond the appeal to the term, to theater, to dreams, and to visions in the opening scenes? This chapter turns to the ways in which these three gestures are narrativized by the texts.

While the latter gestures are conceptually indispensable constituents of literary truth, theater takes precedence narratologically, contributing a generative model for *how* literature can make objects visible. Chapter 2 focuses on this point, exploring what it means for literature to make objects visible, how it achieves this visibility narratologically, and what this tells us about the nature of literary objects. Through a careful reading of how literature as the world of *khayal* makes its objects visible, I argue that literature follows a process that is analogous to theatrical staging, but with a crucial caveat. I refer to this process as "literary staging": a concept that emerges through the careful analysis of how *khayal* arose, during the nineteenth century, as the axis for drawing an analogy between theater and literature as two comparable visual media. Literary staging, therefore, describes the way in which literature makes objects visible.

At its core, chapter 2 follows one main question: How does the literary emerge in this era as the attempt to *make* history *visible?* In this chapter, we will look at the specific ways in which history is visualized in these literary texts, and in the following chapter we will examine how history is conceptualized. The exposition of the specific techniques of visualization/judgment that we began to identify in chapter 1 *and* the probing of the conceptions of history are two inseparable aspects of *how* history is made visible. While, in the texts under discussion, these two aspects are encountered simultaneously, they pose distinct analytical questions. First, the concern with literary staging leads us to an analysis of narrativization, since history will be *staged* precisely through the ways in which these texts are narrativized. On the other hand, the articulation of conceptions of history that are being narrativized once again returns the analysis to the conceptual level. Consequently, this central question is divided over two chapters, reflecting its two main analytical aspects.

This chapter focuses on Francis al-Marrash's "Forest" and Ali Mubarak's *'alam al-din* to show how what I describe as the literary staging of history in the canon of nineteenth-century Arabic literature is achieved narratologically by structuring these key texts as a series of potentially self-enclosed scenes.[1] Each scene, on its own, organizes an object, or several objects, *as if* they are stage objects. The succession of scenes themselves—or the episodes—follows a similar pattern whereby the episodes are arrayed *as if* they are different objects lying on a stage. In other words, the emplotment of the episodes strives to replay the dynamics found within each single episode, and, in so doing, the different episodes sometimes create a single scene and, at other times, become an incessant repetition of a single scene. This episodic structure is motivated by the attempt to deploy all of the stage objects either synchronically to occupy the same scene or to array them as a procession that replays the same scene over and over. Chapter 2 explores literary staging both on the level of the single episode as well as a mode of emplotting episodes. This focalized analysis continues to evoke *khayal* as an image with cognitive, affective, and active dimensions that map out on axes of inside/outside, presence/absence, and exchanges between sensory/sensory or sensory/nonsensory. These different dimensions play out as the interaction between the object onstage as an object of direct sensory experience and another object, or experience, that is evoked through it. I describe the first as an object of direct sensory perception while the latter is a staged object; the interplay between these two is how *khayal* appears in this chapter, continuing to inform our analysis of narrative structure. We begin our exploration by returning to the discussion of theater within the texts and probing how the texts explicate the visual dimension of theater.

Conjunctions: Stage Objects and Their Specters

In their discussion examined in the previous chapter, both Tahtawi and Mubarak emphasize the crucial role played by theater in "educating" both the elite and the masses in order to achieve civilizational progress. The issue is linked to theater's ability to make visible what is otherwise impossible to experience in a direct sensory manner. Their assumption is rooted in an implicit epistemological hierarchy of the senses in which direct sensory experience is thought to be more effective and affective in comparison to abstract disembodied mandates.[2] Consequently, bearing direct witness is better than hearing a report, and, by extension, sight is privileged over aural experiences. Through sight, eyes become vehicles of direct sensory experiences more than any of the other senses. This hierarchy is not born with the *nahda*. Rather, it has a much longer and more nuanced history, some of which was glimpsed through the analysis of *khayal* in the previous chapter. This section grapples with how this hierarchy is redeployed as part of reconceiving of literature as a visual medium; in so doing, it elucidates the way in which both the allegorical and "protorealist—and sometimes "hyperrealist"—texts of the period are underpinned by a shared narrative technique of visualization that I call "staging." To explain staging, let's return to Tahtawi's and Mubarak's discussions of theater, touched upon in the preceding chapter.

Tahtawi focuses exclusively on the portrayal of historical events. Theater offers the opportunity of turning history from a collection of accounts and reports into a direct sensory experience. Mubarak expands the scope slightly to include the depiction of religious narratives, which oscillate between being an ostensible part of history (e.g., stories of previous prophets and peoples) to being a break with time altogether (e.g., judgment day, eternal reward, eternal punishment). Tahtawi's and Mubarak's descriptions strongly suggest that stage settings play a significant role in successfully simulating sensory experience and, thus, in theater's effectiveness as an institution that induces civilizational progress.[3] In other words, stage settings are at the heart of the transformation of history from accounts and reports (aural experiences) to direct experience (sight).[4]

The previous chapter revealed the resonance of these debates regarding theater and *khayal* for the conceptualization of the literary. Yet, by virtue of the difference in media, they highlight interesting nuances concerning the relationship between language and visualization; word and image; performance and text; and language, reading, and performativity. However, it is crucial to note that these terms cannot be neatly divided between theater and literature, whereby, for example, language stands on the side of one and visualization on the side of the other. The point, rather, is that these sets play out *within* literature in one way, and *within* theater in another way. Furthermore, these processes are punctuated by how these sets are worked out in the space of the articulation *between* theater and literature, in both their imbrication and negotiated, tenuous separation.[5]

Yet it is still heuristically useful to deliberately start the analysis here by making a naive distinction between a staged performance of a play and a reading of a literary text. To put it simply, the idea that a play's performance simulates a sensory experience seems, at first, to be self-evident, since watching a play *is* a direct sensory experience. Nonetheless, that is clearly not the point being made by Tahtawi or Mubarak. Instead, the direct sensory experience of watching a play being performed simulates another sensory experience that *is not* directly encountered but that *is* directly staged through the initial one.[6] We have already encountered a version of this interplay in our discussion of the relationship between the object and the shadow in shadow plays. A concise example of this interplay can be found in Tahtawi's discussion of stage settings: "In these spectacles, they represent everything that exists, even the parting of the sea by Moses—Peace be upon him. They represent the sea and create rolling waves so that it completely looks like the sea. One night, I saw that they ended the play (*tiyatir*) with a representation of a sun and its course. The light of this sun illuminated the theatre to such an extent that it outshone the chandeliers; it was as if suddenly morning had broken for people."[7]

One day as he is watching a play in France, Tahtawi witnesses the staging of sunrise at the end of a performance. The object on the stage that is *directly* accessed through an immediate sensory experience is "stage lighting" that is being manipulated to simulate sunlight—judging from the time period, the 1820s and 1830s, Tahtawi is most likely describing the technology of the open gas jet flame and the "gas table." Their light shone so brightly that it was *as if* the audience were outside in the morning light—instead of sitting indoors, in the evening, inside a playhouse. Here, the stage lights do not simply appear to the audience's senses (specifically, sight), but their appearance enables the audience to have another sensory experience—in this case, of sunrise. We are not grappling yet with how this exchange between two sensory experiences (stage lights and sunrise) allows for history to be experienced sensorially; rather we are looking into how this exchange between these two objects, both of which have the potential to be experienced sensorially, occurs onstage. To reiterate, what is being directly staged here is sunrise, but the immediate sensory experience is that of the manipulation of stage lights. The latter are used in such a way, in relation to other elements of the performance, to produce an additional (quasi-)sensory experience. This additional experience is precisely what chapter 1 described as part of the workings of *khayal*. In this chapter, we analyze the ways in which theater offers a prism for nineteenth-century literature in Arabic to grapple with this exchange between object/object, stage lights/sun, as well as to contend with how the latter can enable the turning of history into a sensory experience.

Both sunrise and the lighting of a jet flame are direct and immediate experiences. When we say that watching a play *is* a direct and immediate sensory experience, we are referring both to our experience of the sensory objects themselves (stage lights) and to the additional staged experience they produce (sunrise). The experience of a staged play cannot be reduced to the direct sensory experience, but exceeds it. In fact, the staging depends precisely upon the *seeming* immediacy with which the excess of the direct sensory experience appears to be experienced directly. In other words, the stage lights should be immediately seen to be sunrise. The specific dynamics through which these exchanges and collapses occur is at the heart of the debates on *khayal*, as surveyed in chapter 1. This insight informs the naive heuristic distinction I sketch between theater and literature.

It may have already become obvious that the differentiation is not one of immediacy in the case of theater, as compared to mediation in literature. The point is that literature does not produce this exchange by couching the staged object (sunrise) in a concrete sensory object (stage lights); instead, it must rely on a simulation of the latter. To continue with our reading of Tahtawi's example, we don't have an object-object exchange through which an object-object/history-cum-sensory experience is mediated. In light of this literary canon's insistence on its analogy with theater, this leaves it with two options for thinking and practicing its own version of staging, or literary staging. The first is to drop the first concrete sensory object (the stage lights) in whose shadows we come to access the staged sensory object (the sun or sunrise) and to begin immediately from this sensorially absent and yet present onstage, or staged, object (sunrise). The second is to figure out a literary equivalent to this first concrete object (stage lights) that allows for maintaining the object-object part of the interaction while upholding the implicit differentiation in the mode of presence of these two objects (stage lights vs. sunrise).

These two options are not divided neatly between the texts, but, as we will see in the coming sections, they are both mobilized in different ways *within* each text. Far from being two mutually exclusive options, these two strategies form the axes along which these texts experiment with staging.

In the following section we turn to two seemingly diametrically opposed texts: Marrash's "Forest," with its explicit appeal to theater and the stage, and Mubarak's *'alam al-din*, with its self-fashioning as a narrativized encyclopedia. While these works are in fact quite different, I argue that they both partake in a project of literary staging that conceives of literature as an optic that is narratologically analogous to theater, and discursively comparable to both theater and to micrographs, and yet not reducible to either one, since literary staging offers its own answer to these questions of "evidence."[8]

Staging Allegory and Realism

Marrash's "Forest" and Mubarak's *'alam al-din* are often classified as an allegory and a realist (or protorealist) narrative, respectively. In the early histories of modern Arabic literature, both texts are awkwardly positioned as protonovels—or, at least, as protonovelistic. With the advent of revisionist studies (influenced by various shades of poststructuralist approaches), the concern with genre categorization as well with these texts' place in a literary genealogy has been sidelined. Returning to the division between allegory and realism, this section rereads these attributes in connection with literary staging.

While the critical scholarship on allegory is characterized by its appearance in recurring bursts, it has succeeded in noticeably nuancing our understanding of allegory as a trope, a narrative mode, and a mode of reading (or interpretation). The idea that allegory and realism belong to two opposing narrative poles has not withstood sustained critical pressure, particularly since realism has also undergone a systematic revision.[9] There is no simple one-word translation for "allegory" in Arabic. Just as the conception of allegory has undergone noticeable changes throughout its long history, critical terms describing tropes and techniques of figuration in Arabic have also witnessed significant transformations. Specifically, allegory oscillates between being the name of figuration itself; crossing between different systems, levels, and modes of meaning; and naming a particular technique of figuration. Accordingly, my sense is that, in Arabic, "allegory" would hover between *majaz* as the "figurative" itself and *takhyil* and *tamthil* as two specific techniques of figuration.

Takhyil is derived from the concept of *khayal* discussed at length in chapter 1. A typical definition of *takhyil* is that it grants abstract qualities—usually personal virtues—a perceivable, often instantiated, embodiment. *Tamthil*, on the other hand, gives a concrete example, or analogy, of a description or a state through another description, like saying the cloth was clean to indicate the purity of the soul. If we wanted to be simplistic, we could say that *takhyil* visually captures the essence of the thing, or *what it is* (e.g., courage, generosity), but *tamthil* contributes a concrete analogy of *how the thing is*—in other words, the state of the thing. Needless to say, their actual history of practice was far more complex. My primary concern, however, is not allegory and its equivalents in Arabic, but with the question of how "allegory vs. realism" was used by critical scholarship to describe nineteenth-century Arabic literary practice.

The study of the literature of the *nahda* has not always been able to fully capitalize on these developments in producing readings of the intersection between these two narrative modes (allegory and realism) in, as well as across, specific texts.[10] By extension, it remains unclear how these narrative modes contributed to shaping what we think of as modern Arabic narrative forms despite the attestation to their significance both during the *nahda* and beyond. Consequently, it remains difficult to describe—let alone analyze—forms of modern Arabic narrative.

This difficulty is owed to the way the scholarship of the *nahda* specifically, and the study of modern Arabic literature generally, has unfolded over time. In the introduction to this book, I alluded to the critical trends in this scholarship and do not aim to reproduce that discussion here; I point it out in order to highlight how the idiosyncrasies of the trajectory of the scholarship focusing on the nahda have persistently reproduced a blind spot in the reading of these texts. The skeleton of the issue can be explained as such: the move from conventional and by now disparaged literary histories to variants of poststructuralist analysis is concomitant with an increased focus on ideology (i.e., through the banners of the postcolonial, bourgeois, capitalist, modern). The early fixation on mapping the path of the rise of literary modernity, often capsulized in the novel, has lost its ostensible neutrality as an inquiry into literary development or progression.

Instead, modern Arabic literature is approached as one facet of a wider tumultuous process of social transformation in the wake of capitalist modernity. These social changes include, necessarily, epistemological and conceptual—or, in a word, ideological—vicissitudes. There are such crucial differences and disagreements in this broad-ranging poststructuralist current that it might be more accurate to grapple with them as multiple opposing currents. Yet I group them in relation to a latent tension that draws them together—namely, the elision of the analysis of what the "literary" *is*.[11] I am not referring here to some essential, transcendent, or ahistorical conception of the literary. My point is simple: the conception of the literary, in these studies, appears as an always already given. It is circumscribed; its boundaries lie *outside* of the analytic pursuit, furnished by one theoretical point or another. As a result, the turn to ideology is more of a gesture of intentionality than a methodical exploration. For, in circumscribing the conception of the literary, the analysis has to be repeatedly, forcibly collapsed into what has already been posited as an analytic a priori (i.e., the conception of the literary). In other words, the analysis of ideology—which is also, in this case, the study of the conception of the literary—is rendered inaccessible at the very moment of its supposed analysis. If literature is part of the broader structure of ideology and is *a* particular ideological form, then analyzing it does not hinge on (merely) reiterating the precise portrayals *in* the texts, the opinions (or social positioning) of the authors, but principally on elucidating the conception of the "literary" itself and the struggles to produce and reproduce that conception.[12] To fine-tune the point, it can be said that we are presented with an outline of the literary as an ideological form of capitalist modernity in general. Yet, due to the structure of the analysis itself, the outline continually resists any further abstraction and specification.

The challenge of reading the articulation of allegory and realism in the literature of the Arab *nahda* is one specific level of the broader task of analyzing the conception of the literary. Clearly, a full elucidation of the conception of the literary cannot be accomplished in one chapter or even in a single book. In taking up this challenge, my goal is not to contribute a quick solution, much less another collapse. Rather, the present discussion enables us to grapple with the broader implications of chapter 1, which pursued the conception of the literary in the canon of nineteenth-century Arabic literature. More importantly, with these implications in view, we can dive into the narrative details of the texts with reduced risk of submersion.

In thinking of allegory and realism as they are used to describe this literary canon, I suggest that they in fact capture two broadly conceived approaches to literary staging. The first approach seemingly relinquishes the first object in the object-object exchange while insisting on highlighting its awareness of its own theatricality—precisely at the moment that it seems to desist from producing a stage prop (stage lights). The second, on the contrary, produces a meticulous, micrographic simulation of a series of objects (that operate like the stage lights) and, in its vocal proclamation of kinship to science, produces profoundly theatrical texts. Marrash's "Forest" is a key example of the first type, while Mubarak's *'alam al-din* illustrates the second. Even though the rest of this chapter focuses only on these two texts, creating through them a typology, this move allows us to access the related variations and combinations found in the other texts studied in this book.

Francis al-Marrash's "Forest" contributes the most salient example in this nineteenth-century canon of the literary as an attempt to stage history. Its references to stage, plays, dreams, *khayal*, and spectacles are both explicit and relentless, as we saw in the previous chapter. They do not only abound in the framing narrative but are also used to signal the beginning and end of many of the main chapters of this book. This feature is intimately related to the two levels of staging/narrativization I referred to previously—that is, both within the single episodes as well as in the way the episodes are weaved together.

"Forest" opens with the narrator wandering through his thoughts. Daydreaming, he sees in his mind's eye the ghosts of past eras marching in succession to the tunes of bygone peoples (*naghamat al-shu'ub al-ghabira*). With one ghost after another, the narrator witnesses the course of the history of civilization play out in front of him. It begins with the rise of the ancient Egyptians, immediately followed by the Assyrians and the Phoenicians. Soon afterward, the Persians rise to stardom, overshadowing their predecessors. The Persians themselves are later overcome by the Macedonians, with the Romans after them. Finally, the Roman Empire is split into two parts: one Western, and the other Eastern. The first is constantly expanding into prosperous states and kingdoms while the second is perpetually entangled in repetitive cycles of rise and fall. As the narrator, who is never named, continues to be inundated with these manifestations, which appear to his mind's eye, a door pops open in front of his perception. On the threshold is a written statement: "The intellect rules" (al-'aql yahkum). The narrator crosses through. On the other side of the door lies a vast wilderness. No sooner does he cross over than he sees an approaching flag with blurred writing on it. He puts on his glasses (nazzarat al-ikhtibar) so that he may better decipher it.[13] He looks again, closely, and recognizes the statement: "Knowledge triumphs" (al-'ilm yaghlib). Instantly, the war between civilization and barbarity plays out with the armies of civilization appearing from behind the flag, armed with technology, wisdom, justice, and freedom. They disperse the defeated troops of the kingdoms of darkness, who are stampeding en route to annihilation and oblivion. In this manner, the narrator observes how the State of the Intellect has extended its dominion everywhere, and how peace prevailed. The description is already "theatrical," in part due to its allegorical style and its attendant heavy reliance upon the personification of abstract qualities. Yet the stage is not fully open—visible, and in full action—until the narrator falls asleep.

Intoxicated with these visions he is watching on this "new stage" (marsah jadid), the narrator suddenly sees smoke rising from the west and occluding his vision. Meanwhile, he hears a cacophony of unintelligible noises punctuated by the rumbling of thunder. He can almost make out the glistening of the weapons of war. Finally, the clear voices of the news arise, pronouncing the war on slavery in America. We are told that the "new world" (America) has gone against this coarse habit ('ada) since no remnants of the State of Enslavement could be tolerated.[14] Having considered the meaning and repercussions of these events, the narrator is overwrought with turbulent emotions that roil his body until he gives in to sleep, opening up khayal's dream stage to his eyes.[15]

The reference to theater is already obvious in the first sentences of the text with allusions to "scene," "play," and "curtains." Later on, the narrator refers to his vision, or daydream, as something he is watching in a new theater / on a new stage (marsah jadid). Yet there is a noticeable delay in officially announcing the admission into the stage (of dreams)—it only occurs at the very last sentence of this short framing narrative. Curiously, this delay is replayed in future chapters of the text, with comparable details: the narrator is overtaken by strong, and therefore ineffable, emotions when he suddenly finds himself face to face with a stage.[16] In other words, the opening of the stage is not a one-time occurrence, but a process that is sustained through replaying it. I will return to this detail shortly, but before we can analyze it, we must examine the opening scene. My reading tackles two interrelated questions: With all of these references to theater and stage, what is being staged? And, while I have referred to the text as an allegory that draws extensively on personification, what is it an allegory of?

Three key elements are being woven together here. The first is the daydream, or the narrator's thoughts, percolating in his mind. The second is the diachronic list of "great civilizations," and the third is the reference to contemporary news from the "new world" being broadcast through the wires (hence the reference to lightning and thunder). I have left out the mention of *khayal* and stage of the two statements "The intellect rules" and "Knowledge triumphs," and of the vast wilderness. What I have left out could either be subsumed within the existing three elements, or they could be made to stand alone as additional components. For example, the stage and the vast wilderness could be part of the daydream; it's the setting of the dream, what allows for the staging of "internal" thoughts. The two statements, on the other hand, could be approached as an addendum to the diachronic list. Furthermore, the three elements could be compressed into two: the daydream, and its object (the diachronic list, the statements, the news). In other words, we can produce several different neat lists depending on how we choose to name, categorize, and organize these elements of the narrative. Such an exercise in classification is not very telling, particularly in the absence of a sharp sense of how, and why, these different elements are drawn together. But if we look beyond the cataloging of these elements to what links them, we can see a clear principal relationship connecting them. It can be described with more or fewer details and nuances, shaping the enumeration of the elements, but the basic structure is clear.

We have on the one side the staging of a daydream (the creation of a space, or theater, where the externalization of "internal" thoughts could be played out), and on the other there is the object of the daydream. The latter presents us with separate though successive episodes of history, to which we add the most recent episode taking place in the "new world," as well as the abstract principles that these episodes enact and instantiate. The relationship could be explained in slightly different terms. The daydream is the site where the different episodes could be linked with their undergirding shared abstract principle, enabling a visual experience of these episodes, and of the abstract principles in a way that goes beyond the sensory, but is not entirely abstract either. The daydream, then, signals a particular mode of thinking as envisioning through which the stage becomes the externalization of this particular kind of thinking process. Similarly, the object of the dream is the object of thinking as envisioning.

In either case, there is a "hidden" element: the narrator, who is literally hiding throughout most of the text. Put differently, there is a "subject" whose thinking process is being staged as he grapples with the truth underpinning the movement of history. Strikingly, the moment his thought process is being staged is also the moment he becomes an object of that stage.[17] The two elements could equally be argued to be one single element. We can say that what we encounter, in this opening scene, is the visualization of historical truth: what we see are the actual principles governing the movement of history (here understood as civilizational progress) be it in Phoenicia, America, or nineteenth-century Syria. At stake here is not the mapping out of an internal causal connection leading from one of these civilizations to the next and connecting them horizontally; instead, each civilization constitutes a relatively self-enclosed object whereby the abstract principles governing history are displayed in action. We can approach each one of these objects as enacting a totally self-enclosed scene or investigate their connection as a replay of the same scene, and principles, across different geotemporal sites. In this manner, we have returned to the definition of the conception of the literary in the previous chapter.

To recap, I have started by enumerating the elements in this opening scene in order to elucidate what is being staged and what this text is an allegory of. The previous paragraph has implicitly offered us a response to both these questions. The text sets out to make visible historical truth, which is here understood to be the abstract universal principles governing civilizational progress. Since this staging takes place through narrativization, it is presented as a story of how thinking as envisioning traverses through arid wilderness and dense forests until it cuts its way through to the truth. By extrapolation, it is an allegory of the way thinking grapples with the pursuit of truth (here defined as historical truth). The replayed delay in the opening up of the stage reflects the tension between how the crossing to the literary promises, from the outset, the possibility of making truth visible, and the text's desire to reveal the *process* of visualization and not just its result. This insight offers a preliminary, and clearly fractional, overview of staging in the text—from the vantage point of the opening scene. I describe it as fractional, in part, to anticipate the nuancing of this view as we turn to conceptions of history and characters in the chapters to come. Furthermore, the reading I have offered here clearly elides one of the most long-standing readings of this text as an allegory for the then-contemporary situation in greater Syria. In the following paragraphs, I turn to this concern with Syria by way of moving away from showing staging in general, toward a more careful consideration of what I have referred to before as an arraying of objects. In other words, the discussion hones the interpretation of this staging by specifying allegory in this text, of which I have only provided the general contour so far. I should clarify, from the beginning, that my purpose is to include the long-standing interpretation into my reading rather than dispel or replace it.

Marrash's "Forest" is comprised of eight main chapters in addition to the introduction that I have been referring to interchangeably as the framing narrative and opening scene. These chapters are "The Dream;" "Anxious Thoughts;" (*hawajis*) "The Kingdom of Spirit;" "Politics and the Kingdom;" "Civilization;" "The Commanders of Evil;" "The Trial;" and "The Awakening."[18] The final chapter reads more like an epilogue, where the narrator wakes up to find himself, once again, in a solitary wasteland. The text is habitually described as an allegory as a result of its evident philosophical tendencies. The label often functions to veer the analysis into intellectual history, moving the discussion toward an exposition of the ideas espoused by Marrash in this text.[19] While these studies afford us crucial insights, they leave much to be desired on the level of literary analysis. For one, they do not allow us to understand how the different episodes of the text are arrayed—and, by extension, how allegory works in this text. In answering this question, I offer a brief summary of the plotline, followed by a sample inventory of the objects encountered in the different scenes.

Chapter 7, "The Trial," delivers the event that has been anticipated and delayed since the first chapter, "The Dream." In that chapter, we encounter the King of Freedom (sometimes referred to as the King of Civilization) and the Queen of Wisdom. They are both sitting, anxiously awaiting reports about the war their troops are waging against the Kingdom of Darkness (and Enslavement). Eventually, the good news is reported by the Minister of Love and the Commander of the Army of Civilization: they have triumphed and captured the enemy, which are the seven deadly sins. The party argue over how to deal with the captured nemeses. The King and the Commander contend that the enemy must be fully annihilated, while the Queen and the Minister advocate for reforms. To resolve the matter, they send for the Philosopher, who is to attend and participate in the trial held for the seized foes. This expected main event is delayed until the final chapter. At the same time, the trial is held from the moment the first chapter begins, as the disagreement within the party sets up a "trial" that will be repeated once again in the conversation between the Philosopher and the Commander, who spend the better part of the book debating the best way to deal with the Kingdom of Darkness. The plotline moves through the postponement of the trial and the unfolding of the logic of the Philosopher's argument. In other words, the chapters are divided both in accordance with the movement toward the trial, almost as a journey to a destination, and through signposting the arguments of the Philosopher. The two converge in the seventh chapter, where the official trial finally takes place. By the time the trial transpires, the decision has, in a real sense, already been made, since the characters have been debating it from the first chapter. The issue, at that point, is to specify how each one of the seven sins will be dealt with.

Two details of the narrative are especially key to reading allegory and therefore deepening our grasp of staging. First, Marrash's appeal to theater is not limited to his deployment of a theatrical lexicon (e.g., curtain, ghosts, stage). Rather, theater provides a key form, and therefore limit, of the narrative structure. Most noticeably, the purview of our vision is delimited by the action onstage, and we cannot witness any action that does not take place there. Whatever occurs offstage must be recounted to us through classic theatrical techniques like the reading of letters, the appearance of a messenger, or the existence of signs explicating these details (even the placing of the different characters or objects on the stage and their movements are detailed to us as if we are reading stage directions). These moves occur from the first opening pages of the text, whereby each civilization is identified via an emblem that is closely associated with it, much like the different characters, who are personifications of abstract qualities, hold objects that mark their identity.[20]

Inadvertently, the text's close mirroring of theatrical form results in a series of reversals and inversions that complicate theater's object-object exchange, which is supposedly mimicked here. This point will become clearer as we compare Marrash's deployment of "stage props" to occasion another sensory experience with Mubarak's summoning of "real" objects inside his text. For now, we can say that the explicit emphasis of the theatrical modality of visualization in Marrash's "Forest" complicates its engagement with the abstract and the concrete, which is central for the way it forges an allegory.

The second crucial feature concerns the replayed opening up of the stage.[21] For example, at the end of chapter 1, the King and Queen send for the Philosopher.[22] The action is paused while we wait. The narrator no longer sees or hears anything but the sound of the water stream that had initially led him to the stage in the middle of the chapter: "The royal appearance was drifting into deep thought. I could no longer see anything except for the stature of profound silence, and I could hear nothing but the burble of water."[23]

With these words, chapter 1 of Marrash's "Forest" concludes. The beginning of chapter 2 is once again portrayed like the start of a play:

> As I wandered through the theaters of intellectual ideas, meandering through the theaters of spectral (*khayalat*) deliberations, I suddenly glimpsed a ghost approaching from afar, lolloping through the thick forest. The ghost was submerged by the dense shade as he continued to tear through determinedly until he emerged out of the thick maze, appearing on the theatre of dreams like a moon piercing through dense clouds.[24]

This will not be the last time we see in the text this explicit enactment of theater and staging, nor is it the sole reference to actors on the stage as specters or ghosts.[25] The assembling of this theater, moreover, is not used exclusively at the beginning and end of each chapter; rather, it follows the plotline, framing scenes that move the main action toward the trial and signposting crucial moments when the Philosopher expounds his ideas. In one pivotal moment, the dialogue between the Philosopher and the Commander turns to the prehistorical origins of politics and society. The conversation halts, and a voice explains that the narrator cannot see so far back into ancient history. Yet the voice encourages the narrator to carry on until a stage appears in front of him (again!). At first, the narrator can't see the ghosts (actors) playing because they are so far back in historical time, but when he puts his glasses on, he sees them more clearly. The discussion continues. This is perhaps one of the clearest and most literal renditions of the literary as an optic, specifically as a *staging* of history.[26]

These enactment scenes are deliberate replays of the opening scene (the introduction), which I have considered at length. Across these different replays, the ghosts or actors sometimes represent specific episodes from bygone history, at other times abstract principles (e.g., wisdom, freedom, love), emotions, or even logical deductions, all portrayed in their connection with historical truth. To recap, we have a plot that moves by delaying the official fulfillment of an event (the trial). At the same time, the final event—the trial—is performed from the very first chapter, since its main subject is discussed, debated, and even sealed by the main characters before the formal trial convenes in the end. We have seen that the assembling of the stage is played and replayed at intersections pertaining both to the deferment of the trial as well as to the unfolding of the logical argument. In concluding my discussion of Marrash's "Forest," I argue that this structure is at the heart of how we can understand allegory in this text. In so doing, I continue to elucidate what I mean by arraying objects—a technique that will become clearer as we turn to Mubarak's *'alam al-din*.

I have noted that branding Marrash's text as an allegory has functioned in previous scholarship as a pretext for an exploration of his ideas. Allegory, here, appears to be used in its most rudimentary definition: speaking otherwise. If "Forest" is Marrash's way of saying something indirectly (i.e., an allegory), then the interpretive task is to deallegorize: to explain what it is the author really wanted to say.[27] There are noticeable disagreements in the interpretations produced by these deallegorizing exercises, yet the different studies mostly concede that the text is a patent allegory for Marrash's Syria, and that the question of the relationship between religion, civilization, and progress is the crux of the work. While I do not seek to overwrite this reading, I suggest that the workings of allegory here cannot be read separately from grappling with the way staging mobilizes gestures of visualization and judgement (evidence) and, in a literary context, construct these objects to be examined and therefore to discover truth—specifically, in this instance, historical truth. In other words, what is abstract and what is concrete, in this allegorical exchange, are not stable, given positions. Rather, they are worked out in the dynamics of exchange, at the heart of delineating not only the literary but also truth, and that staging unleashes between object-object/history-cum-sensory.[28]

With this in mind, it might already be clear that Marrash's "Forest" can be read as an allegory of a philosophy of history that draws together the different personified elements of civilization into equilibrium. We see this philosophy of history as it works on multiple levels: as it plays out in the historical trajectory, or diachrony, of "great" civilizations; within a single civilization (America, or Syria—though Egypt is also a possible candidate in the text); among the public of one civilization; or even within a single soul. The constituent elements of these different layers are preencoded and articulated within specific *living* genres and discourses, each of which exists as a distinct system. The text, then, grafts constituents of different systems into levels of a singular principle or universal philosophy of history. The process can be described and approached in different ways, but the analysis of this articulated philosophy of history requires turning to the intersection of epistemological and political questions, issues that must be deferred to chapters 4 and 5. As a first step in that direction, I take up here the interpretation of grafting discrete elements from within the level of narrative structure, which is often dubbed as the genre hybridity of late nineteenth-century Arabic literature.

Viewed from within the narrative structure, we can perceive the distinct constitutive elements, belonging as they do to different systems, to be culled from a range of genres reproduced within the text. These include, but are not limited to, morality plays, *theatrum* of nature, the narrative of slave fugitives, political treatises, and classical and postclassical *adab*. Furthermore, the reading presented here is not very concerned with the genealogy of these constitutive elements, whether that is taken to be their geographic or temporal origin. In other words, I do not draw an a priori differentiation between *theatrum* of nature and *adab* based on their different genealogies, perceived from within a geopolitical prism. Instead, I am concerned with the generative system, or the conception of the literary, that enabled our authors to experiment with grafting them into a single structure. It is within this very process that we can understand what constitutive elements of this emergent system come to be considered internal and external within a geopolitical mapping of "cultures."

Consequently, we are still in the realm of trying to offer a detailed narratological description of the structure of the text and how it works. Thus far, we see the text as trying to *stage* history (which we surmise to be understood as a universal philosophy of history) by arraying literary fragments. In other words, the unifying philosophy of history is performed through culling fragments from seemingly diverse literary systems that are deployed here to encode partial aspects that are drawn together to articulate this new overarching philosophy. The staging of history seems to work here by summoning fragments from a multiplicity of genres and discourses to the stage. Stage props, then, are but one of the objects we see drawn from theater that plays a central role in enframing and narrativizing "Forest." Other genres are likewise drawn upon, bringing with them their literary techniques, tropes, and objects. Ultimately, it is these forms and genres that constitute the object-object/history-cum-sensory dynamics of Marrash's text. In the process, these forms and genres appear both to belong to distinct systems as well as to be grafted into an emergent singular system. This "double membership" is necessary, for to argue that this is a philosophy of history that underpins the world, it must be shown to have always been implicitly present even if in a dispersed form.

What is striking about this text, however, is that it opts for narrativizing the relationship of the constituent elements of this philosophy of history by appealing explicitly to staging and the theatrical form rather than the more common form of the journey that we see in many other narrative allegories, including Mubarak's *'alam al-din* (which we will be turning to shortly). In so doing, "Forest" is, perhaps ironically, the least obviously theatrical text, since the objects it arrays have less simulated concreteness than those found in other texts (its stage lights are not fully subsumed by and hidden behind the sun or sunrise it stages). Rather, the objects here consist predominantly of literary genres and forms and their constituent fragments; they are amassed as the text moves toward the simultaneous performance and deferment of the trial. In this manner, Marrash's "Forest" accumulates fragments and traces of numerous literary—and, by extension, ideological—forms. Yet it does not reproduce any *one* of these forms. Therefore, the exercise of tracing the literary and philosophical influences of the text can only be useful if it is understood from the perspective of the system produced in the text itself, which gives all of its sources, or building blocks, their meaning. The meaning of these parts, here used as staged objects, cannot be deduced by divulging their origin and meaning in another system, but only by working out how they are woven together here. These objects, or literary fragments, are arrayed within each scene and across the movement from one scene to the next to offer a different conception of the literary: the literary as *making* history *visible*, as a *staging* of historical truth.

In this sense, neither slavery in America, the explicit topic of discussion, nor Syria, the implicit topic, need to be present *in* the text. They could easily lie outside of it as episodes that need to be connected with the abstract principles *staged* by the text. This point is crucial for understanding both the prevalence of episodic structure in these texts, and their seemingly encyclopedic tendencies, which arguably result in loosening their plot.

To better understand staging, let's turn to *'alam al-din*, a text that, unlike "Forest," eschews any connection with theater, making strong claims about its relationship to education, pedagogy, and encyclopedias. Nonetheless, Mubarak's text, in fact, contributes a more immediate exchange between object-object/history-cum-sensory. Through analyzing this staging, we can grapple with how the literary could be promoted as a way for training the senses, and we can grasp key features of the narrative structure shared by both of these texts—which in turn can be extended to other key literary texts from this canon.[29]

Mubarak's *'alam al-din* follows the educational journey of its eponymous character from his early days in the village until he becomes a relatively established, but financially unstable, religious scholar in the famous mosque college of al-Azhar. One day, he gets an opportunity to work closely with an English Orientalist who is editing the magisterial lexicon *lisan al-'arab* (The Language of the Arabs) by Ibn Manzur, to be produced in a printed book edition—Edward William Lane drew heavily on Ibn Manzur in his Arabic-English lexicon. Together, 'Alam al-Din, his son Burhan al-Din, and the English Orientalist embark on a journey from Egypt to England via France, traversing myriad places. Over the course of more than 1,200 pages, 'Alam al-Din travels from a small unnamed rural town in Egypt to the suburbs of Paris, passing through Tanta, Alexandria, Cairo, and Marseilles, and by proxy to Senegambia and the Ashanti Empire. Palaces, hospitals, hotels, cafes, gardens, private homes, cultural salons, and educational institutes in these different cities are portrayed, and modes of transport used in commuting between these places are also discussed, with detailed numbers and statistics being used to compare these places.[30] The text also incorporates nonurban space, particularly the natural world, expounding upon various species and their modes of self and spatial organization. In fact, before the main characters ever reach England, the text ends abruptly with a colloquy (*musamara*) dealing with flowers. This kind of ending was not uncommon in literature of the period; Muwaylihi's *hadith* also concludes with a consideration of flowers in a garden just outside of Paris. The dizzying diversity of the episodes in Mubarak's text blurs their linkages and, by extension, obfuscates the structural connections in the text. In fact, for all the reputation acquired by Mubarak as the engineer of the modern, new, and "orderly" Cairo, *'alam al-din* reads like an experiment in hoarding.

According to Darryl Dykstra, there might be more to this comment than irony, since Mubarak appears to have spent more than twenty years collecting material for his book.[31] Dykstra pursues several strands of textual evidence that suggest that Mubarak worked on this book for more than twenty years, researching and gathering the material for *'alam al-din* from as early as the 1860s, if not the late 1850s. Mubarak may, in this case, have actually accumulated such an expanse of material over time that the feeling of it being a space for amassed material is more than justified. This would also be in sync with the encyclopedic pathos that seems to drive so many texts from the *nahda*.[32]

While these circumstantial and biographical details are interesting, the real issue here is the systemic narratological structure that ʿalam al-din shares with "Forest."[33] We have already begun to explore how the episodes of "Forest" are tied individually to an abstract principle, a point I have been referring to as one of staging via arraying objects on the level of the individual scene and the emplotment of scenes. In turning to ʿalam al-din, I offer some final clarification of this idea by focusing on a series of episodes that seem to be total digressions, which intensely challenge any attempt to incorporate them into narrative movement or even into clear concerns with history. These are the long episodes on oysters, bees, and ants.

In their sojourn in Marseilles on their way to Paris, ʿAlam al-Din, his son Burhan al-Din, the unnamed English Orientalist, and their companion Jacob—a French sailor whom they had met on the boat in Alexandria—take a walk through the city. They decide to stop in a café-bar, where they engage in discussion concerning the different pastimes in France (this is a major theme in Tahtawi's *rihla*, and it is there, in fact, that he discusses theater and spectacles). Back at the café-bar in Paris, the characters are abruptly interrupted by an old man who greets them in Arabic. He is an Egyptian who had fled Cairo with Napoleon's defeated troops.[34] He recounts the reasons that drove him out of Egypt and the hardships he encountered due to the tumultuous political events in France. The latter are often glossed over quickly in the text with recurrent statements such as: "Momentous events befell us and all of those who were affiliated with him [Napoleon]; be they foreigners or not. No speech nor report can do these events justice."[35] Over and over, the text declines to detail events from the French Revolution, shrouding them with appeals to ineffability. These omissions suggest that the reader is assumed to be familiar with these renowned occurrences from reading French history and is referred to those works without specification. While these claims to ineffability are repeated in this episode, it still contributes the most detailed account of any of the events of the French Revolution that can be found in *'alam al-din* (in this specific episode, they cover the events of 1814, Napoleon's exile, stretching all the way to the Hundred Days and their aftermath). Nonetheless, the characters' discussion centers on how such barbaric acts could happen in a country as seemingly civilized as France. I will return to this repeated elision of the French Revolution in chapters to come; for now, it is important to note how the specificity of the event is usurped into a dichotomy of light (civility) and darkness (barbarity), like the one we saw in Marrash's "Forest"—even if these two *states* are here *within the same country* (i.e., France)—in fact, for Marrash, the dichotomy could exist within the same person. Furthermore, it is crucial to observe that the dichotomy is coextensive in Mubarak with elision: glossing over details is pivotal for consolidating diverse events into two discrete and dichotomous categories of light/darkness, civility/barbarity, and order/chaos.

To return to the discussion at the café-bar, the French-Egyptian invites the party to lunch at his house. The group splits up: 'Alam al-Din and Jacob accept the invitation, while the English Orientalist accompanies the son to another meeting. At the French-Egyptian's house, they are served oysters, which 'Alam al-Din refuses to eat, since he finds them revolting. This event leads to eleven consecutive chapters dealing with oysters, seashells, and pearls before they branch out into discussions of silkworms, ants, and bees, culminating in a chapter on "Humans and Animals" (*al-insan wa al-hayawan*). This digressive arc is key for grasping staging.

It is evident that the chapters are strung together through digression. Consequently, it is easy to explain the presence of these chapters in terms of Mubarak's overt pedagogical aim. After all, this is the same information one would find in encyclopedias and geography books—two literary forms that have historically been crucial forces in shaping *adab* and were taking new directions in forming the horizons and meanings of *adab* in the nineteenth century.[36] Similarly, one can think of the links between biology and social thought underpinning the philosophy of history and ideas about nature and the connection between society and nature—links that are evident in Marrash's "Forest," too.

While all of these forces are undeniably at work, it is necessary to remember that our goal in this chapter is not to dissolve these texts into their constitutive literary, epistemological, or ideological elements. The purpose, rather, is to describe the literary form they converge to shape as it appears from within the level of narrativization. With this in mind, we can focus on ideas of digression, philosophy, history, and nature, thinking about them from within a concern with narrativization. Specifically, we can proceed to show how ʿalam al-din, much like "Forest," sets out to make history visible, staging a variety of objects in the process, both on the level of the individual scene and the emplotment of scenes.

ʿAlam al-din, like "Forest," is propelled forward through two interrelated forces. The first is furnished via the form of the journey, where spatial travel provides the temporal rhythm structuring the unfolding of events. The second is topical, where the logic of conversations links the various episodes. The titles of the chapters exhibit these two forces: sometimes they name a topic of conversation, while at other times they name a place. Occasionally, the two are conflated, as in the case of theater, which is both a place that they visit and a topic they discuss. Similarly, the journey offers the form that the deferment of the trial provides for "Forest": a yet-to-be-fulfilled aim that carries the action forward. The conversations are comparable to the dialogues with the Philosopher—the pretrial trials. The conversations in Marrash's "Forest" also constitute the second narrativization force. In both works, then, this force is conditioned by the aim: the trial in "Forest," the arrival in England in ʿalam al-din. The spatial journey offers the alibi for all of the other conversations that happen in the space of waiting to arrive.

Having sketched ʿalam al-din's narrative arc and its parallel with that of "Forest," we can zoom in on the aforementioned eleven chapters. To begin at the end, I argue that the move from oysters to seashells to pearls is narratologically comparable to the procession of "great" civilizations in "Forest." Each episode, on its own, is linked to the abstract principle underpinning it, each one constituting a self-enclosed object and scene. The goal is not to weave these specific episodes together or even to posit any direct relationship; the narration in Marrash's "Forest" is not invested in showing the transition from one civilization to the next or the relationships amongst these civilizations. Rather, the point is to see how each civilization manifests the same principle: the war between light and darkness. Likewise, while Mubarak is intensely aware that nature is a delicately intertwined system, the aim is to show how *each* part of it—oysters, seashells, and pearls—exhibits the *same* abstract organizing principles, of order, collaboration, and hard work, which are then posited as natural universal principles that can be extended to "human" sociality. Therefore, this "random" series of episodes culminates in a discussion of human nature and human sociality and, ultimately, of the history of civilizations as the history of the enactment of these abstract principles. In fact, links between these objects, whether ants, oysters, and bees or ancient Egypt, Macedonia, and Persia, might serve as a distraction from their role to stage abstract principles, since that would create another structure that occludes the principal one.[37] In *'alam al-din*, this point also applies to the other episodes that deal with excursions in Paris, Marseilles, Cairo, and Alexandria, which are never unified by state boundaries, even when they are in the same country, but are each treated as an episode that stages abstract principles, crystallizing in concrete discrete sites such as specific train stations, or palaces, or streets.

The eleven "nature" chapters in *'alam al-din* offer a concise example of what is meant here by staging objects from a narratological perspective. On the one hand, within each scene or chapter, the object stages the abstract principles; on the other, the various scenes and chapters are arrayed as if they are different objects on a stage. Taken together, they allow us to see different embodiments of this abstract principle. In other words, while each scene stages an abstract principle as it is directly embodied in an object, the procession of the different objects, from one scene to the next, shows different facets of that abstract principle, and we can read it as a replay of the same scene, or as the drawing of these objects into a synchronic moment, a single scene, that makes the totality of history present. In both cases, this drawing together, via replay or synchronicity, assumes and necessitates an episodic structure.

But what is this abstract principle? Chapter 3 will tackle this question, arguing that the object of literary staging is neither stage prop nor the object of empiricism, but *athar* (the visible trace). In anticipation, the next section of the current chapter offers some concluding remarks on allegory, realism, and staging, and their twinning of theatrics and micrographs, coupled with their simultaneous supersession.

Allegory and Realism under the Literary Microscope

With the preceding discussion in mind, the distinction between allegory and realism, referred to casually in popular literary histories of the Arab *nahda*, can be viewed differently. We can now argue that it rests, in part, upon gradational differences in techniques of staging objects. Taking Marrash's "Forest" to epitomize allegory on the one hand and Mubarak's *'alam al-din* to exemplify realism on the other, it is clear that they do not simply subscribe to two opposing narrative models. Instead, their seemingly contradictory narrative models are underpinned by a shared emerging conception of the literary as the *staging* of historical truth. The narrative arc in these two texts—the general contour of building individual scenes and the emplotment of scenes—is parallel.

Yet it is equally evident that these two texts are anisotropic. In other words, arguing that the texts are connected by a shared emerging conception of the literary does not imply that they are identical. They draw upon a multitude of narrative traditions, techniques, genres, and ideologies, some of which they share and others they do not. More importantly, there are palpable struggles over what it means to stage an object: beyond the basic notion that objects are linked episodically to abstract principles, the gradational differences in technique are at the core of heated conceptual and ideological struggles over defining (and practicing) the literary. Thus, in reading these texts against the backdrop of a shared conception of the literary, my aim is not to eradicate their differences, but to actually see them. In other words, instead of interpreting these differences a priori as the result of diverse literary influences, sensibilities, progression, imposition, or diffusion, it becomes easier to see how these individual authorial traits converge in a field of struggle. Hence, we can learn to read the gradation of differences neither as a chronology, nor as a map of circulation, but as part of a wider struggle—here, specifically, over the conception of the literary.

To see this point more clearly, let's return, once again, to the framing narratives of these texts. Now we can reinterpret the customary distinction between allegory and realism along two main axes. The first axis pertains to the limit of the literary text: what is inside and outside of it. The second concerns the connection between staging techniques and conceptions of history. To restate the point from within the vocabulary of the previous chapter: while both texts converge in approaching the literary as an optic that is narratologically woven through staging techniques, they diverge on assessing whether the optic should be turned to reveal the world outside the text as a theater of history, or inside the text to reveal the world within the text as a theater of history. The dispute over directionality is equally a contention over the conception of history. These two axes converge on the term *athar* (visible trace) as it comes to name the specific modality of bringing objects into visibility through literary staging as well as the conceptualization of history.

Chapter 1 concluded by arguing that key texts from the canon of nineteenth-century Arabic literature mobilize their opening scenes, or framing narratives, to signal unequivocally that one is crossing into the realm of the literary, preparing one to enter a world of ulterior visualization. In light of the previous discussion of literary staging, this argument can be presented more strongly. Crossing into the literary—a move that is repeatedly, explicitly performed by the narrator of Marrash's "Forest" ushers in an experience of making objects visible in a way that exceeds any sensory or empirical experience (this is a facet of the definition of *khayal* developed in chapter 1). The pedagogical telos of these texts cannot be dissociated from their aim to train the senses of the readers to experience everything around them. Over and over again, these texts offer examples of the narrators and main characters using telescopes (Tuwayrani's "Floral Publishing"), spectacles (Marrash's "Forest," Mubarak's *'alam al-din*), and microscopes (Muwaylihi's *hadith*) to better see the world around them. Framed in more skeptical terms, we can say that these texts experiment with different tools for the manipulation of sight—though they often present it as augmenting and enhancing vision.[38] To a large degree, the narrative structure itself moves and is motivated by what we will come to increasingly see to be pedagogy of *seeing*: an experience where the narrator, character, and/or readers learn to use the literary optic, the equivalent of learning how to use telescopes, spectacles, and microscopes. *Hadith* contributes a pithy example.

In a telling scene, the protagonist, Isa, who is a writer by profession, accompanies the resurrected Pasha to a laboratory, where they see germs under a microscope. This event takes place against the backdrop of the two characters' decision to remain in Alexandria for a time because they heard news that the plague was ravaging Cairo. They observe that these breakouts routinely afflict Egypt, and the Pasha remembers one such breakout from his former life. The turn to the microscope is discussed by the Pasha and 'Isa to compare the ways in which their respective periods understood and confronted pathogens.[39] On the level of the narrative structure, however, the episode is a watershed moment in the Pasha's transformation from the arrogance and "blindness" that marked his previous life to a newfound curiosity to learn about and understand what happened to Egypt. For now, we can say that the episode encapsulates the Pasha's realization that he needs to learn to see. Just as he learned how to see pathogens and recognize their truth, he also needs to learn to *see* "A Period of Time" (the text's original title), whereby the literary optic can reveal the world as a theater of history and history both underpins and is therefore also a diagnostic tool for judging everything around him.

The gradational differences between these texts—despite their participation in forging a shared conception of the literary—can be interpreted, from the perspective of narrative structure, through two chief possibilities. The first is that the actual objects staged by these texts are different. For example, some show us real-life animals, while others show us fantastical creatures. Furthermore, they deploy different literary genres and forms: *maqama* versus travelogue versus *theatrum* of nature. Historically and socially, some of these texts deal with specific events in Egypt like the Urabi revolt, some turn to the successive waves of the French Revolution, and others grapple with the sectarian strife in greater Syria in the 1850s and 1860s.

This suggestion would ironically move us from appreciating what we encounter in the texts as stage objects to shrouding them in naive empiricism. In other words, we project an intrinsic meaning to these objects that exercises its force on the literary techniques, instead of directing our attention to the relationalities they participate in and forge them. To give an analogy from our reading of the texts above, this assumption would occlude the series of exchanges that we named staging and that produce the objects in the text—except in this case, we would not just be ignoring their literary dynamic, but also their broader sociopolitical dynamics. In other words, we turn so-called extreme, or naive, empiricism and realism, from being understood as a narrative ideology to an actual force out there *in* objects that write themselves into the texts. It is clear from the argument of the first part of this chapter that the goal of these texts is not to just capture the concreteness of empirical objects, but to array them in a way that enables seeing their connection to an abstract principle. Following this analysis, it might be more fruitful to suggest that the differences among these texts are owed to a combination of variations in conceptualizing the abstract principle (i.e., historical truth) and to devising alternative narrative solutions through which staging can be achieved and objects can be simulated.

These nuanced differences are owed to the minute details of the conception of history being staged, as well as to the specific ways of staging a particular conception through objects. Consequently, the customary distinction between Marrash's "Forest" as an allegory and Mubarak's *'alam al-din* as a realist text (be it hyper- or protorealist) can be analyzed as two specific ways of staging. Both partake in literary staging, but in noticeably distinct manners. I suggest that these differences hinge on the limits of the text, or on what lies inside/outside the text—that is, the direction in which the optic is primarily directed. While the following discussion focuses on Marrash's "Forest" and Mubarak's *'alam al-din*, its implications encompass many of the seminal texts from the canon of nineteenth-century Arabic literature mentioned so far.

Schematically, we can say that Marrash's "Forest" is more explicit in its evocation of theater, while Mubarak's *'alam al-din* insists on presenting itself as offering a series of scientific anecdotes for educational purposes. While Mubarak does not draw any explicit links between *'alam al-din* and theater, the text does define theater, in part, as both a technique for presenting scientific anecdotes and for presenting historical anecdotes scientifically.[40] I have already argued at length that both texts do create literary versions of stage objects. Yet the objects in "Forest" are primarily, deliberately, and transparently stage props and include fragments from other genres and texts. Most of the things Marrash ostensibly sets out to discuss—whether we take that to be slavery in America, or to perceive America as a foil for Syria—are *not* present *in* the text. In other words, the objects inside the text are all elusive, meaning that they are explicitly theatrical, and we cannot encounter them as objects outside the text. We can use the literary optic, however, to better see these phenomena (e.g., slavery, sectarian strife) outside the text. In contrast, *'alam al-din* seems to present us with empirical objects that we could easily encounter outside the text (e.g., trains, hospitals, ants, oysters, and bees).

Narratologically, then, "Forest," imparts the literary optic that we should extend and apply to objects *outside* the text, while *'alam al-din* practices deploying the literary optic *inside* the text with the idea that readers will *repeat* the practice with the same—as well as different—objects they encounter outside it. As such, *'alam al-din* sets out to accumulate more and more objects *inside* the text, in a way that is drastically different from "Forest." Neither seems to say that this is, in fact, how objects appear out there in the world, but that this is how one needs to *learn* to see them. Consequently, while Marrash's "Forest" evokes theater more explicitly and uses stage props, Mubarak's *'alam al-din* is, ironically, more theatrical in the sense that it stages, or simulates, the concreteness of material objects.[41] Consequently, *'alam al-din*, like Tahtawi's stage lights, appears to collapse two sensory experiences directly *within* the text. The pivot for reinterpreting the distinction between allegory and realism in this canon shifts to the issue of the limit of the text—or to whether or not the text is itself a self-enclosed object. This might, at first, strike us as a considerable leap in the argument, yet it has already been gestured toward several times, using slightly different terminology.

The previous chapter concluded by surveying the different ways in which key texts from the canon of nineteenth-century Arabic literature signal the crossing into the world of *khayal*. While they all share the idea of crossing into the literary, the specific dynamics of the crossing vary. Similarly, I have suggested that some of the detailed differences in narrative structure between Marrash's "Forest" and Mubarak's *'alam al-din* lie in whether and how the episodes may extend outside the texts. These two issues conjoin, analytically, around the question of whether the text is a self-enclosed signifying object whose meaning can be understood through a direct personal encounter with it, or whether it necessarily gestures beyond itself. In other words, the two issues conjoin analytically within the question of the conception of textuality, and of the "object."[42]

These issues are intimately entwined with concerns around authorial voice and meaning. In other words, the limit and nature of the text is equally a question of the mode of *presence* of authorial voice and its relationship with meaning. This question was already part of a wider conversation whose most palpable incarnation can be found in debates on *isnad* (chain of transmitters).[43] Both are unmistakably related to authorial voice and meaning, and the ways they circulate and survive in time. I am not suggesting, however, that these debates have their point of origin in the nineteenth century.[44] In this chapter, I simply cannot pursue questions of genealogy, as important as they are. The point here is that they are part of the conceptual purview of these texts, and indispensable for understanding the conception of history in seminal texts from our canon.

In the next chapter, I argue that *athar* is the key concept for grappling with the conceptions of history in these texts. *Athar* ties together questions regarding the conception of the "object," texts (as objects?), authorial voices, and time. Consequently, the turn to conceptions of history here is not a shift outside narrative structure. On the contrary, it is at the heart of the emergence of the literary as a narrative form that makes history visible. This emergence is intimately connected with a deep reworking and redeployment of *athar*: a concept whose history extends far back into Arabic narrative forms and conceptual thought. I do not show this reworking over time, but instead across different texts and different pressure points in the nineteenth century itself.

3

Excavating *Athar*

History through Objects, Traces, and Stage Props

Hassan Husni al-Tuwayrani's "Floral Publishing" follows its narrator, an astronomer, on a journey to trace the history of the present state of Kiwan. The latter is a fictive planet, delineated in the text as a distinct entity from planet Earth, but it is clear that Kiwan is a palpable replica of Earth—specifically, of the Ottoman Empire. After his protracted trips through the universe, the protagonist—who goes by the name of the Eternal Eagle (al-Nisr al-Dahri)—finally returns to his home planet, Kiwan. Troubled by the changes that had struck his home and armed with his telescope and magnifying glasses, the narrator-protagonist sets out on a journey across his planet to uncover the history he missed. He encounters a number of celestial bodies, and it is through conversations with them that the history of the present comes to light.[1]

In a telling scene, an unnamed character suddenly appears. After a brief exchange of greetings with the main characters, the newcomer is asked to introduce himself. The episode repeats previous encounters whereby the characters are asked to identify themselves, including the protagonist-narrator. The stranger, who—unlike the other characters—will remain unnamed, says: "Now, I am today's son. I have arrived through the ladder of the past and I am heading for the hillocks of what is yet to come." When the Eternal Eagle presses him for more information, the stranger adds:

> I am free from conscience-confining passions; I do not love nor do I hate. Rather, it is my nature to be propelled by those who pursue me,

and to be repelled by those who turn their backs on me. . . . Those who pursue me are motivated by the pursuit of themselves; they work diligently, and they tend to their affairs. They provide me with good narrative (*hadith*) that I am not ashamed to retell, for I am the record of time (*dahr*), my notebooks are the visible traces (*athar*) and my input are the deeds. I do not write anything that is not dictated by the Truth.[2]

While this is one of the few characters whose name we are never given, other clues in the text point indubitably to the conclusion that we are in the presence of History.

Like many of the texts surveyed in the previous two chapters, the concerns that undergird "Floral Publishing" include history, the passage of time, and the change and reversal of states and fortunes. From its opening pages, the text embeds a range of genres and literary tropes to play with different ideas of time, its passage, and the emotions time evokes. In fact, history is a direct concern of many—if not all—of the characters; they often discuss it, conjuring feelings of hope and fear. While examples can be found on almost every page, one example will have to suffice here, one whose resonance with the speech of our unnamed character is hard to miss.

In a much earlier episode, the Eternal Eagle attends a conference of a wise man who goes by the name of Sheikh Labad al-Abad (Stayed Forever). It is worth noting that the names of both characters suggest a connection with time. The Eagle's name is linked with eternity (*dahr*), which also bears overtones of time as a natural, and sometimes menacing, force, the closest analogy here being the Fates. The wise man's name can be translated as "He Stayed Forever," capturing the life story of the character who withdrew from the world in the aftermath of the assassination of Omar ibn al-Khattab (d. 644), the second Rightly Guided Caliph (r. 634–44). The name signals the way in which the wise man stands as a witness, both as a contemporary of historical events, as well as an outsider to them. To return to the encounter between the two characters, Sheikh Labad al-Abad commences his speech—which he gives biweekly when he emerges from his seclusion—by placing his audience on a continuum of (genealogical) time. He says: "We are the mark of what preceded us and the foundation for those who will succeed us, we encounter the results of the predecessors' deeds and posterity encounter the results of what we are to do." He then adds, "The pages of history (*tarikh*) were in the hands of the predecessors, they inscribed their visible traces (*athar*) using the hand of their deeds. We read them and see what is inferior and what is precious and so, these are the pages of history (*tarikh*) in our hands, let's write our visible traces (*athar*)."[3]

This quote, together with the excerpt from the unnamed character's speech, define a temporal schema that unfolds as a process of writing. What is being written are deeds (*a'mal*), and the *form* they take are *athar*—the medium in which deeds get inscribed in time. These two quotes offer some of the most distilled examples of how history is conceptualized and narrativized by key texts from the literary canon of the Arab *nahda*. In so doing, they bring the argument advanced in the previous two chapters full circle.

We have already seen how the literary is defined as a *making visible* of history, deploying staging as a technique for focusing on the relationship between a series of objects and their underpinning abstract principle. Taking our cue from Tuwayrani's quotes, we can say that we are invited to see these objects as *athar*, as "records" of history. In this manner, the literary seeks to open up the world as comprised of objects encapsulating history (i.e., comprised of *athar*), and it is in learning this mode of seeing, the literary, that history could come into view.

This chapter pursues the conception of history encapsulated in *athar*. My aim is not to excavate how historical events are represented in the texts, nor is it to adjudicate whether these texts use traditional or European conceptions of history—whatever that may mean. Rather, chapter 3 argues that history is not external to literature, it is not an external object that is represented *within* the text; history here is the form of emplotment produced by the literary mode of visualization, by the particular mode of arraying objects. Consequently, in this chapter, the turn to conceptions of history does not represent a shift outside narrative structure. On the contrary, it is at the heart of how the literary emerges as a narrative form for seeing time as history—what has been dubbed so far as making history visible through staging as a narrative technique. *Athar* furnishes the rubric for discerning the conception of history as it is narrativized by these texts.

It is important to note that the centralization of *athar* does not abrogate the arsenal of terms pertaining to time and history deployed by these texts. Instead, it allows us to probe the ways in which they converge in a literary practice. In arguing that literature and theater are envisioned as a making visible of history, chapters 1 and 2 have already pointed out a number of these terms, the most significant including *waqa'i'* ("grave events" or "happenings"); the turbulence of time (*taqallubat dahriyya*), a term featured heavily in the definitions of theater by Tahtawi and Mubarak; and *zaman* ("time," "season," or "era"). To these we could add *dahr* and *abad* (eternity), as well as words that refer to the recording and transmission of events (*tarikh, hadith, riwaya, khabar*). Nonetheless, in the preceding chapters, this plethora of terms did not prohibit us from unearthing a shared conception of the literary.

Similarly, chapter 3 does not claim a simple correspondence between the lexical and conceptual levels. It adheres to the same approach championed in chapter 1, analyzing how new meanings are produced through summoning and grafting genres, terms, and tropes, reading the latter not as a sign of a simple historical continuity with the past, but as the mechanism for practicing a new vision. To this end, *athar* gains its full significance here because it allows us to understand what I have presented in chapter 2 simply as "object" to be a particular kind of object—one that encapsulates history, regardless of how the latter may be conceived. In this chapter, I begin by asking what is *athar*, and then move to analyzing what conception(s) of history these texts encode in *athar*. This analysis sets the stage for the introduction of the collective as the force literary texts try to capture. Consequently, history is both a singular entity anchored by a universal philosophy of history and an anonym for the collective.

Athar: Immanence and Fraught Permanence

Athar, like *khayal*, has a durable presence across pivotal knowledge-producing discourses in the history of Arabic. In fact, its range of meanings appears to be even broader than that of *khayal*. It is usually translated into English as "monument," "artifact," or "ruin."[4] These three renditions emerge from a variety of semantic fields across historical and cultural contexts. However, from a broader perspective, *athar* is perhaps best translated as "trace." Its range of meanings spans sensory perceptible traces, including a camel's print on the sand, the emotional trace of a phenomenon, an architectural edifice being the trace of its particular patron or of the entire civilization, and a person's legacy. The latter is particularly manifest in the current practice of the publication of the complete works of an author as their complete set of "traces"/edifice—the architectural tone here is hard to miss (*athar kamila*). To put it differently, a civilization, a patron, or a person could inscribe their memory and deeds on time in the form of buildings or writing, rendering the latter two their *athar*.

Moreover, prophetic deeds and sayings (*al-sunna*) are also known as *al-athar*. In this case, al-athar is related to the chain of transmitters whose task was to safeguard the original meaning of the prophetic deeds, and of God's message, against the havoc of time by passing it on through trustworthy personal encounters that go all the way back to the original. In one of its earliest uses, *athar* is implicated with the renowned trope of the lamentation of ruins (*al-buka' 'ala al-atlal*) in the Classical Arabic ode referred to in chapter 1; the encampment's ruin (*talal*) is a specific kind of *athar*. It is the trace the camp leaves on sand in the desert, signaling the once present encampment.

Furthermore, the term *athar* is often encountered in the introduction to works of history as a central pillar for expounding on the importance of history writing. The idea of "tracing" or following the trace (*iqtifa' al-athar*) is central in variants of historical writing. Key examples can be found in al-Tabari's (839–923) tenth-century *History of Prophets and Kings* and al-Jabarti's (1753–1825) early nineteenth-century history, whose title has frequently been translated as *The Marvelous Chronicles: Biographies and Events*, or *The Marvelous Compositions of Biographies and Events* (The Wonders of Athar: Biographies and Narrated Events). The trope takes on added layers of meaning in the topographical genre (*khitat*) where *athar* becomes a fragment that can be mobilized through the assortment and curation of multiple *athar* to grasp a locale's total historical texture.

Taqi al-Din al-Maqrizi's (1364/5–1442) *kitab al-mawa'idh wa al-'i'tibar* is widely believed to be the zenith of the above-described approach to *khitat*. Yet the genre has a much longer history, which extends well into the twentieth century, with *khitat* written about Syria and Jabal ʿAmel in Lebanon, for example, and with ʿAli Mubarak himself writing a renowned example of the genre in the nineteenth century that purports to continue from where Maqrizi had left off. Mubarak appeals to this connection between tracing and history in our canon, and not just in the *khitat*, and specifically in his discussion of theater: "They take what is of benefit and they discard what is harmful and they strive in the same way as those who have achieved goodness and happiness and they trace their *athar*." Marrash addresses this issue from the other side, looking not into how people can follow the trace, but how its executors could make it well known. He discusses the latter as ʾidhaʿat al-athar.[5]

Beyond our canon, the idea of tracing is found in other works from the nineteenth century, with seminal examples from Zaynab Fawwaz's (1860–1914) introduction to her famous biographic dictionary of women, *al-durr al-manthur fi tabaqat rabat al-khudur* (Classes of Ladies of Cloistered Spaces); the poetry of Ahmed Shawqi; and a lesser-known series of articles by Rifaʿa al-Tahtawi, whose title, "baqaʾ al-dhikr bi husn al-al-fikr," may not immediately disclose that its subject is actually Islamic jurisprudence (*fiqh*). These instances indicate the broader resonance and relevance of the concepts we encounter in our canon, not only for other texts but also for other discourses in addition to the literary—an issue that will emerge over the next two chapters.

As if these copious possibilities were not enough, *athar* also referred in premodern times to a particular mode of agricultural-land acquisition. In this case, *athar* does not refer to an inherent quality of the land itself (e.g., level of fertility, or location), but to its status: the relationship between the peasant and his land (*athar*). In Egypt, this land was taxable, and, while it could not be sold or pawned before 1813, it was still inheritable, unless the descendants could not afford to pay the taxes. *Athar*, then, refers to the land's relationship to its possessor, and the possibility for such "possession" to remain through time. However, in the analysis of most historians, the possessor, according to strict legal definitions, is not the owner of the land—primarily because the land had not become fully commodified.[6]

This looks like a potentially endless, and directionless, semantic list.[7] Despite this intimidating expansiveness, however, the forces driving *athar* can be distilled to a coherent relationality. *Athar* encapsulates the intersection between two problems. The first concerns the limits of perceivability: What can be seen, and what cannot be seen? The second is the tension between time as a natural ruinous force, driving everything toward death and annihilation, and as the historical time of culture and civilization.[8] These two broad issues are equally, though differently, present in the new debates surrounding archaeology and antiquities in the nineteenth century. In fact, these two forces shaping *athar* can help explicate the privileging of architectural and archaeological connotations in *athar*'s translation into English as the monument, artifact, or ruin. It is during this same period, of the long nineteenth century, that soaring debates raged concerning the connection and distinction between archaeological, architectural, and art objects. For example, are ancient Egyptian monuments art objects, or archaeological, or even architectural, objects? And how is the difference between them to be arbitrated? In these debates, the sliding of the translation of *athar* between monument, artifact, or ruin bespeaks the imbrication between these discursive objects. I say "discursive objects" precisely because the same object could be appreciated and appropriated as an archaeological, architectural, or art object.[9]

It might be tempting, then, to try to define *athar* by summarizing the encounter between the different discourses, or as it is mobilized by discussions within and surrounding archaeology and fine art, and *athar* as it has existed in historical and literary writings. In this latter instance, it has undergone a long history of variation and, in the nineteenth century, was encountering and seizing upon a new possibility. Perhaps we could also separate out specifically religious discourse, for, even though it exists on a continuum with history and literature, its methods (chain of transmitters, and specific definitions of the text) were becoming increasingly more distinct from other forms of writing.[10] On the surface, this might appear to be a good way to sift through *athar*'s expansive semantic list. But, while this classification is seemingly more orderly, it does not offer an entryway into elucidating how *athar* is deployed by these texts.

Furthermore, we cannot assume that each discourse subscribes to a singular definition of *athar*. If anything, we could argue that each of these discourses gains its apparent stability and distinctness vis-à-vis others by championing a particular combinatory definition of *athar* and history. Consequently, the best way forward is to actually sift through the web woven by these texts, looking for the various ways in which *athar* entwines problems of perceivability with questions regarding the contradictory forces driving time.

With the aim of illustrating this abstract understanding of *athar*, I offer some brief examples of how these two concerns encapsulated within it are deployed in various seminal instances culled from their long traditions. These examples will then facilitate the following reading of *athar* in key texts from the Arab *nahda*.

To begin with a distilled summary of its sprawling semantic list: *athar* denotes an *object* (artifact, including books or a piece of land), a *narrative* (or a collection of sayings), the material or immaterial *effect* of something, or the effect of someone (her sayings or productions) on something or someone. Underpinning these myriad possibilities are concerns with perceivability, and the contradictory pull of time. The two are strongly connected through the understanding of time as a force of erasure and annihilation that induces forgetfulness. As such, time can be resisted by continuing to make visible that which it seeks to erase; alternatively, it can be displayed on visible objects as we witness their ongoing effacement.

The first example lies in the opening verses of the Classical Arabic ode (known as *nasib*). *Athar* in these instances is part of the impossibility of seeing the beloved, who has always already departed. Yet the "I" of the poem has to endure all the reminders—traces—of their prior presence. In this sense, *athar* is a record of absence, of the otherwise invisible force of time as it leaves the traces of its effects everywhere. *Athar* also potentially combats absence, for these traces ensure that absences are never fully realized.[11] *Athar* continues to hold the presence of sensory experiences, despite their actual absence. In this manner, the concern with perceivability here has a strong temporal overtone, intertwined with a question of presence/absence, and understood as both temporal and visual forces.

The study of prophetic sayings and deeds (*'ilm al-hadith*) makes the connection amply clear; it continues the presence of the prophet and of his call, after he had already departed. The prophet's *athar* ensures his contemporaneity to all historical times and periods. In Quranic narratives, *athar* denotes the material traces left by previous civilizations after they have already been annihilated. It is explicitly architectural, and it evokes how we know that these peoples were once present, even though they have now disappeared. It also acts as further proof of the truthfulness of Quranic narratives, since we can see the traces of the peoples whose stories are told in the Quran. By extension, these traces point not only to these ancient peoples and nations but also to the existence of the divine. As such, in both the context of Quranic narratives and prophetic sayings and deeds, *athar*'s function in maintaining perceivability can be described as a question of immanence (the possibility of having an immediate experience of the transcendent). Here, the replayed negotiation between presence/absence and the contradictory forces of time is geared toward seeing the trace of the divine.

Broadly speaking, this negotiation between perceivability and remaining in time can take the form of enquiring after how something, or someone, can continue to be perceivably present after its/their initial disappearance, or, in the case of the divine, eternal invisibility. There is a palpable tension between the unwavering conviction that nothing can remain in time, on the one hand, and the drive to produce cultural artifacts that defy ephemerality, on the other. The latter is a condition for the survival of peoples and civilizations as well as a mode of experiencing the presence of the divine. Artifacts tend both to combat the ruinous force of time and to exhibit it as they themselves fall into ruin. Fittingly, *athar* tends to combat time through exhibiting its force. These two facets, immanence (and perceivability), and the struggle against time are woven together in different ways across specific discourses, periods, and by different authors. Works of topography and much later debates on archaeology are particularly adept at exploring these possibilities.

Finally, I offer an example of how these two forces (visible presence and time) are woven together in Quranic narratives. I do not aim to provide an exhaustive analysis; the epistemological, historical, and ideological origins of this conception are beyond the purview of this chapter. Chapter 4 will resituate these Quranic narratives as they are reworked within historical and literary writing, but, for now, the goal is more modest: to facilitate the introduction of the conception of *athar* in key texts from the canon of nineteenth-century Arabic literature. I chose to give examples from the Quran not because I believe it is the origin in any conventional sense; on the contrary, precisely because these Quranic narratives are interpreted and reinterpreted across various knowledge-producing discourses, they cannot be boiled down to an original essential meaning, but they can be distilled to show, retrospectively, the crux of the concerns they acquired, or were imbued with, through these debates. In fact, while the word *athar* appears in the Quran, the Quranic *athar* becomes a significant trope retrospectively through later engagements with time and history, via *athar*, and the deployment of Quranic narratives in this process.

Before we look at these narratives, it is crucial to note that they are punctuated by a dichotomous view of human nature. The narration of the histories of ancient peoples in the Quran is not concerned with the specification of dates or chronology. Rather, these histories function as the external proof, and the temporal unraveling, of human nature. These narratives are tasked with intervening in this nature to ensure that one side of the dichotomy can triumph. On the level of universal human nature, the struggle is between memory and forgetfulness, blindness (*kufr*) and vision. When performed as a history of a specific people, the struggle is between formation and dissolution, or more accurately, annihilation.

The Quranic *Athar*: The Play of Memory and Forgetfulness

The Quranic narratives of *athar* deal with the rise and fall of ancient peoples. They are mapped in relation to an overarching oscillation between memory and forgetfulness. Humans, by their very nature, are prey to cyclical repetitions of formation and dissolution, culminating in the final cycle, the apocalypse, that would bring the final end/beginning. A particular people (these include the peoples of 'Ad, Thamud, Noah, Lot, and Pharaoh) would exist and rise to prosperity, only to become enchanted with their power, taking their wealth as a sign of immortality.[12] Blinded by their pride in their power, they forget their mortality and grow insolent to the divine message and messengers. Their forgetfulness of their own mortality—and, by extension, of God—leads them to commit grave acts of injustice. Perishing befalls them both as a punishment for their deeds and a reminder of their mortality. This retribution is simultaneously the enactment of what they had forgotten, and, consequently, an admonition. The purpose of these narratives is thus not to clarify the chronological link between these different peoples; the point, rather, is to highlight how these various episodes are underpinned by the same principle driving "human" history, across which the different stories reveal the universal principle, here dichotomy, of memory and forgetfulness playing out. The narrative introduces repeated ruptures in this self-reproducing cycle that induce (some) people to turn from forgetfulness to remembering.[13]

The physical monumental traces, *athar*, of these peoples stand as persisting concrete reminders of their histories, of the inevitability of perishing, and of the truth of Quranic narratives. Echoes of this conceptualization appear in Tuwayrani's text when he signals out *athar* as the medium through which we can see the actions of a specific people: "They inscribed their visible traces (*athar*) using the hand of their deeds. We read them and see what is inferior and what is precious." However, there is no reason to assume that the conception of history in Tuwayrani's text and in the Quran are similar; in fact, as I will argue in the following pages, they are far from it. The idea here is merely that in both cases *athar*, with its range of meanings, encapsulates history—the differences in conceptualizing the latter notwithstanding for now.

The connection between *athar* as an architectural edifice on the one hand, and history on the other, is accentuated through the connection drawn between the creation of an *athar* and the challenge to the divine. In this context, Quranic narrative is at the heart of a shift in how *athar* ought to be perceived and interpreted. *Athar* should no longer simply attest to the success of these civilizations to remain in time, nor should it elicit a contemplation of time as a natural force toward ruin, but it should instead serve as a reminder of God and of mortality. In other words, Quranic narratives reinterpret the meaning of the continuing presence of *athar* by reworking the edifice's relationship to time. This entails grappling with time not just as a natural force often moving toward annihilation, but as one deployed by, and subject to, the divine. In following centuries, both *adab* and history, as fields of knowledge and forms of writing, will mobilize this tension differently and eventually gain their own momentum in dealing with the epistemological and narratological problems posed by this tension.[14]

The play between presence/absence, perceivability, interpretation, and time that lies at the heart of *athar*—and that I outlined briefly in Quranic narratives—is precisely the general movement that this and the previous chapter have been describing so far. In the nineteenth century, the literary emerges as an attempt to give narrative a form that allows history to be perceivable: *staging* history by arraying objects that encapsulate history.

In the following sections, we will discover the conception of history staged by these texts and changing conception of the literary, rendering it a form of staging. I am not trying to follow the process over time so much as I am trying to describe the emergent conception of the literary in a relatively fixed point of time. As such, in turning to describe how history is conceptualized in these texts through the reworking of the term *athar*, it is useful to continue to remember that *athar* might not always tally with our contemporary conceptions of history—though it includes aspects of it. Rather, we are here in the realm of the relationship between immanence and permanence. More accurately, history here is not external to literature; it is not an externality that is represented within the text. History, here, is the form of emplotment produced by the literary mode of seeing. In the following sections, I turn to al-Tuwayrani's "Floral Publishing," Muwaylihi's *hadith*, Mubarak's *'alam al-din*, Marrash's "Forest," and 'Abdullah al-Nadim's 1881 sketch "Medical Council" as key examples for analyzing the transformation of *athar*. Through them, I argue that the biggest change hinges on *whose* deeds we are invited to see. In my earlier examples, time, sometimes as a sign of the divine, seemed to leave *its* mark on *athar*. In this context, however, *athar* does not simply record the deeds of time itself: Tuwayrani's quotes, with which this chapter began, already offer strong indications in this direction.

Athar: Topographies of Cities and Utopias

In chapter 1, we saw that Muwaylihi's text is framed as a dream that 'Isa Ibn Hisham had, recounted by an unknown narrator who was apparently part of a group to whom 'Isa told the dream. In the dream, 'Isa, who is presented as a modern writer, sees himself walking in a cemetery. His little promenade there and his encounter with a resurrected Pasha comprise the first episode of the text. In the serialized version, which was published in the *misbah al-sharq* (Lantern of the East) journal, the different episodes are not given separate titles. Instead, they are published as part of a fixed column entitled *fatra min al-zaman* (A Period of Time). When the episodes are later collected in book form entitled *hadith 'isa ibn hisham* (The Narrative of 'Isa Ibn Hisham), this first episode in the cemetery comes to bear the name *al-'ibra* (The Moral Lesson).[15] While the journal and book titles emphasize different aspects of the narrative—time versus narration, respectively—they both signal the ways in which the relationship between time, narrative, and the *athar* is rethought. Simply put, the relationality of immanence and permanence is sharply recast here as a concern with displaying the trace of the collective. The latter concern cannot be dissociated from leaving a trace *for* the collective.

'Isa is purposefully walking up and down the cemetery to contemplate time as a natural force toward death. He reflects: "In the midst of such sobering notions, I was considering the remarkable things that happen and marveling at the way in which times change. Deep in thought about the extraordinary things which Fate brings about, I was trying to probe the secrets of the resurrection."[16] His contemplations are interrupted by the resurrection of the Pasha, who asks 'Isa why he is in the cemetery. His response is simple—the title of the episode. 'Isa is there seeking a "moral lesson." The latter abound in cemeteries more than they do in religious sermons: "I came here to find inspiration by visiting the tombs. I find it more effective than listening to sermons from pulpits."[17]

This brief exchange presents something of a competition between two different kinds of edifying discourses, sermons and visitations to cemeteries.[18] 'Isa claims that visitations are a more effective form of edifying discourse. It is important to note that the competition does not rest exclusively on one form being ostensibly more concrete—the cemeteries—and the other more abstract, or narrativistic, since religious sermons inhabit certain physical spaces, and the experience of the cemetery is interspersed with narrative fragments that *make* the cemetery *visible*. In fact, the relationship between these two forms of edifying discourse, much like the preceding chapter's comparison of theater and literature, cannot be neatly divided between the visual and the verbal.

Somewhat like Quranic narratives, the opening scene in the cemetery reveals the implication of the lesson with the *athar* of acts that remind us of mortality. In walking through the cemetery, 'Isa's main insight revolves around the erasure of all distinctions through death. In the end, all difference—glory, beauty, or wealth, which people spend their lives competing over in futility—disappears with death. Individual distinctions, be they wealth or power, for which people commit injustices and sins to acquire do not truly remain. People are filled with arrogance inspired by their possessions, temporarily forgetting the looming end. 'Isa's meditations preceding the Pasha's revival focus on individuals and their characteristics, rather than civilizations and ruling dynasties. Nonetheless, the characteristics depict persons with social power and authority that perishes when they die. There is no indication of the loss of power or authority in life. Consequently, the cemetery is the scene, and site, where the truth of human existence appears.

The cemetery is not described simply as a physical space, but in the way in which it stages the truth. This is why 'Isa deems it the most effective edifying discourse. The striking thing, however, is that the opening scene clearly undermines my argument that these texts set out to make history visible. If anything, the cemetery stages the active obliteration of history; all differences that might have distinguished a person, group, or period of time are fully overwritten by the hand of death. The attitude is reminiscent of Quranic narratives whose aim is to relentlessly interrupt flow, forcing people to turn and face their own mortality and, by extension, to face God. The goal is not the drawing of a chronological link between the various peoples and their differences, though the latter is sometimes used to highlight the details of different sins or wrongs. Consequently, it might be hastily inferred from the opening scene that Muwaylihi's text is introducing a "Quranic" vision of history and *athar*, of the interruptive force of death. In fact, one could argue that it takes this vision one step further by abdicating the concern with using particular peoples, like the Quran does, as exemplars.

We might then ask ourselves why the serialized episodes would be entitled *A Period of Time* if they elide the distinction between different periods. The opening episode in the cemetery would suggest that we won't read anything distinctive about that particular period of time. Furthermore, it is already amply clear that the conception of history—if one could call it that, since it stands for time as annihilation—here stands in stark contrast with Marrash's "Forest" and Mubarak's *'alam al-din*. The latter two works, despite their differences, seek to unleash civilizational progress as the force constantly driving cycles of history forward.

These would be hasty conclusions. As episodes continue, it emerges that *hadith* weaves together its conception of history by pitting different articulations of *athar* against each other. Therefore, we can think of the opening scene as one in which a modified version of the Quranic *athar* is staged. The resurrection of the Pasha interrupts this flow, compelling both 'Isa Ibn Hisham and the Pasha to turn in different directions until their outlook is unified into the project of tracing the "history of the present era."

In the first scene in the cemetery, 'Isa can only think of time as an overriding force and movement toward perishing, eliding all difference that may have existed in life. But, with the resurrection of the Pasha, other possibilities emerge that reveal contradictions in the idea of time (death) as the great equalizer. The Pasha is immediately described by 'Isa as being tall, with a broad forehead and a general look of grandiosity and nobility.[19] Aside from physical characteristics, the social status and personal moral attributes of the Pasha are some of the first features noticed by 'Isa. If death really collapses all distinctions of power, wealth, and social status, why are their signs immediately visible on the Pasha when he is first resurrected, at a moment when he is supposedly stripped even of clothes? It seems that the appearance of nobility does not emerge through dress and entourage, but from the Pasha's person. Whether this is because, with the resurrection of the Pasha, all that belongs to life, such as differences and distinctions, are also unearthed, or because one never loses his "character" even in death, but merely accumulated objects of wealth, is not easily discernable.[20] The two readings remain possible and are not, of course, mutually exclusive. Nevertheless, it is only with the resurrection of the Pasha that what is at stake with regard to time expands to include a comparison, and a "period of time" expands to what at first appears to be an encounter between two distinct periods.

In a crucial passage at the Parquet, 'Isa laments the fate of the Pasha, who is completely oblivious to the change in present circumstances:

> I was so worried at the way fate had struck the Pasha down with such a succession of blows. There he was, utterly baffled and bewildered, unaware that time had passed. He was completely unfamiliar with the present state of affairs, and had no idea that, with the passage of time since his own era and the decline of the dynasty of his time into fold of decay, things had changed. . . . I decided not to leave his company until I had managed to show him the things he had not seen, tell him about the things he had not heard, and explain those aspects of *the history of the present* which he did not know. . . . In that way, I would discover what his opinion of the present in comparison with the past, and learn which of the two was of greater worth and brought more benefits.[21]

The question in this instance rests on the change of the state of things from one moment to the next. At stake is showing the Pasha this change, making history present visually. Here we come to the crucial point: change is not narrated chronologically to the Pasha. 'Isa does not simply sit him down and recount to him, year by year, or month by month, the events that had transpired since the Pasha passed on. Instead, we are presented with different scenes that operate like the cemetery. Each vignette presents an object (read *athar*) that, when and if it is seen, can divulge history.

Tuwayrani's text uses a similar strategy, though its depiction of physical space is significantly less tangible than Muwaylihi's. Having returned to his home planet, Kiwan, after centuries upon centuries of exploring the universe, the Eternal Eagle is horrified by the proliferation of wreckage in his once idyllic home. In this sense, the Eternal Eagle, much like the Pasha in *hadith*, lends a perspective through which two periods of time can be compared. For 'Isa and the Pasha, the comparison is between the era of early British Occupation (1881–1956; the text covers the period 1881–1902) and that of Muhammad Ali (r. 1805–48), while for the Eagle, it is between the currently apocalyptic Kiwan versus its once idyllic state. In this sense, Kiwan—whose name literarily means "beauty and grandeur"—is comparable to Marrash's "Forest." It is a utopia-in-crisis that can stand in for a number of possible actual particular places. This observation returns us to the distinction between the so-called allegorical and hyper- or protorealist texts discussed in chapter 2. This time, however, the focus is on what an *athar* is in each of these two discrete narrative strategies—an issue that was already touched upon briefly in the previous chapter in the discussion of the different kind of objects staged by Marrash's "Forest" and Mubarak's *'alam al-din*. In the following paragraphs, I zero in on specific scenes in Muwaylihi's *hadith* and Tuwayrani's "Floral Publishing," reviewing what kind of objects are presented as an *athar*.

I have already argued that in *hadith* each vignette of Cairo and Paris is an *athar*. In other words, each particular place is a site for making the history of the present visible, postponing the exploration of what history means for now. While there are endless examples of this move in the text, the episodes in the pyramids and the Eiffel Tower are particularly suggestive. In fact, the two edifices are compared in the text itself. As such, *athar* does not just refer to ancient monuments and artifacts, but to cultural artifacts more broadly. In other words, *athar* here refers simultaneously to archaeological and architectural objects by grappling with the fact that the Eiffel Tower is a potentially future archaeological object.

'Isa, the Pasha, and an unnamed friend visit the pyramids. This episode begins like others with a description: followed by a vocalization of their immediate response to a direct sensory experience. No sooner is the description completed than it is dismantled and replaced with making history visible—that is, with the reckoning of what the object stages. In this manner, the pyramids are at first described as a momentous *athar*, one that has triumphed in its battle with time.

> Their structure erodes the ongoing freshness of days, and their very permanence obliterates eras of time. They entomb people after people beneath their shadow, and centuries turn grey without affecting them in the slightest. Time's own clothing has become threadbare, and yet there they stand in fresh attire. Ages have been recycled and eras have passed, but they still remain, bumping stars and mocking meteors. As long as

day and night follow each other in turn, they still provide an eyewitness account of man's talent for creating miracles of potential, of the ability of this weak and feeble creature to do amazing things, and to show how such a transitory and ephemeral creature can produce such an abiding and eternal structure."[22]

The terms *mushahada* ("viewing") and *'ayan* ("perceptibility") evoke the visual aspects whereby various *athar* visually manifest abstract temporal principles. However, this laudatory description is soon exposed as the deceptive superficial level, which is falsified once it is connected to the abstract principle. The pyramids are revealed to be an act of arrogance, challenging time, and, as such, God. The critique of the pyramids is directed at this undergirding arrogance and challenge to the divine: "If the poor fool had only realized that the age would come when anyone could blast this building to pieces in a trice and use chemical components to turn it into powder like carded wool and scattered dust, he would not have used as a challenge, a structure that he then committed to the hand of fate—and fate never offers any assurances. God knows, it's a wretched achievement, one that is based on prevalent ignorance."[23]

Muwaylihi evokes here the Quranic intersection between *athar*, memory, and forgetfulness as defining "human" qualities. Crucially, though, the pyramids are not doomed simply because they were left to the corrosive force of time; rather, they are at a constant risk of destruction because they are now at the mercy of a more technologically advanced period of time. In the same vein, the problem with the pyramids is not that there is no point in building anything, but that these buildings encapsulate raw power, one that seeks to constantly point to itself rather than to improve living conditions. Leaving these details aside for now, what is important to note is that the pyramids are approached as an *athar*, an object that encapsulates the relationality between immanence and permeance. Yet it is useful to remember that the latter relationality is now part of an endeavor to stage history, not the divine acting through time—a distinction that I will return to shortly.

The same appraisal extends to include the Eiffel Tower. In a now familiar manner, it is hyperbolically praised at first, only to have its outward appearance dismantled into what it truly manifests. Immediately the comparison is made between the tower and the pyramids:[24]

> We stopped for a while to take a look at this imposing tower, a lofty structure whose sheer height amazed us and whose construction was astonishing. In the category of wonderous sights, amazing rarities, prized entities, lofty peaks, and highest summits, this was certainly a remarkable feat of design and engineering.... In comparison what could one say about the height of the pyramids or Haman's lofty tower? If the Pharaoh had seen it, he would have demolished everything he had built and erected. Nor would he have stated, "I am your lord most high." He would have turned on his builder, Haman, and flayed him a thousand times, and then hung him from a tree. And how could you compare the fabled Tower of Babel with this Parisian tower?[25]

The comparison thus begins with the superior artisanship of the Eiffel Tower vis-à-vis the pyramids before shifting abruptly to their shared vainness. The Eiffel Tower, like the pyramids, is dismissed as a pointless act: "God! It is a false deed and a fleeting shadow."[26] This futility is anchored in the ineffectiveness of the attempts to leave a trace through time, thereby achieving immortality through a spectacular edifice. Such a failure is reminiscent of the narratives I have dubbed as the Quranic *athar*, but it cannot be subsumed by them.

The description of the Eiffel Tower begins with an expression of awe at its magnificence and its industry. Nonetheless, the description does not continue on the path of the tower's representation of progress and scientific advancement; it quickly shifts to follow the same path undertaken in the pyramids episode. The tower embodies the way in which the French, like others before them, try to symbolize their power in a monument meant to stand through time. As such, it does not embody the abstract principle of progress, as Marrash and Mubarak might argue, but represents the way in which the projection of power through an architectural edifice is meant to accrue further power. Yet the move ultimately erodes the actual strength of any civilization that follows such practices.

There are numerous examples of this critique of false, or deceptive, *athar*, including many of the episodes in Paris, for the city itself is considered a prime example of a false *athar*. Back in Cairo, the palace of the Pasha's grandson proclaims the contradiction between the illusory appearance of luxury and the reality of poverty.[27] It appears to exude the wealth in which the grandson lives, but it is soon revealed to hide the poverty of its owner, who is drowning in debts. The examples here might seem wildly different, since the pyramids and the Eiffel Tower echo the desire for permanence found in earlier examples of *athar*—but in what way would the palace of the Pasha's grandson be an *athar*? There are two broad ways of approaching this question. The first approach centers on the manner in which these varying examples stage an abstract principle (tied to a conception of history), and the second pertains to the possibility that an *athar* encapsulates different historical moments. In other words, it allows for experiencing the abstract principle as it plays out in different historical moments. While the first possibility is widely practiced by the different texts studied in this book, the second is more the subject of experimentation and, as such, necessitates a more nuanced reading.

To reiterate the problem, how could the pyramids, the Eiffel Tower, the Pasha's grandson's palace, and the courts, among many other places, all be *athar*? For a broader perspective, let us briefly step outside of Muwaylihi's text without leaving Paris. Specifically, we join 'Alam al-Din, Burhan al-Din, the unnamed English Orientalist, and Ya'qub in Mubarak's "Colloquy 89," where they visit the Palace of Versailles. In visiting the palace, the main characters do not exclusively relate what they perceive through sensory experience; the palace represents another site where the characters learn to see objects as staging an abstract principle. In *'alam al-din*, the principle is explicitly delineated as a relationship between civilizational progress and good governance. As such, the characters see both what the palace looks like and the abstract principles that the particular place manifests. Marrash's "Forest" is equally concerned with staging the connection between the reigning of science, the intellect, and progress. In both "Forest" and *'alam al-din*, the abstract principle is connected to history, since it articulates an abstract philosophy of history; it names the universal principles underpinning how history moves and, furthermore, is entwined with ideas of progress. The latter elucidate historical processes as concerned with being on time, late, ahead of their time, and so forth. In other words, both texts are concerned with staging the principles that enable one to avoid being late, or to succeed at being on time, or even ahead of their time. As such, these different examples are all *athar* because they all teach us to see the principles governing our relationship to historical time. This is the first response.

Yet, in "Colloquy 89" and all of the episodes of Muwaylihi's *hadith*, we see the second response. The link between the object and the principles of history is not contained within the present moment. Rather, *athar* enables us to see how the principle was applied and practiced across different moments, and the effects of these different applications as they play out on the *athar* itself.

The Palace of Versailles is a poignant example. The palace, which has been turned into a museum, is caught in cycles of rise and fall dictating its change from a place of royals to a space for art. As I noted in the previous chapter, Mubarak carefully avoids discussions of the specificity of the consecutive waves of the French Revolution, wrapping them in silence. He merely says, "Many things ensued, too numerous for the tongue to utter and for the mind to grasp, as mentioned in the histories of the French nation."[28] When he expounds on these events, Mubarak tends to focus on the actions of the king and their consequences, but he circumvents the actions of the people through which the consequences were carried out.[29] As such, *athar* here does not only stage an abstract principle but also temporalizes it, seeing it across specific periods of time or through the selection of "grave happenings." The key here is that there is a *selection* of events perceivable via the *athar*, and not an ostensible chronological repetition of what had transpired.

With this in mind, let's return again to the pyramids, the Eiffel Tower, the palace of the Pasha's grandson, the courts: How are they all *athar*? First, they all stage a principle pertaining to history—be it a concern with progress, with the Quranic *athar*, or with something that exceeds both of them. Second, they encapsulate layers of events and grave happenings, enabling an equivalence between the different objects. As I said earlier, the Eiffel Tower is potentially a future archaeological object, and every other place encountered in *hadith*, including the Palace of the Pasha's grandson, is a potential museum, or museum object; the history of the Palace of Versailles is a striking example of this staging.

Our final stop on the tour of *athar* as a medium of staging history—potentially through specifiable events—is the planet Kiwan. Tuwayrani's "Floral Publishing" furnished the starting point for the investigation of *athar* in this chapter, contributing the working definition of the relationship between *athar* and history. I have argued at length that all of the texts are tied to history, but "Floral Publishing" features the only instance where the abstract concept of History is presented as a character that speaks to define itself. Rather fittingly, the character is never named. In these definitions (discussed at the beginning of this chapter), history is linked with *athar*. It is appropriate, then, to conclude this section by inquiring into what objects we are invited to learn to see as *athar* in "Floral Publishing." Much like the Forest of Truth in Marrash's text, Kiwan is the *athar* here. The other "objects" in the texts are, as in Marrash's "Forest," fragments of other literary genres and tropes that weave together the abstract principle we are meant to see through the *athar*, be it Kiwan as an abstract rendition for Planet Earth, the Ottoman Empire, or Egypt, or the Forest of Truth as a stand-in for the "New World," Syria, or Egypt.

History as the Future of the Past

The previous section demonstrated the ubiquity of *athar*, either as it is centralized in a single object or proliferated in a multiplicity of objects. Progress and good governance as aspects of an abstract and universal principle of history were also mentioned. The two issues can be connected, for *athar* is not simply a visible object; it registers the way in which a variety of objects have been rendered into the visible traces of history. Staging history, then, cannot be dissociated from the exploding possibilities of seeing all experiences and events as ultimately historical. This section foregrounds the investigation of the conception of history staged by *athar*, beginning with a return to Muwaylihi's *hadith* and the examples discussed earlier. My focus here shifts from showing that the different objects stand in a relationship to time to investigating what conception(s) of history are in encoded in the *athar*. In other words, our emphasis shifts from the object to the principle without losing sight of either.

I noted that the descriptions of these places—the pyramids, the Eiffel Tower, and the palace of the Pasha's grandson—dramatize a rupture between an apparent and superficial level on the one hand and a "true" one on the other. The accounts of these places begin with hyperbolic praise that quickly crumbles as we learn to see these places as *athar*, to recognize their connection with an abstract principle of history, and to think about how these places have fared over time.

Over and over, in *hadith*, *athar* reveals that this period of time is characterized precisely by the rupture between the apparent and the actual. This dissociation is the distinctive feature of this period, which perhaps renders the need to learn to see even more urgent. The text seeks to dramatize this split as the entryway to its contemporary state, which is characterized by the way in which "people today are caught up in a movement which is neither Eastern nor Western."[30] In learning to see, the Pasha—and the readers—practice recognizing objects as *athar* (i.e., they learn to see everything historically). The latter stage not only how 'Isa's period of time is animated by a split but also how the split breaks with the abstract universal principle driving history. Ultimately, while this period of time seems to blaze toward ever more glory, in actuality it is a global moment of erosion. The activation of the Quranic *athar* cannot be read as an issue of continuity, but as part of the strategy for staging both the split and an abstract principle from which it diverges. In the following paragraphs, we will elucidate the nature of this abstract principle, deemed the cornerstone of the conception of history, and whether it is shared by the different texts.

Ultimately, in evoking the Quranic *athar*, Muwaylihi's critique is not solely rooted in the Quranic attack on human arrogance and forgetfulness, but additionally imbued with a concern for the optimal functioning of the social collective—an issue I will return to in depth in the next two chapters. It can be outlined very briefly here: in directing the energy and resources of a particular civilization toward the construction of an unattainable, everlasting, monumental trace, the civilization is actually weakened. The attempt to project the appearance of grandness risks the entire civilization, for it diverts resources from attainable goals to unattainable ones. Muwaylihi exposes this forgetfulness as an obliviousness to perishing, neglecting that which truly remains: the true *athar*. Pitting a true and a false *athar* against one another, the text problematizes the restriction of *athar* to artifacts, insisting on seeing everything as an *athar*, or a visible trace of history, even if it was not intended as such. The true *athar*, here, is not the afterlife, but the future. It is useful to recall Tuwayrani's evocation of a genealogical vision of *athar* and history, the continuity between predecessors and their successors, where the dichotomous view of human nature is not played out as a struggle between civilization and divine; rather, it is usurped *within* civilization itself—even if that includes the divine.

The concept of *athar* appears in multiple forms in Muwaylihi's hadith. In both the episode of the pyramids and the Eiffel Tower, it evokes the Quranic depiction of *athar* while imbuing it with ideas of progress and then takes both the Quranic and the linear developmentalist vision in a different direction. *Athar* can have a negative impact on civilization if they are empty material signifiers of power rather than useful objects. The details of the criticism of the pyramids contribute crucial insights.

First, the pyramids are part of a deception. Ancient Egyptians are alleged, in Muwaylihi's text, to have lived a primitive life. The energy and skill used to build the pyramids were directed, according to the unnamed friend, to matters not relating to the actual life of the collective inhabiting the civilization. Consequently, in looking at the pyramids, one should see not their triumph against time, but their encapsulation of a history of injustice.[31] The pyramids stand as a material manifestation of and a testament to the injustice befalling the Egyptians as they were forced to exhaust themselves to build something that would not make their lives better, but would further humiliate and subjugate them. The pyramids as a manifestation of injustice extend through Egyptian history; their centuries-long existence makes them witnesses to a long history of injustices perpetually befalling Egyptians at the hand of ephemeral ruling classes, who have not learned to focus on that which truly remains. Napoleon Bonaparte's speech from the top of the pyramids makes them witnesses to yet another "Pharaoh" who used the edifice to deceive his people and to push his soldiers into wars with no benefit for them. Consequently, the pyramids are declared as a site of deception, whose truth can only be seen through literature's ability to make history visible, turning them from a sensory to a stage object. As such, the pyramids stage both the attempt to pursue a futile *athar* and the negligence of pursuing the true *athar*. In the text, the Delta Barrage is offered as an example of a useful, and as such true, *athar*.

What we have seen so far, then, is a move to view these monumental objects as *athar*: objects that record the history encapsulated in them. The *athar* includes an abstract principle underpinning history and potentially, layers of history and memory of happenings or events encapsulated in the *athar* itself. The pyramids do not just stage an abstract principle; they allow one to see key moments and events in the play of this principle over time (here the course of Egyptian history). We observe this in order not only to see the relationship between *athar* and an abstract principle more clearly, but to see the latter through time in texts from this canon that try to accumulate more and more objects within themselves, such as Mubarak's 'alam al-din. As for the more allegorical texts, their centralized *athar* (e.g., Forest of Truth or Kiwan) lays claim to the entirety of civilization's history. In both Marrash's "Forest" and Tuwayrani's "Floral Publishing," the history of civilizations is envisioned as their successive replacement of one another. To these successive cycles, "Floral Publishing" adds the chain of Islamic dynasties.

Can a unifying principle be gleaned through this variety? Both Kiwan and the Forest of Truth offer us an episode of the broader civilizational history they stage. Through each of these episodes, we learn about the principles governing the movements of human history—envisioned as a history of civilizational succession. In other words, we ostensibly learn why civilizations rise and fall by attending to the utopia-in-crisis at hand, which can either be seen as undergoing a fall or attempting to rise back. Marrash's "Forest" opens with the reigning of science and the intellect as the sine qua non of the rise of civilizations. As I argued in chapter 2, the text goes on to play out the details of this principle as it maps on various levels: in the individual soul, in the public, in the history of one single civilization, or across civilizational history. "Floral Publishing" is not as demonstrative, yet there is a perpetual bemoaning—a fitting term, considering the way the text plays with the poetic trope of the cry over ruins—of the lost unity of the people of Kiwan.

To reiterate, in seeing the Forest of Truth, we learn to see how *athar* displays the reign of science and the intellect, or their waning power. Kiwan stages the state of the union. In each case, these are the principles underpinning history. In Muwaylihi's *hadith*, *athar* stages the focus on or neglect of the future. Mubarak's *'alam al-din* is one of the more elaborate texts in drawing a link between history, political rule, and civilization; its *athar* stage the principles of good rulership and their efficient application during a particular period of time. But isn't this ultimately what all *athar* stage in these different texts? In reflecting on the different principles they single out, we begin to see that *athar* focalize something about the principles of rulership whether these are taken to be rationality, unity, justice as a result of bureaucratic expertise, or a preoccupation with the future. The concern with good ruling cannot be adequately understood if it is reduced to a technical political problem; it has to be considered, in the context of these texts, as one pertaining to whose deeds we are learning to see, and what deeds one is learning, through literature (*adab*), to perform. Al-Nadim's renowned sketch "Medical Council" offers a succinct illustration that is also pertinent to the other texts explored so far.

I have already mentioned that the visions of 'Isa and the Pasha are aligned when they join forces. The aim of 'Isa is to help the Pasha perceive the history of the present by comparing their two respective periods of time. Al-Nadim had similarly described the contents of his journal *al-tankit wal tabkit* (Raillery and Reproof) as the "sighs" arising from the act of encounter/comparison (*al-muqabala*) between past and present: "Do not deny what it recounts before applying it to our state and do not think that its jokes intend to ridicule us or mock our deeds. They are but sighs produced through comparing our present to our past."[32] The simultaneous encounter and comparison is produced through engaging the present state, which is perceived as one of complete chaos. The comparison is necessary to explain the present and to attempt to intervene in it and change it. These are mutually dependent goals: the disarray of the present coupled with the desire to reform it result in a turn to comparison.

Al-Nadim articulates explicitly what Muwaylihi's *hadith* and other texts set out to do: compare civilizations (kingdoms of light vs. kingdoms of darkness), as well as cities, periods, and moments within the same civilization. These divergent objects are rendered similar—be they different cities or distinct periods of time—because they are each an *athar*—an object that stages and potentially concretizes the invisible principle of history.

The narrative of al-Nadim's "Medical Council," one of the first entries in the first edition of *al-tankit wal tabkit* is preceded by the announcement of the establishment of the paper, and the first editorial, titled "O Speaker of Arabic."[33] The editorial is the backdrop against which the story is to be read, and it also contributes the rubric for how to approach the new journal. The sketch recounts the story of a beautiful and great young man, whose attributes are not only preserved over time but also continuously increase, due to his people's vigilance in protecting him, their unity in looking after him, and their willingness to die for him.[34]

Things suddenly change when an unknown man appears. At first, the stranger seems worthy of the company of the youth, but it soon becomes clear that he only intends harm. He diverts the attention of the young man's people, devising multiple ploys, including beautiful women and various forms of entertainment.[35] Meanwhile, he leads the young man down misleading roads and paths until he is incapable of escaping the stranger's hold. Having been deserted by everyone, the young man surrenders to his fate, giving in completely to his mysterious companion. The latter then passes the young man off to his friends, who only further exacerbate the young man's misery and exhaustion. He eventually collapses, lying in waste/ruin (*khirba*), after the alien—allegorized as an illness, most likely syphilis—has entirely taken him over.[36] The story can be read as an allegory of Egypt's (*al-watan*, the homeland) history, transitioning from the care of united (Tuwayrani's keyword) Egyptians to the custody of the companion (Ottomans/Muhammad Ali's dynasty), who in turn surrender him to the Europeans.

My concern here, though, is with descriptions of the young man in relationship to time. Prior to his downfall, the young man is depicted as increasing in beauty, youth, and glory through time, as a result of his people's conscientiousness. After his collapse, one of his people, who finally pays attention, comments on his present state, comparing to it the youth's prior vitality and power over time: "Where is your health that used to maintain its youth while time ages?"[37] The portrayal is reminiscent of Muwaylihi's descriptions of the pyramids as well as the "formulaic" phrases deployed to evoke the wonder of (ancient) monuments. Indeed, the power of Nadim's phrases lies in their formulaic overtones. The young man and his health reflect his people's unity. When they are united and working together, his positive attributes perpetually increase; when they are dispersed, he falls prey to illness. To reevoke Tuwayrani's quotes, the young man is the *athar* recording *his people's deeds*—in accordance with, or discordance to, the universal principles of history.

The reading of the young man as the *athar* is fortified by the evocation of monumental traces. Lying ill in the ruin, the youth looks at the palaces and *athar* of his people, which have likewise fallen apart.[38] The story recounts the cycle of rise and fall, and its undergirding reasons. The main reason is the loss of unity, which is also Tuwayrani's explanation for historical changes.[39] The concern with unity, as well as with sociability and socialization, were central during the nineteenth century (a point to which I return in the next chapter). For now, it is crucial to note that the entirety of the social collective is, in this case, posited as an *athar*. Explained otherwise, *athar* records the deeds of *everyone*, and their deeds are understood as occurring *within* the civilization.

Thus, *athar* is still caught amid dichotomous principles (rise and fall, unity and disunity, progression and regression), as was the case with the Quranic *athar*. Yet the struggle here is not between human nature and the transcendent, and the fall is not attributed to the action of time or the divine; rather, it is all subsumed *within* the principles of civilization themselves, exploding a whole new possibility for thinking about action in time. The move, toward the civilization or the social collective, is implicated with the question of whose deeds *athar* record—Pharaoh and Napoleon, ruling Pashas and their grandchildren, as we saw in Muwaylihi's *hadith*, or an anonymous passerby who can call onto everyone indiscriminately.

The cycle of rise and fall, in "Medical Council," is not taken to be performing an inevitable course of history necessitated by the dichotomous human nature. Instead, the cycles follow the deeds of people, and their attempts to intervene. The destabilization of the repetitive cycles—but not their complete elision—hinges upon carving out the place for the action of persons in these cycles. The fall of the young man calls for a collective intervention, because it is not simply a record of the contradictory forces of time. When the present state of the youth is seen by a passerby from among his people, the seeing evokes an act of encounter/comparison between the present and the past. The young man becomes the site of a comparison between his current fallen state and his earlier glorious one, elucidating the cause(s) behind the rise and fall. The explanation (i.e., unity) then furnishes a path for intervention and change.

The body of the youth, the *athar*, stages unity as the abstract principle and records whether or not it has been implemented. Put more sharply, the *athar* records the deeds of the collective, with particular focus on whether or not the deeds are in accordance with unity. The transformation of the youth into a site where abstract principles manifest and where the present and past can be seen at the same moment is crucial. The encounter/comparison between the two images would not be possible if the passerby did not have a memory of the past state of the young man. This encounter and comparison results in a process of questioning the reasons behind the downfall, which implicitly reveals the reasons for the rise. The young man asks the passerby to intervene and help him, and this is when the call for resurrection is sounded. The man runs to the neighborhood and calls out to his and the young man's people, perchance some will come to the rescue: "O silent graves rip open and resurrect the dead. The great calamity has arrived, and judgement day has approached. O idle spirits! Return to your worn-out bodies, raise them from their death, and restore them to existence so that they may look at him; if he were to be annihilated, they would suffer."[40] Rather than call to the inhabitants of the neighborhood to come to the rescue of the young man, the summons are directed at the dead to come back to life. On one level, the appeal can be interpreted as addressing present living Egyptians, figuratively describing them as "dead" to show the extremity of the collapse; on another, the young man's earlier reference to the ruinous *athar* and palaces is taken a step further, depicting them as tombs.

Hadith features both an actual cemetery, with which the narrative begins, as well as a figurative one beneath any actual place. The latter is used as a sign of actual collapse hidden behind a façade. In "Medical

Council," the resurrection of present-day Egyptians is contingent upon their being reminded of their history and their selves. Consequently, resurrecting present Egyptians is entwined with reviving the ones who have already died and rest in tombs. The self in the present remains a potentiality that can only be actualized when the reader encounters their history. Resurrecting present Egyptians, who are like the dead, is an act of reminding them of those older Egyptians buried in tombs now. This reminder is an act of resurrection, not simply of the past, but of a self.

The story ends with a public call for successful action, grafted onto the call for prayer (*hayya 'ala al-falah*). Huge masses respond to the call, taking quick measures to save the young man and protect him as they once did. The narrator of the story—distinguished from its transcriber—also hears the call for prayer and rises to do its duty (*al-fard*) before continuing the service of protecting the homeland with his brothers. The call for prayer as *al-fard* signals both the call for actual prayer, and the plea to perform the duty of serving the young man. This reading is supported by the reference in the call to the young man as the one you are judged upon, pointing once more to judgment on a religious duty (*fard*). The double meaning aims at sustaining both meanings without privileging one over the other.

The two calls might, of course, be grafted onto each other, as both Muwaylihi and Nadim do. Consequently, understanding the conception of history in these texts hinges on working out the relationship between action or deeds (of characters) and *athar*—an issue I take up in the next chapter on characters and characterization. Even though the previous section drew out key elements in the conception of history staged by these texts, we cannot completely articulate it without turning to characterization. While the splinters discovered in this chapter resonate with other discourses of progress, identity, and politics (or political theology), the aim is to grapple with the vision of the literary practiced by these texts.

Similar to the way we are forced to realize that history cannot be grasped without thinking of actors, the resurrected Pasha in Muwaylihi's *hadith* is forced to draw a comparable lesson. Upon his return to life, the Pasha is caught in an altercation with a donkey-driver that lands both the driver and the Pasha in prison. Following a long legal ordeal, the Pasha finally manages to extricate himself from the modern legal system, with which he had no prior familiarity. Yet he is not entirely liberated from all attachments to the legal system, since he still needs to find money to pay his lawyer. Consequently, the lawyer, 'Isa, and the Pasha try to find the Pasha's endowment, which he had left for his progeny. In a discussion with the lawyer, the Pasha is offered a forewarning of what he will repeatedly see in the following episodes in relation to his grandchildren, his endowment, and the great people from his time. The lawyer describes the falling apart of the state of the Pasha precisely as an erasure of their trace: a falling apart of the *athar* (both architectural and otherwise) that they have left behind.

> In fact, worms and inheritors had a race over your buried remains as well as your hoarded ones, and the inheritors beat the worms coming in and out. More and more money disappeared, and in gargantuan amounts. Estate after estate, mansion after mansion, was lost forever, till only the house in which they were living was left. Then they started selling off the furniture . . . until the building was flattened and all vestiges of it disappeared. The name of the owner who had committed so many crimes in order to build it and keep it standing was lost.[41]

The ruin of *athar* is not a result of the contradictory force of time, but the direct consequence of actions. These actions can be summed up in the greed that drove this class to ignore anything other than saving money, from ignoring the responsibility of ruling to neglecting the education of their children. In other words, the ruin follows from the replacement of the future with the pursuit of an illusory immortality. Once they die, their children turn around to sell everything that the greedy parents left behind. Here, not unlike what has been seen with Pharaoh and the pyramids, the injustices of ruling are linked to the negligence of perishing, which results in acts of arrogance and the challenge of time through building monumental traces (*athar*). The latter do not perish because anything left in time will perish; it is not about the natural battle between time as a drive toward death and annihilation and time as the historical time of civilization. Rather, the effacement of these traces is connected with historical action. The lawyer's interpretation of the downfall of the Pasha's dynasty provides the interpretive web through which to read the endowment episode, or to read the endowment as an *athar*.

The endowment is described by the servant of the Pasha as having been built to immortalize the memory of the Pasha and his name. It did not just completely collapse, but also turned upside down from a mosque into a bar:

> Master, not a single trace of your wealth remains. Property, money and estates, everything worth mentioning, they are all gone. For a long time I was able to live on the profits of what you endowed to your household and retinue, and also to this mosque, fountain, and Quran school to perpetuate your memory and keep your name alive. But before too long, the endowment collapsed and became defunct through prolonged neglect. We were all left in poverty and hardship. As you can see now, the school has been turned into a storehouse, the fountain into a wine shop and the mosque into a dyeworks.[42]

The responsibility for this fall is ascribed to the actions of the Pasha's grandsons, whose behavior plays out the lawyer's earlier descriptions, and the warning to the Pasha, of the typical behavior of wealthy men's descendants. The Pasha's class's own attempts to achieve immortality hasten its fall. The Pasha's effort to reinherit the endowment, the trace (*athar*) that he had left for posterity to immortalize his memory, forces him to inherit the consequences of his own actions—the future of the past.

The Pasha's resurrection is not exclusively an estrangement technique; it contributes a rubric for making time visible as the history of the present and not just as the force of death encountered in the cemetery. The "present" moment is for the Pasha the future of his present, or simply the future of the past. It is the *athar* (trace/what is left behind, and also the yield) of the past, which the past cannot recognize as such, and that needs comparison (*muqabala*) precisely to see it as such an *athar* (trace). It holds within it, too, traces of the future; consequently, it is the future's past. Inasmuch as the Pasha's time and its actions held within it traces of the future that it could not see, and, as such, the Pasha could not recognize anything in a completely transformed Cairo, the acts of making history visible offer lessons for reading the traces of the future in the textual present moment.

Because Cairo has changed tremendously, the Pasha is incapable of finding his *waqf*. Even after he first sees it, it takes him time to actually recognize it. In fact, he only really identifies it as his own when he perceives one of his old servants. The inability of the Pasha to recognize the present is not restricted to things that happened after his time, despite the fact that they are posited as the result of his time; it also includes things of his time, which have themselves changed. This forces the Pasha to eventually come to terms with the fact that this time is not merely a bizarre, topsy-turvy period, but also the trace (*athar*) of his own time and of his own actions.

The Pasha's repeated comments that living in this period of time is more of a punishment than death itself is more than an exaggeration.[43] The Pasha's introduction to the history of the present era is an act of inheriting the future of his past, as its *athar*. The agony the Pasha experiences does not just result from his series of misfortunate events, but is exacerbated when he becomes aware of the direct causal links between the actions of his own class and his state, and the period of time he is resurrected in. It is this experience that he finds more painful than even his first encounters. He is forced not only to compare the two periods but also to discover their links: history. These encounters truly teach the Pasha something about the mistakes of his era and the mistakes of his lifetime. The Pasha's era, of which (no) traces can be found, is made visible only through linking his actions to the new present in which he is resurrected. Like Quranic narratives, the punishment befalling the Pasha is a reminder: it is as if in experiencing this new world, the Pasha is reminded of his own world, of his own actions, and of their own meaning. Meaning here is defined precisely as *athar*, as what remains in time. The "moral lesson" is about the future. Peculiarly, the punishment of the Pasha is meted out through reminding him of the future through the comparison, which results in him seeing the "history of the present era." In this way, inheriting the future is an act of remembering the future.

The meanings of the actions of the Pasha and his class cannot really be understood except through his attempt to inherit the future of these actions. Here the possibility of a different future is opened up, precisely through reinterpreting the position of memory in Quranic narratives in a way that posits meaning as a question of the future and suspending the repetitive cycles as an extension of the dichotomous human nature. The act of reminding in Quranic narratives formed part of the notion of time crystallizing around *athar*, focused on invoking the past, for the sake of the present and of the future. The Quranic reminder pertains to perishing, intervening in the human tendency to forgetfulness, and making sure that memory triumphs against forgetfulness in the temporal unfolding of the dichotomous human nature. In *hadith*, however, what is being narrated is not merely a story of the fall of a people. Through positing A *Period of Time* as the future of the past, reminding becomes not just about perishing, but about the relationship between perishing and the future. Peculiarly, the act of reminding is an act of reminding of the future, not of the past. The Pasha is reminded of the question of the future, which he had taken so lightly. In assuming that they live forever, or in accumulating wealth or building monuments thinking that they would immortalize them, this class did not leave the *athar* they thought they were. Rather, their trace is forged out of their relinquishing of the actual future, in pursuit of an unattainable immortality: the play between the false and the true *athar* occurs in the slippages between pursuing an illusory immortality versus chasing after the future. In envisioning what is yet to come as an impossible continuation of a necessarily fleeting present, the Pasha and his class forget their own children, and the social collective more broadly, which results in the destruction of everything as well as their own downfall. In touring Cairo, we are invited to see the history of the Pasha and his class as it is being staged, inscribed on every object we encounter.

Time in *hadith* is thus worked in a strictly oppositional manner to that iterated by great men from the Pasha's time. After talking about Muhammad Ali and his rule, they quickly say, "May God have mercy on what is past, may He protect us from the present, and give us a safe refuge against the future."[44] It is against this attitude to time that *hadith* is to be read. In fact, the Pasha immediately tries to point his contemporaries to their mistakes. Their assumptions about time, to which he had also previously subscribed, have been proven through his journey to be completely wrong. The link between remembering, perishing, and working for the actual future are here collapsed together much like the call for prayer and action in Nadim's "Hurry to Success" sustained the call for prayer, and for action for the collective. The move from futile attempts to immortalize a fleeting present toward the "future" is intertwined with the turn from immortalizing the self to the true *athar* (the future of the collective). In playing with the Quranic, archaeological, and other *athar*, the texts entwine contemplations of time as a ruinous force with time as history, as the record of actions or deeds on time itself.

History, good ruling, and the collective are strung together through *athar*—this much is clear. What is less certain, however, is whether the action for the collective is taken by them, or at the hand of a new reformed ruling body. In other words, are the deeds encapsulated by *athar* of the collective, or are they enacted upon the collective, constituted as the population, the public, or the commoners? In turning to characterization in the next chapter, we take up the collective as *al-nas*, analyzing the conception of the collective and the bifurcation therein. Consequently, we continue to explore how literature (*adab*) is reconstituted as a pedagogy of, and in, seeing.

4

History's Actors and the Collective Sovereignty of *al-Nas*

Chapter 1 intimated a link between the three gestures of visualization that form the literary optic—bringing objects to stand in front of the mind's eye, placing them under an optic device, and putting them onstage—and the purpose of this visualization: judging the connection between seemingly discrete events and their undergirding universal principles of civilizational progress. We posited that the object of both visualization and judgment is history, while noting that what we see in the texts as history would be refined as our analysis deepened. Chapter 3 nuanced this idea as *actions* in history: what is being judged are actions through which the seemingly distinct events and their underlying governing principles are either brought together harmoniously or violently riven. *Athar* (the visible trace) makes this relationship between events, actions, and principles observable; in so doing, it contributes the potential for change, for, in learning to see history, we also learn to align our actions in it with the abstract principles of civilizational progress. *Athar*, then, can be seen not so much as a particular kind of object (archaeological, architectural, artistic, or natural) as much as the *effect* of the literary optic that enables us to approach any object as *athar*. Literature helps one see every object as encoding actions that either cohere disparate events and abstract principles or tear them apart.

The previous chapter made the case that learning to see history via *athar* entails grappling with the meaning of actions from the vantage point of the future, judging what of this meaning will remain—what its outcome, or "yield," will be. Furthermore, the latter vantage point necessarily exceeds the specific position of the actor, since they (although in our canon it is mostly he) has to project a future in which they are not there, but their traces are. In other words, since the trace outlasts the actor, its meaning is not delimited by the actor's intentions or position, but necessarily exceeds them. Consequently, in learning to see history via *athar*, one is learning about the position from where intention, action, and meaning can be aligned with something that exceeds the confines of one's direct personal experiences. Narratologically, this ulterior position is carved out through a host of estrangement techniques that result in marking the future as the locus for engaging with the meaning of action as well as with the possibility of inducing changed actions. The point is quite clear when some form of time travel is involved; often a character from the past comes back to a place they haven't been to in a long time and takes stock of the changes in this future-present, excavating the relationship between the past and the future-present. Yet this is equally true in cases of geographical travel, because, as we saw in the preceding chapter, traveling between places is also traveling through time, since the diagnostic dimension of history enables us to judge places as being ahead, behind, or on time. As a result, literature has a pedagogic dimension that is not extraneous to its literariness but is at the heart of how the literary is conceptualized and practiced by the canon of nineteenth-century Arabic literature.

Within this understanding of the literary optic, chapter 4 argues that while the future is presented narratologically as the vantage point from where the meaning of action can emerge, this move is predicated upon the advent of the collective (*al-nas*) as a conceptual category underlying a concern with modern political sovereignty. The possibility that the future also stands in for the collective was suggested in the previous chapter; still, the connection between this future-collective and sovereignty requires further unpacking, and it can be broken down into two interrelated points. First, the narratological focalization of the future enables our canon to narrativize the totality that emerges out of sociality, or the society (*hay'a ijtima'iyya*)—and this is *because* of the texts' "episodic" structure, not in spite of it. We have already seen that the adjudication of what remains in time is not just a question of autonomous continuity; rather, it is shown in the texts to be the consequence of the actions of others and for others (e.g., Muwaylihi). In other words, *athar* is not exclusively what lasts in time, but what lasts through and for others. Therefore, the evaluation of actions does not merely exceed the actor's position temporally, but postulates others—in the form of what I will argue in this chapter is a social "whole," which I refer to as a totality—as the backdrop against which her actions can be assessed. Taking this a step further, to the second point, this narratological move (the superimposition of the future and the social whole) is underpinned by a critical conceptual shift in defining the origins of society.

To give a brief outline of what will be explored in more detail, society has a long intellectual history of being traced back to human nature itself (i.e., to sociality), which necessitates the coming together of persons as a condition for survival. In the same vein, human nature demands that the formation of society is concomitant with the concentration of power in a political head or sovereign. In Arabic, this is the debate on the nature of the relationship of *sultan* and *ra'iyya* (literally, "power"/ruler and his dependents, but can be conceptually captured in "sovereign and subjects"). For our nineteenth-century canon, the congruence of human nature (sociality), society, and the concentration of power in a political head proves a slippery matter.

While almost every single text studied in this book touches on this debate, the engagement with it is complicated by the emergence of the collective as both object and potential subject of political power. In the process, the criteria for dividing any given society between *sultan* and *ra'iyya* become muddled, and in need of accurate and truthful judgment that can discern the heart of human nature. Literature as making history visible is forged in the face of this challenge, presenting itself as a tool, an optic, for this desperately needed judgment of human nature as it is encoded in traces of history. The recourse to history is rooted in the assumed invisibility of the collective, which precludes encountering it directly as an object of empirical knowledge. Literature redresses this impasse by making the collective visible through the traces of history. With this, we can finally discard history as a placeholder for what is yet to come. History is the visible anonym for the invisible collective.

Chapter 4 uncovers this play of visibility and invisibility. It begins by revisiting *athar*, discovering its entwinement with human nature (including both sociality and its ensuing need for sovereignty) and the future. It then reveals the future in this canon to be both temporal and social, enabling the projection of society as a totality. We explore this point by widening our lens to perceive the mode of characterization (how characters are drawn) in this canon, discovering that it assumes the collective (*al-nas*) as its backdrop while continuing to uphold the impossibility of turning it into a visible object—either "inside" the text or "outside" it. In fact, the mode of characterization, with its reliance on social types and the personification of abstract virtues and principles, is deployed expressly to address the collective's invisibility. This chapter, then, resolves the mystery that the characters of this canon, with their seeming "lack of" interiority or "psychological depth" and "weak" plot continuity, have continued to present to us. In doing so, it unravels the "origins" of this canon—not by demarcating a temporal point or a geographic source, but by revealing the question of sovereignty in the wake of the rise of the collective as the crucible of this canon.

History: The Interplay of Sociality and Sovereignty

Chapter 3 emphasized that, in this canon, the dichotomous view of human nature does not play out as a struggle between (human) civilization and the divine. Rather, it is usurped within the dynamics of civilization itself. This transformation, however, is neither sudden nor absolute. I have already pointed out that *athar* played a vital role in history writing long before the nineteenth century. The notion of "tracing" or "following the trace" (*iqtifa' al-athar*) was often deployed to explain and justify history writing as a knowledge producing and edifying discourse.[1] Consequently, *athar* must have been used to encode actions in history—however these may have been conceived—long before our nineteenth-century canon. Thus, the distinction between *athar* and action (in the nineteenth century) contra *athar* and time as an abstract force (prior to the nineteenth century) is a generalizing schema that helped us delineate broad tendencies as a step in historicizing the canon of nineteenth-century Arabic literature.[2] In this section, this schema is nuanced by turning to the relationship between *athar*, action, and time in Abd al-Rahman ibn Khaldun's (1332–1406)

Muqaddima, a work that has long been believed to profoundly influence various intellectual currents in Arabic during the nineteenth century. In fact, our canon has frequently been associated with Khaldunian thought.[3] Analyzing the intersection between Ibn Khaldun and this canon is a necessary step in grasping the superimposition of the future and social totality in our texts.

However, instead of constructing a reading of Ibn Khaldun that attempts (impossibly) to be all inclusive, we approach "Ibn Khaldun" here as a namesake for a layer *inside* the canon of nineteenth-century Arabic literature. In other words, we are not primarily concerned with Ibn Khaldun as a fourteenth-century historical figure and offering an exhaustive sense of his work, let alone of its intricate history of reception up to the nineteenth century. In the same vein, I do not aim to present a full historical documentation of the relationship between history, action, and *athar* prior to the nineteenth century. Our focus remains on our canon itself, historicizing moments within the texts and, in the process, touching upon earlier articulations that are mobilized by these texts without confusing that with offering a chronological emplotment of historical change.

We begin with two direct quotes from Ibn Khaldun's *Muqaddima* that appear in Mubarak's *'alam al-din* that deal with the relationship between history (of civilization), human nature, and sovereignty. Contrary to studies that tend to highlight the continuing influence of Ibn Khaldun on the nineteenth century, I show that the moment at which Ibn Khaldun seems to be reproduced in Mubarak's text is also the moment of a radical break with him. This break is both epistemological and political, involving rethinking human nature at the intersection of sovereignty and sociality, and it reaches beyond a single text—in this case, Mubarak's *'alam al-din*. This is not to suggest that Ibn Khaldun was not influential, but to offer a more precise sense of his importance, arguing that he is engaged by our authors from within an already transformed conceptual universe—much like *khayal*, as discussed in chapter 1 of this book.

Mubarak's *'alam al-din* charts the journey of 'Alam al-Din and his son Burhan al-Din with an unnamed English Orientalist from Egypt to London through France (Marseilles, then Paris). Upon arriving in Marseilles, Burhan al-Din hands his father a letter that he had written to send home to his mother in Egypt.[4] While Mubarak's text incorporates numerous snippets from other written works and documents, the way in which this particular letter is shared with readers is distinctive. The other written works were read aloud by one of the characters to their companions. As readers, we can only access those written texts within ʿalam al-din if they are voiced by one of the characters. In this way, Mubarak's work deploys explicitly theatrical techniques whereby the narrative perspective is strictly aligned with what is externalized by the conversing characters, as we discussed at length in chapter 2—and this theatricality applies to other texts as well. In the case of Burhan al-Din's letter, however, there is no narratological justification for how we see it: it is not read aloud by one of the characters in the middle of a conversation. Instead, the letter is shared directly: "Once they settled in the house, the Sheikh said to his son, where is your letter to your mother? The son handed him a letter. This is its image."[5] The next six colloquies, or chapters, contain the reproduced letter.[6] With the conclusion of the letter, part 1 of ʿalam al-din comes to an end. The fact, then, that the son's letter is reproduced through a markedly different strategy and is uninterrupted by any other narrative event is striking, and so is the fact that it marks the end of part 2. But what is most remarkable about this letter are its contents, which offer a macrocosm of Mubarak's entire book.

Colloquy 21 bears the title "Burhan al-Din's Letter," and each of the subsequent episodes through Colloquy 26 has a new title announcing its focus: "Burhan al-Din and His Friend," "History and Geography," "Acts of Worship" (al-ʿibadat), "Humans and the Form of Society" (al-insan wa hayʾat al-ijtimaʿ), and "The Conclusion of Burhan al-Din's Letter," respectively. The topical titles are followed by a subtitle between brackets: "Continuation of the Letter." The coupling of the titles with a fixed subtitle preserves the topical arrangement of the book while confirming that we continue to read the same letter. While I will zoom in on how Ibn Khaldun is cited in the text, I begin by giving an overall sense of the letter to better understand Ibn Khaldun's position in it, before turning to the Muqaddima to analyze where these quotes are taken from.

The letter begins with Burhan al-Din's effusive expression of his longing for his mother and his home. His style and word choice are reminiscent of nostalgia tropes from the Classical ode, as touched upon in chapter 1. In fact, Burhan al-Din explicitly evokes that poetic tradition, claiming to finally have a firsthand experience of the emotions poets customarily express. Like them, he is overcome by a powerful yearning; he loses sleep, and, when he does sleep, he is haunted by alternating dreams and nightmares. His father helps him cope with these consuming passions by teaching him how to recognize truthful from illusory perception; much of the advice given by the father here resonates with the discussions of theater that we analyzed in chapters 1 and 2. It is useful to remember that while the letter concludes part 1, part 2 will begin immediately with the colloquy exploring theater, further reentrenching the association between theater, *khayal*, and dreams that we have seen before.

Following the tropes of nostalgia, Burhan al-Din shares with his mother something else that had helped him cope: he met James (whose name he translates into Arabic as Ya'qub) on the boat, and the latter joined them on their journey. Thus, Ya'qub becomes the companion of the son, just like the unnamed English Orientalist is the father's. The rest of the letter is dedicated to the encounters between the son and his newfound friend. Their discussions distill the pedagogic agenda of the whole text, offering a snapshot of the topics covered both before as well as after these episodes, with the added advantage that, due to the letter's brevity relative to the entire text, we can better observe the relationality between these topics, tying all of them to the interplay of sociality and sovereignty at the core of human nature.[7]

Ya'qub and Burhan al-Din begin by talking about geography. This leads into a discussion of "ethnography"—a term they do not use explicitly, but geography and ethnography were not fully separated out during the nineteenth century. They map out ethnicities, dissecting the habits, cultures, and religious beliefs of the various groups inhabiting the diverse parts of the world. Ya'qub explains that geography's importance lies in its indispensability for history, which itself enjoys an uncontestable status in the realms of knowledge and progress:

> [Ya'qub] said, it appears that you have not read the science of Geography, so I replied and what science is that? He laughed saying it is the

science of the Earth's surface, its length and width, what it contains: seas, cities, and rivers, and what is particular to each region including the religion of its people, their type of government and what their ethical dispositions and state of affairs are like among other things. I said I never heard about this except from you. He replied how could this be when it is the Arabs who first recorded it and founded it, I wonder if they have deserted it and forgotten it now even though knowing it is considered by people of all religions to be the duty of every human being because through it one knows the creatures inhabiting Earth, and discovers the truth of so many beings, and without it, knowing history would be challenging. . . . The *millet* has no power without the power of its men, and the power of its men is incomplete without history and other sciences.[8]

In the following colloquy, "Humans and the Form of Society," geography and history culminate in a discussion of human nature, through which the different social groups studied by geography and history are assumed to have emerged. The letter, then, moves on an arc that excavates the shared singular source manifesting through the world's diversity, unearthing the human propensity toward sociality as the crux of the different social groups encountered in geography and history. Ibn Khaldun is featured in this penultimate installment of the letter dealing with sociality.

Having elaborated on the different ethnic groups and their beliefs, Ya'qub and Burhan al-Din continue their journey from the multiple manifestations to their singular source, encapsulated in the drive to form social groups:

So, he said, we have already discussed the groupings of the humankind and the religions they uphold as was deemed appropriate for that point in the discussion and now we say that it is in the nature of this human species to love closeness with others and to lean towards sociality and *that's why they say that Man is "social" by nature, that is to say he must conjoin others which is the meaning of civilization in their terminology*.[9]

In this definition, sociality is highlighted as the sine qua non defining feature of the human nature. Ya'qub argues that there are two reasons that demonstrate that this depiction of human nature is incontestable. First, no one person can satisfy all her basic survival needs on her own, and, second, the human species is weaker than others in the animal kingdom and, as such, needs to collaborate to fend off predators. Yet—and this is where we begin to see the dichotomous dimension of human nature—sociality is constantly at risk of being undercut because of the equally strong propensity toward intrahuman aggression. Consequently, there is a need for a member of the species to assume sovereignty, ruling over others and protecting them from one another. Thus, sovereignty is the product of quelling through one localized position the force of intra-aggression that was dispersed among the group. The cohesion of society is then actualized and maintained by guarding against the ever-present risk of self-implosion. Both sociality as a drive toward harmonious coexistence with others on the one hand and antisocial aggression (or the turn against sociality) on the other are conceived of as constituents of human nature, though the tendency toward aggression is often relegated to more base, or "animalistic," inclinations that humans share with other animals.

Chapter 3 touched upon this oscillation, explaining it as the dichotomy between memory and forgetfulness at the core of human nature. The movement between two antagonistic sides of human nature is maintained in the canon of nineteenth-century Arabic literature, but, in addition to memory and forgetfulness, sociability and aggressiveness, we also observe the following binaries: the fully human/animalistic, order/chaos, love (*mahabba*)/animosity (*'adawa*), competition (*muzahama*)/collaboration (*musa'ada*), and civilization/ barbarity, to name just a few. Once both sociality and antisocial aggression are asserted as defining aspects of human nature, the need for a sovereign—as a suppressor of aggression and a site where aggression is concentrated—becomes naturalized; it is necessitated by human nature and the latter's oscillation between the need for forming society as a condition for survival and the propensity towards destroying them. These ideas are far from unique to Mubarak's *'alam al-din*, or even to the select canon studied by this book, but are dispersed throughout numerous writings from this period. For our purposes, it is crucial to note that, in the above definition of human nature, the sentences in bold are culled from Ibn Khaldun's *Muqaddima*. In fact, it is one of the early definitions offered by this fourteenth-century luminary of his new science (*'ilm al-'umran*), to which we will turn soon. For now, we explore another example from our canon, Marrash's "Forest," where these ideas are echoed with a degree of explicitness akin to what we saw in Mubarak.

Marrash's "Forest" invites its readers to step into the meandering thoughts of the unnamed character-narrator, which unfold as a theater-trial between the Kingdom of Light and the Kingdom of Darkness. We have already seen in chapter 2 the way in which the anticipated grand trial is preceded by side-discussions that operate like small-scale rehearsal trials; in fact, these rehearsals occupy the bulk of the text. Of these, the longest is the conversation between the Philosopher and the Commander of the Army of Civilization. In the fourth chapter of "Forest," entitled "Politics and the Kingdom," the latter two characters touch upon the origins of politics. Much like Burhan al-Din's letter, the discussion begins with tracing the origins of sovereignty back to human nature itself.[10]

Unlike in *'alam al-din*, however, the oscillation is given a historical actuality; it is not just part of human nature, but has been actualized in the distant past. In other words, the oscillation is construed as the deep history—perhaps prehistory—through which civilization emerged. Thus, there is an assumption in "Forest" that there was an actual period of fighting that was quelled by the rise of a ruler whose power was at first restricted solely to the family, and it is out of this model of ruling the family (i.e., patriarchy) that more expansive forms of politics gradually grew.[11] In discussing this episode in chapter 2, I pointed out that a voice suddenly intervenes in the text, announcing that the Philosopher cannot reach so far back into history.[12] The sudden voice is distinct from the narrator, who acts as a character hiding in order to watch these events, though in actuality he is dreaming it all. The voice encourages the Philosopher to carry on and to keep trying, and it is only then that the latter dons new glasses and a stage is opened up again.[13]

We previously discussed this crucial scene in relationship to visualization, mentioning in passing that the Philosopher was in pursuit of the origins of politics, which lie far back in history. In returning to it here, I am arguing that this moment of tracing the origins of politics (as sovereignty) is not merely one among many where the stage of history is opened in

Marrash's text. Rather, the process we witness at this precise moment is key to understanding how the literary stage of history is opened in "Forest," as well as in texts from this canon, as an optic that makes human nature visible and, as a result, enables it to be truthfully and accurately judged, thus aligning the mode of rule with human nature in a way that ensures civilizational progress.

It comes as no surprise, then, that in both Mubarak's and Marrash's texts the tracing of the origins of sovereignty is followed by an exploration of the other necessities that ensue from this concentration of power in a sovereign. They each scrutinize the conditions necessary for the founding of sovereignty and managing of sovereign power that are most conducive to preserving society and ensuring that it continues to flourish. They both sketch out a series of steps that flow one from the other, forming circles that begin with the emergence of sovereignty, charting out what is needed to maintain sovereignty and therefore strengthen sociality against antisocial aggression. Yet the accompanying terms in each writer's circle are noticeably different. Marrash branches out of sovereignty into cultivating the mind (*tathqif al-'aql*), improving habits and customs/traditions (*tahsin al-'adat wa al-taqalid*), reforming the city/polis (*islah al-madina*), and, finally, love (*mahabba*). In fact, the entire theater-trial is meant to enact the accurate application of these principles on the level of the individual soul and the entire city by defeating, or balancing out, the antagonistic forces that undercut the harmony of this circle. Mubarak, on the other hand, uses a prominent maxim that is often quoted in classical *adab* works and is sometimes known as the circle of eight wise words, or the circle of justice.[14]

While Mubarak uses two versions of the circle, they are both drawn out of Ibn Khaldun's magnum opus. We now turn to explore how Ibn Khaldun worked out the relationship between human nature (Mubarak's first quote on sociality) and the circle (Mubarak's second quote). This will lead us into an exploration of Ibn Khaldun's notion of *athar*, which crystallizes its difference from the nineteenth-century rendition in the emergence of the potential of collective self-rule. While, on the surface, human nature is discussed in comparable ways, and the oscillation between sociality and antisocial aggression is maintained, the political possibilities that grow out of that shift in the nineteenth century are entirely new. In fact, right after the circle, the conversation shifts to republican versus monarchical modes of ruling, splitting the latter further into absolute and restricted (i.e., constitutional) monarchies.[15]

The *Athar* of Ibn Khaldun

Ibn Khaldun's *Muqaddima* famously sets out to institute a new science that verifies and corroborates the reported accounts and narratives (*al-akhbar wal-riwayat*) of which history writing (*tarikh*) is formed. The new science, known as *'ilm al-'umran* (the study of the laws of civilization), discloses the laws underpinning the movement of history by revealing those that govern the formation and dissolution of civilizations and their ruling dynasties. Because these laws map out the general phases that each civilization necessarily passes through, therefore one could carve out a methodology for corroborating accounts and narratives, discerning whether they conform with what is to be expected at this stage in the civilization's life cycle, which is also the life cycle of its underpinning group solidarity (*'asabiyya*).[16] We will turn to these details later, analyzing them through Ibn Khaldun's use of the concept of *athar*; for now we focus on his introduction of this new branch of knowledge (from which Mubarak's first quote is extracted).

In presenting his newly discovered science, Ibn Khaldun links it both to human nature and history, speaking those links from within their incomplete—from his perspective—articulation by other fields of knowledge. This is where we encounter the excerpt Mubarak quotes: "Man is 'social' by nature, that is to say he must conjoin others which is the meaning of civilization in their terminology."[17]

In this statement, Ibn Khaldun explicitly engages the Arabic "Aristotelian" philosophic tradition with its strong Neoplatonic tinge. When he says, "in *their* terminology," the philosophers are the anonymous plural.[18] He soon moves on, however, to surveying other knowledge-producing discourses in which the centrality of human nature is partially glossed, but not adequately confronted. These include legal theory (*usul al-fiqh*, "the principles of [Islamic] Jurisprudence"), and in the latter's "subfield" of *maqasid al-shariʿa* ("the purposes of the law") as well as in rhetoric and politics (from the aforementioned philosophic tradition), and *adab*.

Ibn Khaldun's survey notes that the contemplation of human nature (i.e., their sociality, their tendency to conjoin forming societies) underpins both legal theory (*usul al-fiqh* and *maqasid al-shariʿa*) but is never, according to him, tackled explicitly at length. That said, *Muqaddima* also points to other fields that have confronted human nature unequivocally: rhetoric (*al-khataba*), politics (*ʿilm al-siyasa al-madaniyya*), and *adab* literature.[19] The examples he mentions of the latter belong to a genre called mirrors for princes. In his brief discussion of these three fields, he is keen on emphasizing that his new science is distinct from all of them; while rhetoric and politics share some similarities with his work, they are ultimately rather different, because their aims and purview diverge drastically. Rhetoric is concerned with convincing or deterring people. Politics is utopian, concerned with the ethical principles according to which people *should* organize their lives, and, in so doing, premised on an unrealizable possibility of "self-rule" (specifically, that each person is the guide and ruler of themselves). Ibn Khaldun is quick to dismiss the latter idea because it simply has no evidence from real life (history)—an important point to keep in mind for when we return to our canon. Ibn Khaldun concludes his survey with *adab* literature, which he believes comes closest to his own insights, but with a major drawback that his work remedies.

Specifically, Ibn Khaldun acknowledges a resemblance between his science and the circle of eight wise words or circle of justice discussed in *adab* literature.[20] (Mubarak takes his second quote from this section.) Ibn Khaldun identifies *adab*, particularly the circle, as the most serious attempt—prior to his own—to grapple with how human nature unfolds in patterned rhythms that undergird history. It is perhaps not surprising, then, that he, too, reaches a complex cyclical vision. The pivotal difference, according to Ibn Khaldun, lies in the ability of *ʿilm al-ʿumran* to explicate its own cyclical structure, while *adab* is relentlessly caught in the reproduction of words of wisdom, with no prospect for their theorization.

We can thus say that one way of reading the *Muqaddima* is to see in it an attempt to radically deploy the conception of "Man" *al-insan*, as it implicitly exists in various knowledge-producing discourses in Arabic for the production of historical knowledge in a wide spectrum of "human" (read social) practices.[21] Ibn Khaldun tackles issues ranging from philosophy to artisanal production as aspects of 'umran, which encompasses everything that emanates out of human nature. It makes sense, then, that one of the first definitions of this new science encountered in the *Muqaddima*—and quoted by Mubarak—could equally be read as a definition of *al-'umran* and as an elucidation of a key aspect of the nature of *al-insan*. The vital point is that *'umran* is equally a question of history and of "human nature" inasmuch as history is the performance of human nature.[22] *'Ilm al-'umran*, the new science undergirding the study of history, is therefore also an articulation of a metahistorical principle and a summation of a human nature that is orchestrating the movement of history.[23] In the following paragraphs, I show how Ibn Khaldun deploys human nature to theorize *adab*'s circle, and how he manages to reveal why it is a circle at all. To show his theorization, I focus on his use of the term *athar*.

In addition to *'umran* (civilization), *'asabiyya* (group solidarity) is probably the other most famous concept presented by Ibn Khaldun. *'Asabiyya* refers to the solidarity among a kin group that enables them to form a dynasty that extends its rule over others whose group solidarity is not as strong. This group is key to Ibn Khaldun's understanding of the patterned rhythms undergirding history. We do not need to deal in this book with the intricacies of the term; it suffices to note here that its rendition as group solidarity or the blood tie among a kin group does not fully capture the universe in which this idea moves. Briefly put, *'asabiyya* is the site where Ibn Khaldun works out the relationship between a series of antonyms, drawing together and also supplanting diverse knowledge-producing discourses. These dyads include formation (*huduth*) and dissolution (*fana'*), form (*al-sura*) and matter (*al-madda*), and Bedouin identity (*al-badawa*) and settled civilizations (*al-hadara*). At the core of these dyads in the *Muqaddimma* is the sovereign/subject dyad that *'asabiyya* is able to explain. *Athar* is critical in showing the centrality of the sovereign/subject (*sultan/ra'iyya*) and in disclosing the latter's role in Ibn Khaldun's theorization of the *adab* circle.

Athar (here, "ancient monuments") does not occupy a central position in Ibn Khaldun's *Muqaddima*. Ancient monuments are described in passing as the *athar* (traces) of *al-'umran*.²⁴ This statement is presented as an intervention decrying fantastical beliefs in ancient lore and the mystification of ancient civilizations: Ibn Khaldun faults people for attributing the wonder of ancient monuments to magical abilities and supernatural qualities rather than to the magnificence of the civilization (*al-'umran*) of their founding dynasties.²⁵ Consequently, in experiencing an *athar*, one should relate all its perceivable aspects to the *'umran* of its builders. Ibn Khaldun argues that the failure to *see* the laws of *'umran* in perceiving *athar* is due to the fact that these laws have not been elucidated by anyone before him. Furthermore, the weakness that he sees in the then-contemporary *'umran* in comparison to the *athar* of older civilizations occluded the relationship between *'umran* and *athar*, forcing an appeal to the magical.²⁶ This proposed mode of encounter is one we have already seen in our canon, except that its scope is now expanded beyond ancient monuments to include all the other things that emanate from *'umran*. This expansion was not suddenly born in the nineteenth century, but has a longer history in the *khitat* topographic genre—especially in the momentous work of Taqi al-Din al-Maqrizi (d. 1442), who met Ibn Khaldun in Cairo and studied with him.

There is another more general sense in which *athar* is used, and it subsumes *athar* as "ancient monuments." Numerous passages in Ibn Khaldun's *Muqaddima* feature a variation on this phrase: "Its trace was effaced"; the words for "trace" include both *athar* and *rasm*; and "erasure" is expressed as *mahw* (erasing), *ta'attul* (stopping/seizing/halting/suspending), and *ikhtifa'* (disappearance).²⁷ He uses these phrases not only to discuss the disappearance of architectural objects but also—and more often—to point to a large variety of phenomena that grow out of *'umran*, including particular modes of ruling with the specific political positions and institutions, as well as to crafts, trades, and industries associated with the prosperity of the civilization. This broad, and diverse, use of these phrases reflects Ibn Khaldun's grappling with "ruination" as the very rhythm of history, one that is tightly entwined with the way in which the circle of eight words articulates how power reproduces and expands itself by dispersing its sites.

To explain these connections, let's revisit the first quote, where Ibn Khaldun defines *'umran* via human nature, and that Mubarak also uses to highlight sociality as the very definition of humanness. Ibn Khaldun explains the origins of sociality in much the same way as Mubarak: the oscillation of human nature between the need for sociality and intra-aggression that perpetually risks the actualization of a cohesive society spawns a need for a sovereign. To this overall explanation, Ibn Khaldun adds details that are glossed over in Mubarak's discourse—though, as we will see shortly, they are confronted narratologically. For Ibn Khaldun, the sovereign enforces his will over other persons and, in so doing, subjects them to his will, which is, at its core, an unjust act. However, it is also at the heart of the possibility of justice, since it is necessary to curb intra-aggression and enable the formation of sociality, which is inevitable for survival. That said, no one can extend their rule over others without appeal to group solidarity or kinship. This is because the sovereign, as a person or personalizable entity, is ultimately quite weak in comparison to what he needs to achieve. Consequently, while the sovereign is the originator of the political power necessary for drawing sociality out of its potentiality into actuality, he is also ultimately an emblem of the strength of his group-kin.[28] His task is to transfer this union of blood into political power and, in the process, becomes the originator of political power as the enframing— and therefore actualization—of sociality. In so doing, however, he also begins the process of fragmenting the union of blood transformed into political power that underpins his power. At this very moment of formation, the process of disintegration is set into motion, for it is one and the same as the process of transforming kinship into political power. The circle of eight words is crucial for understanding this rhythm of forming as undoing.

The sovereign, according to Ibn Khaldun, is actually weak when we think of him as a person. His strength lies in the way his presence becomes an emblem of the strength of his group, and his role is to transfer the blood union into political power and actualize society (matter) by enframing it (giving it form).[29] This framing, however, is not merely constituted out of announcing the presence of the sovereign; it also requires the delineation of sites of power necessary for the optimal functioning of society. These sites or locations of power are where Ibn Khaldun uses the term *khitat*, referring to them as *al-khitat al-sultaniyya*: they are official positions of power that emanate out of the emergence of the sovereign, and I believe that they name the specific ways, and sites, key to transforming 'asabiyya into political power.³⁰ Ibn Khaldun names four general (from his perspective, perhaps universal?) tasks that could be further subdivided, depending on the particular dynasty. These tasks tally perfectly with the necessities the circle-of-eight-words names. Without going into the minutiae of the debates and just focusing on their general arc, we can say that the presence of the sovereign sets off a process of disintegrating group solidarity by divesting the power condensed in him—which is an intersection of the quelling of intra-aggression in the sociality and the active force of his group—into particular locations. The more prosperous the civilization, the more intricate these sites of power (*khitat sultaniyya*) become, and, as a result, the closer we are to a complete disintegration of the union of blood that had founded the sovereign as originator and emblem. The duration through which his emblematic presence could last depends on a number of factors that lie beyond our interests here.³¹

Previous scholarship has often suggested that Ibn Khaldun's idea of group solidarity (*'asabiyya*) played an important role in Tahtawi's coinage of "love for the *patrie*" or patriotism (*hubb al-watan*). This is in part justified by the heavy deployment of Ibn Khaldun as well as by the use, and abuse, of the image of the nation as a family, shrouding the former in a pseudokinship. Consequently, the love of the *patrie* is perhaps an expanded form of Ibn Khaldun's group solidarity whereby the bond extends from within the dynasty to encompass the entirety of the sociality. In the process, we also move from direct kinship to its semblance—a move that is already implied in Ibn Khaldun when he refers to dynasties that don't rely on kinship, like the Mamluks, and in a more diluted way in other dynasties that rely heavily on military slavery.³² Nonetheless, such an expansion is not possible without gravely eroding the naturalness of the ground through which society is split between sovereign/subject. 'Asabiyya offers a natural explanation: the *sultan* is an emblem of his group's solidarity and of the natural tendency of people to overpower each other. Consequently, the *sultan* is an emblem of that process, a token of injustice as the condition of possibility of justice. However, once we remove natural group solidarity, what then grounds the divide between sovereign and subjects that Ibn Khaldun has tried to demystify? Once 'asabiyya is "expanded," it actually loses its ability to offer a "natural" explanation—and perhaps legitimation—of the division of society into ruler and ruled. Our canon is born in the throes of this problem, and it is complicated by the realization that there are multiple competing possibilities for the division of society. Consequently, one needs to "judge" the best mode of organizing society. In the following section, I show two key attempts at grappling with the ruler/ruled relationship. Once again, these are the series of debates that I call "the rise of the collective"; the reason for naming them in this way will become apparent with our first example, where we return to Paris with Tahtawi.

The Rise of the Collective

We have already encountered Tahtawi in chapters 1 and 2, where he connected *khayal* and theater to history. In the same text, his travel narrative, he documents the events of the July Revolution of 1830, since he was in Paris at the time. He outlines the competing groups, offering a sense of their vision of political rule. We may already begin to point out that while human nature oscillates between sociality and antisocial aggression, the ensuing form of ruling is not given; on the contrary, there are different options. These are habitually glossed by the other texts of our canon, and the implications of the existence of different historically actualized modes of ruling cannot be overstated. His explanation of the "Republican" stance (he renders them as *al-hurriyyin*: the upholders of freedom/liberty) is worth particular attention. He notes their dedication to the rule of the "subjects" (*al-ra'iyya*). In Tahtawi's rendering, it peculiarly sounds like the rule of the ruled—a point that he is acutely aware of, since he proceeds to address it using precisely the terms ruler (*hakim*)/ruled (*mahkum*). He asserts that, since one cannot be both ruler and ruled at the same time, the principles of the Republicans (*al-hurriyyin*) necessitate electing representatives.[33] In this brief passage, Tahtawi grapples with the tensions arising from the possibility for the "subjects" (as the object of a ruling power) to also assume the position of the subject of a ruling power. Consequently, the subjects' position as the object of a ruling power is no longer as conceptually stable (clearly this relationship was never absolutely socially or politically stable) as it might have appeared to be, in part because there are different forms of dividing the relationship between ruler/ruled—or, perhaps more profoundly, because there is the possibility for self-rule, to occupy the position of subject and object simultaneously and to be both the source and object of power. This conceptual problem is what I refer to as "the rise of the collective," wherein the position of the subjects as the object of power is destabilized and therefore up for debate, but it is also a conceptual problem that emerges against the backdrop of the possibility—and, for many, the "threat"—presented by the rise in social and political movements aiming at instituting collective self-rule. Tahtawi already tells us that instituting this contradiction requires some form of political representation (*tawkil*) to function. Muwaylihi's critique of *takhyil hukm al-malik*, discussed in chapter 1, is born out of wrestling with what it might mean for subjects to be viewed as the collective. The terms of representation are reversed in Muwaylihi's case, however, since it is the king, and not the collective, who needs to be represented in the president. Thus, we come back to *khayal*, seeing now that the possibility of the rise of the collective is the core problem to which making history visible (the literary optic) is offered as a solution—an issue that I take up in more detail in the second half of this chapter and in the chapter that follows.

Having explored various vignettes of Cairo, the Pasha and 'Isa Ibn Hisham decide to go to Paris to better understand the history of the present. There, they befriend a French wise man, or philosopher, and the Pasha explicitly asks him to expound upon the roots of French "civilization"/polis (*madaniyya*), with particular attention to the king (*al-malik*). The Philosopher's response that the king has no name (*ism*) or body (*jism*) takes the characters on an exploration of the mode of rule in France that starts with the president (*al-ra'is*) at the top and ends with elections among the inhabitants (*al-ahali*), from which the power of ruling both begins and ends.[34] This diffusion of sovereignty aims at realizing freedom and equality and is in fact not idiosyncratic to France, as the Pasha's reactions in these episodes may have us believe. Early on in *hadith*, the Pasha quarrels with a cabbie named Mursi who tells the Pasha that they are now living in the age of freedom (*zaman al-hurriyya*). In fact, the Pasha's violent brush with modern institutions of administering justice (institutions of the law) reveals the new form of power that begets this age of freedom and equality. The juxtaposition between the Pasha as the embodiment of old forms of power that were just that—"embodied"—and newer ones in which ruling is not condensed into a name and a body is key in every vignette.

A quick survey of the definitions of some of these institutions as they are offered by the text will help us to see this point more clearly. In the altercation between the Pasha and the cabbie, the latter calls to the police after the Pasha physically assaults him. Confused as to who this "police" might be, the Pasha asks Ibn Hisham if he is some kind of saint (*wali*) that people call on in times of distress. Since the term *wali* could also mean something like "lord" or "overlord" (it was the title of the Ottoman ruler of a province *vali*), Ibn Hisham responds in the affirmative: "This police is the caretaker (*wali al-amr*), and the ruling power resides in him (*ihtallat fih al-quwa al-hakima*)."[35] The Pasha cannot quite follow this definition, and, so to simplify the matter, Ibn Hisham tells him that this is what he knew during his era as *al-qawwas*. This translation results in absolute chaos, for the Pasha assumes that the police will follow his orders, and it takes the entire journey of the book for him to fully internalize the difference between the embodied form of power he took part in and the new system. This incident adds another layer to the reason why Ibn Hisham couldn't just tell the Pasha the history of the present, but had to make it visible for him: language itself was reformulated in this process, so key words no longer meant the same thing as they used to mean. This provides us with a good analogy for what the arguments of *Literary Optics* show on the level of conceptual language and how we need to reperceive it in order to historicize this canon beyond the idea that it combines the old with the new.

Later, when the Pasha's case is referred to the parquet, the same pattern unfolds in trying to define the institution. Ibn Hisham defines it in the following way: "The parquet in this new system is a judicial power (*sulta qada'iyya*) charged with pursuing criminal lawsuits against criminals, they represent society (*bi-l-niyaba 'an al-hay'a al-ijtima'iyya*)."[36] The two characters go into further detail about what "society" denotes, the process by which the representatives are chosen, and the role of educational degrees in the process. These definitions of the "new system" and how it functions are repeated throughout the early episodes of the text before the two main characters turn their attention to entertainments and social institutions, focusing on the society in whose name these institutions rule. At the same time, society is also the product of these institutions. Conceptually, this is the pattern through which the text unfolds, and that the plot enables. Moreover, the preoccupation with the relationship between systems of ruling and society is not unique to *hadith*; we have already seen in chapter 3 that *athar* is a site for judging whether or not the abstract universal principles governing history are applied. We can now think of it not just as a concern with history, but with ruling, and, in particular, with judging the best mode of splitting society into ruler/ruled in a way that ensures its prosperity—as evidenced by the *athar*.

I turn to one last example from Mubarak's *'alam al-din*, with which this section started: to Mubarak's characters in Versailles, where we left them in chapter 3, tiptoeing around a discussion of the French Revolution. I have already pointed to the fact that the events of the revolution are often quickly glossed over and absorbed into dichotomies of light (civility) / darkness (barbarity) in Mubarak's *'alam al-din*. Here, we will look at this process of elision more closely and view how it aims at focalizing the actions of the king while circumventing those of his "subjects." However, this does not indicate disregard for the question of judging the best mode of ruling—read also as the rise of the collective—as much as it demonstrates a particular stance toward it, since it is only against the backdrop of the rise of the collective that it would make sense to aggressively wipe them out of the text. Through this reading, we come to our last clue that Ibn Khaldun is written into the text not as a sign of continuity, or for the purpose of domesticating "imported" ideas, but to forge the language with which to give form to a problem.

In colloquy 89, "Versailles," the characters explore the palace and its attached gardens. Only the first couple of paragraphs are dedicated to a description of the palace interiors and the objects within it. The conversation shifts swiftly to the vicissitudes of time underpinning the rise and fall of the palace that we saw in chapter 3. Upon closer examination, we discover that these formulaic phrases about the passage of time are ultimately concerned with political history and, specifically, with questions of sovereignty.

The conversation centers on explaining the history of the place as a manifestation of sovereign power—in other words, the palace is an *athar* whose rise and fall is dictated by the actions of the king both in relationship to his advisors and in terms of how he organizes his time, dividing it among learning, working, and relaxing. Such a division guarantees that his actions are in line with the necessities of good ruling. Once this is disrupted with the ascension of a new king, the status of the palace starts to dwindle; the king's *adab* and *tarbiya* are necessary for his ability to manage everything that emanates from his power, as encapsulated in the circle of eight words.

> He used to divide up his time, allocating some time for sleep, other for perusing the news regarding his state and his people, and time to be alone and another to socialize with his loved ones. . . . When it was time for him to wake up, his servant would go in, wake him up, then leave, and he would invite the wiseman . . . then, his son succeeded him, but he did not uphold his father's practices pertaining to how he divided his time that we stated earlier. Rather, he spent it all on his pleasures. . . . Many things resulted from this, too numerous for the tongue to utter it all and for the mind to encompass. . . . As a consequence, the French political laws were charted, and Napoleon Bonaparte appeared.[37]

While the text does distantly allude to the fact that this "dwindling," or undoing, of the palace took place at the hand of the rise of the French, their actions are overwritten as "the hand of history" or time, smoothing over the details through which a constitution was written and an entirely "new system"—to use Muwaylihi's expression—was born.

The insistence on overemphasizing the acts of the sovereign and his advisors at the expense of "inhabitants" is striking in Mubarak. But this is no oblivion of the collective—it is rooted in the very realness, and threat, of their presence, which Mubarak chooses to actively obscure at key moments. In this way, the conceptual problem he faces is quite distinct from that of Ibn Khaldun, who seeks to demystify *adab* discourses, revealing the sovereign as an emblem of another power (group solidarity, often based on blood kinship). For Mubarak, however, the rule of the king is peculiarly unanchored—or, if anywhere, then anchored in his *adab* as his ability to organize himself and his time in accordance with abstract universal principles of civilizational progress, with the help of his advisors, those entrusted with educating the king (his *adab* and *tarbiya*). That said, this is not a return to the types of *adab* edification Ibn Khaldun criticizes and transforms, but a reaction to the emergence of the collective on the stage of politics in ways that seem unavoidable. The following section confronts the emergence of the collective from the vantage point of characters. Taken together, this section and the one that follows show how *athar* as history and as a stand-in for social totality are drawn together.

Al-Nas as Hermeneutic

The previous section argued that, while human nature has a long history of being connected with sociality and the division of society between ruler and ruled, the emergence in our canon of competing forms through which society could be divided and of the possibility of self-rule complicates the former connection. Specifically, it becomes possible to conceptually envision society *separate from* its traditional division into ruler/ruled. In other words, one could bring human nature (the oscillation between sociality and antisocial aggression) prior to its political enframing to stand in front of the mind's eye, putting it under an optical device and placing it onstage. This possibility is clearly linked both to the distant past as well as to a gleaming potential in the present. We have already seen how Marrash's "Forest" projects such a nondivided society onto the prehistoric past. In this case, however, the political form of the social would not have been historically actualized, but would rather remain as a potential, due to the constant inner fighting (i.e., the dominance of antisocial aggression). As for the future prospect, it pertains to the possibility of self-rule. For our purposes here, what is of most immediate concern is that a conceptual ground emerges through which the always already social nature of human beings does not lead to a division into a form of power (political form) that is concomitant with it and seemingly innate; instead, a space forms between these steps that necessitates judgment as a means for crossing over this rift. In this case, judgment would lead to a decision on the form of rule (political form) that would be most conducive to society's prosperity, and what needs to be judged is human nature itself. In other words, we need to bring the social, as an expression of human nature, to stand before us so that we may judge the best way for organizing it through a political form. I refer to the emergence of this ground and to the perplexing questions that stem from it as the rise of the collective, a process that at its core is profoundly political, pertaining to a changing horizon of possibilities. Yet we focus here on the way it appears from within the position of the canon of nineteenth-century Arabic literature.

I suggest that this ground, which I have described as the rise of the collective, crystallizes in late nineteenth-century Arabic literature around a single concept: *al-nas*.[38] On the surface, *al-nas* is simple: it is the plural of *al-'insan* (human being). Looking closely, we will find that *al-nas* is more complex, denoting something closer to the collective. Ultimately, *al-nas* is a collective defined by nothing other than its collectivity alone, with no regard to any other aspect, unlike other terms in Arabic that denote groups (and there are many of these). Nonetheless, *al-nas* is quite unlike *khayal* and *athar*, the two other concepts engaged by this book; I do not argue that *al-nas* is an already delineated concept whose hermeneutical provenance—however scattered or complex, as in the cases of *khayal* and *athar*—can therefore be gathered from extant scholarship. Rather, I view *al-nas* itself as a hermeneutic, a problem of rule posed anew in the wake of sweeping sociopolitical and epistemological transformations, that gives rise to this canon's definition of literature and, in the process, enables the retrospective working-out of *al-nas* as a concept *now* rather than in the past. In the process, we also come to see that it has "always" existed, but was not necessarily abstracted—again, the example of Ibn Khaldun in the previous section is a case in point.

Al-nas is an extremely elusive concept. The difficulty in defining it resides paradoxically in its assumed obviousness. It is the plural of *al-insan* (human being), the meaning of which is so conspicuous that it often does not warrant an explanation. When Ibn Manzur (1233-1311) defines *al-insan*, in *lisan al-'arab*—the lexicon that 'Alam al-Din and the Orientalist are editing—he says: "والإنسانُ معروفٌ" ([the meaning of] *al-'insan* is well known).³⁹ By extension, the meaning of *al-nas* is ostensibly equally self-evident. In tracing *al-'insan* to its root, its initial obviousness and that of its plural is obscured. At first, *al-'insan* is presented under the root '-n-s, which indicates the enjoyment of the company of others; this, then, is what it means to be *'insan*. *Al-nas*, by extrapolation, are either a group of those who enjoy the company of others, or the collective formed through the nature of *al-'insan*. In both cases, the central axis for understanding *al-nas* is sociability. The implications of defining *al-'insan* thus surpass the boundaries of lexicography to reach the core of conceptualizing history (as a process and as a field), as well as conceptualizing the social and the political; we briefly explored this point in the previous section through Ibn Khaldun's *Muqaddima* as an example of this link.

To return to Ibn Manzur's entry on '-n-s, he mentions within it that *al-'insan* could additionally be traced to n-s-y. That is to say, it could be linked to "forgetting" rather than to the "enjoyment of company"—*al-'insan* is the one who forgets. The case of Ibn Khaldun, as it relates to Quranic narratives, already suggests that the issue is inextricable from the act of linking *al-'insan* semantically to central conceptual tropes regarding the oscillating nature of *al-'insan*. The attempt to connect *al-'insan* to *'ins* ("human" as an order of being, in contradistinction to *jinn*) supports this inference. In the same entry, the possibility that *al-'insan* is linked to the notion of visibility through *'ins* is also mentioned (*'ins* are those who are visible, whereas *jinn* are the concealed ones). Thus far, *al-'insan* is linked to enjoyment of company, forgetfulness, and visibility. Crucially, all these possibilities are debated in the interpretations of *surat al-nas* in the Quran, particularly in relation to verse 6. The debates on conceptualizing *al-'insan* have a direct bearing on thinking *al-nas*. With each potential root, there is a different interpretation that demonstrates how *al-nas* is derived from *'anas*, *'ins*, and *nasa*. There were also those who argued that while *al-nas* is used as the plural of *al-'insan*, it does not share its root. According to this view, *al-nas* is derived from n-w-s, which is defined as a movement of oscillation. The possibility is mentioned in most major dictionaries, though it is often hastily dismissed.⁴⁰

Al-nas could be traced back to '-n-s (enjoyment of company), I-n-s (visibility), n-s-y (forgetting), and n-w-s (oscillation). The disputes over defining *al-'insan* clearly show that comprehending the stakes in these disagreements requires tuning in to the conceptual realms within which they are thought, and that are shaped by them. In other words, defining *al-nas* is not now, nor has it ever been, an exercise in locating and fixing one root to one word; the heated debates concerning *al-'insan* and *al-nas* already prove the unfeasibility of such an approach. Rather, *al-nas* can be understood when it is recognized as a hidden knowledge-producing category, underpinning thinking the political, the social, the historical, and the literary. The lexicographical disputes are reimmersed in the conceptual deliberations they participate in. The previous section argued that this is one keyway through which to read Ibn Khaldun's intervention. We might already note, however, that all of these possibilities relate *al-nas* to a quality that is deemed to be the core of human nature, and that the latter is linked to sociability either directly or indirectly. *Al-'insan* and *al-nas* could either be derived from the enjoyment of company (i.e., direct sociability), or some other quality related to it, such as visibility, which enables socializing, or forgetting, which is linked to the propensity to forget the importance of the sociality (or the divine), and, finally, to the oscillation itself which expresses the dichotomous nature of humans.

In continuing to show that *al-nas* is best understood as the collective that arises from the act of coming together itself, I will focus on a grammatical point before turning to an example from our canon. Unlike other terms describing groups, *al-nas* does not denote any other qualities of this group; it has no other markers of belonging be it scale (how large or small the group is), identity (i.e., religious, ethnic), createdness (vis-à-vis their creator), or social status (as in '*amma* and *khassa*).[41] Furthermore, adjectives cannot be used to modify it, so we cannot add a national or gendered qualifier to it—but we can add markers of social status and goodness to describe *al-nas* as bad or good. This is not to suggest that some of the terms that denote these other more specific markers cannot be used in the more general sense I am ascribing to *al-nas*; *khalq* and '*ibad allah* are often used in this way in general, and in particular in Muwaylihi's *hadith*. The point is not just about a term used to refer to people in general, but that *al-nas* is a concept that connotes not just a plural but a general collective that does not refer to an original specific quality other than collectivity itself. We can then understand why such a term could be deployed both for those who have such high status we do not even need to specify them because of their renown, as well as for the "riffraff" who do not deserve to be specified.[42] In the canon of nineteenth-century Arabic literature, we will see this possibility play out on axes of general and particular, public and private, and tacit "individuation" against the backdrop of the collective. To anticipate what will emerge in the following paragraph, *al-nas*, unlike other images or visual objects made visible via *khayal* is not an ontologically groundless image that is epistemologically necessary. Rather, *al-nas is the ground* of both politics and literature, and yet it can only be perceived via *khayal*. This is the heart of the change we see in this canon, which will return us at the end of this chapter to Ibn 'Arabi's crossings *within khayal*, encountered in chapter 1.

Our final example takes us back to Muwaylihi's iconic introduction to his published book (1907) where he tells his readers that, in preparing this book edition, he aims at "explicating the ethical dispositions and states, describing what people (*al-nas*) are like in terms of the vices that should be avoided, and the virtues that should be upheld."[43] The ascription of a pedagogic objective to literature is common to texts from this period. Both in our canon and beyond it, authors claim that their texts offer an instruction in virtues and vices that propels people to act in accordance with virtues. We can link this to the project of making visible that is not concerned with a passive visualization, but it is—as we have seen in chapter 1—connected to affective and active dimensions that drive people to act in accordance with what is made visible to them. We have now come to recognize the latter as both history and the collective, or history as the visible anonym for the invisible collective. As a result, the pedagogic function of these texts plays out on an axis of general and particular and public and private. In other words, the edificatory function of these texts cannot be adequately understood as a replay of eulogy (*madih*) and lampoon (*hija'*); the virtues and vices are extracted from their embodied examples drawn out of particular historically existing persons—and they do not refer to just abstract valorized ideals. Consequently, they tempt readers to think that these embodied examples of virtues and vices refer to specific people. Let's turn to the discussion of newspapers in *hadith* comparing it to an editorial by Muwaylihi in his "Lantern of the East": the editorial holds several clues for understanding this interplay, which will be crucial for grappling with characters as the collective. His intervention will reintroduce *waqa'i'* (historical events), with which we started our exploration of history in chapter 1.

In introducing the Pasha to modern-day newspapers (*al-jara'id*), Ibn Hisham says that these papers gather and recount public reports (*akhbar*) and reported narratives (*riwayat*) so that *al-nas* may become aware of the states of *al-nas*. He then adds that they (newspapers) are an *athar* of Western civilization originally intended to spread the praise of virtues and the censure of vices—claiming this pedagogic agenda was then common to literature, theater, and newspapers. Furthermore, papers are entrusted with letting the community (*'umma*) know about the acts of the government that represents it.[44] This is hardly an isolated reference to the connection between *al-nas*, the government, and institutions that are meant to connect *al-nas* with themselves as well as with their representatives. To anticipate the arguments of the following section, we can highlight the need for *al-nas* to know *al-nas* as a critical key to understanding how characters function in these texts, highlighting that this knowledge is historical in the way we have been explaining thus far: it connects particular events or instantiations with abstract principles. This is explained at length in one of his editorials and is equally palpable throughout the practice of the newspaper.

In the 150th edition of the journal, and in celebration of its third anniversary, Muwaylihi dedicates the editorial to outlining its pillars, or what he terms "the practices of the paper" (*sunnat al-jarida*).[45] The editorial offers a succinct articulation of the journal's overarching aims and of the sources for its articles. The central aim is to benefit people through moral lessons.[46] This is a generic enough goal, also shared by theater and schools, as modern institutions embroiled in the process of rethinking *adab*. The moral lesson is to be ascertained via "the criticism of deeds through exhibiting what we see and witness from the happenings pertaining to individuals (*waqa'i' al-ashkhas*)." This is rooted in the efficacy of particularity: he assumes that the publication of a particular incident pertaining to a particular person enables inspiring change in people more efficiently. This stance is in complete opposition to Ibn Sina, who views panegyric poetry's particularization of its addressee as problematic.[47] Needless to say, Muwaylihi's attitude resulted in numerous personal feuds and serious libels. Yet it tallies perfectly with Mubarak's argument on the efficacy of history; it is precisely the theater-*khayal* ability to stage virtues through particular histories of individuals that render *khayal* an apt training for the senses. Put more simply, the shift to characters, to virtues and vices, is not a shift outside history, but to it.[48] The texts need to exhibit particularized historical examples of *al-nas* in a way that brings the latter out of its invisibility. As such, the negotiations of characters are not simply between abstract and example, but transpire within a world where these examples are culled from "real life"; the examples are *waqa'i'*. What occurs on the level of characters is comparable to what we have been discussing with regard to history as the connection between specific instantiations and the abstract universal principles. Yet there is one crucial difference to notice: the collective is not invisible because it is an abstract principle—rather, its invisibility is owed to a different reason, and, as such, its relationship to the instantiations is slightly different to the connection between events and laws in history.

Throughout, Muwaylihi's *hadith* often refers to the connection between *naf'* (benefit, or good) and *al-nas*. The connection also recurs in other sites in our canon and period.[49] One crucial example is Ibn Hisham's criticism of the behavior of a couple of characters running for parliamentary elections: "People are distracted with each other, away from each other. Those who work for the benefit of people have lessened."[50]

This is the core problem of this new period: each institution depends on *al-nas* working for *al-nas*, and yet at every tangent this possibility is undercut, as each person seems to work for their own interest.[51] We see this from the very first episode where the policeman is too busy forcefully collecting fruits from vendors to care about the altercation between the Pasha and the cabbie, and we see it in every other episode afterwards. Slowly the Pasha discovers that the chaos of this new period of time does not rest in its disembodiment of power, but in the way in which its basic new principle of *al-nas* working for *al-nas* in a disembodied way is thwarted off.

The above problem seems to introduce another problem to the rise of the collective. We are no longer merely discussing how to judge human nature to discern the best way to rule, but we are also discussing the inability of members of the social collective to recognize their own embeddedness in a totality which results in their tendency toward "selfish" actions. This complete disregard for the broader social totality results in the failure of their own selfish acts, since their success hinges on others, depending on a position that exceeds their own. There are two distinct acts of judgement in relation to the social totality. The first wishes to make them visible in order to adjudicate how to organize rule. The second wishes to make them visible to guide the action of seemingly monadic persons in accordance with the good of the social collective. While these are two conceptually discrete kinds of judgements, they are narratologically inseparable in our texts because the collective cannot be made visible (made to stand in front of the mind's eye, placed under an optic device, and put on stage) *except* through curating its fragmented instantiations in what have been described in this book so far as making history visible. Nonetheless, *al-nas* is neither an empirical object—either in the text or outside it—nor a principle (law of civilizational progress) abstracted from all the fragmented events, it is both the originator and result of learning how to see the fragmented events. This distinction is crucial as we turn to characters, tuning to the negotiation between general and particular, public and private, and inside and outside the text.

In the first chapter of this book, we saw the way in which Shidyaq tied utterance to meaning via a *khayal* image. The latter is the trace of prior sensory experience whose "image" can be brought to stand in front of the mind's eye. No such image could be found of the collective as the social totality; one can call forth the image of persons, groups, crowds, but not of the collective as a totality—in this sense, it cannot be an object of empiricism. This applies to whether we wish to bring forth this totality prior to its division, which is a conceptual potential rather than a historical actuality, or whether we call it in its current political form—once again the problem here is not one of the collective being abstract but rests on it being a totality whose sensory embodiments are necessarily partial. Either way, one does not have a direct experience, which is defined here as a direct empirical experience, of the collective totality, but merely of certain groups from it. Consequently, and to use Shidyaq's line of argument, when one says the collective (*al-nas*), these are mere sounds that quickly dissipate because they do not call forth an image formed through prior sensory experience. But what if we could do that precisely through the magic of (poetic) discourse—what Shidyaq referred to as *sihr al-kalam*? I argue that this is exactly what our texts aim to do. The association between the collective (*al-nas*) and the image ("conceptual content" and also visualization as containing within it an affective and active dimension) of the collective as the totality of the sociality is achieved in our texts through their episodic structure, which makes history visible. It also requires that the boundary between the texts and their world be blurred so that the way the texts' structure the world could be extended outside it. This allows the collective to be made visible not just as a fantastical textual phenomenon, but as something out there in the world however immune to direct sensory experience it may be—hence the importance of *waqa'i'*.

The next section explores how characters blur the boundaries of the texts in order to take the final step in making the collective visible. It also shows why the two distinct kinds of conceptual judgement (the best mode of ruling, the best way of acting) are narratologically inseparable. I pursue the latter point in more detail in the next chapter as the "origins" of the canon of nineteenth-century Arabic literature. Yet, it might already be suggested that, since making the collective visible starts from the specific historical examples toward projecting the historically existing collective, literature cannot extract either of the two processes— judging a "general," nonspecific collective or preparticular collective (the concept) versus judging the particular collective (action).[52]

Below I analyze two broad typologies of characterization. These do not exist in absolute form in our texts, but coexist within them. Nonetheless, it is heuristically useful to separate them out. The first rests on periphrasis and metonymy (*kinaya*) and is closely aligned with the realist or hyperrealist approach explored in chapter 2. The second pivots on the personalization of abstract virtues and is heavily mobilized in the texts described in chapter 2 as allegorical. We will turn to Muwaylihi's *hadith* as an example of the first type, and to Marrash's "Forest" as an example of the second.

The Anonymized Particular as Social Type

In the early episodes of Muwaylihi's *hadith*, the Pasha spends his first night back to life in prison. Torn by guilt, 'Isa Ibn Hisham vows not to leave the Pasha's side until he has shown him the "history of the present." Ibn Hisham meets the Pasha at the police station and later follows him to the parquet. They wait a long time for the Pasha to be admitted to the public attorney's office for interrogation. With no end in sight to their waiting, 'Isa (much like Marrash's narrator-character) takes shelter in a hidden corner, peeping and eavesdropping on the public attorney, whom we discover is converzing with two visitors on matters that are completely unrelated to work:

> SECOND VISITOR: Have you heard that X has married his girlfriend?
> FIRST VISITOR: Have you ridden in Y's car?
> ATTORNEY: Have you heard why the son of B, the financier, committed suicide?
> FIRST VISITOR: I've found out why Z quit his job.⁵³

Two details are particularly noteworthy. First, the exchange between the characters is narrated through direct discourse—we "hear" them speak to each other with no intervention on the part of the narrator or the main character. Neither the narrator nor 'Isa recount to us what had transpired; we hear it just like 'Isa did, momentarily occupying his position in the text—the readers and 'Isa occupy the position of the audience. The characters appear as if they are speaking on a stage, which is in line with our analysis of narrative structure in chapter 2.

The second point is that the characters are nameless. One character is identified by his vocation: the Public Attorney (*al-na'ib*). His interlocutors are distinguished by their relationship to him as his visitors (First Visitor, and Second Visitor, respectively). While it is tempting to postulate that the characters are unnamed because 'Isa does not know them, and the readers are made to stand in his position, this hypothesis is belied by the ubiquity of this practice in the text. Characters are often identified by their vocation, social position, relationship to other characters, or a particular quality— for example, the Merchant (*al-tajir*), the Dancer (*al-raqisa*), the Lawyer with whom they have direct dealings (*al-muhami*), the Physician (*al tabib*), and the Playboy (*al-khali'*). Even the Pasha's grandson's name remains a mystery, despite his intimate filial connection with the Pasha. This applies to the two main characters as well: while we know their names, 'Isa Ibn Hisham is presented as *al-Katib* (the Writer) while Ahmed el-Manikli is simply referred to as the Pasha.[54]

While al-Makari's (the cabbie) name, Mursi, is also slipped in once in the text, he is otherwise referred to simply by his vocation. Looking beyond our select canon, we can find more examples in the early scholarly studies of this literature that noted the ubiquity of this pattern. The references in early literary histories suggest that most of the period's texts relied upon social types, stock characters, and personification in their portrayal of characters, such as Hafiz Ibrahim's *layali sitih* (1906), Nadim's plays and short dialogues, the plays and dialogues of Ya'qub Sannu' (1839–1912) and Marun al-Naqqash's (1817–1855), and 'Uthman Jalal's translated plays (d. 1889).

The most playful exploration, if not exploitation, of these techniques of characterization is found in Shidyaq's *Leg over Leg* (*al-saq 'ala al-saq*). The Fariyaq, much like 'Isa Ibn Hisham, is a personification and characterization of the voice of the author. In Shidyaq's text, this voice is splintered into multiple other iterations; the *Fariyaqiyya*, Harith Ibn Hisam (almost the name of the narrator of Harriri's *maqama*, but with a lisp). As in Muwaylihi, the other characters are stock characters or types (e.g., the Clergyman, and the Orientalist); this is blatantly obvious in the short *maqamas* in the text itself, where these types are brought together to converse and debate. I describe Shidyaq's use of this mode of characterization as the most playful because it shows these multiplying potential positions of authorial voice only to destabilize them as impossible positions of authority and authorship. This impossibility manifests in the way language splits between utterance and meaning, and there is no position from where utterance and meaning could be brought back together. For now, what matters is that we can see the use of these types everywhere in these texts. Here, much like in earlier chapters, we can see both diversity and different articulations that rely upon similar narratological techniques.

This anticipates our turn toward the end of this chapter, and then again in the next, to how *al-nas* comes to shape authorial voice as a position within the text as well as a position vis-à-vis what lies outside it.

To go back to our characters, there is yet another dimension to this pervasive namelessness. When conversing characters mention others they know, they do not specify their names. Rather, they elide them, replacing them with *fulan* "so-and-so." The use of *fulan* contributes a crucial clue for understanding the approach to characters in Muwaylihi's *hadith*, helping us interpret the elision of names as well as the carving out and mobilization of social types. In other words, these social types are not just general; they continue to suggest the possibility that they have a particular referent whose name was merely anonymized, replaced with the profession or with *fulan*. The point is key to blurring the boundary between the text and the world it writes, which is also the one where it is read.[55] This is further supported by the fact that Muwaylihi will progressively edit out names, as the text moves from the journal to book form, and then between the different editions of the book.

In the above excerpt, the last *fulan* is a *kinaya* of 'Uthman bey Raghib, who was explicitly named in the journalistic editions before the name was elided in the book version. In another significant example, the name of the controversial statesman Nubar Pasha (1825–1899) was removed. In edition 44 of the paper, he was cited as an example of the emirs and ministers (*al-umara' wa al-wuzara'*) who ruled Egyptians but did not know their language.[56] In the book form, the name is dropped, but the social positions are maintained. The increasing disappearance of proper names of historical figures can be explained in various ways, all pointing to a complex process of negotiation underpinning the question of characterization as a concern for blurring the limits between the text and what lies beyond it.

The first possibility is censorship. The text allegedly underwent a softening of its criticism of rulers—this includes both Muhammad 'Ali's dynasty and the British occupation. The gradual process is claimed to have reached its climax in the 1927 (fourth) edition, prepared specifically for schools.[57] The second pertains to the discrepancy between a journal and a book, as they relate to time. This is a central point for al-Muwaylihi's editing of the narrative. As he explains in his own introduction, what is crucial for a paper that deals with the immediate might be irrelevant for a book that is intended to stand through time, or, in the language of *Literary Optics*, become an *athar*.[58] The third issue pertains to legal concerns or libel. Al-Muwaylihi got himself, and his paper, in a lot of trouble by insisting on mentioning the names of distinguished figures.[59] He asserted in his numerous editorials that he never intended the naming of actual contemporaries as a personal attack; it was a necessary part of both his literary and journalistic practice. What people think of as a breach of their privacy is for him public news, whose publication is important for the ways in which *al-nas* can come to know the states of *al-nas*. We have already mentioned this regarding his editorials in the preceding section; for now, we turn to the connection between these three possibilities and *kinaya*.

Like many other concepts describing rhetorical tropes, *kinaya* has a long history, and its meaning has experienced shifts that justify its translation as both "metonymy" and "periphrases." To give a large brushstroke sense of it: *kinaya* came to be understood through its ability to twine both the veridical (*haqiqa*) and nonveridical (*majaz*) sense of an expression. This ability to combine, via oscillation, what are otherwise opposing positions is a logical feat accrued through a long history of debating a cluster of crucial verses in the Quran—and, therefore, much like my discussion of *khayal* and *majaz* in chapter 1, is embroiled in protracted epistemological and political debates. What matters for the purposes of our discussion here is how *kinaya* and *fulan* came to be entwined when the former's typical definition does not explicitly focus on the elision of names, though they do deal with implicit intimation. It appears, however, that it is in conjunction with one specific verse of the Quran: verse 28 of *surat al-furqan* (The Differentiator), where *fulan* is used to refer to a person anonymously. In the process *kinaya* becomes woven with characterization via fulan, and in so doing the use of *fulan* is understood either along the axis of implicit/explicit, or, as the understanding of *kinaya* itself comes to be reshaped, as an expression that can be equally grasped in its veridical and nonveridical sense. This suspension and conjunction between the two will prove key to the analysis of characterization in nineteenth-century texts, and the way it results in blurring the boundaries of the text.

Muhammad al-Tahir ibn 'Ashur's (1879–1973) work on this verse is particularly thought provoking. Ibn 'Ashur was no stranger to the world of late nineteenth-century debates on poetic language. In fact, as a young scholar in the college mosque of Zaytuna, he wrote a letter to participate in a long debate on poetry in Muwaylihi's newspaper.[60] The debate was spurred by a discussion of Hafiz Ibrahim's poetry, and Ibn 'Ashur's contribution focused on the difference between the language of poetry and of the Quran. To return to Ibn 'Ashur's insights on *kinaya*: in verse 28 of *surat al-furqan*, fulan is used as a *kinaya*, and it is widely believed that it refers to Umayya ibn Khalaf in particular.[61] Ibn 'Ashur expands in his analysis on what is already mentioned in other major works of Quranic exegesis (*tafsir*), contributing a pithy rhetorical exploration of *fulan*. He delineates four possible reasons for the use of *kinaya* through *fulan*: 1) fear-induced withholding of identity; 2) unawareness of the name; 3) the inconsequentiality of its specification; and 4) the fact that the concern does not lie with the specific individual, but the type they represent. Most interpretations locate the significance of using *fulan*, in the verse, in a combination of the last two reasons. As such, *fulan* does not just achieve anonymity, but a generalizablity—through anonymization—while continuously pointing to the particular.[62] In other words, kinaya's suspension between the veridical and nonveridical is recast, from the perspective of characterization via fulan, as a suspension between the particular and the general. *Fulan* is suspended between an anonymous particular and the general created through its extraction or abstraction from a specific particular reference that has supposedly been anonymized—I say "supposedly" because the technique can be used to suggest the existence of a specific character regardless of whether or not it is true.[63] In other words, the creation of the general social type through its supposed extraction or abstraction from an actually existing particular referent also operates in the opposite direction, whereby the general social type creates an experience of extratextual referentiality; the point is key for pedagogic designs for social reform typical of this literary canon and of this period more broadly. This is what I suggest happens in characterization, and it is one central way in which the impossibility of making the collective visible is mitigated.

There are discernible echoes between these three possibilities for why Muwaylihi increasingly wiped out the names of specific persons and the general reasons for using *kinaya* cited by Ibn 'Ashur. Nonetheless, they are not mere reproductions of each other. The three possible explanations for using *fulan* in Muwaylihi's *hadith* point toward additional discourses to the lexicographical and Quranic mentioned earlier, and they push the analysis into diverging directions. The first is political in the immediate sense of political context; the second is literary; the third is juridical—or at the intersection of the juridical and the literary.[64] Yet they incessantly signal a core underlying issue, which expands *fulan* into a mode of characterization. The various potential causes can be read as different articulations, from within diverging discourses, of a core undergirding matter; in order to make the collective visible one has to start from the already existing particular fragments. However, the latter fragments are split between a public and private whose boundaries are always contested, whereas *al-nas* needs to precede, and therefore subsume, these divisions.

The three potential justifications exhibit difficult negotiation processes, in different "fields," that all converge within literary texts, between what is deemed personal, private, or particular and between what is read as collective, public, or general. Depending on the field from which the question is posed, the terms change. At one tangent, legal rights might be brought to the fore as the rubric through which to read and configure the terms and their relationship; at others, it might be the social, the institutional, or the economic. The modality of reading the negotiation processes might itself vary between a political, a social, a historical, or a literary one. It could also be a combination of these categories, as is often the case.[65] The terms are defined in the process of negotiation, which is equally the process of their differentiation. In other words, they are not already separate and discrete categories that are drawn together; rather, the negotiation is likewise their process of historical and conceptual separation. The difficulty of capturing the negotiation process, and the terms with which to read it, stems from the fluidity of the process and its terms. As a result, the core concern can be framed differently from within each possibility, coalescing around the question of characterization as a multi-layered process of negotiation.

Let's look at this process from different vantage points before connecting it once again to the rise of the collective. For censorship, the point is when the portrayal of a character—be it Muhammad 'Ali, a merchant, a sheikh, or a dancer—becomes "political." This cannot be thought away from asking what the political means in this context. More accurately, what does the mode of a character's portrayal reveal about how the political is conceptualized? As emphasized earlier, the definition of the terms lies within the contours of the process of negotiation. The different texts in our canon share this negotiation between the public and the private.

There is a parallel interaction in the case of libel. What is the boundary between the personal and the private on the one hand, and the collective and the public on the other? This is the core disagreement between al-Muwaylihi and his opponents. What they perceive as their own "personal" affairs is for him a way for the collective to get to know its truth—through particularized examples, since there is no other way; the collective can only be made visible through its particularized examples.

In pulling in the character of 'Uthman bey Raghib mentioned above, is it a personal, private matter that is being woven into the text, or a collective social one? The issue is part of a larger trend in Muwaylihi (both in his literary text and in his journalism). In a remarkable example, the journal launches a scathing attack on a certain Ahmad Sayf al-Din, who was one of the grandsons of Muhammad 'Ali. His name is the title of a short entry in the section devoted to local affairs, *al-hawadith al-dakhiliyya* (Internal Affairs). The character is criticized for being a "miser" and compared to the incidents mentioned by Abu 'Uthman al-Jahiz (776–868/869) in *kitab al-bukhala'* (*The Book of Misers*). The contrast resonates with a later incident whose *anonymous* protagonist (*la nusammih*) is compared with the misers of both al-Jahiz and Molière (1622-1673); it additionally ties with the criticisms of the Pasha's class, analyzed in chapter 3. The story of Ahmad Sayf al-Din continues in fragments in later editions, where one discovers that he is imprisoned, as the details of his trial are published.[66] Here again the definition of the personal and the private on the one hand, and the collective and the public on the other, occurs through the contested continuous drawing of the boundary between them. The debate is not exclusive to Muwaylihi's journal, and there was a growing interest in the publication of court cases, which was couched in concerns with the social and collective through the publication of the particular.[67]

For example, al-Tabib (the Physician) in Muwaylihi's *hadith* is supposed to be a general portrayal of a doctor. Nonetheless, the generality points to a particular society at a specific *fatra min al-zaman* (a period of time). In other words, it is a socially specific generality, not solely a vocational one. Consequently, al-Tabib embodies a potential particular referentiality whose actualization forces the text to gesture beyond itself, and, as such, to its own boundaries. This effect is often what early scholarship has referred to as a lack in the text's literariness, but it is perhaps best understood as a literary effect that deceptively makes the text appear as a direct experience of its society. The Physician is a *fulan*. He is suspended between an anonymized particularity, whose supposed specific reference is always hidden (therefore my insistence on understanding *kinaya* as both periphrasis and metonymy) and a generality, which is based in the peculiar mode of anonymized particularity. What occurs with the doctor recurs with almost every character (social type). The collective is produced through the crossing between the anonymized particular as social type and the potential of actualizing its referent "outside" the text, thus blurring the boundaries between what lies within and without the text.

Consequently, characterization through anonymous reference encompasses character *in* the text, and the text's positionality *in* and *from* the "world" lying "outside" it with the readers, since the latter have to actualize this anonymized particular, placing them into their world. Consequently, *al-nas* is neither an object of visibility lying strictly within the text nor outside it, but at their confluence; thus, ultimately, *al-nas* is a mode of seeing, or a hermeneutic for reading the social activated both within and without the text through their encounter.

Personifying the Abstract

At the other extreme from this overemphasis on the particularized lies the insistence on personifying abstract principles and nonmaterial virtues. Marrash's "Forest" invests heavily in this approach. For example, the Philosopher (*al-Faylasuf*) characterizes philosophic thought, illustrating how philosophy (*al-falsafa*) perceives the abstract principles underlying civilizational progress. The character embodies the vision of *al-falsafa* in the voice of a character. The same dynamic can be seen with other characters such as the King of Freedom/Liberty (*al-Hurriyya*) and his wife, the Queen of Wisdom (*al-Hikma*). Each character embodies an abstract quality of "civilization" (*al-tamaddun*), making it visible and unearthing the principles underlying the performance of history.[68] This is complemented by the translatability between civilizations, whereby we begin with a parade of "great" civilizations before the character-narrator turns his attention to the ongoing war against slavery in America and finally wakes up by envisioning the rise of Greater Syria. I have already referred in chapter 2 to the way in which the text could be read as an allegory of Egypt, Syria, America, or basically any other civilization. This is a dramatically different play between the general and the particular, but one that is actually closely related to what we saw with *kinaya*.

Since one cannot make the social totality visible, one can instead make the general principles driving history visible as a stand-in for the collective. In other words, if history is the visible anonym for the invisible collective, *al-nas* can be characterized either through its instantiation via particular examples that should cumulatively show the whole, in an analogy to the relationship between event and principle in history. Alternatively, one could allegorize through personification historical principles that should in turn reveal the collective, since these principles are articulations of the action of the collective on time. In this way, the allegory inside the text is actually a reading of the world outside the text, specifically a reading that seeks to reveal the invisible collective shaping that world. The success of allegory as a reading hinges on its applicability to different particular cases standing outside the text. The picture here seems rather flipped, in comparison to what we saw with *kinaya*, but perhaps not really, for, as we saw earlier, the Physician is actually a generality that appears particular enough but gives rise to a broader generality (the entire collective) beyond it. Similarly, the personification of these virtues enables each reader to read the totality of the sociality they inhabit, which may have otherwise continued to elude them, as they could not cross from the fragmented incidents to what binds them. The text gives the reader the optic: the glasses the character-narrator wears over and over to see the totality tying the fragments together. Both approaches envision a crossing between the general and the particular as a way to mitigate the collective's invisibility. It should be remembered that neither of these types exist in absolute forms.

To give one final example of their intermixing, in *'alam al-din*, Mubarak's characters merge personification with *kinaya*—a "merger" that is the result of us distinguishing between the two types that often coexist in this canon. For instance, 'Alam al-Din (the father) and Burhan al-Din (the son) are as much the names of characters as they are personifications of the qualities described by the names; to "know"/sign ('Alam) and to "evince"/sign of religion. Through the characters/ideas and their journeys, what it means to know and evince knowledge (tied to the roots of 'Alam and Burhan) of *al-Din* (religion) is intertwined and reconfigured through the encounter with the principles of history as a question of settling and populating the world (*'imara*).[69] The unnamed English Orientalist is yet another example of the characterization of a type. At the same time, the often-commented-upon resonance between the plot of *'alam al-din* and the encounter between Ibrahim al-Desuqi and Edward William Lane (1801-1876) implicates the narrative with a potential particular referentiality.[70] In all of these instances, characterization is at the crux of a process of negotiation between the general and the particular, which equally plays out as a negotiation of the "limits" of the textual: the boundaries between the literary texts and the world of its readers. The deliberate playing with these boundaries is what gives these texts their seemingly abrupt endings, their "weak" characters and plots. These seeming lacks are the sign of literary artifice, but one that is forged in the encounter with the problem of the rise of the collective.

Al-Nas as a Crossing

Chapter 1 showed the way in which Ibn 'Arabi reenvisions the relationship between *khayal* and truth. He reinterprets the latter from the strive to grasp the "thing-in-itself," to rethinking it as incessant crossing between images that ultimately reveals relationality. This latter mode of seeing comes close to al-Farabi's understanding of the importance of *khayal* for *al-'amma* (the commoners) who cannot grasp the thing-in-itself but can see it in relationality to other things. Consequently, *khayal* has a crucial role to play in al-Farabi's polis because it gives the inhabitants a semblance and simulation of Truth through which they could be led, and as such is important for maintaining the polis. I am tempted to say that what we see in this canon is both a combination of these two tendencies and their transformation.

Khayal as a site of convergence à la Ibn 'Arabi is activated, but in this case it is placed within concerns pertaining to the polis. This positioning is born out of the fact that the collective is not a thing in itself, or an object, but a relationality. While one can explain the matter in this way, we also have to recognize that this transformation—as we have been seeing in this book—alters the conceptual underpinnings of whatever preceded it. In other words, this potential combination between 'Ibn 'Arabi's *khayal* and Farabi's *khayal* is ultimately an overcoming of the two. What combines the three instances of *khayal*, however, is its role in enabling a crossing toward what would otherwise be impossible. In our nineteenth-century canon, the crossing is toward *al-nas*, and it is a crossing between what lies inside the text and what lies beyond it to offer *al-nas*, not as an ontologically ungrounded image, but as the "invisible" ground (i.e., the social as a relationality) of both literature and "politics." Chapter 5 tackles this crossing, offering some final conclusions on what literature is as conceptualized and practiced by the canon of nineteenth-century Arabic literature.

5
Literature as a Political Problem

The previous chapter culminated in the definition of this literature as a making visible of history to be superimposed on a problem of sovereignty, a problem that is rooted in the fraught assertion that the collective is both the object and potential subject of sovereign power. Consequently, to adjudicate the best mode of ruling—the one that would be conducive to a prosperous civilization—one must adjudge the nature of the collective itself, from whom ruling power is derived and to whom that same power is applied. In this way we return to the parallelism between nature and society and science and history alluded to in chapter 1, as they converge on a quest for a truthful judgment of human nature that uses history, and historicism, to grapple with how to know the nature of the collective—as an entity that is immune to typical empiricist procedures.

It is crucial to remember that the nature of the collective in these texts stands in for a universal human nature at the core of sociability and collectivity, as we saw in chapter 4. In other words, these texts are not concerned with charting out pluralities of natures inherent in the supposed particularities of actually existing collective groups. This is not to say that the question of particularities, which must necessarily be answered in order to determine what is truly universal, was not heavily contested. Yet these disputes still assumed a universal nature that could be discovered.

Despite these texts' insistence on the existence of the universal, they still deploy various techniques to delimit the inclusion into the universal. Racism is the most obvious way for exclusion-though culturalism also plays an equally significant role. This is not unique to this body of texts, and systematic racism plays a structural role in delimiting the applicability of universal postulations. In these texts, the gap between the universal and those who are barred from accessing it is often projected as a historical distance that needs to be traversed, leading to "stagist" conceptions of history—not in its ostensibly Marxist guise, but as a more general conception underpinning ideas of civilizational progress.[1]

The fact that history in this canon is both a recognition of historicity and a diagnostic tool bespeaks these inclinations to organize civilizations in accordance with their full or partial realization of the universal nature. In fact, the key terms in this period's political lexicon, such as order, unity, and justice—which we have already encountered in the previous chapters as stable fixtures in our literary canon—are subsumed within these ideas of civilizational progress, embedded in universal laws. Therefore, deciphering the universal nature of the collective is crucial for aligning any given particular collective with the laws and virtues that beget civilizational progress. This process of aligning is precisely the role of ruling, in which literature plays a crucial role; it is precisely here that we encounter the "origins"—to use these two terms in a new way, outside of their usual cartographic and chronological underpinnings—of the canon of nineteenth-century Arabic literature.

This chapter homes in on the inner contradiction produced by literature's resolution of the problematic presented by sovereignty in the wake of the rise of the collective. Chapter 4 explained this problematic as the increasing need to make the collective visible so that one could judge its nature and by extension decide the best mode of ruling it in accordance with its nature, coupled with the intensifying realization that the collective (as a social totality) is not a sensorial object—whether inside or outside the texts. The arguments presented here show that the tension between the need to make the collective visible and its invisibility forges the deliberate form that we have been studying in the previous chapters. Chapter 5 focuses on how the process of rendering the invisible collective visible complicates literature's intervention, from a concern with making visible as a prelude to accurate and truthful judgment toward an enactment of a judgment that has already been made.

Only then, having analyzed these texts by revealing their driving question—which I present here as an inner contradiction or problematic—will we be able to widen our scope to deal explicitly with questions of literary history. We start by revisiting the idea that the collective eludes direct perceivability, which we saw in the previous chapter. In so doing, I highlight the ways in which the collective's invisibility gives this canon its form, while also complicating conceptions of what literature is or does.

In analyzing characters, the preceding chapter outlined two main typologies: the first embodies abstract universal laws via personification, moving them within a highly allegorical narrative world, whereas the second relies on *kinaya* (periphrasis, metonymy) to create a generalizable social type that tantalizingly promises easy specification because it moves within a seemingly hyperrealist narrative world. In practice, neither of these types exist in absolute or isolated form. Rather, they are a typological schema, an analytical tool that reveals their coexistence in our canon—even as some texts seem to lean more toward one end of this continuum than to the other. Furthermore, both techniques work together against the backdrop of the task of making the collective visible, bringing it to stand in front of the mind's eye, placing it under an optic device, and putting it on stage so that its nature may be judged and, by extension, the best mode of ruling it can also be ascertained.

The task of "staging the collective" is indispensable because, while one could directly perceive persons, groups, crowds, and mobs, the collective as a social totality cannot be an object of direct perception.[2] Rather, direct perception can only reveal fragments of that totality (i.e., persons, groups, crowds, mobs and the like). Therefore, an impasse is reached between the need to subject the collective to scrutiny in order to determine the best mode of ruling—and the increasing configuration of scrutiny within a strong empiricist impulse is important to remember here—and the impossibility of encountering the collective as a totality. The form of the canon of nineteenth-century Arabic literature is born from this impossibility.

In encountering the seeming impossibility of perceiving the collective, literature is devised as a mode of making visible that is capable of revealing the traces of history on every object (I use "object" here in its most general sense as an object of literary perception, which, as we saw in previous chapters, includes people, places, and events). In the terms of our authors, literature shows every object to be an *athar*, and lurking behind every *athar* we see the specter (*khayal*) of the collective as the force enacting *athar*, whose action is not reducible to a single moment, but extends through time. The history of the *athar* is not reducible to its moment of formation because it continues to encode the actions of the collective in time. The crystallization of actions on *athar* allows us to perceive the latter as a sign standing for collective action, and as a consequence for the state of the collective more broadly; in this way, social totality can come into visibility encoded in signs all around us. In other words, the transformations in *khayal* and *athar*, with which this book has been concerned in its early chapters, are subtended by the emergence of the collective as both the object and potential subject of power, and as an entity that evades direct perceivability and therefore both emphasizes the need for thorough scrutiny and also complicates it. As a consequence, *khayal* and *athar* are reworked in response to this challenge. By uncovering the specter of the collective through its traces, literature propounds to solve the challenge presented by the collective's invisibility, contributing to the resolution of the problematic posed by sovereignty through the making visible of the collective.

In this manner, the canon of nineteenth-century Arabic literature is part of a broader current through which fields and practices are restructured against the backdrop of new conceptions of the collective as a social totality. We can then, in retrospect, recognize that the process of restructuring is evident from the first chapter of this book, when we saw how history was demarcated as *the* objective of *khayal*, becoming the crucial force in the latter's transformation. The following chapters continued to explore history as the pivot of these text's literary universe—this is evident even from the titles of the chapters, since they wed history to *khayal*, *athar*, and, finally, *al-nas*. Yet the implications of this insight could only be fully recognized after we pursued the conception of history, reading it as both the convergence of fragmentary events and abstract laws as well as an anonym for the collective. In this way, we have come full circle, identifying the way in which the emergence of the collective is our analytical end point, or conclusion and, therefore, also the founding problem of this canon that we have been grappling with since chapter 1, but that we could only fully recognize after we have entered the world of this canon and learned its language.

Chapter 5 argues that the solution literature poses for the problematic presented by sovereignty is foiled from its inception. To anticipate what will be analyzed more thoroughly in the coming pages, this literature's attempt to carve out a "prepolitical" space through which an adjudication of human nature, as the nature of the collective, could offer the ground for political organization—discussed in the previous chapter—is thwarted from the beginning because the question of nature and its adjudication is revealed to be doubly political. On the one hand it is embroiled in debates on sovereignty, which we discussed in the previous chapter as the rise of *al-nas*, and on the other the literary procedures for making the collective visible as a precursor for distinguishing between law and accident, or the universal and the particular, are always already politically, and socially, positioned.

However, this is not a sign of failure as much as it is the result of the inner contradiction that defines literature from the position of this canon, both as a form and as a field. In the coming paragraphs, I turn to this inner contradiction, exploring the two axes it moves across, both of which hinge on the details and procedures through which literature makes the collective visible. The first pertains to the relationship between the fragmented part (characters) and the whole (the collective as a social totality), and it leads directly into the second, which is concerned with literature's interventionist designs.

The Duplication of Fragmentation as Totality

Thus far, we have seen that literature's contribution to the problematic posed by sovereignty lies in its ability to make the collective visible, staging it so that it seems *as if* the collective can be directly perceived. In so doing, literature offers the preconditions for drawing accurate conclusions regarding the nature of the collective and the best way for ruling it. We might then assume that literature contributes a neutral ground that anchors and therefore conceptually precedes any epistemological or sociopolitical conclusions concerning the nature of the collective, because its role is primarily restricted to making it visible. It is only *after* literature has performed its task that conclusions can be drawn. Yet this presumed separation of the literary, the epistemological, and the sociopolitical is betrayed by the form of this canon itself. In fact, the possibility of making the collective visible depends on the intricate inseparability of this trio. Consequently, literature's contribution toward a solution presupposes an unattainable neutral position, abstracted from any prior epistemological or sociopolitical imbrications. At the same time, however, literature's solution depends on their inseparability. This is the problem of part and whole, which is most obvious in/through the characters, though, as we are about to see, it encompasses the canon's form in general.

While our body of texts strives to make the collective visible, the collective as a social totality—what we described in the previous chapter as *al-nas*—is not a literary object *inside* the text, nor is it a sensory object *outside* it. Unlike other objects, or *athar*, such as the pyramids, the Eiffel Tower, the Palace of Versailles, trains, streets, arcades, and courts of law, or even oysters, ants, and bees, the collective is not an object that we encounter in our texts. At the same time, it is not an allegorized entity, such as *al-watan* (the homeland), which is personified as the youth in Nadim's "Medical Council," or Wisdom and Civilization/Freedom that become the Queen of Wisdom and the King of Civilization/Freedom in Marrash's "Forest." Rather, as chapter 4 argued, the collective as a totality emerges through the various combinations of the two typologies of characters and the literary mode of making history visible more broadly. The latter do not turn totality into an object that can be directly perceived inside the text as much as they arrange an encounter between characters inside the text and readers outside it that produces the collective as a focal point, through a series of "crossings." This encounter depends precisely on the seemingly facile and simple referentiality of the texts as a whole, and of characters specifically, since they both seem to offer little more than a loose literary framing for social commentaries that draw on their actual contemporary occurrences or allegorize their author's opinions about social conditions, or what is often dubbed as these texts' "episodic" structure. The previous chapters made the case that this episodic structure is deliberate and in fact key to making history visible. To this, we can now add that, because the narrative structure toys tantalizingly with the idea that it lacks literary artifice, it facilitates the slippage between text/world and character/reader, which is the key to making the collective visible. Put more bluntly, the form of these texts is not an indication of the lack of literary artifice, or even of a fumbling of it, but is actually its apex. In unpacking this idea, we come to a fuller understanding of this canon's form, which has often been dubbed as its "episodic" structure. This enables us to turn to the foundational contradiction at the heart of this structure.

Al-nas, the collective as a social totality, coheres the multiple and seemingly disjunctive episodes that constitute these works, converging them in a singular focal point that is the collective itself. This focal point is neither entirely within the text nor outside of it, but produced through the doubling—or the mirroring, to use an optical term—of the fragmentary nature of direct experiences outside the texts. The texts' iconic episodic structure repeats, if not intensifies, the fragmentation of personal experiences of the social totality. The episodes divide up space into discrete sites that we can scrutinize one by one, in a move that is strongly reminiscent of topographic genres and travelogues and is widely practiced across this body of texts. That we should see this as an intentional technique is supported by the fact that we often encounter a similar repertoire of spaces across these texts. Similarly, time is parceled into distinct sequential moments both on the level of the moments encoded in the *athar* as well as on the level of narrative temporality, where each episode presents us with a seemingly self-enclosed textual moment that could be easily removed or reshuffled with minimal disruption to the narrative flow. The same could be said of characters: we often meet a character, be it the personification of an abstract principle/virtue or a social type, who disappears after the encounter—regardless of its length—and seldom returns. Characters, much like spaces and moments of time, present seemingly disconnected persons with faint, if any, relationality among them.

These features have often been assumed by early scholarship to be the manifestation of the incomplete transition to modern literature, supposedly obvious in the texts' weak plots and their professed privileging of social reform agendas over literary and artistic concerns. More recent studies have thoroughly written over the stigma of this assessment, referring in passing to how Arabic narrative forms, unlike their "Western counterparts," rely heavily on episodic rather than teleological patterns of unfolding. The move naturalizes this feature, but it does not explain it; supposed historical continuities require as much explanation as change. Neither continuities nor breaks in literary history—much like those in history itself—are either natural or unnatural.

Chapter 3 offered us a partial reading of this feature, arguing that fading out the connections among *athar* enables the focalization of the relationship between it and the abstract historical principle undergirding it and, in so doing, enables us to see the same principle over and over with every encounter with an *athar*. Consequently, we come to see how this principle governs myriad instantiations. With the advent of *al-nas*, we can better understand this repetition as a duplication of the fragmentary nature of experiences. The enticing slippery identification between character and reader is vital here: it evokes the idea that what is being read is little more than an assortment of contemporary events that are just subjected to surface periphrasis or allegorizing, an issue that we explored extensively in the previous chapter. Yet, as we saw there, the creation of these characters, through *kinaya* and allegory, that at first seem to invite simple identification with what lies beyond them (i.e., between character/reader, and text/world) is in fact an elaborate literary undertaking whose different facets have been explored throughout the chapters of this book. In this manner, what the previous chapters have been describing as a making visible of history can now be seen to be ultimately a mode of focalizing the collective, staging the collective. The projected focal point of the collective—rather than plot, to cite a counterexample—weaves the episodes of each text together. Consequently, the fragmentation or episodic structure of these texts is not a vestige of transition or continuity from premodern to modern, but is, on the contrary, a defining feature of their literariness and of their narrative logic.

We have already seen that, even though Muwaylihi's *hadith* starts with the declared aim of comparing two distinct periods of time, the era of Muhammad Ali versus the era of British occupation—both key for the history of modernity in Egypt—the narrative quickly turns in the direction of showing their connection, and how the actions in the first period resulted in the second one. From the Pasha's initial perspective, this is outlandish, since these two moments could not be more different for him.

Nonetheless, the connections between the two periods become increasingly more apparent throughout the narrative. However, the connections are not narrativized with a linear chronology. On the contrary, the relationship pivots precisely on this episodic structure. The story of the Pasha is a case in point.

In learning that every object is an *athar*, the Pasha is compelled to align his judgment of action with what it has left behind for the future of the collective in its totality. This is tied to his realization that the outcome of his own actions does not emanate from, nor does it fully coincide with, his will and intentions. Rather, actions are susceptible to the forces of history, read here as the collective. The episode of the endowment, which we examined closely in chapter 3, offers us a poignant example. While the Pasha intended to build the endowment to immortalize his name, this did not materialize in a durable institution because his children and grandchildren—whose proper education he had ignored—ended up dismantling it out of ignorance. Moreover, this pattern is not restricted to the genealogical sphere, but repeats in various other episodes whereby the totality of Cairo and, later, Paris are produced via that ignorance of the future. Eventually, the Pasha realizes that the acts of the lawyer, the doctor, the '*Umda*, and the police officer are all connected, as evidenced by every single *athar* he and Ibn Hisham see. This is true even though those actors themselves might not be able, or willing, to see that. By reduplicating the seeming isolation of the characters' actions throughout the episodic narrative structure, while revealing their actual interconnectedness through *athar*, the narrative structure enables the readers to project a cohering focal point for their own seemingly sequestered actions and, as such, allows them to see and know themselves as *al-nas*.

This coherence of characters into the collective, through the identification of characters and readers, does not occur simply inside or outside the text, but through their encounter, whose dynamics are coordinated by the narrative structure itself. The latter functions as a lens—to continue with this canon's fascination with optical devices—through which the fragments focalize to show something that exceeds both direct sensory experiences of objects as well as the textual one, even though it is produced at their limit and through their encounter. We can observe this pattern in

Mubarak's *'alam al-din*, even though the scope of actors is considerably more constricted.

In the visit of the four characters ('Alam al-Din, Burhan al-Din, the unnamed Orientalist, and Ya'qub) to the Palace of Versailles, which we analyzed in chapters 3 and 4, the collective appears narratologically, despite its discursive absence. The fate of the palace-turned-museum is played out at the hands of the social collective, whose agency is elided by the overwriting of their rise as an effect of the king's actions. As we saw earlier, the conversation bypasses the discussion of the French Revolution, hypostatizing the king as the actor from whom original actions emanate, the rest being relegated to derivative effects of this original action. Despite this attempted discursive sleight of hand, we see here clearly that the collective was already an actualized force, since it is only in the wake of its actual presence that one may try to elide it. Furthermore, while the text is keen to ascribe the chief role in history to the king as the prime mover, it still cannot circumvent the action of the collective, or the fact that history is carried at its hand, even as it continues to insist on pointing to the king as its ultimate originator. In other words, *athar*, in Mubarak's text, reveals the force of the collective even though he adds another further point of origination that is the king: that the collective acted in this way *because* of the king is Mubarak's intervention in this literary vision. This is an important point, and one that we have already touched upon in the previous chapter, grappling with the question of whose *athar* we see as our rubric for clarifying the ways in which each text frames the scope of history's actors and, by extension, maps out a series of hierarchies within the collective, because some actions, and some types, belong to the collective more than others—and, therefore, some are more representative of law and the universal and others of accident and the particular.

In this chapter, we explore another layer of the issue of the collective. I am less focused here on whom the texts demarcate as belonging to the collective as I am on the very idea that making the collective visible cannot conceptually precede the hierarchal bifurcations within it.[3] This means that the literary mode of seeing cannot dissever itself from the epistemological and the sociopolitical. Consequently, its attempt to offer itself as the ground for these broader debates, standing both before them and

Literature as a Political Problem 191

at a remove from them, is already frustrated because the fragments with which the texts commence are thoroughly saturated with sociopolitical implications. This is what I have referred to earlier as the problem of part and whole.

The literary vision of the collective as a social totality is premised upon the duplication of fragments that promise easy direct referentiality. The whole (collective) is constructed through the parts (characters/readers), as an effect of the arrangement of these parts in relationship to one another within the narrative structure. This means that while literature promises to bring the collective (whole) into visibility so that we may judge the best way of ruling it—that is, on how the parts (characters/readers) should be arranged in relationship to one another (structure of society/socialization, order, or even civilization, in the political lexicon of this period)—it can only show the collective (whole) by organizing the parts (characters/readers) that are already embedded in a particular social structure into a relationship (literary structure). In other words, there is a tension between the promise that literature can bring the whole to stand in front of us so that we can *afterward* judge the best mode of ruling it or organizing it. According to this logic, the whole is postulated as preexisting, and therefore outside, the specifics of sociopolitical and epistemological dynamics. Literature is meant to offer the ground from where judgments upon the collective (the nature of the collective, how to rule it, and why it is split between ruler and ruled does or does not tally with the nature of the collective) can follow. At the same time, the fragments (character/reader) with which literature makes the collective visible are already embedded and positioned within the social totality. This is actually a condition for the seemingly facile identification. In other words, the positioning of characters/readers does not *follow* from the literary mode of seeing enabling seeing the collective. Rather, the fragments are already socially embedded before the literary could ever make the collective visible. While this literary contribution to the problem of sovereignty would conceptually demand that the whole precede the division of parts, in actuality the parts are already in place before we could ever constitute the whole conceptually or narratologically. The notion that literature can bring the collective into visibility so that one may judge its nature, the best mode of ruling it, and whether it can rule itself, so that *after* we see it, we can decide how to position the parts in relationship to one another is foiled by its own form that begins with already positioned parts and already existing relationalities.

At the same time, this tension does not negate the prospect of repositioning the parts in light of having seen the whole. While these fragments are always already embedded in a particular relationality, the literary mode of seeing invites reforming or changing that relationality or structure. We see this in numerous texts from this canon, whose ethos is overwhelmingly reformist and pedagogic. Nonetheless, the formative contradiction still holds between the aspiration to offer the ground for judgment—furnishing the equivalence of the conditions of the scientific experiment—and the way in which the parts literature deploys to constitute the whole are already socially positioned before literature's supposedly neutral ground could ever come to emerge. The possibility for comparing literature to science is evident from chapter 1, where literature's three gestures of visualization entail a scientific one. We can now grasp how literature construes its relationship to the collective in terms that are analogous to science's relationship to nature.

Yet this analogy is not as seamless as the discourse of these texts suggests. There is no "before" or "outside" social totality from where seeing-as-knowing could categorically precede, or temporarily evade, positionality. By implication, the conception of literature as a making visible of the collective does not stand before or outside rivaling political visions and epistemological contentions of and for the collective. On the contrary, the conception of the literary is born in the throes of this struggle. As such, literature's relationship with its broader social continuum is always in medias res. This insight will prove critical when we return to questions of literary history at the end of this chapter. For now, it suffices to point out that wrestling with literary history revolves on our ability to attune to literature's changing relationship to its broader social continuum. This relationship is how literature becomes defined, often not so much as a discrete object, or a set of prescriptive features, but as a position in a social relationality.

When looking at this issue from the perspective of our nineteenth-century canon, the picture is quite complex. On the one hand, literature emerges as the site that promises to resolve political disputes by offering the ground that legitimizes social and political practices in line with their effects on the collective, whose nature literature helps us judge. On the other, as we have seen, the literary form of this canon betrays this promise. Instead of laying the ground on which political debates could then unfold, its narratological structure reveals the impossibility of this "neutral" ground. In other words, the form of the canon narrativizes the impossibility of standing outside the totality in a nonaligned position. Of course, the narrativization of this impossibility does not contravene the continuing discursive insistence on it. Thus, the outcome of this founding contradiction is mixed and, as we are about to see, key to understanding its history: on the one side, the pursuit of ways to bring the social as a totality into visibility is instituted—because of broader sociopolitical and epistemological struggle, and literature's position in it—as the defining objective of this literature. At the same time, literature is constituted as a site for the perpetual, though obviously fraught, translation of the sociopolitical and epistemological struggles posed by the rise of the collective into primarily ethical issues.[4] Unpacking this dynamic will return us once more to our earlier insight into this canon's narrative structure.

While this canon sets out to offer a neutral ground that stands outside the sociopolitical struggles over the collective, its own form betrays the impossibility of this positionality, exposing the fact that debates on sovereignty are always already positioned in this struggle. It aims to mitigate the increasing seeming groundlessness (obviously, it would seem groundless only because the authors insist that a true ground must be unpositioned) by continuing to suggest that if one could really come to see the collective, everyone would act in accordance with its interest, which necessarily coincides with the interest of every member of the collective in the most profound sense. The implicit assumption in this case is that there is a singular definition of interest and collective interest regardless of where one is positioned, because true interest is the one that is best aligned with the true nature of the collective and the true universal laws governing the history of the collective. Therein lies the real conundrum, as literature seems to want to simultaneously offer a "neutral" ground—which we have already seen to be impossible—as well as to instill and propagate the true judgment.

Grappling with the impossibility of standing beyond the social totality and mitigating the impasses caused by it, this literature oscillates between offering a *mode* of seeing that makes the social totality visible and a *pedagogy* of seeing that seeks to reveal to its readers the true nature of the collective, to show them how to align their behavior with the interest of the collective. The next section turns to this oscillation, arguing that, through it, we can view the pedagogic project of these texts in a new light. To anticipate what is yet to come, I argue that this pedagogic project marks both the ways in which literature engages with the broader social struggle over sovereignty, and the ways in which literature becomes a distinctive site of this struggle, one that has its own internal logic. As such, the struggle over the collective is not restricted to the content and statements of vision but also includes formal issues that do not have *direct* correlation with a specific sociopolitical content—this is more of a tacit than absolute distinction, since the previous chapter argued that the negotiation of the limit of the political versus the literary versus the juridical is a complex process.

Mode of Seeing, Pedagogy of Seeing

This canon's body of texts often lay an overt claim to a pedagogic agenda that is sometimes expressed in moralistic edifying terms, other times as an assistance in learning encyclopedic information, and others as a vision of political futurity. These three dimensions are usually woven together because knowledge-morals-politics are part of the same circle we saw in the previous chapter. As people come to know better about the true nature of sociality, they will act better, and this is precisely what politics sets out to do: lead people to act in accordance with the good of the collective. Per this view, literature as a mode of seeing offers the knowledge that will improve behavior (morals), bringing about political change, and therefore resulting in civilizational progress. This can be viewed as the nineteenth-century version of the circle of justice.

Looked at this way, we can see that the canon of nineteenth century Arabic literature sets out to encircle morals-knowledge-politics against the backdrop of the emergence of the collective. However, because making the collective visible is not a neutral scientific experiment, this circle oscillates between seamless success and utter failure; the literary oscillates between offering a mode of seeing that people—here as *al-nas*—can use to know themselves, judge themselves, and perhaps rule themselves, and between inculcating an already made judgment in its readers, whereby it is specific actions, and not modes of seeing, that this literature instills. Similarly, morals hover between being a result of literary seeing (it is after seeing that *al-nas* decide how to act) and being the necessary precursor to seeing *al-nas*, because people need to be taught to turn towards *al-nas* first in order for *al-nas* to be made visible so that they may then pass true and accurate judgments. Yet, in teaching people to turn, they have already been taught to act in a way that precedes them making a judgment from a neutral ground. In other words, people need to be taught how to act to construct their vision of the collective. Finally, there is no judgment about politics that comes *only after* making the collective visible, because what people learn about how to act is already political: it is the product of a political vision about the dynamics within the collective. These three examples are specific instances in which the impossibility of having a neutral ground manifest itself. Looked at in this way, what is truly pedagogic about these texts is not their propensity to share information about institutions of the state and micrographs (in Muwaylhi's *hadith*); about oysters, ants, and bees (in Mubarak's *'alam al-din*); the history of the respective Islamic dynasties (in Tuwayrani's "Floral Publishing"); or the origins of sociality (in Marrash's "Forest"). Rather, the information is already methodically placed within a circle of knowledge-morals-politics, and it is through this "circle" that this information comes to acquire its value as an optimizer of sociality because as people learn to see, they also learn to act.

This is what I refer to as the translation of the sociopolitical onto an ethical plane by assuming an unrealizable epistemological neutrality. This circle, much like the earlier iterations we saw in the previous chapter, sets out to create an unattainable harmonious circle whereby knowledge is the precursor of a "scientific" judgment that in turn grounds politics. Yet it also demonstrates that every step of this circle is always already political, that there is no outside or before. Consequently, the canon of nineteenth-century Arabic literature fluctuates between offering a mode of seeing and a pedagogy of seeing; both are equally present, for they are born out of the same contradiction and are two facets of a single response. We will turn to one final example from Muwaylihi to grapple with this literary pedagogic as it functions within what we have been describing as a narrative literary structure.

Turning to the episodes with the 'Umda, the longest continuing episodes with a single character in *hadith*, the main characters conclude that the problem is that "people (*al-nas*) are distracted with each other, away from each other. Those who work for the benefit of people (*al-nas*) have lessened."[5] This statement reveals how the invisibility of the collective results in the inability of the collective itself—which doesn't know itself as the collective (because it can't see)—to act for the collective. The point was key in the analysis presented above of the duplication of fragmentation as totality. What the text offers, then, is a mode of seeing that will enable people to turn and face one another and work for the benefit of the people and therefore form durable *athar*.

This basic insight encompasses all of the texts we have analyzed in this book. However, this mode of seeing is intimately entwined with principles through which we judge the *athar* and the totality. We do not see and then discover what the principles are; the principles are already encoded for us in everything we see (because history itself is a diagnostic tool). As such, the question of the best mode of rule in line with the collective's nature and therefore conducive to the prosperity of society is already answered—a structure reminiscent of the postponed narrative objective that is also already present from the beginning that we discussed in chapter 2, through the trial in Marrash's "Forest" and the arrival at England in Mubarak's *'alam al-din*. The readers are taught this answer not only because they are instructed into an already demarcated abstract principle, but because they are also taught ethical dispositional, virtues, and behaviors that are steps toward aligning them to turn to see the collective. In other words, what one should learn after having seen the collective is actually a precondition for being able to see the collective. This is the contradiction this literature narrates through the interplay of part and whole, mode of seeing and pedagogy of seeing. Throughout, literature continues to move across two interrelated arcs: the first weaves epistemological and sociopolitical concerns to give us the literary mode of seeing (what has been described in this book through the concepts of *khayal, athar, al-nas*), while the second translates epistemological and sociopolitical concerns into ethical ones that mitigate the impossibility of having a neutral ground from where to judge the collective.

In other words, literature makes this problem appear and disappear simultaneously, postponing dealing with the gravity of realizing that there is no neutral ground by continuing to present a form that assumes there is one, even as it narratologically exposes its absence. Consequently, to the first arc weaving epistemological and sociopolitical concerns to give us the literary mode of seeing, there is a second arc that presents literature as a pedagogy of seeing through a cluster of terms such as *adab, ta'dib, tarbiya* (education), *tahsin al-'adat wal taqalid* (improving habits and traditions/customs), to name a few, with *'ibra* (yield / moral lesson) and *naf'* (benefit/good) being close associates of this second arc. The second arc has been heavily studied in our field: from a literary perspective as a site of continuity with premodern Arabic literature, and from within social and intellectual history as a site for studying the rise of the middle class between nationalism and colonialism. Although we won't delve into further details about this second arc, it suffices here to note that from the position of literary studies, this arc has to be read in its relationship to a "new" founding problem—what this book has been describing as the rise of the collective. The issue is of particular importance not just to literary studies proper, where we might study forms and narrative techniques, but is key in grappling with how this second arc creates a particular discourse that can be mobilized within political disputes. This "literary" discourse can be used to authorize certain political interventions by eschewing their sociopolitical positionality, shrouding their political interventions in the guise of ethical ones. I will give just one example of this kind, by way of suggesting the implications of the work undertaken by *Literary Optics* and anticipating some of its conclusions, but a full mapping out of this literary discourse is clearly beyond the purview of this book.

Both Nadim and Muwaylihi wrote brief biographic entries about Colonel Ahmed 'Urabi (1841–1911), whose name was attached to the popular movement from 1879 to 1882. The revolt erupted in the wake of Egypt's declaration of its bankruptcy in 1876, and the subsequent institution of "dual control": a joint British-French colonial forceful management of the Egyptian state budget in the name of the European creditors on whose debt Egypt had defaulted.[6] The period witnessed percolating political mobilization, but it was on September 9, 1881, that what appeared to be a factional voicing of grievances by the lower-rank members of the Egyptian army crystallized into a sweeping mobilization demanding constitutional reforms, and less vociferously economic ones. A year later, the British army had squashed the revolt and began its occupation of Egypt—the legal status of the latter notwithstanding.

Nadim was famously involved in these events, but so were many of the main protagonists of this book—though they didn't always stand on the same side of it: Muhammad al-Muwaylihi took part in the revolt and was exiled to Istanbul in the wake of the defeat where he spent his time editing and printing old Arabic manuscripts with his father, Ibrahim, a renowned journalist and litterateur in his own right, and Muhammad 'Abduh, the religious scholar who was to become a towering figure of modern thought in Arabic, exercising influence across competing political and ideological factions. In a peculiar detail in Tuwayrani's biography, however, we learn that he was a disciple (*murid*) of al-Sheikh Abu al-Huda al-Sayyadi (1850–1909), a close religious counselor of Sultan Abdulhamid, becoming his advisor as of 1879. Al-Sayyadi is the subject of a long scathing lampoon written by Nadim and published posthumously. The lampoon, *kitab al-masamir*, attacks al-Sayyadi as an anti-reform figure who was responsible, according to Nadim, for Al-Afghani's (1838–1897) death. Ibrahim al-Muwaylihi, Muhammad 'Abduh, and al-Afghani were also mentioned by Muhammad al-Muwaylihi in the introduction to his book. Meanwhile, it was Shidyaq's journal *al-jawa'ib*, based in Istanbul, that published the Sultan's condemnation, and "ex-communication," of the leaders of the movement. These details will prove key as we read Nadim's and Muwaylihi's articles.

In 1881, Nadim wrote a brief biographic sketch about 'Urabi, published in his journal "Raillery and Reproof"—this is where "Medical Council" was also published. The short biography was titled "*nubdha min tarikh al-humam* Ahmad Bek 'Urabi" (A Snippet from the History of the Brave Ahmad Bek 'Urabi).[7] What it communicates is not information, but the deep connection between the military man and the land of Egypt—often in a literal territorial sense. 'Urabi's relationship with the homeland (*al-watan*) is intertwined with his knowledge of the people, ultimately qualifying him to lead. It is this connection, not his opinions or vision, that are highlighted as what enables his successful political leadership. Clearly, this is one entry, and the rest of the journal often expounds on a more detailed political vision. Consequently, I am not here making claims about the movement itself or about the entirety of Nadim's journal. The point is more specific: that there is a particular kind of intervention that can turn political concerns onto a plane of knowledge of the sociality-turned-ethics. This kind of intervention is what I think of as a mobilization of a literary discourse beyond the contour of a specifically literary form.

To see this more clearly, let's jump forward to Muwaylihi's intervention twenty years later. In the aftermath of the revolt, the participants were put on trial, with many of them being sentenced to exile in Palestine and Istanbul for varying periods of time. 'Urabi and his closest associates, however, were banished to Sri Lanka for just under twenty years (1881–1901). By the time they were allowed to return, some had already died. 'Urabi did return, however, causing a media frenzy, with waves of criticism flooding the papers. Muwaylihi writes his entry against the backdrop of this whiplash, responding to it. He critically titles it "ihda al-'ibar" (A Moral Lesson, or, alternatively, An Exemplar of the Yield).

The article completely elides any mention of its author's own participation in the revolt. Instead, he says that, despite the ongoing accusations, 'Urabi was not a corrupt person. Nonetheless, his leadership was doomed to fail. If the Colonel had committed any acts of hubris, it was his assumption that he could lead when he—as Nadim had told us earlier, but with a dramatically different conclusion—is drawn out from amid the people themselves. According to Muwaylihi, 'Urabi is a member of the *'amma* (the public but also commoners in contradistinction to the elite, *khassa*), and, as a result, he was never fit for leadership. Muwaylihi's position does not hearken us back to a world that precedes the rise of the collective. Instead, much like Mubarak's overemphasis of the actions of the king, it represents not a world that pre-dates the rise of *al-nas*, but a response to it. This is obvious in the way Muwaylihi's—just like Nadim's—judgment of 'Urabi hinges on grappling with the colonel's position in the collective. Crucially, they appeal to a similar set of terms, one that bears clear affinity with the modes of judgment in these texts. Yet, they reach completely different conclusions, couching both of them as disinterested conclusions that follow from the evaluation of 'Urabi's "objective" position. In other words, they both present us with diametrically opposed political interventions that appear as judgments made on the grounds of 'Urabi's ethical dispositions (*adab*), instead of what they are—political arguments.

Moreover, in diagnosing 'Urabi's "lacking" (i.e., why he is judged to be part of the public-as-commoners rather than the elite), Muwaylihi's answer is: education. Here we return once again to the question of pedagogy, where the relationship between the literary as a mode of seeing and a pedagogy of seeing reveals its political stakes. If the distinction between the public-as-commoners and the elite, which prohibits the collective from assuming the position of the subject, is rooted in education, this always raises the possibility that this distance could be traversed, unless there is knowledge suited to each class by its "nature" that it cannot trespass—a point that is actually often made in discussions of *tarbiya* (education) in the nineteenth century. The point returns us to the way in which universal postulations are delimited; here, education is both a practice for overcoming hierarchies within the collective and for their social reproduction, turning the collective into the commoners. While the pursuit of these connections between this literary discourse, politics, and education, beyond the contour of literary form, is beyond the scope of this book, it is still crucial to emphasize the fact that different political positions emerge out of this tension or problematic between axis 1 and axis 2. The relationship between the two is much more complex, as is evidenced by the history of education as much as it is in the oeuvre of these authors themselves, for, as we began to glimpse, just because they all deal with the rise of the collective in a shared (aesthetic) vocabulary does not in any way mean that they took shared positions on the challenges posed to them by the collective's oscillation between subject and object, and by literature's oscillation between mode and pedagogy. These two axes do not pan neatly onto each other because, while all of these texts subscribe to a pedagogic function, they do not all occupy the same political positionality.

What we see here is not just political conflict between Nadim and Muwaylihi that plays out over a period of time, but, more importantly for our purposes here, the latter dispute takes the form of a struggle over the nature of the collective: Is it the object of power, or its subject, and, therefore, does belonging to the collective imbue one with power or erode its foundation? Furthermore, this disagreement regarding the collective is presented as an apolitical adjudication, despite its obvious political stakes; it is the ground of a political position rather than its motivation. Writing his memoirs (*mudhakkirat*) twenty-five years after the events, 'Urabi will take a different approach to that of Nadim and Muwaylihi, stressing his "noble" descent from land-owning classes that belong to the prophet's bloodline (*al-ashraf*).[8] What we glimpse here are the shifting positions emerging through both the rise of *al-nas* as a founding political and epistemological problem, and the emergence of the literary as a particular formal and discursive formulation of it.

To return to Nadim, and specifically to his "medical council," when the possibility that history's cycles of rise and fall could be intervened in by the collective because it is figured by the collective. The call for intervention ushers in the collective as an actual mobilizable social collective and a concept into a new universe. While both the living and the dead are called upon, the respondents who emerge from their grave (resurrected specters of older times who bring with them the conceptual language of those times) are positioned in the present. They partake in shaping the shared social and aesthetic questions of the present by searching for a shared vocabulary and struggling over its meaning. In so doing, they also participate in forging the different social and ideological positions from these shared social and aesthetic questions. It is precisely on this note of (literary) positionality that this chapter ends.

Our canon is forged in the wake of the rise of *al-nas* offering a mode of literary seeing (arc 1) that exceeds its discursive limits (arc 2), but one that is also always already contained within the latter (arc 2). This formative contradiction, or oscillation, will prove key as we turn to what of this conception of the literary remains. This oscillation reformulates "*adab's*" double-meaning as narrative and dispositional virtues. Yet, far from continuing what *adab* meant, it positions the relationship between narrative and dispositional virtues within a new universe—this is what we have been seeing in the past chapters. This knot between narrative and dispositional virtues will be tied and untied in new ways by future literary practice. Of the form these texts propose for staging the collective, it is this canon's grappling with authorial position that will continue to inspire future literary endeavors. The author as an image of voice, and a hidden position from where the totality could be seen, is one crucial legacy of this literary experimentation, and one that could continue to be reformulated with grave political and pedagogical stakes. This is what I mean when I say that these fights continue with their own literary logic that may not always pan out linearly on a specific sociopolitical position, but still has sociopolitical stakes.

This gives us a clue into future transformations: I suggest that narratologically the image of the voice of the author as a nonposition from where the whole appears will continue to be grappled with and discursively, this sleight of hand through which the sociopolitical could be rendered a question of ethics observed from a neutral ground is also one of the "legacies" of this canon. Finally, methodologically, our experiment with this body of texts helps carve out a path for grappling with literary history in Arabic, one that necessarily passes through the realization that the problem of historicizing modern Arabic literature is the problem of historicizing premodern Arabic literature, too. In this way, the story this book tells is not one that enables us to pinpoint a different ground for understanding the foundational status of these texts, but that explodes this idea of founding (with its implicit ideas on textuality and temporality) as a replacement for historicizing. Rather, situating the implications of this reading of the form of nineteenth-century literature in Arabic is a work of the future, not of the past.

Epilogue

Literary Optics is an exploration of the world of the canon of nineteenth-century Arabic literature anchored by a single perspectival shift: we desist from deploying the trope of the encounter as the interpretive framework for grappling with this body of texts. In doing so, the book offers a reading through which these texts no longer appear to be transitional, riven between—or, more mildly, "mixing"—traditional Arabic narrative forms with modern European ones. Rather, the canon *gives form to* a question on sovereignty and the nature of the collective arising against the backdrop of sweeping sociopolitical and epistemological transformations. Thus, we move beyond approaching the history of modern Arabic literature as the drama unfolding in the wake of the encounter between Europe and its others, whereby the "present" (in this case, our "analytic present"—the canon of nineteenth-century Arabic literature) is the site of the encounter between two stable turned ahistorical objects (traditional Arabic literature and modern European literature). Instead, the "present" emerges as the site for reconfiguring forms, discourses, and concepts in the wake of "new" problems, where the texts do not simply seek to resolve them, but to forge a form through which they can be posed at all. With this we move from ahistoricity perpetually appearing as history to the possibility of encountering history.

In concluding this book, we replay three parallel critical scenes from contemporary thought in Arabic where the disappearance of the present is encountered (the present here connotes both the object of study that is the analytic present and the present in the historical sense; of course, the two are often related in complex ways). While readers familiar with the works of these three intellectuals might be able to discern their traces throughout this book—captured not necessarily in the content of their arguments as much as through their distinctive intellectual "chess moves"—I do not call to them here by way of contemplating their *athar*. Rather, replaying these scenes helps us perceive the relationship between the disappearance of the present and the institutionalization of *nahda*—read via the trope of the encounter—as the origin of modernity. In other words, through these three moments we come to better understand how *nahda* is a position in contemporary thought that enables enfolding history into the trope of the encounter and, in so doing, continuously thwarts attempts at historicizing the present. Taking a wider lens to the methodological challenge confronted by this book, we also encounter its wider implications.

In 1974, prominent intellectuals from around the Arab world met in Kuwait for a conference concerning the crisis of Arab civilization (*'azmat al-hadara al-'arabiyya*). Mahdi 'Amil (1936–1987), the renowned Marxist from Lebanon, wrote a book in response to the proceedings of the conference. His main claim revolved around the terms of the debate. Once one accepts the diagnosis of the present (of a civilizational crisis), the produced analyses—despite their seeming differences—relinquish the ability to ask questions, but merely proceed to produce answers regardless of supposed theoretical, ideological, or disciplinary differences. Put differently, the characterization of a civilizational crisis is not a question from which debates may begin; it is an answer. Instead, 'Amil proposes that the crisis is the crisis of the Arab bourgeoisie classes who present their "crisis" as an all-encompassing civilizational one. The disagreement pivots on how to approach the present: as an expansive civilizational crisis whose origins lie in whichever moment one chooses to demarcate as decay (*inhitat*), and therefore in the failure to redress the latter, or, alternatively, the present needs to be read through its structural dynamics. This is our first scene.

Throughout his eventful career, Nasr Hamid Abu Zayd emphasized the historicity of textuality in its connection with interpretation. His engagement with the Quranic utterance produced a strong modality of attuning to the historicity of texts, interpretations, and (conceptual) language. In the process the interpretive act is revealed "as always already a historicizing act."[1] He contributed a pithy critique of approaches to the body of works known as *turath*—literally "inheritance," but it has come to denote "tradition" as a textual canon that is often juxtaposed to modernity (*hadatha*) or contemporaneity (*muʿasara*). According to Abu Zayd, intellectuals from the radical left to the conservative right encounter *turath* as an object preserved from time and shielded from its force. Consequently, it can be encountered as an "essence," a stable object that is then bended in accordance with leftist or right-wing interpretations. Both groups, despite their clear opposition, approach *turath* as an ahistorical essence in two interrelated ways: they ignore the historicity of the body of texts known as *turath*, and they occlude the historicity of their own interpretive act, sidelining how the present shapes their encounter with *turath*. Both the "analytic" and historical present are violently wiped out here in our second scene.

Hani Shukrallah wrote a series of insightful articles about the Egyptian Revolution of 2011; his engagement centered on the relationship between the palpable aversion to self-organizing that was dominant at the time and the cognizance of the political project or agenda, however implicit, driving collective political mobilization. In pursuing the causes of the contradictions, he perceives, between what the movement is about and the skewed vision harbored and cultivated by key political figures playing a leading role in it, that Shukrallah is led back to an excavation of *nahda*. Specifically, he homes in on the segment of the Egyptian middle class known as *effendiyya*, who project their sense of class crisis, mapped out as civilizational identity crisis, onto the history of modernity in Egypt, painting the latter as the struggle between the "East" and the "West"; Selim's description of the *nahda* as a foundational cultural problem, quoted at the beginning of this book, echoes Shukrallah's description of this class's self-perception.[2] This is scene three; it is strongly akin to ʿAmel's general reading, where a particular crisis is rendered as a civilizational one between "East" and "West," or "rise" (*nahda*) and "fall" (*suqut* or *inhitat*), and it is equally suggestive of Abu Zayd's reading regarding the entrapment he intervenes in between *turath* as a body of texts lying in the past on the one side, and modernity on the other. Together, they suggest that the elision of the analytic and historical present are parts of the same process.

What we see here are comparable patterns through which the present is fractured between two dichotomous points, perhaps not too dissimilar to Mubarak's reading of the French Revolution through light and darkness or civility and barbarity. This pattern is at the heart of the insistence in this book that the problem of historicizing modern Arabic literature is also the problem of historicizing premodern Arabic literature, for the issue lies in the imposition of this fracturing rhythm. The latter renders both modern and premodern literature in Arabic ahistorical points that elide the present. The latter elision is then presented as history by continuing to read the present as the site of the encounter between two dichotomous points (i.e., the modern and the premodern). In moving beyond the deployment of the trope of the encounter as the interpretive framework for approaching this canon, *Literary Optics* takes a step toward imploding this rhythm, carving out a space for the possibility of *turning to face the present*.

Notes

Bibliography

Index

Notes

Introduction

1. The critique of the trope of the encounter is expansive, cutting across the different confrontations with Eurocentrism. Here I offer some key texts that have been deeply generative for my understanding of the way the trope conditions the scholarly reception of nineteenth-century Arabic literature: James Morris Blaut, *The Colonizer's Model of the World: Geographical Diffusionism and Eurocentric History* (New York: Guilford, 1993); Samir Amin, *Eurocentrism: Modernity, Religion, and Democracy: A Critique of Eurocentrism and Culturalism*, trans. Russell Moore and James Membrez, 2nd ed. (Cape Town: Pambazuka, 2011); Gayatri Chakravorty Spivak, "Can the Subaltern Speak?," in *Marxism and the Interpretation of Culture*, ed. Cary Nelson and Lawrence Grossberg (Champaign: Univ. of Illinois Press, 1988), 271–313; Edward Said, *Orientalism* (London: Penguin, 1978); Sadiq Jalal Al-'Azm, *al-istishraq wa al-istishraq al-ma'kus* (Beirut: dar al-hadatha li al-tiba'a wa al-nashr, 1981); Nelly Hanna, *In Praise of Books: A Cultural History of Cairo's Middle Class, Sixteenth to the Eighteenth Century* (Syracuse, NY: Syracuse Univ. Press, 2003); Nelly Hanna, *Artisan Entrepreneurs in Cairo and Early-Modern Capitalism* (Syracuse, NY: Syracuse Univ. Press, 2011); Sabry Hafez, *The Genesis of Arabic Narrative Discourse: A Study in the Sociology of Modern Arabic Literature* (London: Saqi, 1993); Saad Albazei, *istiqbal al-akhar: al-gharb fi al-naqd al-'arabi al-hadith* (Beirut: al-markaz al-thaqafiyy al-'arabiyy, 2004); and Thomas Bauer, "Mamluk Literature: Misunderstandings and New Approaches," *Mamluk Studies Review* 9, no. 2 (2005): 104–32.

2. There are numerous examples of this assumption, dispersed across the study of literature, history, and positive law—and, in a different way, education. For literature, this has most famously been articulated as the "*maqama*-novel" debate. See Paul Starkey, *Modern Arabic Literature* (Edinburgh: Edinburgh Univ. Press, 2006), 98; Anshuman A. Mondal, "Between Turban and Tarbush: Modernity and the Anxieties of Transition in Hadith 'Isa Ibn Hisham," *Alif: Journal of Comparative Poetics*, no. 17 (1997): 220; Matti Moosa, *The Origins of Modern Arabic Fiction* (London: Lynne Rienner, 1997), 180–92; Roger Allen, "The Beginnings of the Arabic Novel," in *The Cambridge History of Arabic Literature; Modern Arabic Literature*, ed. M. M. Badawi (Cambridge: Cambridge Univ.

Press, 1997), 180–92; Mohamed-Salah Omri, "Local Narrative Form and Constructions of the Arabic Novel," *Novel: A Forum on Fiction* 41, nos. 2–3 (2008): 244–63; Jeffrey Sacks, "Futures of Literature: Inhitat, Adab, Naqd," *Diacritics* 37 (December 1, 2007): 32–55; Stephen Sheehi, *Foundations of Modern Arab Identity* (Gainesville: Univ. of Florida, 2004); Yoav Di-Capua, *Gatekeepers of the Arab Past: Historians and History Writing in Twentieth-Century Egypt* (Berkeley: Univ. of California Press, 2009), 37; and Samera Esmeir, *Juridical Humanity: A Colonial History* (Stanford, CA: Stanford Univ. Press, 2012).

3. Abdallah Laroui, *mafhum al-'aql: maqala fi al-mufaraqat* (Beirut: al-markaz al-thaqafiyy al-'arabiyy, 1996); Elias Khoury, "For a Third Nahda," in *Arabic Thought against the Authoritarian Age towards an Intellectual History of the Present*, ed. and trans. Jens Hansenn and Max Weiss (Cambridge: Cambridge Univ. Press, 2018), 357–69; Muhammad Misbahi, *jadaliyit al-'aql wa al-madina fi al-falsafa al-'arabiyya al-mu'asira* (Beirut: muntada al-ma'arif, 2013).

4. In thinking about problems of historicizing acts, I have benefited tremendously from being in conversation with the works of Etienne Balibar, Mahdi 'Amel, Nasr Hamid Abu Zayd, Roberto Schwarz, Massimiliano Tomba, and Michael McKeon. The debates on world literature offer a site for grappling with the intersection between history and the formation of our objects of knowledge (national literatures vs. world literature) as both a historical and theoretical problem.

5. Franco Moretti, "Conjectures on World Literature," *New Left Review*, no. 1 (February 1, 2000): 54–68; Ayman A. El-Desouky, "Beyond Spatiality: Theorising the Local and Untranslatability as Comparative Critical Method," in *Approaches to World Literature*, ed. Joachim Küpper, vol. 1 (Berlin: Akademie Verlag, 2013), 59–86; Nirvana Tanoukhi, "The Scale of World Literature," *New Literary History* 39, no. 3 (2008): 599–617; Emily Apter, *Against World Literature: On the Politics of Untranslatability* (New York: Verso, 2013); Emily Apter, "Untranslatables: A World System," *New Literary History* 39 (June 1, 2008): 581–98; Maya Kesrouany, *Prophetic Translation: The Making of Modern Egyptian Literature* (Edinburgh: Edinburgh Univ. Press, 2019); Frederic Jameson, "Third-World Literature in the Era of Multinational Capitalism," *Social Text* 15 (Autumn 1986): 65–88; Frederic Jameson, *Allegory and Ideology* (New York: Verso, 2019); Qin Wang, "Fredric Jameson's 'Third World Literature' and 'National Allegory': A Defense," *Frontiers of Literary Study in China* 7, no. 4 (2013): 654–71.

6. Mohamed-Salah Omri, "Local Narrative Form and Constructions of the Arabic Novel," *Novel: A Forum on Fiction* 41, nos. 2–3 (2008): 244–63; Samah Selim, *Popular Fiction, Translation, and the Nahda in Egypt* (London: Palgrave Macmillan, 2019).

7. Michael McKeon, *The Origins of the English Novel 1600–1740* (Baltimore, MD: Johns Hopkins Univ. Press, 1987). The debates on historicizing capital and the capitalist world system are another critical site where these comparable questions are also asked. See note 1 for some examples that have direct relevance for the history of modernity in the Arabic-speaking world.

8. Jonathan Kramnick and Anahid Nersessian, "Form and Explanation," *Critical Inquiry* 43 (Spring 2017): 650–69; Michael Allan, *In the Shadow of World Literature: Sites of Reading in Colonial Egypt* (Princeton, NJ: Princeton Univ. Press, 2016); Moretti, "Conjectures on World Literature."

9. Samah Selim, *Popular Fiction, Translation and the Nahda in Egypt* (London: Palgrave Macmillan, 2019), 2; emphasis mine.

10. Dipesh Chakrabarty, "Labor History and the Politics of Theory: An Indian Angle on the Middle East," in *Workers and Working Classes in the Middle East: Struggles, Histories, Historiographies*, ed. Zachary Lockman (New York: State Univ. of New York Press, 1994), 321–34; Dipesh Chakrabarty, *Provincializing Europe: Post-Colonial Thought and Historical Difference*, 2nd ed. (Princeton, NJ: Princeton Univ. Press, 2007); Timothy Mitchell, *Colonising Egypt* (Cambridge: Cambridge Univ. Press, 1988); Shaden M. Tageldin, *Disarming Words: Empire and the Seductions of Translation in Egypt* (Berkeley: Univ. of California Press, 2011); Isam al-Khafaji, *Tormented Births: Passages to Modernity in Europe and the Middle East* (London: Bloomsbury, 2004).

11. For a similar critique of how conflicting positions could be anchored by the same vision, see Mahdi 'Amel, *azmat al-hadara al-'arabiyya am azmat al-burjuwaziyat al-'arabiyya?* (Beirut: dar al-farabi, 1974); Nasr Hamid Abu Zayd, "qira'at al-turath fi kitabat ahmad sadiq s'ad," in *ishkaliyat al-takwin al-ijtima'iyy wa al-fikriyat al-sha'biyya fi Misr* (Damascus: dar kan'an li al-dirasat wa al-nashr, 1992); and Nasr Hamid Abu Zayd, "Nasr Abu Zayd yaktub 'an fashl al-tanwir al-hukumiyy nushirat fi akhbar al-adab 2005: suqut al-tanwir al-hukumiyy," Ruwaq Nasr Abu Zayd, April 11, 2009, https://rowaqnasrabuzaid.wordpress.com/2009/04/11/.

12. Ayman El-Desouky, *The Intellectual and the People in Egyptian Literature and Culture: Amāra and the 2011 Revolution* (London: Palgrave Pivot, 2011), 62.

13. Roberto Schwarz, *A Master on the Periphery of Capitalism: Machado de Assis*, trans. John Gledson (Durham, NC: Duke Univ. Press, 2001), continues to offer one of the most inspiring examples for grappling with ideas of the center and periphery while by-passing its culturalist trappings for literary studies and intellectual history.

14. Bauer, "Mamluk Literature"; Ahmed El Shamsy, *Rediscovering the Islamic Classics: How Editors and Print Culture Transformed an Intellectual Tradition* (Princeton, NJ: Princeton Univ. Press, 2020).

15. This position—aligning ourselves with or inside the canon—is not a stable one, existing outside of the analytic movements. Rather, I understand it as both a step in the analysis and a result of it. Michael McKeon, "A Defense of Dialectical Method in Literary History," *Diacritics* 19, no. 1 (1989): 83–96.

16. Muhammad Al-Muwaylihi, *hadith 'isa ibn hisham*, ed. Roger Allen (Cairo: al-mjlis al-a'la li al-thaqafa, 2002); Muhammad Al-Muwaylihi, *A Period of Time: A Study and Translation of* Hadith 'Isa Ibn Hisham *by Muhammad al-Muwaylihi*, ed. and trans. Roger Allen, 2nd ed. (Reading: Ithaca, 1992); Francis bin Fathallah Marrash, *ghabat al-haqq*,

2nd ed. (Beirut: matba'at al-qidis jawrijiyus li al-rum al-urthudhuks, 1881); Ali Mubarak, *'alam al-din* (Alexandria: matba'at jaridat al-mahrusa, 1882); Hasan Al-Tuwayrani, *al-nashr al-zahriyy fi rasa'il al-nisr al-dahriyy* (dar al-khilafa: matba'at mahmud bek, 1889); 'Abdallah al-Nadim, *majlis tibbi 'ala musab bil ifranji*, in *al-tankit wa al-tabkit* ("Raillery and Reproof"), no. 1 (June 6, 1881): 4–6. Also available in 'Abd al-'Azim Ramadan and 'Abd al-Mun'im Ibrahim al-Jumay'iyy, eds., *al-tankit wa al-tabkit* (Cairo: al-hay'a al-misriyya al-'amma li al-kitab, 1994), 37–39.

17. We, unfortunately, do not know much about the journal other than it was published in Istanbul and probably ran from 1880 to at least 1886, but we are yet to find issues from it. Project Jaraid, https://projectjaraid.github.io/pages/chrono.html (accessed January 6, 2023).

18. Ahmad Ibrahim Al-Hawari, *naqd al-mujtama' fi hadith 'isa ibn hisham li al-muwaylihi*, 2nd ed. (Cairo: dar al-ma'arif, 1986); Allen, *A Period of Time*; M. M. Badawi, *Early Arabic Drama* (Cambridge: Cambridge Univ. Press, 1988); Muhammad Mustafa Badawi, ed., *Modern Arabic Literature* (Cambridge: Cambridge Univ. Press, 1995); Jurji Zaydan, *tarikh 'adaab al-lugha al-'arabiyya* (Windsor: Hindawi, 2017); Ahmed Taymur Pasha, *tarajim a'yan al-qarn al-thalith 'ashar Wa 'awa'il al-qarn al-rabi' 'ashar* (Cairo: dar al-'afaq al-'arabiyya, 2001); Albert Hourani, *Arabic Thought in the Liberal Age, 1798–1939* (Cambridge: Cambridge Univ. Press, 1983); Jens Hansenn and Max Weiss, eds., *Arabic Thought beyond the Liberal Age: Towards an Intellectual History of the Nahda* (Cambridge: Cambridge Univ. Press, 2016); Tageldin, *Disarming Words*; Samah Selim, *The Novel and the Rural Imaginary in Egypt, 1880-1985* (London: Routledge Curzon, 2004).

19. These features were read by the early histories as indicators that these texts are not yet modern, but somewhere between the traditional and the modern. Revisionist scholarship tended to focus on questions of "ideology" without necessarily paying close attention to issues of narrative form. One thing that is not spelled out in either body of scholarship is that the importance of, for example, plot, characters, and character development, is owed to the way in which they have come to mark what is unique to modern literature as the modern novel in variants of formalist and structuralist thought from Mikhail Bakhtin to Northrop Frye to contemporary historical narratology. In fact, the "*maqama* novel" debate is actually a "replay" of the "romance novel" debate in English literature. The formal features of the *maqama* have not always played a central role in that debate; it is primarily a placeholder for the novel's premodern "negative."

20. See Mahdi 'Amel, *muqaddimat nazariyya Li-dirasat athar al-fikr al-ishtirakiyy fi harakat al-taharrur al-watani* (Beirut: dar al-farabi, 1980) for a discussion of a similar idea, particularly in the introduction; Nasr Hamid Abu Zayd, *al-ittijah al-'aqliyy fi al-tafsir: dirasa fi qadiyat al-majaz fi al-qur'an 'ind al-mu'tazila*, 3rd ed. (Beirut: al-markaz al-thaqafiyy al-'arabiyy, 1996), also brushes with this idea in his treatment of the historical context of the emergence of Mu'tazalite thought.

1. The Literary Optic

1. This is a simplified typology that we often find dispersed across works of formalism and early structuralism. Historical narratology is particularly apt at fleshing out this idea, which we locate in a more dispersed form elsewhere. We also implicitly find this typology in the studies of nineteenth-century Arabic literature itself. Monika Fludernik, *The Fictions of Language and the Languages of Fiction* (London: Routledge, 1993); 'Abdullah Ibrahim, *mawsu'at al-sard al-'arabiyy*, 9 vols. (Dubai: qindeel li al-tiba'a wa al-nashr wa al- tawzi', 2016).

2. Eve Trout Powell, *A Different Shade of Colonialism: Egypt, Great Britain, and the Mastery of the Sudan* (Los Angeles: Univ. of California Press, 2003); Samah Selim, "Languages of Civilization: Nation, Translation and the Politics of Race in Colonial Egypt," *Translator* 16 (April 2009): 139–56. Translations of geography books offer a good site for analyzing this cartographic imaginary of linear time of civilizational progress. See, for example, Rifa'a Rafi' Al-Tahtawi, *al-kanz al-mukhtar fi kashf al-aradi wa al-bihar*, 2nd ed. (Torah: matba'at al-tubajiya, 1835); and 'Ali Mubarak's various geographic works in *rawdat al-madaris (Cairo: 1870–1877)*, ed. Ali Fahmy. Mubarak's *haqa'iq al-akhbar fi al-kashf 'an asrar al-bihar* was serialized from the first year of the journal but with some intermissions. Peter Hill, *Utopia and Civilization in the Arab Nahda* (Cambridge: Cambridge Univ. Press, 2019), especially chapter 3.

3. The relationship between these three categories—"history," "science," and "literature"—is central to modern literature and is often meticulously studied in works on the history of modern English literature. See Michael McKeon, *The Origins of the English Novel, 1600–1740* (Baltimore, MD: Johns Hopkins Univ. Press, 1987); Jonathan Kramnick, "Empiricism, Cognitive Science, and the Novel," *Eighteenth Century* 48, no. 3, special issue, "Empiricism, Substance, Narrative" (Fall 2007): 263–85; and George Levine, *Dying to Know: Scientific Epistemology and Narrative in Victorian England* (Chicago: Univ of. Chicago Press, 2002). To my knowledge, the connection is not the focus of extended studies on narrative structure and form in nineteenth-century Arabic literature, but we see snippets about changes in history and science in these works: Yoav Di-Capua, *Gatekeepers of the Arab Past: Historians and History Writing in Twentieth-Century Egypt* (Berkeley: Univ. of California Press, 2009); Mitchell, *Colonising Egypt* (Cambridge: Cambridge Univ. Press, 1989); Marwa Elshakry, *Reading Darwin in Arabic, 1860–1950* (Chicago: Univ. of Chicago Press, 2013); and Omnia El-Shakry, *The Great Social Laboratory: Subjects of Knowledge in Colonial and Post-Colonial Egypt* (Stanford, CA: Stanford Univ. Press, 2007). The connection between these trends and literature is yet to be fully explored.

4. Elshakry, *Reading Darwin in Arabic*.

5. Marrash, "Forest," 1–5. We will return to this scene in more details in chapter 2, where we will also explore the consistent use of these terms throughout Marrash's "Forest."

"أما أنا فرأيت المحل الذي أشغله لم يعد مناسباً لحق المعاينة والاستماع .6
لكون انظاري لا يعود أن يمكنها الإحاطة بجميع الأشباح وآذاني صارت تعجز عن إيفاء حق السمع لما
استجد من الضوضاء فتركت هذا المحل وأطلقت خطوات التجسس حتى بلغت الجمهور المحتفل
وانخرطت في سلك الأشخاص اللاحقين من حيث لم يشعروا بقدومي." (Marrash, 95–96)

"As for me, I saw that the place I am occupying was no longer suitable for adequate sensory apprehension because my vision is no longer capable of perceiving all the ghosts and my ears became unable to properly hear because of the noise that was being made now. And so, I left this place, and I followed the steps of wonder until I reached the gathered audience, and I mingled with these persons without them sensing that I had arrived."

7. James E. Montgomery, *The Vagaries of the Qaṣīdah: The Tradition and Practice of Early Arabic Poetry*, Gibb Literary Studies, no. 1 (Oxford: E. J. W. Gibb Memorial Trust, 1997). In his *kitab al-shi'r*, Averroes famously touches on the importance of the ruin and the specter of the beloved to Arabic poetry, a connection relevant to our discussion of *khayal* later in this chapter. Ibn Rushd, *talkhis kitab al-shi'r*, ed. Charles Butterworth and Ahmad 'Abd Al-Majid Haridi (Cairo: al-hay'a al-misriyya al-'amma li al-kitab, 1986), 94–97; Averroes, *Middle Commentary on Aristotle's* Poetics, trans. Charles Butterworth, 2nd ed. (Chicago: St. Augustine, 1999).

8. Al-Tuwayrani, "Floral Publishing," 4–5.

9. Al-Tuwayrani, 23.

10. Al-Tuwayrani, 32.

11. Al-Tuwayrani, 5–6, 9, 16, 17, 35, 41, 66, 126. This is not an exhaustive list of all the instances where these terms appear. Rather, it is a small selection of particularly suggestive moments that offer condensed examples of relationships that are otherwise dispersed throughout the text and require reading the text in its entirely to fully grasp. The point is equally true of the examples I select from other texts.

12. During this long history, the genre underwent numerous changes, if not reinventions; see Jaakko Hämeen-Anttila, *Maqama: A History of a Genre* (Wiesbaden: Harrassowitz Verlag, 2002); James T. Monroe and Mark F. Pettigrew, "The Decline of Courtly Patronage and the Appearance of New Genres in Arabic Literature: The Case of the Zajal, the Maqāma, and the Shadow Play," *Journal of Arabic Literature* 34, nos. 1–2 (2003): 138–77; and James T. Monroe, *The Art of Badi' Az-Zaman al-Hamadhani as Picaresque Narrative* (Beirut: American Univ. of Beirut, 1983). Allen shows that Muwaylihi used this framing technique for some of his articles prior to embarking on the series we now know as *hadith*. For more on the reception of the *maqama* in the nineteenth century, see Bilal W. Orfali and Maurice Pomerantz, *The Maqamat of Badi' Al-Zaman al-Hamadhani: Authorship, Texts, Contexts* (Berlin: Reichert Verlag, 2022), 2–9, 39–41. The book also offers a more general history of the formation of the canon of Hamadhani's *maqamat*. I am grateful to Bilal al-Orfali and Maurice Pomerantz for generously sharing the book with me prior to its publication.

13. Ahmed Pasha al-Manikli appears to be part of Muhammad 'Ali's close circle, according to Afaf Lutfi Al-Sayyid Marsot, *Egypt in the Reign of Muhammad Ali* (Cambridge: Cambridge Univ. Press, 1984), 78–79.

I haven't been able to dig up too much information on him, although he is regularly—though briefly—mentioned in works on the "Egyptian rule" of al-Sudan. I found his dates of birth and death through looking his position as the governor (*hikimdar*) in Sudan between 1844 and 1846. https://www.worldstatesmen.org/Sudan.html (accessed January 12, 2022). He fought as part of Egypt's wars in Syria, Qurm (Crimea), and Sudan, but was removed from all positions by Said Pasha (1822–1863, r. 1854–63). These details complicate the timeline offered by Muwaylihi's *hadith*, where Ahmed Pasha assumes that he is still living in the reign of Muhammad 'Ali, when the latter clearly passed away before Ahmed Pasha. This detail, however, is actually helpful, because it halts any simple equation between the narrative and historical lines and allows us to understand the function of the Ahmed al-Manikli pasha to rest on the fact that he comes from the past, in particular from the era of Muhammad Ali.

14. Roger Allen, ed. and trans., *A Period of Time: A Study and Translation of* Hadith 'Isa Ibn Hisham *by Muhammad al-Muwaylihi*, 2nd ed. (Beirut: Ithaca, 1995), 117; Al-Muwaylihi, *hadith*, 140.

15. I am not merely referring to the use of word but to its suggestive conceptual moments that enable us to read instances where the term is mentioned more passingly such as these two:

(Muwaylihi, 123) ."وشاعر يشعر فيه بمثل طيف الخيال من لطف الخيال"

And "وتركوا الحقيقة إلى الخيال" (152).

In the next section, we will see how these two instances are reminiscent of the ode and shadow play, respectively.

16. Roger Allen traces the history of the book's publication (*Period of Time*, 32–48).

17. Muwaylihi does not tell us much about these characters in his dedication, but we do know that their paths crossed in the 1870s and, more violently, during the 'Urabi revolt (1881) whose effects on political thought unfolded on the scale of the Ottoman Empire, not just Egypt, and also beyond, as Egypt's bankruptcy and occupation offered a model for Marxist thinkers, like Rosa Luxemburg and others, to rethink imperialism and its functioning. To return to our characters, Afghani, Abduh, and the Muwaylihis (father and son) were all exiled at around the same time to Istanbul—Ahmed Faris al-Shidyaq, whom we will encounter later in this chapter, was already based there. Together, Abduh and the Muwaylihis started a venture for publishing classical works of Arabic literature while they were there. Barudi, a famous poet and political activist, died in exile in Sri Lanka in the wake of the defeat of the 'Urabi revolt by the British and their occupation of Egypt. Al-Shanqiti appears to be the least studied member of this group. Tracing substantial information about him was difficult, though I believe he is the linguist and Azharite mentioned by Rashid Rida in *al-manar* as the person who read Abduh's *risalat al-tawhid* and

debated him on some of its ideas, particularly those pertaining to the positions taken by the Mu'tazalites. *al-manar*, 25 (September 6, 1898); Julian Ricardo Cole, *Colonialism and Revolution in the Middle East* (Princeton, NJ: Princeton Univ. Press, 1992); AbdelAziz EzzelArab, "The Experiment of Sharif Pasha's Cabinet (1879): An Inquiry into the Historiography of Egypt's Elite Movement," *International Journal of Middle East Studies* 36, no. 4 (November 2004): 561–89; Latifa Muhammad Salim, *al-quwa al-ijtima'iyya fi al-thawra al-'urabiyya* (Cairo: dar el shorouk, 2009); Terri de Young, *Mahmud Sami Al-Barudi: Reconfiguring Society and the Self* (Syracuse, NY: Syracuse Univ. Press, 2015).

18. The combination of *takhyil* and *taswir* has a long history in Arabic. It pertains to the comparison between poetry and painting—which will be briefly touched upon in this chapter through the conceptual history of *khayal*. Muwaylihi refers to this comparison in a series of editorials on the modern press, "Kalam fi al-matbu'at," *misbah al-sharq* 157 (June 7, 1901), where he refers to painting as *taswir*. Later in this chapter, we will see how Shidyaq also references this comparison. Significantly, in Farah Antun's (1874–1922) famous novel *al-mudun al-thalath: al- 'ilm, al-din, al-mal* (1903), which has close formal and thematic connections to Marrash's "Forest," the main character, Halim, is presented as a *musawwir* (painter). In another important debate, *misbah al-sharq* discusses the difference between poetic and Quranic language *misbah al-sharq* 175 (September 20, 1901)

19. Al-Muwaylihi, *hadith*, 525. Going by the tendency to translate *takhyil* not just as the evocation of images, but also as "make-believe," one could translate this as the make-believe of the rule of the king. But I have opted for emphasizing the spectral and haunting sense involved here, since the point revolves on how the attempt at self-rule ironically finds itself forced to resurrect a spectral form of the rule of the king (i.e., a presidential system), as if the king returns to haunt the new regime of power that had replaced him.

20. Working specifically with *takhyil*, Wolfhart Heinrichs charts out five main locations where the term is used: 1) philosophical poetics, which he defines as the creation of an in image by the poet in the mind of the listener, though it also includes affective and active dimensions that we will discuss later; 2) the rhetoric of poetry (giving the impression of praising while one is lampooning and vice versa; e.g., the poetry appears to be doing something but is in fact doing the opposite); 3) the theory of imagery as a part of poetics, he defines (takhyil in this instance) as a "phantasmagorical re-interpretation of a fact in poetry"; 4) Quranic exegesis, where it refers to the visual anthropomorphic representation of an abstract notion, or what I will describe as a transaction between the nonsensory and the sensory; and, finally, 5) a rhetorical figure, used as a synonym of *tawriya*. See Heinrichs, "Introduction," in *Takhyil: The Imaginary in Classical Arabic Poetics*, vol. 2, ed. Geert Jan Van Gelder and Marle Hammond (Oxford: Oxbow, 2008), 1–14. For more on how the equation between *takhyil* and *tawriya* might have started in Arabic through Farsi as an attempt to avoid extending *takhyil* to the Quran that ironically results in the equivocation of *takhyil, iham,* and *tawriya*, see Ahmad Sakhr Achtar, "Contact between Theology, Hermeneutics, and Literary Theory: The Role of Majaz in the Interpretation of the

Anthropomorphic Verses in the Quran from the 2nd AH/8th CE until the 7th AH/13th CE" (PhD diss., London, SOAS, Univ. of London, 2012), 261–62. That the disagreements over the term are not just "technical" but political is an issue that will continue to pop up in our discussion. In his entry in the *Encyclopedia of Islam*, Heinrichs focuses in particular on the theory of imagery, where he discovers irreconcilable differences within this single field and consequently concludes that the different iterations he examined have little to do with one another. He makes the point once more in his introduction to the *takhyil* volume, arguing that al-Razi and al-Sakkaki's use of the terms (in the adjectival form *isti'ara takhyiliyya*) "has little do with al-Jurjani's notion" (13). In other words, even the same term within a single field could come to accrue different connotations through time or in shifts in the intellectual concerns of the specific thinker(s). In the context of our canon, this challenge appears in an amplified form, as we saw above. Wolfhart Heinrichs, "Takhyil," *Encyclopaedia of Islam*, accessed January 20, 2022, https://referenceworks.brillonline.com/entries/encyclopaedia-of-islam-2/takhyil-COM_1156?s.num=157&s.start=140; Wolfhart Heinrichs, "'Takhyil' and Its Traditions," in *Gott Ist Schnund Er Liebt Die Schnheit Festschrift Für Annemarie Schimmel*, ed. Alma Giese and J. Chr. Bürgel (Berne: Peter Lang AG, 1994), 227–47. I suggest that we expand Heinrichs's category of "philosophic poetics" to include both other works within this tradition that deal with the soul (of the *De Anima* variety), with epistemology (this includes logic, but also books of rhetoric in addition, of course, to (Poetics), and politics (this includes both Ethics and the Virtuous City) as well as philosophic strands of Sufism, particularly the work of Ibn 'Arabi. Yet one of the challenges of the schema presented by Heinrichs is that sometimes it registers a use by a single author. For example, number 2, in the rhetoric of poetry, is used in this sense only by Abu Hilal al-'Askari. While this type of rhetorical reversal between the apparent and real is discussed both before him and after him, he is the only example, mentioned by Heinrichs or others, who uses *takhyil* in this sense. Similarly, use number 3 is accredited exclusively to 'Abd al-Qahir al-Jurjani, since Heinrichs argues that the later uses (by al-Razi and al-Sakkaki, for example) are different. Per Heinrichs's argument, Jurjani is the only one who uses *takhyil* in the theory of imagery in this way. Heinrichs makes the same argument about use 4 in Quranic exegesis, saying that the term's use by al-Zamakhshari "is clearly not related to al-Jurjani's" (13), a point that Achtar argues against showing the term's use in Quranic exegesis to be a deployment of al-Jurjani's notion of it, but in a different site (216–17). The possibility that some of these uses might be connected—particularly use 1 in philosophic poetics, and use 3 in theory of imagery—has also been tacitly suggested by Margaret Larkin in *The Theology of Meaning: 'Abd al-Qahir al-Jurjani's Theory of Discourse* (New Haven, CT: American Oriental Society, 1995); and Lara Harb, *Arabic Poetics: Aesthetic Experience in Classical Arabic Literature* (Cambridge: Cambridge Univ. Press, 2020). We find the same suggestion—though in a different way—in Gabir Asfour, *al-sura al-fanniyya fi al-turath al-naqdiyy wa al-balaghiyy 'ind al-'arab*, 3rd ed. (Beirut: al-markaz al-thaqafiyy al-'arabiyy, 1992). In her review of the *takhyil* volume Rebecca Gould points to the long-held belief in the nonconvergence between the two separate paths charted by *Balagha* "Arabic literary theory" based on grammar and philology and philosophical poetics influenced by Neoplatonic and Aristotelian traditions. The decision, then, to juxtapose the two in the volume "may be seen to argue for the fundamental interrelatedness, which is not yet isomorphism, between *balagha* and *falsafah*. Though best known to scholars of comparative literary theory as one of the Arabic terms for Aristotelian mimesis (other equivalents being *tashbih* and *muhakah*), *takhyil* also entered *balagha* as the equivalent of *iham*. Watwat is our first and one of our best sources for the convergence between *iham* and *takhyil*, and thus between *falsafah* and *balagha*." Rebecca Gould, "Book Review: Takhyīl: The Imaginary in Classical Arabic Poetics. Volume 1: Texts Volume 2: Studies by Geert Jan van Gelder; Marlé Hammond," *Journal of Arabic Literature* 41, no. 3 (2010): 327–30.

21. *Takhyil* "literally" lacks an original in as much as its advent through philosophic poetics is a translation for a "nonexisting" original in Aristotle; the point is often attributed to the inclusion of the *Poetics* in the Organon, which resulted in carving out a poetic syllogism to justify its inclusion. Deborah L. Black, *Logic and Aristotle's Rhetoric and Poetics in Medieval Arabic Philosophy* (Leiden: E. J. Brill, 1990); Anne Sheppard, "Preface," in *Takhyil: The Imaginary in Classical Arabic Poetics*, ed. Marle Hammond and Geert Jan Van Gelder (Oxford: Oxbow, 2008), 1:ix–xv.

22. Such as *mimesis* or the *phantasma*, and in the nineteenth-century imagination or fancy—and, by extension, the fictional. My point is not that *khayal* is disconnected from these terms, but that simply rendering it into one or the other does not actually historicize it and therefore cannot explicate it.

23. In its canonical form, the ode is comprised of three thematic units: 1) *nasib*; 2) *rahil*, or departure, where the poet embarks on a lone journey with his camel as his sole companion; and 3) the *madih*, eulogy, made to a famous leader or patron—or even to the poet himself—ascribing to the eulogized seminal valorized virtues. *Tayf al-khayal* belongs to the first thematic unit, the *nasib*.

24. The problem of identity and identification is, as expected, a big motif here: Renate Jacobi, "The 'Khayal' Motif in Early Arabic Poetry," *Oriens* 32 (1990): 50–64,; Renate Jacobi, "Al-Khayalani-a Variation of the Khayal Motif," *Journal of Arabic Literature* 27, no. 1 (1996): 2–12. This trope is suggestive for thinking about Heinrich's use 2 in the rhetoric of poetry, where something appears one way but then shifts to another. This point is crucial for grasping *khayal* not so much as a still image (*sura* in the sense of both the form of an idea, and a visual object), but as one that entails movement of thought—an issue that I will discuss later as "crossing." In fact, we can see the movement of thought or crossing as the conceptual anchor of *khayal*'s visual and linguistic dimensions in as much as visuality, and vividness, prepare the audience for the reception of the meaning of ideas. The connection between the visual, vividness, and thought is discussed in the Greek context in Sheppard, "Preface." I won't exhaust this point here, though it will come up once more in relation to the nineteenth century.

25. Li Guo, *Arabic Shadow Theatre, 1300–1900: A Handbook* (Leiden: E. J. Brill, 2020). *Khayal* also seems to have potentially referred to live performance in general. This point is also made in Arnoud Vrolijk, ed., *Bringing a Laugh to a Scowling Face: A Study and Critical Edition of the "nuzhat al-nufus wa-mudhik al-'abus" by 'Ali Ibn Sudun al-Basbugawi (Cairo 810/1407-Damascus 868/1464)* (Leiden: Research School CNWS, School of Asian, African & Amerindian Studies, 1998). Ibn Daniyal used both *khayal* and *khayal al-dhill* synonymously to refer to shadow plays, though the common scholarly consensus is that eventually the latter came to refer to shadow plays replacing the use of *khayal* on its own.

26. Guo, *Arabic Shadow Theatre*, 3–5. Ibn al-Haytham discusses shadow plays as an attempt to explain perception as part of his contribution to the field of Optics. Paul Kahle, "The Arabic Shadow Play in Egypt," *Journal of the Royal Asiatic Society of Great Britain and Ireland*, no. 1 (1940): 21–34; Shmuel Moreh, "The Shadow Play ('Khayal al-Zill') in the Light of Arabic Literature," *Journal of Arabic Literature* 18 (1987): 46–61.

27. Li Guo, *The Performing Arts in Medieval Islam: Shadow Play and Popular Poetry in Ibn Daniyal's Mamluk Cairo* (Leiden: E. J. Brill, 2012) has a translation of Ibn Daniyal's *The Phantom*.

28. Guo, *Performing Arts in Medieval Islam*, 220. Li Guo's translation of *majaz* as metaphor, rather than its more accurate translation as the tropical or the figurative, highlights how Ibn Daniyal's discourse "combines" the lexicographic/grammatical stream of *khayal* discussions with the supposedly more idealistic (philosophic) stream, uniting the two around questions of narration-performance. One thing to keep in mind is that poetry is also performative. That the two streams may be more connected than was first assumed is something Lara Harb suggests several times, particularly as she touches upon Aristotle's own discussions of metaphor. It is useful to point out that the use of the term *khayal* to refer to performance in general in Arabic as well as its configuration around shadow plays might contribute to how we approach their preceding critical debates from the perspective of their "afterlife."

29. Guo, 105–7; Guo, *Arabic Shadow Theatre*, 5–7.

30. Heinrichs also mentions this meaning in Gelder and Hammond, *Takhyil*.

31. This is a point that is both made and performed by Nasr Hamid Abu Zayd throughout his intellectual oeuvre; for a particularly suggestive (and lesser-known) work, see Nasr Hamid Abu Zayd, "The Hermeneutic Aspect of Sibawaihi's Grammar," *Alif: Journal of Comparative Poetics* 8 (Spring 1988): 82–117. For another thought-provoking discussion on how to write intellectual history—though it actually deals with the history of ("Western") philosophy—see Sadiq Jalal Al-'Azm, *difa'an 'an al-madiyya wa al-tarikh: thalath muhawarat falsafiyya, mudakhala naqdiyya muqaraba fi tarikh al-falsafa al-haditha wal-mu'asira* (Beirut: dar al-fikr al-jadid, 1990).

32. These are the seminal studies I draw on for the following discussion, in addition to my reading of the primary sources. Since our principal aim is to provide background

for the nineteenth-century debates, I have opted to use the following footnotes strategically, pointing readers to which sources they might want to consult to further pursue a point I make, or to respond to some "confusion" that may arise for readers familiar with these discussions because of the large brushstroke approach undertaken here. Wolfhart Heinrichs, "On the Genesis of the Haqiqa-Majaz Dichotomy," *Studia Islamica*, no. 59 (1984): 111–40; Wolfhart Heinrichs, "On the Figurative (Majaz) in Muslim Interpretation and Legal Hermeneutics," in *Interpreting Scriptures in Judaism, Christianity, and Islam: Overlapping Enquiries*, ed. Mordechai Z. Cohen and Adele Berlin (Cambridge: Cambridge Univ. Press, 2016), 249–65; Wolfhart Heinrichs, "The Classification of the Sciences and the Consolidation of Philology in Classical Islam," in *Centers of Learning: Learning and Location in Pre-Modern Europe and the Near East* (Leiden: Brill, 1995), 119–39; Wolfhart Heinrichs, *The Hand of the Northwind: Opinions on Metaphor and the Early Meaning of Isti'ara in Arabic Poetics* (Wiesbaden: Deutsche Morgenlandische Gesellschaft, Kommissions-verlag Franz Steiner GmbH, 1977); Wolfhart Heinrichs, "Contacts between Scriptural Hermeneutics and Literary Theory in Islam: The Case of Majaz," *Zeitschrift Fur Geschichte Der Arabisch-Islamischen Wissenschaften* 7 (92 1991): 253–84; Wolfhart Heinrichs, "Isti'arah and Badi' and Their Terminological Relationship in Early Arabic Literary Criticism," *Zeitschrift Für Geschichte Der Arabisch-Islamische Wissenschaften* 1 (1984): 180–211; Alexander Key, *Language between God and the Poets: Ma'na in the Eleventh Century* (Berkeley: Univ. of California Press, 2018); Mustafa Shah, "The Philological Endeavours of the Early Arabic Linguists: Theological Implications of the Tawqif-Istilaḥ Antithesis and the Majaz Controversy-Part I," *Journal of Quranic Studies* 1, no. 1 (1999): 27–46; Mustafa Shah, "Classical Islamic Discourse on the Origins of Language: Cultural Memory and the Defense of Orthodoxy," *Numen* 58 (2011): 314–44; Robert M. Gleave, "Conceptions of the Literal Sense (ẓāhir, ḥaqīqa) in Muslim Interpretive Thought," in *Interpreting Scriptures in Judaism, Christianity and Islam: Overlapping Inquiries*, ed. Mordechai Z. Cohen and Adele Berlin (Cambridge: Cambridge Univ. Press, 2016), 183–203; Robert M. Gleave, *Islam and Literalism: Literal Meaning and Interpretation in Islamic Legal Theory* (Edinburgh: Edinburgh Univ. Press, 2013); Peter Adamson and Alexander Key, "Philosophy of Language in Medieval Arabic Tradition," in *Linguistic Content: New Essays on the History of Philosophy of Language*, ed. Margaret Cameron and Robert J. Stainton (Oxford: Oxford Univ. Press, 2015), 75–108; Hossein Modarressi, "Some Recent Analyses of the Concept of Majāz in Islamic Jurisprudence," *Journal of the American Oriental Society* 106, no. 4 (1986): 787–91; Bernard G. Weiss, "Medieval Muslim Discussions of the Origins of Language," *Zeitschrift Der Deutschen Morgenlandischen Gesellschaft* 124, no. 1 (1974): 33–41; Bernard G. Weiss, "Text and Application: Hermeneutical Reflections on Islamic Legal Interpretation," in *The Law Applied: Contextualizing the Islamic Shari'a—A Volume in Honor of Frank E. Vogel*, ed. Peri Bearman and Wolfhart Heinrichs (New York: I. B. Tauris, 2008), 374–96; and Abu Zayd, *al-ittijah al-'aqliyy fi al-tafsir: dirasa fi qadiyat al-majaz fi al-qur'an 'ind al-mu'tazila*.

33. Music is analyzed using linguistic tools, and painting and writing are often compared.

34. Assuming that expressions in language can unfold in two principal ways: the first uses language in accordance with its original configurations (regardless of whether the latter was instituted through divine ordinance or per a primordial social agreement), and the other changes, or reconfigures, the original—either by deploying already existing reconfigurations (these may be ancient, but they still diverge from the postulated original) or by introducing new reconfigurations. These are often the debates on *majaz* and *haqiqa* or *istilah wa tawqif*, but I have not referred to them in those terms because I am after the general schema and not the specifics of these debates as they unfold across different knowledge producing discourses through time.

35. Alexander Key, *Language between God and the Poets: Ma'na in the Eleventh Century* (California: Univ. of California Press, 2018).

36. Another way of explaining this is that I am not necessarily assuming an autochthonous conceptual world, or a shared cultural sensibility of which what I analyze here are examples. In other words, we do not begin with an original meaning, but we can abstract a core meaning. These are two very different ideas about how to write intellectual history, whereby in the first case we have an original meaning whose history of transformations we can trace—and in the absence of such an original founding meaning for *khayal*, it becomes difficult to think any possible connection of its myriad instantiations. The other assumes that seemingly original meanings are not absolute givens, but abstractions that are forged out of the different activations of the term that may or may not lead to a seemingly settled conceptual delineation that appears to be the original. In other words, the core meaning I present here is not the predecessor of the debates on *khayal*, but a retrospective abstraction of the different instantiations that I read not as "examples" of this already existing abstract sense, but as sites and instances that forge this abstract sense. This might be a useful way of thinking about conceptual language in general, where its abstract meaning is never fully embodied in any given one example (the debates on a seemingly more removed example like "class" are incredibly useful in this regard). In a very different vein, the seeming difficulty of defining "realism" or "the novel" in Arabic is a related instance in which we treat these texts as "examples" rather than as sites of intervention through which we forge and nuance an abstraction.

37. Shah, "Philological Endeavours of the Early Arabic Linguists"; Abu Zayd, *al-ittijah al-'aqliyy fi al-tafsir: dirasa fi qadiyat al-majaz fi al-qur'an 'ind al-mu'tazila*; Heinrichs, "On the Genesis of the Haqiqa-Majaz Dichotomy."

38. Li Guo refers to how Jurjani, Ghazali, Ibn 'Arabi used ideas of the "shadow" to describe metaphorical meanings for Jurjani and metaphysical world view for the latter two. These examples are crucial for *khayal*'s indexical field (*Performing Arts in Medieval Islam*, 106).

39. There are other issues pertaining to the likelihood of the image. In other words, while we understand that it did not happen, is it likely that it could? Yet these standards of "logical" probability and poetic canonicity are not absolutely separate, for the realm of what is acceptable, and passable within the logic of poetry, is also conditioned by canonized poetic examples. Harb, *Arabic Poetics*, 35–44.

40. Harb, 35, 41.

41. Harb, 43.

42. Gelder and Hammond, *Takhyil*; Harb, *Arabic Poetics*; Larkin, *Theology of Meaning*.

43. I do not intend to hearken back to the typical argument that, save for Ibn Rushd, the Arabic philosophic tradition did not fully engage with Arabic poetry; Lara Harb already demonstrates a different way of factoring in the effect of poetic production on their ideas.

44. The conception of *khayal* in Jurjani and the philosophers is rarely thought of alongside Ibn al-'Arabi, which might be due to issues of periodization.

45. Allen, *Period of Time*, 140–42; Al-Muwaylihi, *hadith*, 164–68.

46. Ideas about *khayal* are dispersed throughout Ibn al-'Arabi's oeuvre and are thoroughly studied by Nasr Hamid Abu Zayd, *falsafat al-ta'wil: dirasa fi ta'wil al-Quran 'ind muhyi al-din ibn 'arabi*, 5th ed. (Beirut: al-markaz al-thaqafiyy al-arabiyy, 2005). The classic study remains Henry Corbin, *Creative Imagination in the Sufism of Ibn Arabi*, trans. Ralph Manheim (Princeton, NJ: Princeton Univ. Press, 1969). For readers unfamiliar with Ibn al-Arabi's work, this quote is a distilled introduction into his reconfiguration of *khayal*:

"الخيال هذه حقيقته، أن يجسد ما ليس من شأنه أن يكون جسداً، وذلك لأن حضرته تعطي ذلك، وما ثمَّ في طبقات العالم من يعطي الأمر على ما هو عليه سوى هذه الحضرة الخيالية، فإنها تجمع بين النقيضين، وفيها تظهر الحقائق على ما هي عليه . . . هذه الحضرة كالجسر بين شطين، للعبور عليه من هذا الشط إلى هذا الشط . . . ولهذا قال الله أموراً واقعة في ظاهر الحس وقال: (فاعتبروا) وقال (إن في ذلك لعبرة) أي جوزوا واعبروا مما ظهر لكم من ذلك، إلى علم ما بطن به وما جاء له"

The excerpt above taps into and reconfigures various Arab knowledge producing discourses including Fiqh, Sufism, Arabic language sciences, and Quranic exegesis. Their discussion in this chapter will tackle these layers. Ideally, their translation would capture both their resonance and divergence from other discourses. What I offer here is not such a translation, but a paraphrasing of their meaning into English. "This is the truth/actuality of *khayal*; it enables the embodiment of the noncorporeal. That is because its *hadra* (presence) offers that. There isn't a thing in the orders of the world that offers the matter for what it is except this *khayali hadra* (presence). It brings together opposites. In it, the actualities appear for what they are. This *hadra* is like a bridge between two shores, for crossing through it from this shore to this shore. . . . That is why God spoke of matters occuring in the apparent sensory realm and said: 'Learn (cross) from this'; meaning traverse (*juzu*) and cross from what appears to you to the knowledge of what lies beneath and what it came for." This passage is quoted in Mahmud Ghurab, *al-khayal: 'alam al-barzakh wa al-mithal: min kalam al-shaykh al-akbar, muhyi al-din ibn al-'arabi*, 2nd ed. (Damascus: dar al-kitab al-'arabiyy, 1993), 63–64. Ibn al-'Arabi's use of both khayal and khayal al-dhill is discussed by Guo, *Performing Arts in Medieval Islam*, 106.

47. Muhammad Mahjub, *al-madina wa al-khayal: dirasat farabiyya* (Tunis: dar al-'ahd al-jadid, 1989).

48. Syed Rizwan Zamir, "Tafsir Al-Quran Bi-l-Quran": The Hermeneutics of Imitation and 'Adab' in Ibn 'Arabi's Interpretation of the Quran," *Islamic Studies* 50, no. 1 (2011): 5–23.

49. For a discussion of "original human disposition" (*fitra*) at the intersection of jurisprudence (*fiqh*) and politics, see Abdallah Laroui, *mafhum al-dawla* (Beirut: al-markaz al-thaqafiyy al-'arabiyy, 2011), 134–41. Ibn al-'Arabi's "*fitra*" is a crossing toward *al-insan al-kamil* as the one "in the image of God".

50. This is quite literally what a *hadra* is for Ibn al-'Arabi; that's why he often says *hadrat al-khayal*, but the understanding of presence and what is made present could not be more different.

51. Abu 'Ali Ibn Sina, *sharh kitab al-musiqa*, ed. Ghattas 'Abd al-Malik Khashaba (Cairo: al-majlis al-a'la li al-thaqafa, 2004), 21, 25–26, 93–94, 143–56.

52. Ibn Sina, *sharh kitab al-musiqa*, 149.

53. These terms often exist in a cluster: "*waqa'i'-'ibra-'umran-madaniyya-adab*."

54. Rifa'a Tahtawi is an iconic figure of the Egyptian and Arab Enlightenment. He started his momentous career as a translator, an educator, and a modernizer when in 1826, his mentor Hassan al-'Attar (1766–1835), who was a prominent scholar at al-Azhar, secured Tahtawi a position as the assigned religious scholar accompanying the first student delegation sent to Paris, by Muhammad Ali (1769-1849) the ruler of Egypt at the time (1805–48). Once there, Tahtawi succeeded in also becoming a student, spending five years studying language and humanistic sciences in France (1826–31). His famous travelogue, from which I quote, documents this period. While it is often simply referred to as *Rihla* (Travelogue), it bears the title *takhlis al-ibriz fi talkhis bariz* (1834) [*The Extraction of Pure Gold in the Summation of Paris*].

55. Daniel L. Newman, "An Imam in Paris: Account of a Stay in France by an Egyptian Cleric (1826–1831)," in *An Imam in Paris: Account of a Stay in France by an Egyptian Cleric (1826-1831)*, by Rifa'a Rafi' Al-Tahtawi, ed. and trans. Daniel L Newman (New York: Saqi, 2012), 229–31. I have added in the Arabic original in brackets at key moments.

56. The earliest reference to theatrical performance in Arabic that I am aware of is from the early seventeenth century, from the journey of the prince Fakhr al-Din the second (1572–1635) to the palaces of Tuscany, Sicily, and Napoli between 1613 and 1618, where he was in exile seeking to shore up support against his competition back in Mount Lebanon.

57. *Tawassu'* sometimes appears in conjunction with *takhyil* in classical literary theory since it is one of the tools of *majaz*. What we see here, however, is not its use as a semantic or rhetorical trope, but as a conceptual one. Newman translates *tawassu'* as enlargement in the prefatory excerpt used in this chapter. Yet, as I argue in my reading of *khayal*, the issue is not one of enlarging the scope of meaning of an unchanged utterance. As such I prefer the term expansion to enlargement—this is also the translation opted for when rendering *tawassu'* from classical literary theory though this is not my primary reason of choosing this translation. Rather, I prefer expansion because it seems to me to suggest not just the increasing the size or number of referents, but also the conceptual connection between the different connotations.

58. Ahmad Matlub, *mu'jam al-mustalahat al-balaghiyya wa tatawwuriha*, 2nd ed. (Beirut: maktabat lubnan, 2006), 2:438; Bilqasim Bil'arj, "zahirat tawwasu' al-ma'na fi al-lugha al-'arabiya: namadhij min al-qur'an al-karim," *majalat al-'ulum al-insaniyya* 6, no. 9 (2006), July 4, 2023. https://www.asjp.cerist.dz/en/downArticle/97/9/16/37791 (accessed July 4, 2023).

59. This passage is rather famous and has been analyzed through the prisms of both translation studies, and the history of theater, yet it is rarely connected to the meanings of *khayal* itself. Tageldin, *Disarming Words*; Sameh Hanna, *Bourdieu in Translation Studies: The Socio-Cultural Dynamics of Shakespeare Translation in Egypt* (New York: Routledge, 2016).

60. Shortly after describing theatre as a great school for learning, Tahtawi claims that "if it were not for the *satanic* leanings in the French theatre, it would have to be considered an institution with highly beneficial virtues" (231; emphasis mine). *naza'at shaytaniyya* literally means "satanic tendencies"; however, in this context, it must be read as "naughty" or even "devious" tendencies. The statement contradicts the initial description of theater as a school for the education of virtue for all. The same institution both is and is not an institution of great virtue. In this textual "tension," Tahtawi's reading act becomes apparent. The tension does not represent self-contradiction, but a space between what he glimpses as a potentiality in the practice of French theater, and his actual experiences of it. The description can then be reinterpreted not as a simple account of an actuality, but of a potentiality seized upon. The latter potential cannot be detached from Tahtawi's overarching process of reading theater and spectacle in which he critically deploys *tawassu'* to access and rearray a myriad of Arabic literary practices encapsulated in an *expanded khayali*. In other words, the call for the *expansion* of *khayali* is inextricably intertwined with the *expansion* occurring for "theater" and "spectacle"—in the very process of their reading and interpretation, or their seemingly immediate reception. He does not encounter a concept and practice of French theater insulated from the tools of its reception, and he does not proceed to insert the insulated French theatre in a dialogue with a similarly shielded classical concept of *khayal(i)*. Rather, the process of *expansion*

is all encompassing. Theater and spectacle are read via a notion of *khayal(i)*, which is *expanding* in its attempt to read the former as a practice in *expansion*.

61. Rifa'a Rafi' Al-Tahtawi, *al-diwan al-nafis fi iwan baris aw takhlis al-ibriz fi talkhis bariz*, ed. 'Ali Ahmad Kan'an (Beirut: al-markaz al-'arabiyy li al-dirasat wa al-nashr, 1977), 102; Newman, "Imam in Paris," 201. Shaden Tageldin also reads these two episodes together, arguing that both display a universalization of French epistemes through translation, placing Paris at the center by placing Egypt and France (via Greece) on a footing of inequality. Tageldin, *Disarming Words*, 113–15.

62. The first attempt to translate the *Iliad* (from the original Greek) was by Sulayman al-Bustani in 1904.

63. The term receives its most serious treatment in the works of Muhammad 'Abid Jabri and 'Abdullah Laroui on Ibn Khaldun, the towering judge and thinker who lived during the fourteenth century. In different ways, both Jabri and Laroui argue that *waqa'i'* is at the heart of the tensions entailed in Ibn Khaldun's attempt to turn and face his present-day reality. In failing to work through these challenges that inhere in the term's vision of time, Ibn Khaldun's project was bound to collapse in upon itself. For now, a brief summary will do. *Waqa'i'* shares the same linguistic root from where the words for reality, the realistic, and the real are drawn (I am using these terms here in their plainest semantic meaning). Typically, the term denotes a grave happening, such as a huge military battle, or even doomsday. It is rooted in a cosmology where occurrences seem to befall humans, to literally fall upon them from above—this is the crux of Jabri's and Laroui's argument. While Ibn Khaldun wants to turn to his reality, the latter was understood as that which befalls us, producing a series of contradictions in Ibn Khaldun's theorization of history. Mohammed Abed Al-Jabri, *fikr ibn khaldun: al-'asabiyya wa al-dawla: ma'alim nazariyya khalduniyya fi al-tarikh al-islamiyy*, 6th ed. (Beirut: markaz dirasat al-wihda al-'arabiyya, 1994), 289–306; Laroui, *mafhum al-'aql: maqala fi al-mufaraqat*. What concerns us here, however, is to what extent *waqa'i'*, much like *khayal*, has become embroiled in a different kind of relationality, particularly as the term came to be used in the title of Egypt's first official state newspaper, *al-waqa'i'al-misriyya* (The Egyptian Happenings). The same title was adopted by the official gazette of Iraq in the 1920s (*al-waqa'i'al-'iraqiyya*). The first police gazette in Egypt in the 1890s was also entitled *waqa'i' al-bulis*. This presents interesting implications for reading al-Tahtawi's translation of *Les Aventures de Télémaque* (1699), composed by François Fénelon (1651-1715). The word *waqa'i'* features in al-Tahtawi's translated title *mawaq' al-aflak fi waqa'i' tilimak* (The Orbits of the Celestial Bodies in the Adventures of Telemachus). For a definition of the conceptions of temporality (*zaman*) and history linking them to *waqa'i'* and *ahdath*, particularly in the work of Mu'tazilites, Ash'arites, and grammarians, see Mohammed Abed Al-Jabri, *binyat al-'aql al-'arabiyy: dirasa tahliliyya naqdiyya li nuzum al-ma'rifa fi al-thaqafa al-'arabiyya* (Beirut: markaz dirasat al-wihda al-'arabiyya, 2009), 190–92.

64. Mubarak, 'alam al-din, 2:408–9. Ali Mubarak is one of the most famous high-ranking bureaucrats in Egypt from the second half of the nineteenth century. His career is tightly linked with the modernizing projects of Muhammad 'Ali's dynasty. He was educated at government schools and served a number of ministerial positions, most prominently as the minister of public works during Khedive Isma'il's (r. 1863-79) ambitious and rather incautious plan to renovate Cairo. Darrell I. Dykstra, *A Biographical Study in Egyptian Modernization: 'Ali Mubarak (1823/24–1893)* (Ann Arbor: Univ. of Michigan Press, 1993).

65. Mubarak, 406. *Abo Rabya* is a name the conversationalists in the text use to refer to popular performers in Egypt. They seem comparable to Tahtawi's '*Awalim* (dancers, performers, singers), but I have not been able to locate other references to them that might give us historical information about this specific group.

66. For an example of each, see Mubarak, 408–9, 411–12, 415–16.

67. Mubarak, 411. "ثم لا يقتصر حكمه على الوقت الحاضر بل يسري أيضًا إلى الزمن الغابر فيجول في تواريخ الأمم الماضية ويستخرج منهم من ذكروا بفعل قبيح أو حسن فيستحوذ عليهم ويكلهم لرجل من رجاله يكسوهم ملابسهم ويبرزهم في صورهم ويهيئهم بهيئاتهم التي كانوا عليها وأسمائهم التي كانوا يذكرون بها حتى كأنهم نشروا من قبورهم قبل آوان نشورهم فيعرضهم كذلك على أعين الناس مع ما كانوا عليه في زمنهم من فعل خير ممدوح أو عمل شر مذموم ومكرمة تبقى آثارها وافتخارها أو معرة يخلد عارها وشنارها فيكون ذلك من أعظم البواعث على تربية النفس وتأديبها وحسن تهذيبها"

"Its [theater] judgment is not restricted to just the present; it also extends to the past. It traverses through the histories of the past communities and chooses from them those who were mentioned for committing a bad deed or a good one, and it possesses them, authorizing one of its men [playwrights] to dress them in their usual attire and to show them in their images and appearances that they once had and in their names that they were called by. As if they have been resurrected before their time [judgment day] and it displays them in this way to the eyes of people in the way they were in their times, be it that they committed good deed that should be eulogized or bad deed that need to be lampooned, an honorable deed whose traces remain becoming a source of pride or a shameful one whose disgrace and scandalous nature is immortalized. In so doing, it [theater] becomes a great motivator for educating and disciplining the self."

68. Ahmad Faris Al-Shidyaq, "*fi al-mukhayyila wa al-takhayyul*," in *kanz al-ragha'ib fi muntakhabat al-jawa'ib*, by Ahmad Faris Al-Shidyaq, ed. Salim Faris (Istanbul: matba'at al-jawa'ib, 1871), 1:10. I am grateful to Marle Hammond for referring me to Shidyaq's entry when I first started working on *khayal* and the nineteenth century.

69. In earlier formulations, *al-mukhayyila* as a faculty that lies somewhere between the senses and the intellect was often given an intermediary role; it mitigates the lack of "memory" functions in the senses, enabling the continuing presence of what is sensible so that the intellect could subject it to thinking. Consequently, while the faculty of *mukhayyila* is indispensable, it does not have direct access to the certainty afforded to

sensory experience (provided the senses are not impaired) or the intellect (provided it uses sound logic).

70. There is a long history of this example in Aristotle and the philosophers. See, for example, Adamson and Key, "Philosophy of Language in Medieval Arabic Tradition." Shidyaq's use of it, however, is rather idiosyncratic.

71. 'Abd al-Basit Likrari, *dinamiyat al-khayal: mafahim wa aliyat al-ishtighal* (Rabat: ittihad kuttab al-maghrib, 2004), 72–82.

72. Al-Shidyaq, "fi al-mukhayyila wa al-takhayyul," 10–11. For more on *sura* and *khayal*, see Likrari, *dinamiyat al-khayal*, 376–79.

"فأنك اذا قلت مثلا زاوية مثلثة ولم تصور لنفسك صورة زاوية مخصوصة فلا يكون ذلك الا مجرد صوت واذا كنت لم تر أو تلمس من قبل زاوية مثلثة لم يكن لك ان تتصور كيفية واحدة منها . . . واذا حسبت كان لا بد لك من ان تتصور احادا ينضم بعضها الي بعض والا فان عقلك لا يدرك شيئا مما تفعله يدك."

73. Nabil Matar, "Alfārābī on Imagination: With a Translation of His 'Treatise on Poetry,'" *College Literature* 23, no. 1 (1996): 100–110.

74. Deborah K. W. Modrak, *Aristotle's Theory of Language and Meaning* (New York: Cambridge Univ. Press, 2001), 250–61.

75. Al-Shidyaq, "fi al-mukhayyila wa al-takhayyul," 10–12.

76. Al-Shidyaq, 12–13.

77. Kramnick, "Empiricism, Cognitive Science, and the Novel"; Rüdiger Campe, "Shapes and Figures—Geometry and Rhetoric in the Age of Evidence," *Monatshefte* 102, no. 3 (Fall 2010): 285–99.

78. Unsurprisingly, this seems to be related to his theory of metaphor.

79. Al-Shidyaq, "fi al-mukhayyila wa al-takhayyul," 11.

80. Al-Shidyaq, 11. He specifically discusses a laborer (*'amil*) asking for his wage (*ujratuh*) through the concept of justice (*'adl*).

81. Al-Shidyaq, 11. Sensory experiences in this case would be of a negation; this is how antonyms are created around a single experience and its negation.

82. Al-Shidyaq, 13.

83. Al-Shidyaq, 12–13.

84. This flips older ideas about the faculty of *khayal*, where, if it could just be a repository of images, it would be more trustworthy, but it is in fact its tendency toward generative combinations and associations that poses a threat to its truth, or that makes it bypass any consideration of truth. That said, what Shidyaq is describing here, vividness, is a big part of what, since late antiquity, including later in Arabic, has been part of assessing the power of language, particularly poetic language, where the comparison to painting played an important role. I have already mentioned in footnote 18 how Muwaylihi reproduces this comparison (between poetry and painting, though for Muwaylihi it is writing in general) in one of his editorials.

85. Al-Shidyaq, "fi al-mukhayyila wa al-takhayyul," 12–13.

86. Al-Shidyaq, 13.

87. Abu 'Ali Ibn Sina, "fann al-shi'r min kitab al-shifa,'" In *aristutalis fann al-shi'r*, ed. AbdulRahman Badawi (Cairo: maktabat al-nahda al-misriyya, 1953), 161–63.

88. Al-Shidyaq, "fi al-mukhayyila wa al-takhayyul," 13.

89. There is a parallel in Muwaylihi's discussions of Socrates and what he terms the occurrences of persons, which we will discuss further in chapter 4, when we turn to characters.

90. Al-Tuwayrani, "Floral Publishing," 4–5.

2. Khayal

1. These texts have often been described by the histories of modern Arabic literature as having an episodic structure. The point is sometimes extended to premodern Arabic narrative forms in general. For an example of this latter move, see Maya Kesrouany, *Prophetic Translation: The Making of Modern Egyptian Literature* (Edinburgh: Edinburgh Univ. Press, 2019), 27.

2. Rifa'a Rafi' Al-Tahtawi, *al-diwan al-nafis fi iwan baris aw takhlis al-ibriz fi talkhis bariz*, ed. 'Ali Ahmad Kan'an (Beirut: al-markaz al-'arabiyy li al-dirasat wa al-nashr, 1977), 165–66.

"وفي الحقيقة أن هذه الألعاب هي جد في صورة هزل، فإن الإنسان يأخذ منها عبرًا عجيبة، وذلك لأنه يرى فيها سائر الأعمال الصالحة والسيئة، ومدح الأولى، وذم الثانية، حتى إن الفرنساوية يقولون: إنها تؤدب أخلاق الإنسان وتهذبها، فهي وإن كانت مشتملة على المضحكات، فكم فيها من المبكيات. ومن المكتوب على الستارة التي ترخى بعد فراغ اللعب باللغة اللاتينية ما معناه باللغة العربية: ⟨قد تصلح العوائد باللعب⟩ . . . وبالجملة (فالتياتر) عندهم كالمدرسة العامة، يتعلم فيها العالم والجاهل." While Mubarak weaves the idea throughout his colloquy on theater, it is especially spelled out in Ali Mubarak, *'alam al-din* (Alexandria: matba'at jaridat al-mahrusa, 1882), 408–9, 411–12, 415. Mubarak focuses on bringing things before the eyes, both in the sense of moving them from the aural to the visual and from what is internalized and concealed to an externalized and palpable space. This quote, cited in chapter 1, distills his core insight (408–9):

"ومن أعظم ما يقوي ذلك في أذهانهم ويمكن تأثيره من قلوبهم هذا التياتر لأنه يصور جميع تلك الصور للعين ويجلوه للعيان ويخرجها من قوة التخيل إلى حيز المحسوس المشاهد."
"كل هذه الأحوال لا يخفى تأثيرها في القلب وفعلها في النفس وليس لها غير التياتر ما يكشف حقيقتها ويعطيها قوتها فإنه هو الذي يضعها موضعها وينزلها منزلها ويوفيها حقها ويكسوها ما يليق بها من ثياب الحسن والكرامة والنعمة أو القبح والمهانة والنقمة حتى يرى الرائي حالة العظماء المتكبرين والأشقياء المتجبرين والكبراء المشهورين كيف تقلبت بهم حادثات الليالي." (418–19)

3. Daniel L. Newman, *An Imam in Paris: Account of a Stay in France by an Egyptian Cleric (1826–1831)*, by Rifa'a Rafi' Al-Tahtawi, ed. and trans. Daniel L. Newman (New York: Saqi, 2012), 229–31; Mubarak, *'alam al-din*, 408–16.

4. The evocation of the distinction between directly witnessing something and reading about it occurs in countless introductions to premodern histories written in Arabic. While the issue could be simply dismissed as formulaic, its intellectual interest in fact lies in its seeming continuity coupled with the subtle introduction of ruptures in the meaning of "witnessing" and, by extension, in the position occupied by history in a hierarchy of knowledge production. Two examples are particularly striking for their brevity, their evocation of seemingly similar formulaic appeals, and their clear difference: Taqi al-Din al-Maqrizi (d. 1442), *ighathat al-'umma bi kashf al-ghumma*; Al-Sharif al-Idrissi (d. 1251), *anwar 'ulwi al-ajram fi al-kashf 'an asrar al-ahram*. Their introductions can be compared to the analysis in the previous chapter, particularly to Mubarak's hierarchy of the senses as they pertain to theater. While Mubarak seems to be repeating the same formulaic appeals, he is expanding and reinterpreting those phrases from a concern with a firsthand witnessing to include also the "externalization" of an interiority. For Mubarak—and, less explicitly, in Tahtawi—it is also about externalizing an image from the mind, fancy, or imagination, making it "concrete," or embodied in an object standing in front of us on a stage. Abu Ja'far Al-Idrisi, *kitab anwar 'ulwiyy al-ajram fi al-kashf 'an asrar al-ahram*, ed. Ulrich Haarman (Beirut: Franz Steiner, 1991); Taqi al-Din Al-Maqrizi, *igathat al-'umma bi kashf al-ghuma*, ed. Karam Hilmi Farahat (Cairo: 'in li al-dirasat wa al-buhuth al-insaniyya wa al-ijtima'iyya, 2007).

5. The complexity is not just theoretical: it pertains to the social practices of reading and textual consumption at the time. To give but one example, in the nineteenth-century Arabic-speaking world reading aloud for a group of people was still a widely practiced mode of reading. Furthermore, it was not uncommon for plays to be read in a similar fashion. In the process, stage settings were "transformed," de facto, into a literary description of setting. Ziad Fahmy, *Ordinary Egyptians: Creating the Modern Nation through Popular Culture* (Stanford, CA: Stanford Univ. Press, 2011).

6. There is a long theoretical tradition of engaging with the aesthetic and theoretical problematic posed by theater as distinct issues as well as using them as a foil for thinking about questions of temporality (asynchronicity, anachronicity, and repetition), the relationship between the part and the whole, the connection between epistemology, ideology and "reality," and even the "theatricality" of the revolutionary event. For this chapter, I focus on how the elaboration on theater can illuminate key features in literary narrative structure, leaving aside—for now—concerns with other issues. Maaike Bleeker, *Visuality in the Theatre: The Locus of Looking* (New York: Palgrave Macmillan, 2008); Rebecca Comay, *Mourning Sickness: Hegel and the French Revolution* (Stanford, CA: Stanford Univ. Press, 2010); Mladen Dolar, "The Endgame of Aesthetics: From Hegel to Beckett," *Problemi International* 3, no. 3 (2019): 185–214; Etienne Balibar, "Althusser Dramaturgy and the Critique of Ideology," *Differences* 26, no. 3 (2019): 1–22. For an argument that modern literature draws on drama's techniques for scene shifts, see Monika Fludernik, "The Diachronization of Narratology," *Narrative* 11, no. 3 (2003): 331–48.

7. Newman, *Imam in Paris*, 227; Rifa'a Rafi' Al-Tahtawi, *takhlis al-ibriz fi talkhis bariz*, ed. 'Alaam Mahdi, Ahmed Ahmed Badawi, and Anwar Loqa (Cairo: sharikat maktabat wa matba'at mustafa al-babi al-halabi wa awladih bi misr, 1958), 166.

"وهذه السبكتاكلات يصورون فيها ما يوجد، حتى إنهم قد يصورون فرق البحر لموسى عليه السلام، فيصورون البحر ويجعلونه يتماوج حتى يشبه البحر شبهًا كليًا، وقد رأيت مرة في الليل أنهم ختموا التياتر بتصوير شمس وتسييرها وتنوير التياتر بها حتى غلب نور الشمس هذه على نور النجف حتى كأن الناس في الصباح."

8. Rüdiger Campe, "Shapes and Figures—Geometry and Rhetoric in the Age of Evidence," *Monatshefte* 102, no. 3 (Fall 2010): 285–99; Jonathan Kramnick, "Empiricism, Cognitive Science, and the Novel," *Eighteenth Century* 48, no. 3, special issue, "Empiricism, Substance, Narrative" (Fall 2007): 263–85; Jonathan Kramnick, "Presence of Mind: An Ecology of Perception in Eighteenth-Century England," in *Mind, Body, Motion, Matter: Eighteenth-Century Literary Perspectives*, ed. Mary Helen McMurran and Alison Conway (Tornoto: Univ. of Toronto Press, 2016), 47–71. I am grateful to Betty Rosen for brining Campe's work to my attention and to Michael Allan for suggesting that I read Kramnick's work.

9. While I do not pursue these questions of the history of debates on figuration, my discussions of *khayal* and *athar* could be useful for those who wish to address these questions on the figurative. In thinking about allegory, allegoresis, and realism, I have benefited tremendously from the following works: Frederic Jameson, *Allegory and Ideology* (New York: Verso, 2019); Tara Mendola and Jacques Lezra, eds., *The Year Book of Comparative Literature: Allegory and Political Representation*, 61 (Toronto: Univ. of Toronto Press, 2015); Paul De Man, *Allegories of Reading: Figural Language in Rousseau, Nietzsche, Rilke, and Proust* (New Haven, CT: Yale Univ. Press, 1979); Stephen Greenblatt, ed., *Allegory and Representation: Selected Papers from the English Institute, 1979–1980* (Baltimore, MD: Johns Hopkins Univ. Press, 1981); Northrop Frye, *Anatomy of Criticism: Four Essays* (Princeton, NJ: Princeton Univ. Press, 1957); Susan Buck-Morss, *The Dialectics of Seeing: Walter Benjamin and the Arcades Project* (Cambridge MA: MIT Press, 1989); Walter Benjamin, *The Origin of German Tragic Drama*, trans. John Osborne (New York: Verso Books, 2009); Michael McKeon, *The Origins of the English Novel, 1600–1740* (Baltimore, MD: Johns Hopkins Univ. Press, 1987). On the Arabic side, I did not only learn from the many theoretical discussions of language and *majaz*, touched upon in the previous chapter, but also found the following texts, which deploy the critical terms and their discussions around Quranic exegesis, as well as literary and historical works, to be immensely helpful: Abu al-Qasim Al-Zamakhshari, *al-kashshaf 'an haqa'iq al-tanzil wa 'uyun al-'aqawil fi wujuh al-ta'wil*, 2nd ed., vol. 3 (Cairo: al-maktaba al-tijariyya al-kubra, 1953); Nadwa Dawud, "mustalahat 'al-taswir' wa 'al-tamthil' wa 'al-takhyil' 'ind al-Zamkhashari fi 'al-Kashshaf'," *Journal of Qur'anic Studies* 10, no. 2 (2008): 142–77; Paul Kahle, ed., *Three Shadow Plays by Muhammad Ibn Daniyal* (Cambridge: Trustees of E. J. W. Gibb Memorial, 1992); Muhyi al-Din Ibn al-'Arabi, *The Bezels of Wisdom*,

trans. R. W. J. Austin (Mahwah, NJ: Paulist, 1980); Binyamin Abrahamov, *Ibn Al-Arabi's Fusus Al-Hikam: An Annotated Translation of the "Bezels of Wisdom"* (London: Routledge, 2015); E. M. Sartain, ed., Jalal Al-Din al-Suyuti, vol. 2, al-tahadduth bini'mat allah (Cambridge: Cambridge Univ. Press, 1975); Farid al-Din al-'Attar al-Nisaburi, *mantiq al-tayr*, trans. Badi' Muhammad Jum'a (Beirut: Dar al-Andalus, 1984).

10. Peter Heath makes a similar argument though in relation to both modern and premodern Islamic literature. Peter Heath, "Allegory in Islamic Literatures," in *The Cambridge Companion to Allegory*, ed. Rita Copeland and Peter T. Struck (Cambridge: Cambridge Univ. Press, 2010), 83–100.

11. For an approach that diverges from this pattern:, see Michael Allan, *In the Shadow of World Literature: Sites of Reading in Colonial Egypt*, Translation/Transnation (Princeton, NJ: Princeton Univ. Press, 2016). The literary in this case is defined as a modern and always already international disciplinary practice of reading.

12. Pierre Macherey and Etienne Balibar, "Literature as an Ideological Form: Some Marxist Propositions," *Oxford Literary Review* 3, no. 1 (1987): 4–12.

13. *Ikhtibar* is a key word here and shows the relationship between these analogous gestures of visualization. I will return to this issue at the very end of this chapter and in the chapters to come, where we will discover the way in which rallying these gestures of visualization is not only the result of empiricism and its questions suffusing the horizon of these texts but are also used to grapple with a political-cum-epistemological conundrum.

14. For more on the idea of habit (*'ada*) in these texts, see Nadia Bou Ali, *Psychoanalysis and the Love of Arabic: Hall of Mirrors* (Edinburgh: Edinburgh Univ. Press, 2020).

15. Marrash, "Forest," 4–5.

"فعندما استوعبت هذه الحوادث ووفيت التمعن حقه تلاعبت يد الاضطراب في جهاز الحياة ومالت الأعضاء إلى الارتياح ولم أزل فريسة ترتعد بين مخالب تلك الانفعالات إلى أن أخذتني سنة المنام وانفتح لدى أعيني مرسح الأحلام."

16. Marrash, 49–53.

17. Repeatedly, after the stage of the dream appears, the narrator uses the phrase "and I saw myself" or "I found myself" (Marrash, 5-6): (ورأيت نفسي) (وجدت ذاتي). The phrases are particularly interesting because they are deployed as part of a stylistic and rhetorical arsenal that play with the position of the subject and object. This kind of play is often referred to in classical rhetorical theory as grammatical shift for rhetorical purpose (*iltifat*), although the above cited examples do not directly fall into the traditional renditions of the trope.

18. *Hawajis* refers to the immaterial forms that intrusive thoughts and ideas take when they besiege their subject, especially during moments of anxiety or vacillation. They are often associated with the nighttime and with sleep more generally. In "Forest," *hawajis* is often used interchangeably with the "dreams of *khayal*" (أحلام تخيلية). For example, see 1-2.

19. The most recent example of this approach can be found in Peter Hill, *Utopia and Civilization in the Arab Nahda* (Cambridge: Cambridge Univ. Press, 2019).

20. Marrash, *ghabat al-haqq*, 1–2, 6, 17–18, 95–99.

21. See Marrash, 6–11, for descriptions of characters and how their names or identities are inscribed on objects they are holding. For the repetitions of the opening scene, see 19–20, 49–53, 86–88, 96.

22. There is a deeply disturbing racial tension in this text, for the king and queen often send their Black slaves to run their errands, and, much like the kingdom they ostensibly fight, they seem to own slaves. These tensions are central for understanding the ways in which the different levels of the allegory in this text don't always fall together seamlessly.

23. Marrash, *ghabat al-haqq*, 19–20.

"وأخذ المظهر الملوكي يضرب في أغوار التفكرات. وماعدت أرى سوى هيبة السكوت المتعمق ولا أسمع سوى هدير الماء المتدفق."

24. Marrash, 20.

"وبينما كنت أجول في مراسح الأوهام العقلية وأطوف في مسارح الخيالات الفكرية اذ استلمحت شبحاً يتقارب من بعد وهو يخب في بطن الغاب غائصاً غمر الظلال المتكاثف ومازال يعسف على قدم الاقدام حتى نفذ من تلك الغمرات المدلهمة وظهر في مسرح الأحلام ظهور القمر في كبد الغمام."

25. Marrash, 100, 132.

26. Marrash, 49–53.

27. Mendola and Lezra, *Year Book of Comparative Literature*, 1–9.

28. Clearly, this argument could be reversed—as it has already been, particularly by poststructuralist readings—to say that allegory is one of the ways in which systematicity is created, since the crossings sanctioned by allegory draw into equivalence, or at least into parallel, discrete, coexisting modes of producing meaning, fusing them by arguing that they are different levels of an already interlinked system. In other words, it actively produces what it claims to be merely portraying.

29. Mubarak, *'alam al-din*, 416.

"يحملنا لا محالة على توجيه انظارنا وازدياد ميلنا للحسن الممدوح واعراضنا وازدياد نفرتنا عن السيء المذموم فتتسع دائرة معلوماتنا وتستقيم طرق فهمنا وترسخ الأمور في نفوسنا بصورها الحقيقية وهيئاتها الصحيحة فتتميز عن اضدادها ولا تلتبس بغيرها فمتى وقعت تحت حواسنا عرفناها وعرفنا أصحابها فنأخذ ما يوافق لحالنا بالنظر لتحصيل المنافع ودفع المضار."

30. I am not aware of studies that look holistically into the use of diagrammatic representation in this period in pedagogic works in Arabic and how that would relate to what we are terming "staging" here as a specific technique of bringing word and "image" against the backdrop of empiricism and other related challenges.

31. Darrell I. Dykstra, *A Biographical Study in Egyptian Modernization: 'Ali Mubarak (1823/24-1893)* (Ann Arbor: Univ. of Michigan Press, 1993).

32. Bou Ali, *Psychoanalysis and the Love of Arabic*; Dykstra, *Biographical Study in Egyptian Modernization*, 8.

33. It is crucial to note that both have often been faulted by early scholarship for being too pedagogical. *'Alam al-din* reads like an attempt to impart factual knowledge by wrapping it up in a "weak" narrative plot. In fact, Mubarak himself says as much in his introduction to the book (7):

"وقد رأيت النفوس كثيراً ما تميل إلى السير والقصص وملح الكلام بخلاف الفنون البحتة والعلوم المحضة فقد تعرض عنها في كثير من الأحيان لا سيما عند السآمة والملال ومن كثرة الاشتغال وفي أوقات عدم خلو البال فحداني هذا في أيام نظارتي لديوان المعارف إلى عمل كتاب أضمنه كثيراً من الفوائد في أسلوب حكاية لطيفة ينشط الناظر فيها إلى مطالعتها ويرغب فيها رغبته في ما كان من هذا القبيل فيجد في طريقه تلك الفوائد ينالها عفواً بلا عناء حرصاً على تعميم الفائدة وبث المنفعة."

34. The episode seems to be inspired by Tahtawi's encounter in France with Joseph Agoub, whose poetry is the first French poetry translated into Arabic by Tahtawi. Agoub was part of the small community of Egyptian-French people who left with Napoleon, including Ellious Bochtor, who laid the groundwork for one of the most important French-Arabic dictionaries in the nineteenth century. For more on this community, see Ian Coller, *Arab France: Islam and the Making of Modern Europe, 1798-1831* (Berkeley: Univ. of California Press, 2011).

35. Mubarak, *'alam al-din*, 519.

36. There is an increased interest in the premodern "Encyclopedic" tradition in Arabic. See, for example, Elias Muhanna, *The World in a Book: Al-Nuwayri and the Islamic Encyclopaedic Tradition* (Princeton, NJ: Princeton Univ. Press, 2017).

37. Michael McKeon, "Romance Transformation II: Bunyan and the Literalization of Allegory," in *The Origins of the English Novel, 1600-1740* (Baltimore, MD: Johns Hopkins Univ. Press, 1987), 295–314.

38. In Mubarak's *'alam al-din*, there is an entire colloquy entitled "Spectacles" (al-nazzarat) (441–45). Fittingly, it follows directly after the long colloquy dedicated to the discussion of theater (397-440). In terms of plot, the flow is informed by how the characters use spectacles to watch the play and then discuss them along with other optical issues in the following days. For our analysis, however, the flow is revealing for the analogy between the uses of lenses to enhance or manipulate vision and the appreciation of theater—and, by extension literature—as visual media. In Tuwayrani's "Floral Publishing," the narrator is an astrologer, and the text is presented as epistles detailing his astrological discoveries. As such, there are repeated appeals to telescopes (*al-nazzara*); see 5–6, 9. I will turn to microscopes in Muwaylihi's *hadith* in the following sections.

39. The Pasha's memories are actually taken from Abdulrahman al-Jabarti's chronicles. This clearly tallies with the analogy between nature/society/science/history that we see running both throughout and across these texts. Since this chapter focuses on

narrative structure, we will not deal with this issue except from within its narratological effect. For more on this, see Marwa Elshakry, *Reading Darwin in Arabic, 1860–1950* (Chicago: Univ. of Chicago Press, 2013); Khaled Fahmy, *In Quest of Justice: Islamic Law and Forensic Medicine in Modern Egypt* (Berkeley: Univ. of California Press, 2018); Yoav Di-Capua, *Gatekeepers of the Arab Past: Historians and History Writing in Twentieth-Century Egypt* (Berkeley: Univ. of California Press, 2009).

40. Mubarak, *'alam al-din*, 406. "وعلى الجملة فليس التياتر عندنا من قبيل ما ذكرت من العاب اولاد رابية ونحوها بل هو كما ذكرناه عبارة عن أمثال علمية على حسب الحوادث التاريخية والتقلبات الدهرية وهو بهذه الكيفية مما يساعد على تقدم الأمة وتمدنها ويوسع دائرة ثروتها وفخرها."

41. The implication of my reading is that what we often think of as realism should be aligned with theatricality in the sense I am using here, where it is a technique of visualization that collapses the sensory object and the staged object, whereas allegorical narratives continue to point to their distinction even as they invite us to see their connection. This fits with McKeon's argument concerning the "literalization" of allegory in Bunyan's *Pilgrim's Progress*.

42. For an analysis of the relationship between text and object in *nahda* literature, see Allan, *In the Shadow of World Literature*.

43. Abdulrazzak Patel, "Language Reform and Controversy in the Nahda: Al-Shartuni's Position as a Grammarian in Sahm," *Journal of Semitic Studies* 55, no. 2 (2010): 509–38, investigates a series of debates in the wake of al-Shidyaq's supposed "simplification" of Arabic grammar. Customarily, the debates on language and grammar during this period are read through the lens of traditional versus modernizing tendencies. Yet both "traditional" and "modernizing" scholars seem to draw on the same canonical texts. As such, their feuds cannot be accurately understood by simply appealing to the importance they place on "tradition." Rather, it is best considered with regard to debates concerning the relationship between meaning, text, author, and the institutions entrusted to safeguard and reproduce their relationality. In fact, the conflict between Shidyaq and al-Shartuni seems to rest precisely on the place of the instructor of grammar and whether a student can learn from a text without needing a teacher. In a different but related vein, modern philology was also reshaping the relationship between "original" text and "derivative commentaries" as extratextual apparatuses rather than as integral constituents of the text. Consequently, the issue of who is the "author" of the text, and how the original meaning he intended could be retrieved, was being raised as well. Islam Dayeh, "From Tashīh to Tahqiq: Toward a History of the Arabic Critical Edition," *Philological Encounter* 4 (2019): 245–99; Ahmed El Shamsy, *Rediscovering the Islamic Classics: How Editors and Print Culture Transformed an Intellectual Tradition* (Princeton, NJ: Princeton Univ. Press, 2020). For an example of recent attempts to reuse what were thought to be "derivative commentaries," see Khaled el-Rouayheb, *The Development of Arabic Logic, 1200–1800* (Berlin: Schwab Verlag, 2019).

44. There have been debates and satirical treatments of these topics since the ninth century, including in the *maqama* itself, the genre we touched on in the previous chapter.

3. Excavating *Athar*

1. Tuwayrani's "Floral Publishing" is clearly in conversation with the twelfth-century Sufi work by Farid ud-Din Attar, *The Conference of the Birds*, trans. Afkham Darbandi and Dick Davies (London: Penguin, 1984). Though Tuwayrani's work is less of an allegory of the soul's journey, its affinity to Attar's work is palpable in their shared use of birds as main characters. Yet the allegorical elements in Tuwayrani's work are more akin to Marrash's "Forest," analyzed in the previous chapter.

2. Al-Tuwayrani, "Floral Publishing," 91–90. "انا الآن ابن اليوم اقبلت من سلم الماضي وابتغي احقاف الآتي فأنا اطوي بسط الفضاء والتحف رداء الظلما [sic] فلا يستوقفني مسلم ولا يستفزني مودع ... قال انا مجرد الوجدان عن علايق الهوى لا أحب ولا أبغض وانما طبيعتي الرغبة في من أقبل علي والرغبة عمن أعرض عني ... وانما يرغب في الراغب في نفسه العامل على جده المقبل على شأنه الذي يزودني حديثاً حسناً لا يخجلني إن رويته عنه فإنما أنا مكاتب الدهر دفتري الآثار ومدادي الأعمال فلا أكتب إلا ما يملي علي الحق."

"Ahqaf" is the title of a sura in the Quran, the word refers to the dwellings of the people of 'Ad. The significance of this passing reference will become clearer in this and the following chapter.

3. Al-Tuwayrani, 20–19. "نحن عنوان ما قبلنا واساس لمن بعدنا فنحن نلاقي نتائج اعمال السلف ويلاقي الخلف نتائج ما نحن عاملون كانت صحف التاريخ بيد السلف فكتبوا آثارهم بيد أعمالهم ونحن نتلوها فنرى الغث والثمين ثم هذه اوراق التاريخ بين ايدينا فلنكتب آثارنا."

In this quote, the Arabic plural of *athar* is used. However, I have chosen to keep to the singular, *athar*, in all translations and transliterations to simply the variations.

4. Elliott Colla, *Conflicted Antiquities: Egyptology, Egyptomania, Egyptian Modernity*, illus. ed. (Durham, NC: Duke Univ. Press, 2007), 81. The book surveys *athar*'s range of meanings; see 80–86.

5. Abu Ja'far Al-Tabari, *tarikh al-rusul wa al-muluk*, ed. M. J. de Goeje, vol. 1 (Leiden: E. J. Brill, 1879); 'Abd al-Rahman Al-Jabarti, *'aja'ib al-athar fi al-tarajim wa al-akhbar*, ed. Hasan Muhamad Jawhar, 'Abd al-Fattah al-Sirinjawiyy, and Ibrahim Salim al-Sayyed (Cairo: lajnat al-bayan al-'arabiyy, 1958); Taqi al-Din Al-Maqrizi, *kitab al-mawa'idh wa al-i'tibar bi-dhikr al-khitat wa alathar, al-ma'ruf bi al-khitat al-maqriziyya*, ed. Muhammad Zinhum and Madiha al-Sharqawi, 3 vols. (Cairo: maktabat madbuli, 1998); Muhammad 'Ali Kurd, *khitat al-sham*, 2nd ed. (Beirut: dar al-'ilm lil malayin, 1969); Muhsin Al-Husseini and Hasan Muhsin Al-'Aamiliyy, *khitat jabal 'amel* (Beirut: matba'at al-insaf, 1961); Ali Mubarak, *al-khitat al-tawfiqiyya al-jadida li misr al-qahira wa muduniha wa biladiha al-qadima wa al-shahira*, 20 vols. (Cairo: bulaq, 1889); Ali

Mubarak, *'alam al-din* (Alexandria: matba'at jaridat al-mahrusa, 1882), 409; Francis bin Fathallah Marrash, *ghabat al-haqq*, 2nd ed. (Beirut: matba'at al-qidis jawrijiyus li al-rum al-urthudhuks, 1881), 50.

6. *Zaynab Fawwaz, al-durr al-manthur fi tabaqat rabat al-khudur* (Bulaq: al-matba'a al-kubra al-amiriyya, 1895). Shawqi's poem is entitled "jam' al-taksir." Tahtawi's article is in edition 3 of the first year of *rawdat al-madaris* (1870). Reference to this type of agricultural land acquisition abounds in studies of the development of agricultural land ownership in Egypt. This type of land acquisition pre-dates the Ottoman rule of Egypt, but I am not sure whether the term itself—referring to this land as *athar*—was also in use throughout that period, or if it's a technical Ottoman term, or even one linked to the bureaucracy of Muhammad Ali's dynasty. For example, see Raouf Abbas, and Assem El-Dessouky, *The Large Landowning Class and the Peasantry in Egypt, 1837–1952*, ed. Peter Gran, trans. Mona Zikri and Amer Mohsen (Syracuse, NY: Syracuse Univ. Press, 2011).

7. It would be even more complex if we were to add Farsi and Ottoman Turkish, since the three languages were conceptually related.

8. We can find comparisons between what is being described above and Baroque, romantic, or even critical theory's engagements with the "ruin." While I do think it is premature to jump into these comparisons, it is worth noting how critical engagements with the ideas of the "ruin" tended to look at the complex interplay between "secularization" and a "religious" worldview. Walter Benjamin, for example, argued that the ruin in the Baroque period registers secularization from within a religious world view, while Romanticism might then by extrapolation engage in a lament of a what is already a fully secularized world. It would be immensely challenging to graft these critical articulations on what we are seeing with *athar* here, since such a comparison cannot be done without an excavation of political theology in Arabic, particularly in the lesser studied periods of the thirteenth to the seventeenth centuries, twined with an analysis of economic history. Walter Benjamin, *The Origin of German Tragic Drama*, trans. John Osborne (London: Verso, 1998).

9. Colla, *Conflicted Antiquities*; Donald Malcolm Reid, *Whose Pharaohs? Archaeology, Museums, and Egyptian National Identity from Napoleon to World War I* (Berkeley: Univ. of California Press, 2002); Adam Mestyan, "Arabic Lexicography and European Aesthetics: The Origin of Fann," *Muqarnas* 28 (2011): 69–100. Mestyan notes the use of the terms *athar* in the first catalog of the Egyptian museum, composed by Auguste Mariette and translated by Abul Su'ud Effendi (1820–78). He also observes the absence of *fann* as a translation for "art." Instead, the beautiful *athar* (*al-athar al-jamil*) and the grand *athar* are used (*al-athar al-fakhm*). Significantly, the catalog was titled *The Pleasure of the Spectator* (*furjat al-mutafarrij*), with a longer subtitle referring to its subject matter as the description of the objects held at the khedival museum. While such incidents do signal the importance of these discourses for *athar* in the nineteenth century, they also emphasize the ways in which no stable meaning could be simply found in any one single

discourse. If anything, the distinction between these discourses is being worked out in the space of distinguishing their respective renditions of *athar*.

10. We can see the entire project of an intellectual like Nasr Hamid Abu Zayd as an attempt to dissolve the increasing polarity between the methods of literary reading and those of exegesis. Abu Zayd views himself as standing in a long line of attempts to achieve this goal, not just as an important methodological concern, but as part of a broader attempt to dismantle modern forms of ideological power. In a strikingly different way, Michael Allan's work on disciplines of reading and Zeina Halabi's critique of the intellectual as a prophet offer significant contributions for understanding this problematic of reading. Yet, unlike Abu Zayd, they are quick to conflate dominant theoretical trends (secularist readings) with the exercise of institutional power in society, granting them the position of dominance. In the process, the struggle between different dominant ideologies and their coexistence within a regime of power is missed. Abu Zayd tried to reveal this coexistence in his double critique of modern intellectuals' project of "Enlightenment" as well as ultraorthodox conceptions of textuality via the Quranic text. Nasr Hamid Abu Zayd, "Nasr Abu Zayd yaktub 'an fashal al-tanwir al-hukumiyy nushirat fi akhbar al-adab 2005: suqut al-tanwir al-hukumiyy," ruwaq Nasr Abu Zayd, April 11, 2009, https://rowaqnasrabuzaid.wordpress.com/2009/04/11/; Zeina Halabi, *The Unmaking of the Arab Intellectual: Prophecy, Exile, and the Nation* (Edinburgh: Edinburgh Univ. Press, 2017); Michael Allan, *In the Shadow of World Literature: Sites of Reading in Colonial Egypt*, Translation/Transnation (Princeton, NJ: Princeton Univ. Press, 2016).

11. The idea is sometimes developed as an underpinning force in the forms of modern Arabic literature and language. Jeffrey Sacks, *Iterations of Loss: Mutilation and Aesthetic Form, al-Shidyaq to Darwish* (New York: Fordham Univ. Press, 2015). Significantly, *khayal* is linked to this process of combatting absence; it is often defined as the trace of (prior) sensory experiences (*athar al-mahsusat*).

12. Colin Turner, "Wealth as an Immortality Symbol in the Qur'an: A Reconsideration of the Mal/Amwal Verses," *Journal of Qur'anic Studies* 8, no. 2 (2006): 58–83.

13. Ayman A. El-Desouky, "Heterologies of Revolutionary Action: On Historical Consciousness and the Sacred in Mahfouz's 'Children of the Alley,'" *Journal of Postcolonial Writing* 47, no. 4 (September 1, 2011): 428–39; Tarif Khalidi, *Arabic Historical Thought in the Classical Period* (Cambridge: Cambridge Univ. Press, 1994); Yedullah Kazmi, "The Notion of History in the Qur'an and Human Destiny," *Islamic Studies* 37, no. 2 (1998): 183–200; Yedullah Kazmi, "Historical Consciousness and the Notion of the Authentic Self in the Quran: Towards an Islamic Critical Theory," *Islamic Studies* 39, no. 3 (2000): 375–98.

14. A historical analysis of the development of this tension in Arabic narrative forms is beyond the scope of this study. Also, it would be misleading to assume that there is an original problem that is reworked rather than new problems that repostulate older ones. I opted for simplicity here, though, and for showing how this Quranic narrative is

mobilized in the texts themselves. In a famous *hadith qudsi*, a specially designated group of prophetic sayings whose meanings were directly driven from the divine even if the actual wording was the Prophet's, people are prohibited from cursing time (*dahr*). The ban is explained by claiming that God *is* time. Yet I do not think that the point hinges on a singular saying so much as it is woven across discourses on will, language, and meaning.

15. Allen translates the Arabic title *al-'ibra* as "The Admonition." In another interesting agricultural coincidence, the term *ibra* was also used during the Mamluk and early Ottoman period to designate the "tax-yield" of cultivated lands. It suggests another apt translation of the term as the yield, what one derives from a situation, economic or "moral."

16. Roger Allen, ed. and trans., *A Period of Time: A Study and Translation of* Hadith 'Isa Ibn Hisham *by Muhammad al-Muwaylihi*, 2nd ed. (Reading: Ithaca, 1992), 107; Muhammad Al-Muwaylihi, *Hadith 'Isa Ibn Hisham*, ed. Roger Allen (Cairo: al-majlis al-a'la li al-thaqafa, 2002), 130.

"وبينما أنا في هذه المواعظ والعبر، وتلك الخواطر والفكر، أتأمل في عجائب الحدثان، وأعجب من تقلب الأزمان، مستغرقاً في بدائع المقدور، مستهدياً للبحث في أسرار البعث والنشور."

17. Allen, *Period of Time*, 108; Muwaylihi, *hadith*, 131.

"وقد جئت لأعتبر بزيارة المقابر فهي عندي أوعظ من خطب المنابر."

18. For more examples of this "competition," see Mohammed Abed Al-Jabri, *al-'aql al-siyasiyy al-'arabiyy: muhadidatuh wa tajaliyatuh*, 4th ed. (Beirut: markaz dirasat al-wihda al-'arabiyya, 2000), 47, 65–66.

19. Allen, *Period of Time*, 107; Muwaylihi, *hadith*, 130.

20. In a later scene, the Pasha's old servant recognizes him through his birthmark. These are common and heavily exploited motifs in romances. Michael McKeon, *The Origins of the English Novel, 1600–1740* (Baltimore, MD: Johns Hopkins Univ. Press, 1987). McKeon reads them in relation to an aristocratic ideology of virtue whereby nobility is taken to be a marker of both social status and moral superiority, with the latter justifying the social status. The use of the motif here, however, does not necessarily bring with it the same ideology; instead, it becomes a plot device within a rather different literary ideology.

21. Allen, *Period of Time*, 117; Muwaylihi, *hadith*, 140.

22. Allen, 136–37; Muwaylihi, 371.

"تبلي ببقائها جدة الليالي والأيام وتفني بدوامها أعمار الأعوام وتدفن تحت ظلالها أقواماً بعد أقوام شابت القرون ولم يلحق قرنها المشيب وبليت الدهور وهي في ثوبها القشيب قائمة على كرور الأعصار ومرور الأدهار تناطح النجوم وتسخر بالرجوم وتقيم الدليل والبرهان وتحدث حديث المشاهدة والعيان ما توالي الملوان وتعاقب الفتيان عن قدرة الإنسان على عجائب الامكان وقوة هذا الضعيف الضئيل على هذا العمل العظيم الجليل وكيف بلغ هذا الفاني البائد أن يصدر عنه هذا الباقي الخالد."

Compare these descriptions to the ones found in al-Maqrizi, particularly in the section on the pyramids though descriptions of other antiquities feature similar formulas. For example, the pyramids are described in these words:

"ليس من شيء الا وانا ارحمه من الدهر الا الهرمين فاني لارحم الدهر منهما."

"There is nothing for which I do not ask for mercy from Time, except for the two pyramids, I ask them to be merciful with Time" (100). This idea is reiterated throughout the section, see particularly al-Maqrizi, *kitab al-mawaʿidh wa al-iʿtibar bi-dhikr al-khitat wa al-athar, al-maʿruf bI al-khitat al-maqriziyya*, 340–43.

23. Allen, 140–41; Muwaylihi, 373.

"ولو عقل هذا المسكين أنه سيأتي عصر من العصور يمكن فيه لأحقر صعلوك أن ينسف هذا البناء في لمحة واحدة فيجعله كالعهن المنفوش والهباء المنثور بمقدار قبضة اليد من الأجزاء الكيماوية لما اغتر بالقوة والسلطان ولما تحدى بشيء سلمه ليد الحدثان وليس للحدثان من أمان اللهم إنه عمل ضائع من جهل شائع."

24. The friend accompanying the Pasha and ʿIsa Ibn Hisham expresses frustration with their early description of Paris. He urges them not to project what they think they know of the city of Paris onto its space, preventing them from actually seeing it. They proceed to produce a critical typology of Arabic travel narratives of Paris, dispelling the already assumed knowledge of Paris, which obstructs experiencing the city. As such, the description Kamran Rastegar stresses where a panoptic view of the city emerges is soon dismantled in the text; see *Literary Modernity between the Middle East and Europe: Textual Transactions in Nineteenth-Century Arabic, English, and Persian Literatures* (New York: Routledge, 2007). The three characters decide to look at Paris and see what it reveals to them. What they see, however, is not an experience or a description of space. They attempt to approach space as embodying abstract values that can be seen rather than reproduce assumed knowledge. Consequently, they proceed to approach Paris the way they had approached Cairo earlier.

25. Allen, *Period of Time*, 314–15; Muwaylihi, *hadith*, 449.

26. Allen, 450.

27. Allen, 199–200; Muwaylihi, 219–20.

28. Mubarak, *ʿalam al-din*, 1052.

"فنشأ من ذلك أمور لا يحصرها لسان ولا يحيط بها جنان كما هو مذكور في تواريخ الأمة الفرنسية."

29. Mubarak, 905, 1052.

30. Allen, *Period of Time*, 229; Al-Muwaylihi, *hadith*, 249.

"والناس اليوم في حركة لا شرقية ولا غربية."

31. A variant of this critique was later developed by pan-Islamist political currents as a reaction to the burgeoning articulations of a purely Pharaonic identity, particularly in the 1920s-1930s. Colla, *Conflicted Antiquities*.

32. ʿAbd al-ʿAzim Ramadan and ʿAbd al-Munʿim Ibrahim al-Jumayʿiyy, eds., *al-tankit wa al-tabkit*, no. 1 [June 6, 1881] (Cairo: al-hayʾa al-misriyya al-ʿamma li al-kitab, 1994), 36.

"ولا تنكر علينا ما تحدثك به قبل أن تطبقه على أحوالنا ولا تظن مضحكاتها هزئا بنا ولا سخرية بأعمالنا فما هي إلا نفثات صدور وزفرات يصعدها مقابلة حاضرنا بماضينا."

33. *al-tankit wa al-tabkit*, no. 1 (June 6, 1881), ed. Ramadan and al al-Jumiʿi, 34–49.

34. Al-Nadim, «Medical Council,» in *al-tankit wa al-tabkit*, 1 (June 6, 1881), ed. by Ramadan and al al-Jumiʻi, 37–39.

35. The choice of distractions suggests that the people (*qawm*) of the young man are assumed to be predominantly men.

36. The term *khirba* was widely used. Peter Hill, "Utopia and Civilisation in the Arab Nahda" (PhD diss., Univ. of Oxford, 2015).

37. Al-Nadim, "Medical Council," 38. "أين صحتك التي اشابت الدهور وأنت في عنفوان الشباب."

38. Al-Nadim, 39. "آثار أهلي وقصورهم المتهدمة".

39. A similar gesture can be found in Hafiz Ibrahim's proposition of a university (*al-jamiʻa*; whose root calls forth unity) as a solution to Egypt's present-in-crisis in Hafiz Ibrahim, *layali sitih* (Cairo: kalimat, 2011).

40. Al-Nadim, "Medical Council," 39. "أيتها القبور الصامتة انشقي وانفرجي وابعثي من فيكي من الأموات فقد أتت الطامة الكبرى وأنكدرت النشور. ويا أيتها الأرواح الخامدة هلمي إلى أجسامك البالية فأقيميها من موتها وابعثيها في الوجود لتنظر هذا الذي تشقى بعدمه."

41. Allen, *Period of Time*, 152; Muwaylihi, *hadith*, 177. "فيسبق الورثة الدود في الصدور والورود، فتذهب البدرة وراء البدرة والضيعة بعد الضيعة والدار عقب الدار حتى اذا لم يبق الا بيت السكن أتوا علي ما فيه من الأثاث بيعا... الي ان يندك بناؤه ويعفو أثره ويزول اسم بانيه الذي ارتكب ما ارتكب من الذنوب لتشييده ودوام بقائه."

42. Allen, 157; Muwaylihi, 182. "ولم يبق لك أيها المولى من أثر يذكر في ثروتك ومتاعك وأموالك وضياعك، وقد عشت دهرا وانا متمتع بريع ما وقفته أيها الأمير علي حاشيتك واتباعك وعلي هذا المسجد والسبيل والكتاب لتخليد ذكرك واحياء اسمك، فما لبث الوقف ان تهدم وتخرب بطول الترك والإهمال فوقعنا كلنا في الفاقة والإحتياج وانقلب الكتاب مخزنا والسبيل خمارة والمسجد مصبغة."

See also the Pasha's description of why people of his time chose to build *awaqf* (sing. *waqf*): Allen, 155; Muwaylihi, 182.

43. Allen, 118–21, 152–54; Muwaylihi, 141–43, 176–77.

44. Allen, 168; Muwaylihi, 193. "رحم الله الماضي، وعاذنا من الحاضر، وأجارنا من المستقبل."

4. History's Actors and the Collective Sovereignty of *al-Nas*

1. See note 6 in chapter 3. Tarif Khalidi, *Arabic Historical Thought in the Classical Period* (Cambridge: Cambridge Univ. Press, 1994); Aziz Al-Azmeh, *al-kitaba al-tarikhiyya wa al-maʻrifa al-tarikhiyya: muqaddima fi usul sinaʻat al-tarikh al-ʻarabiyy* (Beirut: dar al-taliʻa, 1983); Yoav Di-Capua, *Gatekeepers of the Arab Past: Historians and History Writing in Twentieth Century Egypt* (Berkeley: Univ. of California Press, 2009).

2. This schema is comparable to the one through which we define modernity in contradistinction to everything that preceded it. It is helpful because of its ability to draw large brushstroke trends and draw general conclusions from them, but, instead of a historical picture, it remains a schema that helps in historicizing.

3. Albert Hourani, *Arabic Thought in the Liberal Age, 1798–1939* (Cambridge: Cambridge Univ. Press, 1983); Anwar 'Abd al-Malik, nahdat misr: takawwun al-fikr wa al-aydiyulujya fi nahdat misr al-wataniyya (1805–1892) (Cairo: al-hay'a al-misriyya al-'amma li al-kitab, 1983); Julian Ricardo Cole, Colonialism and Revolution in the Middle East (Princeton, NJ: Princeton Univ. Press, 1992); Peter Hill, "Utopia and Civilisation in the Arab Nahda" (PhD diss., Univ. of Oxford, 2015).

4. Ali Mubarak, *'alam al-din* (Alexandria: matba'at jaridat al-mahrusa, 1882), 347. At a later point, we are told that the son gave the letter to the English Orientalist, not the father, to mail it (386). It is unclear whether the letter was given to the father or to the English Orientalist.

5. Mubarak, *'alam al-din*, 347.

6. Mubarak, colloquy 21 to colloquy 26, 347–86.

7. These follow the pattern of educator/educated. In retelling these conversations, Burhan al-Din occupies the position of educator to his mother (educated) who, in turn, is going to be the educator to his siblings (educated). There is a chain of educator/educated, that starts with Ya'qub/Burhan al-Din and is reproduced among the characters within the text, and then in the readers' (educated) relationship to the text's characters (educator). The topics covered by the letter offer us an overview of the entire text and delineate its literary, and educational, program.

8. Mubarak, *'alam al-din*, 357–58.

"قال كأنك لم تقرأ علم الجغرافيا فقلت وأيّ علم هذا فضحك وقال هو العلم بسطح الأرض وهيئاتها في الطول والعرض وما فيها من البحار والمدائن والانهار وما اختص به كل بقعة منها وأديان أهلها وكيفية حكومتهم وما هم عليه من الأخلاق والأحوال وغيرها فقلت لم أسمع بهذا إلا منك ولم أروه إلا منك فقال كيف هذا مع ان العرب هم الذين دونوه وأسسوه أفتراهم الآن تركوه ونسوه مع ان معرفته عند جميع أهل الأديان من أهم الواجبات على كل إنسان اذ به يعلم ما على الكرة من مخلوقات ويقف على حقيقة كثير من الكائنات وبدونه تكون معرفة التاريخ عسرة ثم قال فاذا يكون علم التاريخ عندكم مفقودًا فقلت لا إلا أننا لا نجعله من الأمور الضرورية اللازمة بل نعده من ضمن القصص والاخبار اذ ليس علمًا يحتاج إلى معلم فيمكن ان يقرأه الإنسان من نفسه فلما سمع ذلك مني عبس واعرض وطأطأ رأسه إلى الأرض وسكت مليًّا ثم رفع رأسه وقال الآن علمت سر تقهقر الملة الإسلامية وسبب ضعف أهل البلاد المشرقية وهو انها لما هجرت علم التاريخ بمدارسها زال من بين رجالها معرفة سير الماضين الذين كانوا سببا في سطوتها وعظم بطشها وتمكن قوتها وحيث لا قوة للملة الا بقوة رجالها ولا تكمل قوة الرجال الا بالعلم كان ترك علم التاريخ وباقي العلوم مما يضعف قوة الملة ويضيع شهرتها ويجعلها تحت اسر غيرها فيجور عليها ويذلها واعلم يا ولدي ان فن التاريخ جم الفوائد عظيم الفرائد اذ هو يوقفنا على أحوال الماضين من الأمم في أخلاقهم والانبياء في سيرهم والملوك في دولهم وسياستهم حتى **يقتفي اثرهم** من يروم الاقتداء بهم في احوالهم الا انه محتاج إلى مآخذ متعددة ومعارف متنوعة وحسن نظر وتثبت يفضيان بصاحبهما إلى الحق لأن الاخبار اذا اعتمد فيها على مجرد النقل فربما لا يأمن فيها من مزلة القدم فمنفعة علم التاريخ عامة للخاصة والعامة (. . .) فهو اليعسوب لكل فن **والمفتاح لكل أثر حسن** وغير حسن فنأخذ منه ما يلزمنا فنعلم الممدوح فنحبه والمذموم فنجتنبه."

9. Mubarak, 376.

"فقال قد قدمنا القول على أقسام نوع الانسان ودياناته بما انساق به القول إلى هذا المقام والآن نقول إن هذا النوع الإنساني من طبعه حب الألفة والميل إلى الجمعية **ولذلك يقولون الإنسان مدني بالطبع** أي لا بد له من الاجتماع الذي هو معنى المدنية في اصطلاحهم."

Rosenthal translates the section in bold from Ibn Khaldun in this way: "Man is 'political' by nature. That is, he cannot do without the social organization for which the philosophers use the technical term 'town' (*polis*)." Franz Rosenthal, *The Muqaddimah: An Introduction to History*, abridged ed. (Princeton, NJ: Princeton Univ. Press, 2005), 45. The translation is challenging because it includes two layered acts of reading. On the one hand, Ibn Khaldun reads the philosophers, reconfiguring what they meant by those terms, and on the other hand Ibn Khaldun (including his reading of the philosophers) is read in the context of the nineteenth century. Leaving aside the technicalities of the terminology, I understand the main difference between reading 1 (Ibn Khaldun reading the philosophers) and reading 2 (nineteenth-century reading of Ibn Khaldun, which includes his reading of the philosophers, or reading 1) to center on the relationship between the social and the political. In reading 1 *ijtima'* (the act of coming together through which society is formed) and *madaniyya* (the polis, or the political structure of society) have a relationship of matter (society) to form (political structure); one cannot exist without the other. This is noticeable in Rosenthal's move from "political" to "social organization": politics is the organization of the social. In the nineteenth century, the multiplicity of forms (competing modes of political power, or "social organization;" absolute monarchy, constitutional monarchies, representational democracies) raise the question of whether society can be made to exist "without" political form, both as an object of cognition as well as an object of history; the latter entails projecting anarchical moments in the distant "prehistoric" and "prepolitical" past or in the uncertain future (postpolitical?). This point will be explained at length later in this chapter. I mention it here briefly by way of elucidating my translational decisions, opting to render *madaniyy* as "social" rather than Rosenthal's "political."

10. Francis bin Fathallah Marrash, *ghabat al-haqq*, 2nd ed. (Beirut: matba'at al-qidis jawrijiyus li al-rum al-urthudhuks, 1881), 41.

"كما أن نظام هذه الكرة الأرضية لا يمكن قيامه بمجرد حركتها اليومية على نفسها بل يحتاج إلى الحركة الشمسية حول فلكها أيضًا. هكذا الإنسان بما أنه محمول على ظهر تلك الكرة وآخذ جميع مواده ومقوماته منها فهو تابع بجميع اطواره لأحوالها. فلا يمكنه القيام بمجرد اقتصاره على ذاته فقط وذلك لعدم مقدرته على حفظ نظام حياته الشخصية بل يحتاج إلى الدوران حول مركز المجموع الإنساني. وكما أن القوة الجاذبة التي تتبادلها جميع الأجرام السماوية لا تسمح بوقوع خلل في نظام الفلك العام هكذا يحتاج ذلك المجموع الإنساني إلى قوة تحفظه من الوقوع في الخلل والتبديد. وإذا اخذنا نفتش على قوة مثل هذه فلا نراها سوى في السياسة والشريعة. أما ينبوع ظهور السياسة والسيادة والشرائع فهو جار من تغلب الناس بعضهم على بعض منذ القديم وهو الأمر الذي أنتج التملك والمملكات على وجه الأرض."

11. Per this view, politics grows out of patriarchal models. Crucially, poetry, in this vision, is born from the need to rally the group within one tribe or clan to fight another

one (an enemy), in turning to face his people, to call on to them as a cohesive group, poetry emerges, and so do poets. Marrash, *ghabat al-haqq*, 45–52.

12. This voice is described as *al-rawi* (the narrator). Yet the narrator here simply means the speaker: the person speaking at this tangent in the text rather than the narrator as a narratological position and norm. Questions of speaking and voice, as well as the management and deployment of narrative time, is yet to be studied thoroughly in this canon and in Arabic narrative forms more generally.

13. Marrash, "Forest," 49.

"ولما كان لا يمكن لنظر الراوي أن يدرك جليًا كيفية امتداد تلك السياسة على العالم ولا أن يستوضح حقيقة المسلك الذي نهجته لها الأقدار لما يعارضه هناك من ظلمات الأحقاب والأعصار وجب عليه حينئذ أن يستخدم العقل كمصباح لكي يمكن لأعينه أن تنفذ في تلك الظلمات الدامسة فتفوز بمشاهدة ما وراء ذلك. فهلمّ إذًا أيها الراوي واتل علينا بقية ما جرى هنالك وأخبرنا عما عثرت عليه من المواقع بعد ان استطلعت العقل نيّرًا في أوج الغوامض. انني بعد أن أولجت نظري طويلًا في بحر زاخر من الظلام الهائل حيثما كانت أمواج التيه والمعاثر تتلاطم تحت مهب عواصف الأيام والليالي انفدته أخيرًا من هذه اللجج العميقة إلى سهل فسيح الأمد يعانق بباع نهايته أفق البداية. وإذا مسرح عظيم قد انفتح أمامي. وإذ كنت عاجزًا عن استجلاء الأشباح اللاعبة فيه تمامًا لشدة توغلهم في عباب القدمية وضعت على أعيني نظارة الاستقراء وجعلت أتأمل."

14. Mubarak, *'alam al-din*, 378–79.

"لكن لا يتم عز هذا الملك إلا بالشريعة والقيام لله بالطاعة والتصرف تحت أمره ونهيه ولا قوام للشريعة إلا بالملك ولا عز للملك إلا بالرجال ولا قوام للرجال إلا بالمال ولا سبيل إلى المال إلا بالعمارة ولا سبيل للعمارة إلا بالعدل والعدل هو الميزان المنصوب بين الخليقة نصبه الرب وجعله له قيمًا وهو الملك ولذا يقال لا ملك إلا بالجند ولا جند إلا بالمال ولا مال إلا بالخراج ولا خراج إلا بالعمارة ولا عمارة إلا بالعدل ولا عدل إلا بإصلاح العمال ولا تصلح العمال إلا باستقامة الوزراء وراس الكل تفقد الملك أحوال رعيته بنفسه واقتداره على تأديبها حتى يملكها ولا تملكه وقد وضع في هذا المعنى دائرة جامعة لثماني كلمات حكمية سياسية ارتبط بعضها ببعض وارتد اعجازها على صدورها فلا يتعين طرفها."

Compare this to the versions below from Ibn Khaldun's references to *adab*; the first version is quoted by Ibn Khaldun from al-Mas'udi and he attributes the second to Anshruwan, 'Abd al-Rahman Ibn Khaldun, *al-muqaddima*, ed. 'Abdallah Muhammad Darwish (Damascus: dar ya'rib, 2004), vol. 1, 129–30.

"أيها الملك إن الملك لا يتم عزه إلا بالشريعة، والقيام لله بطاعته، والتصرف تحت أمره ونهيه، ولا قوام للشريعة إلا بالملك، ولا عز للملك إلا بالرجال، ولا قوام للرجال إلا بالمال، ولا سبيل للمال إلا بالعمارة، ولا سبيل للعمارة إلا بالعدل، والعدل الميزان المنصوب بين الرب والخليقة، نصبه وجعل له قيما وهو الملك."

"الملك بالجند والجند بالمال والمال بالخراج والخراج بالعمارة والعمارة بالعدل والعدل بإصلاح العمال وإصلاح العمال باستقامة الوزراء ورأس الكل بافتقاد الملك حال رعيته بنفسه واقتداره على تأديبها حتى يملكها ولا تملكه (...) فهذه ثمان كلمات حكمية سياسية ارتبط بعضها ببعض وارتدت أعجازها إلى صدورها واتصلت في دائرة لا يتعين طرفها."

15. Mubarak, 379.

16. The scholarship on Ibn Khaldun in Arabic and English is extensive and therefore prohibits any attempt at including it all. The works of Muhammad 'Abid al-Jabiri

and Abdullah Laroui offer a crucial entryway into the world of the fourteenth-century luminary. I have also benefited from Nasser Rabbat's work on Maqrizi, in which he often touches on the latter's mentor and teacher: Ibn Khaldun. Rosenthal's work remains a classic for its thorough philological engagement, though later scholarship's critique of Rosenthal's reading is crucial. Importantly, I find the scholarship on Ibn Khaldun's importance for Ottoman historiography key to breaking the perplexing siege on Ibn Khaldun, wherein his work seems to stand outside any historical (including conceptual and intellectual) historical trajectory. Kenan Tekin, "Reforming Categories of Science and Religion in the Late Ottoman Empire" (PhD diss., Columbia Univ., 2016); Marinos Sariyannis, "Ottoman Ibn Khaldun Revisited: The Pre-Tanzimat Reception of the Muqaddima from Kinalizade to Sanizade," in *Political Thought and Practice in the Ottoman Empire*, ed. Marinos Sariyannis (Rethymnon: Crete Univ. Press, 2019), 251–86; Vefa Erginbas, "Ibn Khaldunism in the Seventeenth Century: Khaldunian Concepts in Katip Celebi's 'Fadhlaka'" (MESA, Sheraton New Orleans Hotel, November 14–17, 2019); Kenan Inan, "Avrasya U–Tursun Bey's Tarih-i Ebü'l-Feth (1488) and Ibn-i Haldun's Mukaddime" (MESA, Sheraton New Orleans Hotel, November 16, 2019); Yeliz Cavus, "Between Ibn Khaldunism and Ottoman Exceptionalism: Abdurrahman Seref Efendi's 'Tarih-i Devlet-i Osmaniyye' ('History of the Ottoman State')" (MESA, Sheraton New Orleans Hotel, November 16, 2019). Incidentally, Kınalızade's *Ahlak-i Ala'i*, which is deemed critical for the link between Khaldunian thought and later Ottoman historiography, was published by Bulaq in 1833.

17. Ibn Khaldun, *muqaddima*, 137. Rosenthal translates the excerpts as: "Human social organization is something necessary. The philosophers expressed this fact by saying: 'Man is "political" by nature.' That is, he cannot do without the social organization for which the philosophers use the technical term 'town' (*polis*)." Ibn Khaldun, *The Muqaddimah: An Introduction to History*, ed. and trans. Franz Rosenthal, vol. 1 (New York: Pantheon, 1958).

18. In Mubarak's *'alam al-din*, however, "their" loses the specificity of this identifiable referent (the philosophers). Rather, one would have to read it as pointing to a widely accepted, and therefore general, definition of civilization, or *madaniyya*. The grammatical slippage in the transplanting of the quote, which suddenly introduces a plural whose referent is not identified, thus reveals the changing status of *madaniyya*, which shifts from being a term that is historically located in a particular discursive language, and which Ibn Khaldun supplants with *'umran*, to becoming a keyword that is equated with *'umran*—and in Mubarak's case, with *'imara* as well.

19. Ibn Khaldun, *muqaddimah*, 1:128–29.

20. Ibn Khaldun, 1:129–31.

21. Abdallah Laroui, *mafhum al-dawla* (Beirut: al-markaz al-thaqafiyy al-'arabiyy, 2011).

22. Mohammed Abed Al-Jabri, *nahnu wa al-turath: qira'aat mu'asira fi turathina al-falsafiyy*, 6th ed. (Beirut: al-markaz al-thaqafiyy al-'arabiyy, 1993).

23. This might explain the seemingly tautological nature of the definition. It appears as an amalgamation of concepts, which are offered as a delineation of Ibn Khaldun's new science. These concepts point to the position of the *muqaddima* at the intersection of multiple knowledge-producing discourses that it seeks to subsume and, as a result, supplant; this includes Quranic narratives pertaining to the rise and fall of peoples (i.e., civilizations) that were touched upon in the previous chapter.

24. For example, see Ibn Khaldun, *muqaddima*, 1:288, 345–47.

25. Ibn Khaldun, 1:345–53.

26. Ibn Khaldun, 1:346. A similar criticism is found in the work of al-Baghdadi, cited in Colla, *Conflicted Antiquities*, 85. Ibn Khaldun refers to ancient monuments as *al-ʿadiyat* (in reference to the people of ʿAd mentioned in the Quran whose famous dwelling the *ahqaf* are the title of a sura in the Quran). Interestingly, when Tuwayrani refers to the "hillocks of the future," he uses the term *ahqaf* as well (*ahqaf al-aati*), suggesting that there is as much of a strong connection between the people of Ad, *ahqaf*, and ancient monuments as there is between Pharaoh and pyramids (the latter is more well studied). See Ibn Khaldun's discussion of *iwan kisra* that follows a very similar pattern to the challenge of the pyramids analyzed in chapter 3; the latter challenge is also discussed at length by Maqrizi (Ibn Khaldun, 345). Some of the fantastical narratives criticized by Ibn Khaldun are also reproduced and ridiculed in Muwaylihi's *hadith*. The stories told by the merchant (*al-Tajir*) in *al-ahram* are a good example. He mentions ʿAwj ibn ʿUnuq (sometimes ʿAwj ibn ʿUnaq), who in *hadith* is a fantastical survivor—along with the pyramids—of Noah's flood; Roger Allen, ed. and trans., *A Period of Time: A Study and Translation of* Hadith ʿIsa Ibn Hisham *by Muhammad al-Muwaylihi*, 2nd ed. (Beirut: Ithaca, 1995), 356–57; Muwaylihi, *hadith*, 370–76. The same character (ʿAwj ibn ʿUnuq) and the narratives linking him to greater Syria—not the pyramids—are attacked by Ibn Khaldun, *muqaddima*, 1:345–46.

27. There are numerous examples; some of the most suggestive moments can be found in Ibn Khaldun, 1:418–39; and 2:45–49, 56–58, 96, 124.

28. These excerpts are from Ibn Khaldun, 2:45.

"وذلك أن الدولة والملك صورة الخليقة والعمران، وكلها مادة لها من الرعايا والأمصار."

He makes the point once more a couple of pages later (52, 53).

"أن الدولة والملك للعمران بمثابة الصورة للمادة، وهو الشكل الحافظ بنوعه لوجودها وقد تقرر في علوم الحكمة أنه لا يمكن فكاك أحدهما عن الآخر." "الدولة بالحقيقة الفاعلة في العمران إنما هي العصبية والشوكة، وهي مستمرة على أشخاص الدولة. فإذا ذهبت تلك العصبية ودفعتها عصبية أخرى مؤثرة في العمران ذهب أهل الشوكة."

29. Ibn Khaldun, 1:418.

30. This point takes out a long section of his work, but this example where he talks about the lack of sophistication of these *khitat* because the state is till nascent will make the point (1:425):

"فلا أثر عندهم لشيء من هذه الألقاب ولا تمييز الخطط، لبداوة دولته وقصرها."

31. The Sultan (Power of which the Sovereign is an emblem and an embodiment) splits into *wizara* (this manages issues pertaining to security, protection and the military), *kitaba* to enact his will to matters that are spatially and temporally far, tax collection (*jibaya*), and, finally, his "guard" or *hajib*.

32. Ibn Khaldun, 2:55.

33. Rifaʻa Rafiʻ Al-Tahtawi, *al-diwan al-nafis fi iwan baris aw takhlis al-ibriz fi talkhis bariz*, ed. ʻAli Ahmad Kanʻan (Beirut: al-markaz al-ʻarabiyy li-l-dirasat wa al-nashr, 1977); Daniel L Newman, "An Imam in Paris: Account of a Stay in France by an Egyptian Cleric (1826-1831)," in *An Imam in Paris: Account of a Stay in France by an Egyptian Cleric (1826-1831)*, by Rifaʻa Rafiʻ Al-Tahtawi, ed. and trans. Daniel L. Newman (New York: Saqi, 2012), 114–16.

"ومن الفرقة الثانية طائفة عظيمة تريد أن يكون الحكم بالكلية للرعية، ولا حاجة للملك أصلا. ولكن لما كانت الرعية لا تصلح أن تكون حاكمة ومحكومة، وجب أن توكل عنها من تختاره منها للحكم، وهذا هو حكم الجمهورية، ويقال للكبار مشايخ وجمهور."

34. *misbah al-sharq*, 193 (February 21, 1902), published in the Arabic book edition as an appendix, 524–31.

"وها انا انتهي بكم الي باب الانتخاب بين الاهالي الذي تبتدئ منه سلطة الحكم وتنتهي.".

35. Al-Muwaylihi, *hadith*, 134; Aziz al-Azmeh, *Muslim Kingship: Power and the Sacred in Muslim, Christian and Pagan Polities* (London: I. B. Tauris, 1997); Jacques Derrida, "Force of Law: The 'Mystical Foundation of Authority,'" in *Deconstruction and the Possiblity of Justice*, ed. Drucilla Cornell, Michel Rosenfeld, and David Grey Carlson (New York: Routledge, 1992), 1–67; Pierre Bourdieu, "The Force of Law: Toward a Sociology of the Juridical Field," trans. Richard Terdiman, *Hastings Law Journal* 38, no. 5 (1987): 805–13; Kantorowicz Ernst, *The King's Two Bodies: A Study in Medieval Political Theology* (Princeton, NJ: Princeton Univ. Press, 2016); Eric L. Santner, *The Royal Remains: The People's Two Bodies and the Endgames of Sovereignty* (Chicago: Univ. of Chicago Press, 2011).

36. Muwaylihi, 143. In one of the dialogues between Nadim and the student (*al-tilmidh*), the concept of *al-hurriyya* is linked to a parliament formed across the class spectrum. The conversation is framed allegorically as a discussion of how to choose a parliament (*mahfal al-nuwab*) for the school the student attends. In this instance, *al-hurriyya* is thought of as an attribute of the collective, interlinked with "new" institutional practices—much like we see in Muwaylihi's *hadith*. At stake are questions of *hukm* (entailing a question of political rule and making "judgments") and *siyasa* (as politics and leading), especially since the two articulations bear some echoes. The latter pertain once again to *tarbiya* and the distinction between *al-insan* and *al-bahima* as well as to defining *al-hurriyya* as an observance of "limits" (*hadd*), distinguishing the *haqq* of various persons. Nadim terms the latter a "figurative" (*majazi*) *hurriyya*, for actual liberation from all limits is unfeasible for *al-insan*. See the 4th and 17th editions of *Al-tankit wa al-tabkit*. Marrash makes a similar argument about the impossibility of absolute freedom, but he

describes it as *hurriyya 'ala al-shabah*. That *tashbih* (simile) and *majaz* would be used to make conceptual points, much like *tawassu'* for Tahtawi, is suggestive for studying conceptions of language at the time.

37. Ali Mubarak, *'alam al-din* (Alexandria: matba'at jaridat al-mahrusa, 1882), 1042–44.

"فلما خرجوا قال الإنكليزي للشيخ أيها الأستاذ كيف ترى فيما فعلت حوادث الزمان وخطوب الحدثان وتحول الأشياء عما كانت عليه وخروجها عن موضوعها فقال الشيخ كيف ذلك وما الذي خطر ببالك فقال إن هذا القصر كان محلًّا للملوك لا يصل إليه شريف ولا صعلوك فلما تقلبت به الأيام وامتدت له يد الزمان عامًا بعد عام اضمحل حاله وآل إلى ما ترى مآله ... فكان يقسم أوقاته فيجعل وقتًا لنومه ووقتًا للمطالعة في أخبار دولته وقومه ووقتًا لخلوته واجتماعه بأحبته ... اذا جاء وقت قيامه من نومه دخل عليه الموكل بخدمته فينبهه ثم يخرج ويدعو بالحكيم ومن يلوذ به ... ثم أتى ولده من بعده فلم يجر على سنن والده في تقسيم أوقاته على ما قدمنا بل صرفها جميعًا في حظوظه النفسية ... فنشأ من ذلك أمور لا يحصرها لسان ولا يحيط بها جنان ... فترتب على ذلك تدوين الأحكام السياسية والقوانين الفرنساوية وظهر نابوليون بونابرت."

38. In addition to studying how *al-nas* is used in our canon in comparison to other terms denoting groups like *jumhur*, *khalq*, *'ibad allah*, *'umma*, *al-ahali*, *tabaqa*, *'amma*, *khassa*, to name just some of the key terms. I have also consulted lexicons (*kutub al-furuqat* were particularly helpful) and works of Quranic exegesis, looking into their interpretations of *surat al-nas* and of other instances where the word is used in the Quran and comparing it with other terms for groups—focusing in particular on the ones I found in our canon. I have also explored how early *adab* works use the term. While these varied sources are key for writing a more comprehensive history of the term, my goal here is more modest. One thing to note is that the word used to refer to criminals in official police records in Egypt during the nineteenth century was *al-nas al-ashrar*; see Khaled Fahmy, "Prostitution in Nineteenth Century Egypt," in *Outside In: On the Margins of the Modern Middle East*, ed. Eugene Rogan (London: I .B. Tauris, 2002), 77–103. As a technical term, *al-nas* will probably be most familiar to readers in its reference to the sons of Mamluk emirs who were not allowed to become emirs themselves and were known as *awlad al-nas*; the term is still used in contemporary Egyptian Arabic to refer to "good" people who could equally be of good social standing (wealth and power) or of good upbringing ("morals"). There are ongoing debates in Mamluk studies regarding who exactly were *awlad al-nas* and what their social status was. "In Search for a Hidden Group: Where Are the Awlād al-Nās" (Anne-Marie Schimmel Kolleg Conference, Bonn & Online, December 17, 2022), https://www.academia.edu/44668381/_In_search_for_a_hidden_group_Where_are_the_awlād_al_nās.

39. Muhammad ibn Mukarram Ibn Manzur, "'-n-s," in *lisan al-'arab*, Al-Warraq Online Classical Arabic Books, accessed January 24, 2022, http://www.alwaraq.net/Core/waraq/coverpage?bookid=89&option=1; Rida al-Din al-Saghani, "'-n-s," in *al-'abab al-zakhir*, Al-Warraq Online Classical Arabic Books, accessed January 24, 2022, http://www.alwaraq.net/Core/waraq/coverpage?bookid=3133; Abu Nasr al-Jawhari, "'-n-s," in *taj al-lugha wa sihah al-'arabiyya*, Al-Warraq Online Classical Arabic Books, accessed

January 24, 2022, http://www.alwaraq.net/Core/AlwaraqSrv/bookpage?book=273&session =ABBBVFAGFGFHAAWER&fkey=2&page=1&option=1; Abu Mansur Muhammad ibn Ahmad al-Azhari, "'-n-s," in *tahdhib al-lugha*, Al-Warraq Online Classical Arabic Books, accessed January 24, 2022, http://www.alwaraq.net/Core/AlwaraqSrv/bookpage ?book=3134&session=ABBBVFAGFGFHAAWER&fkey=2&page=1&option=1; Ibn Manzur, "'-n-s." Abu Hilal Al-'Askari, *al-furuq fi al-lugha*, accessed January 24, 2022, http://www .alwaraq.net/Core/waraq/coverpage?bookid=3270; Al-Khalil Ibn Ahmad al-Farahidi, *al-'ayn*, accessed January 24, 2022, http://www.alwaraq.net/Core/waraq/coverpage?bookid =62; Abu al-Hassan 'Ali Ibn Syduh, *al-mukhasas*, accessed January 24, 2022, http://www .alwaraq.net/Core/waraq/coverpage?bookid=277. In the context of the nineteenth century, Niqula al-Turk's and Jabarti's use of *jumhur* in their engagement with French liberal thought in an imperial context (during the French invasion of Egypt and Syria in 1789), and Tahtawi's use of *nas* to engage these same ideas during his time in France, are equally key in my discussion of the concept.

40. *surat al-nas* appears as the last *sura* in the contemporary organization of *al-Qur'an*. It's seen as part of a couple, along with its preceding *surat al-falaq*. They are known as *al-Ma'uzatan* or *al-Mushaqshiqatan*. The disputed verse is the last one: ".مِنَ الجِنَّةِ وَالنَّاسِ" Abdel Haleem translates it as: "whether they be jinn or people." The contention concerns the referentiality of jinn and people in relation to the rest of the sura. Muhammad al-Tahir Ibn 'Ashur, *tafsir al-tahrir wa al-tanwir* (Beirut: mu'asasat al-tarikh, 2000), 30:556–58; Abu al-Qasim Al-Zamakhshari, *al-kashshaf 'an haqa'iq al-tanzil wa 'uyun al-'aqawil fi wujuh al-ta'wil*, 2nd ed. (Cairo: al-maktaba al-tijariyya al-kubra, 1953), 4:303; 'Imad al-Din Isma'il Ibn Kathir, *tafsir al-qur'an al-'azim* (Beirut: dar al-ma'rifa, 1987), 4:616.

41. I am grateful to Kristen Brustad for pointing this out to me.

42. This reading is supported by works of *furuqat al-lugha*, in which we find many examples of this pattern. For example, al-'Askari says:

"البوش هم الجماعة الكثيرة من أخلاط الناس."

He also describes *al-jiblah*, 49, in a similar way:

"الجبلة اسم يقع على الجماعات المجتمعة من الناس."

In following these sections closely where he differentiates between *al-nas* and other terms, it becomes clear that *al-nas* is the more general term. This is not necessarily the pattern he follows with other words because their differentiation could rest on other factors than what I describe here as an axis of more general versus more specific. He also points out that *al-nas* encompasses the dead and the living, and he raises the possibility that *al-nas* is a plural that has no singular form from within the same root (141). This pattern seems to hold in narratives, too. In studying *al-nas*, I found Abu Hayyan Al-Tawhidi, *al-imta' wa al-mu'anasa* (Book of Enjoyment and Bonhomie), accessed January 28, 2022, www.alwaraq.net/Core/waraq/coverpage?bookid=11, particularly inspiring. His use of the following terms is particularly noteworthy: *talaqi al-nas* (45–49), which I read in contradistinction to his definition of sovereign/subject (*sultan/ra'iyya*) as two

Notes to Pages 165–67   249

interdependent categories (*al-ahwal al-mutadayyifa wal asma' al-mutanasifa*); 154. His description of the Battle of the Yarmuk with the Byzantine Empire uses this pattern of using *al-nas* as a general category before splitting it (178)—though this pattern is dispersed through his book.

"وماج الناس بمدينة السلام واضطربوا، وتقسم هذا الموج والاضطراب بين العامة والخاصة، وصارت العامة طائفتين."

He also uses the division sometimes as خاصة الناس vs. عامة الناس which confirms that *nas* on its own does not entail an intrinsic division of the collective (168).

43. Allen, *Period of Time*, 103; Muwaylihi, *hadith*, 127.

44. Muwaylihi, 161. "(عيسى بن هشام) – (. . .) الجرائد هي أوراق تطبع في كل يوم أو كل أسبوع أو كل شهر تجمع وتسرد فيها الأخبار والروايات العامة **ليطلع الناس على أحوال الناس** وهي **اثر من اثار المدنية الغربية** انتقل الينا فيما انتقل، والأصل في وضعها انتشار الحمد للفضيلة والذم للرذيلة والنقد على ما قبح من الأعمال والحث على ما حسن من الأفعال والتنبيه الى مواضع الخلل والتحضيض على إصلاح الزلل **وتعريف الأمة بأعمال الحكومة النائبة عنها حتى لا تجري بها الى غير المصلحة وبتعريف الحكومة بحاجات الأمة لتسعى في قضائها**، وبالجملة فإن أصحابها هم في مقام الأمرين بالمعروف والناهين عن المنكر الذين اشارت الشريعة الإسلامية اليهم."

The pasha responds in this manner: "فلا بد ان لا يكون قد اشتغل بها واهتم بأمرها كبراء العلماء والأعلام وعظماء المشايخ الكرام ولنعمة الوسيلة وحسمت الطريقة في تبليغ الناس ما يصلحهم في معاشهم وينفعهم في معادهم. فعلي بواحدة منها."

45. "sunnat al-jarida," *misbah al-sharq*, April 19, 1901.

46. "sunnat al-jarida." "انتفاع الناس بحسن الاعتبار."

47. Abu 'Ali Ibn Sina, "fann al-shi'r min kitab al-shifa'," in *aristutalis fann al-shi'r*, ed. AbdulRahman Badawi (Cairo: maktabat al-nahda al-misriyya, 1953), 161–98, 178.

48. In the article right after the editorial, "kalima fi al-falsafa" (A Word on Philosophy), Muwaylihi explains philosophy through the example of Socrates' biography. Furthermore, the latter's contribution hinges on his move from the abstract (*al-mujaradat*) to the "existents" (*al-mawjudat*)—the latter clearly indicating a move toward actual happenings and occurrence, since Muwaylihi focuses on how Socrates converses with people about their lives and events that take place and talks to them on the street. In a similar fashion, when Muwaylihi discusses Jahiz's *kitab al-bukhala'* (*Avarice and the Avaricious*) on its own and later in association with Molière, he also treats their works like they are reports of actual occurrences, comparable to what he includes in his newspaper: "al-hawadith al-dakhiliyya" [Internal Affairs] (*misbah al-sharq*, June 9 1889). At this time *risalat al-jahiz fi manaqib al-turk* was being serialized. It was later collected and sold in book form by the journal's press; "bukhl bil-qalil and tafrit fi al-Din." *misbah al-sharq*, December 29, 1898. "sunnat al-jarida," April 19, 1901, also discusses miserliness detailing once more the importance of using examples culled out of real life.

49. In the same episode discussing newspapers, the characters dissect the newspaper scene, offering another lens onto market competitions and consumption as both the way people express their judgment as well as a way to judge people themselves and how

accurate their judgment is. They conclude with another reference to *al-nas*, this time a Quranic one. Allen, *Period of Time*, 158; Muwaylihi, *hadith*, 162:

"والحكم كله للقارئين في الإقبال على ما ينفع والانصراف عما يضر فأما الزبد فيذهب جفاء وأما ما ينفع الناس فيمكث في الأرض."

The way the Quranic verse is deployed here is strongly suggestive of what we saw earlier in relation to *athar*, where what is "beneficial" to people, in the sense of the social totality, will remain, while everything else is eroded. This intersection between literary and market value and their relationship to "judgment" is still with us today. We do not deal directly here with how this entire canon is placed within other modes of social judgements of value; instead we look into how these are internalized from the position of this canon—in a sense, looking into their literary effects from within the texts.

50. *misbah al-sharq* 91 (February 8, 1900). For an alternative translation see Allen, 331.

"فالناس مشتغلون ببعضهم عن بعض وقل بيننا من يشتغلون للناس في نفع الناس."

51. Muwaylihi, 151–53.

52. I understand this interplay to be central to modern fiction in general, a category that is complexly implicated with modern history, standards of historical veracity, and the possibility of having a specific referentiality. What we are observing here is the specific dynamics through which these entanglements emerge in this canon. In other words, this is an act of historicizing that should cumulatively contribute to our theoretical understanding of modern literature broadly conceived—a goal to be achieved by the discipline (i.e., collectively) and not necessarily by a single thinker.

53. Allen, *Period of Time*, 124; Muwaylihi, *hadith*, 147.

(الزائر الثاني) -هل بلغك زواج فلان بمعشوقته
(الزائر الأول) -هل ركبت مع فلان في الدراجة الكهربائية؟
(النائب)-قد وقفت لكما على سبب انتحار ابن فلان المتموّل [...]
(الزائر الأول) -وأنا وقفت لكما على سبب استعفاء فلان من وظيفته.

54. Matti Moosa, *The Origins of Modern Arabic Fiction* (London: Lynne Rienner, 1997); M. M. Badawi, *Early Arabic Drama* (Cambridge: Cambridge Univ. Press, 1988), 339–44.

55. When the Pasha finally meets someone in these institutions who is willing to take him seriously it's because he has read his story in *misbah al-sharq* and consequently believes the news. This metafictional element, blurring the line between news, published trials, and stories, is pervasive in both Arabic literature from the period and modern literature in general. What I am interested in, however, in this section, is the resultant mode of characterization.

56. Muwaylihi, *hadith*, 192. 'Uthman Raghib is named in *misbah al-sharq* 34 (December 8, 1898); 44 (February 23, 1899).

57. Allen, *Period of Time*, 42.

58. Allen, 127.

59. Allen, 10–11.

60. *misbah al-sharq* 175 (September 20, 1901). The insights of this debate were used in my discussion of *khayal* in chapter 1 of this book.

61. "يَا وَيْلَتَى لَيْتَنِي لَمْ أَتَّخِذْ فُلَانًا خَلِيلًا". "Woe is me! If only I had not taken so and so as a friend" in M.A.S Abdel Haleem, trans., *The Qur'an: A New Translation by M. A. S. Abdel Haleem*, 2nd ed. (New York: Oxford Univ. Press, 2005), 228. The reference to *Fulan* has also been interpreted as pointing to Satan, since he is mentioned in the next verse. As Ibn Manzur notes in his entry, the two interpretations are not mutually exclusive.

62. One way of thinking about this is the way in which the veridical and nonveridical, when it comes to persons, pans out as a question particular versus general.

63. Suspension is a suggestive way for thinking *kinaya*, and its position between the veridical and the nonveridical, and the particular and the general.

64. Michael McKeon, *The Secret History of Domesticity: Public, Private, and the Division of Knowledge* (Baltimore, MD: Johns Hopkins Univ. Press, 2005) analyzes the contribution of "libels" to the rise of realism—as a modern literary mode of representation in the English context (49–109).

65. Laroui, *mafhum al-dawla* actively deploys the different methodological approaches from within different fields to probe the concept of the state, revealing what is at stake in each field's particular mode of asking questions. He distinguishes between a juridical, a philosophical, a historical, and a sociological mode. The humanities do not contribute a fifth mode, since they are a combination of the historical and the sociological, according to Laroui (9). The debate concerning the category of "Right" between Hegel and Marx illustrates the contentiousness of reading the relationship between the individual and the state, panned out on the category of "Right." Laroui's discussion of this latter debate further emphasizes the point of modalities of reading.

66. *misbah al-sharq* 9 (June 16, 1989); 11 (October 27, 1889).

67. McKeon, *Secret History of Domesticity*; Samera Esmeir, *Juridical Humanity: A Colonial History* (Stanford, CA: Stanford Univ. Press, 2012); *majalat al-ahkam al-shar'iyya* 1 (April 24, 1902) explains its own necessity by arguing that despite the proliferation of other specialized juridical magazines, none deal with the sharia courts. The characters in Mubarak's *'alam al-din* follow the trial of such a case in the papers.

68. Muwaylihi, *hadith*, 7.

69. Rather amusingly, in 1994, the prominent Egyptian writer Usama Anwar 'Ukasha (1941–2010) depicts two characters named 'Alam al-Din and Burhan al-Din in the famous television series *Arabesque*, which uses the then-recent earthquake in Egypt to grapple with the country's history and identity mapped onto its architecture, as captured in the title of the show. The earthquake and ensuing collapse of buildings is taken to signal the incompatibility of the layers of history and identity, at the root of the present-in-crisis. 'Alam al-Din and Burhan al-Din are in this case twin brothers, whose perspective

renders the history of the present visible, as well as dramatizes the crisis of intellectuals in their relationship to people. Lest these connections be lost on viewers, another main character is named 'Imara—Mubarak's preferred word for *'umran*. The series offers one clue of the relevance of the literary modes analyzed here to later practices.

70. Wen-chin Ouyang, "Fictive Mode, 'Journey to the West,' and Transformation of Space: 'Ali Mubarak's Discourses of Modernization," *Comparative Critical Studies* 4, no. 3 (2007): 331–58.

5. Literature as a Political Problem

1. These issues have been fiercely debated in discussions of Eurocentrism and the ways beyond it, whereby the universal and racism have sometimes been placed on the same side, or even equated. In the process, the political stakes of debates on historical method, broadly conceived, become explicit—a welcome move, but one that has sometimes resulted in curtailing the debates on method to either the deconstruction of existing ones or their defense in the name of the universal. What this ironically leaves out is an engagement with methods as they are necessitated by a political intervention in the present, not in response to the supposed already achieved hegemony of the "universal," but to weave an alternative. The issue is too wide ranging to be covered by this footnote or this book. Yet I point to the oeuvre of Muhammad Farid Wajdi (1878–1954) from the late nineteenth and early twentieth century, through which we can see the problems of the implicit stagist view in ideas of civilizational progress through the example of an "Islamist" response to it. The response is more culturalist than racist. In another vein, both Ghali Shukri and Khaldun al-Naqib offer crucial ways for tackling questions of method in the face of the present—rather than an abstract sense of hegemony—and it is to these two examples that I would like to draw attention. Ghali Shukri, "min al-ishkaliyyat al-manhajiyya fi al-tariq al-'arabiyy ila 'ilm ijtima' al-ma'rifa," *al-mustaqbal al-'arabiyy* 77 (July 1985): 126–36; Khaldun al-Naqib, "bina' al-mujtama' al-'arabiyy: ba'd al-furud al-bahthiyya," *al-mustaqbal al-'arabiyy* 79 (September 1985): 4–41.

2. This is a particular manifestation of the problem of representation in democracies whose purchase is not restricted to democratic systems; it becomes a foundational problem of modern politics in general, even in autocratic regimes. It is also a problem of national liberation, in as much as the latter needs to assume a nation in whose name one speaks or acts. This problem of representation becomes particularly obvious in revolutionary moments. A key example from the period studied by this book pertains to the problematization of the use of the term *hizb* (what we now understand to be a political party, but it literally means "faction") by the proponents of the 'Urabi movement. Its couching here in relationship to problems of sovereignty is worth further exploration, but is beyond the scope of this book. The scholarship on this problem of representation in politics is immense, though not much deals with it as a conceptual problem in our

period, which is more often read through the prism of the interplay of nationalism and colonialism, though the latter clearly implicitly assumes a conceptual and political problem of the collective.

3. A serious engagement with the details of those fissures—in other words, with who is or isn't part of the collective—cannot be reduced to an itinerary of characters, but necessitates adding another lens to the conceptual one mobilized by this book. At the very least it requires grappling with political and economic history, not as a relationship of text and context, drawing on the content of those histories, but twining the latter with questions of methods among these disciplines. To answer the question of who, then, is to undertake a different project to the one pursued by this book.

4. We see this double meaning in the maintaince of a reformist agenda that fixates on *akhlaq* (morals), in Marsafi's definition, and also in two literary histories (Jurji Zaydan and al-Rafi'i). We also see the ways in which a new ground for thinking both narrative and ethical disposition is constituted (revisit the part on Ibn Khaldun). To my mind, this is how *adab* reproduces its double entendre of narrative/comportment but with a dramatically changed cosmology. "Commitment" literatures will continue to reimagine this problem, both within Arabic and beyond, but this time inversing the motion. In this way, the sense that *adab* is both narrative and ethical disposition is simultaneously maintained and transformed, more accurately the seeming continuity is belied by change in the relationship between, as well as conceptions of, the literary, the political, and the ethical.

5. *misbah al-sharq* 91 (February 8, 1900); for an alternative translation see Roger Allen, ed. and trans., *A Period of Time: A Study and Translation of* Hadith 'Isa Ibn Hisham *by Muhammad al-Muwaylihi*, 2nd ed. (Reading: Ithaca, 1992), 331.

6. This episode was crucial for the understanding of the imperialist dimension of monopoly capital. Around the same time, Greece and the center of the Ottoman Empire were encountering similar issues with their debt, but with different political outcomes.

7. *al-tankit wa al-tabkit* 17 (October 9, 1881), 319–20. See also 'Urabi's own speech to the same effect in the same edition (318).

8. 'Urabi, *mudhakkirat ahmad 'urabi*, 87–91.

Epilogue

1. Ayman El-Desouky, *The Intellectual and the People in Egyptian Literature and Culture: Amara and the 2011 Revolution* (London: Palgrave Pivot, 2011), 40.

2. He cites the work of Lucie Ryzova, *The Age of the Efendiyya: Passages to Modernity in National-Colonial Egypt* (Oxford: Oxford Univ. Press, 2014).

Bibliography

Abbas, Raouf, and Assem El-Dessouky. *The Large Landowning Class and the Peasantry in Egypt, 1837–1952*. Edited by Gran Peter. Translated by Mona Zikri and Amer Mohsen. Syracuse, NY: Syracuse Univ. Press, 2011.

'Abd al-Malik, Anwar. *nahdat misr: takawwun al-fikr wa al-aydiyulujiyya fi nahdat misr al-wataniyya (1805–1892)*. Cairo: al-hay'a al-misriyya al-'amma li al-kitab, 1983.

Abdel Haleem, M. A. S., trans. *The Qur'an: A New Translation by M. A. S. Abdel Haleem*. 2nd ed. New York: Oxford Univ. Press, 2005.

Abrahamov, Binyamin. *Ibn Al-Arabi's Fusus Al-Hikam: An Annotated Translation of the Bezels of Wisdom*. London: Routledge, 2015.

Abu Zayd, Nasr Hamid. *al-ittijah al-'aqliyy fi al-tafsir: dirasa fi qadiyat al-majaz fi al-qur'an 'ind al-mu'tazila*. 3rd ed. Beirut: al-markaz al-thaqafiyy al-'arabiyy, 1996.

———. *falsafat al-ta'wil: dirasa fi ta'wil al-qur'an 'ind muhyi al-din ibn 'arabi*. 5th ed. Beirut: al-markaz al-thaqafiyy al-'arabiyy, 2005.

———. "The Hermeneutic Aspect of Sibawaihi's Grammar." *Alif: Journal of Comparative Poetics* 8 (Spring 1988): 82–117.

———. "Nasr Abu Zayd yaktub 'an fashal al-tanwir al-hukumiyy nushirat fi akhbar al-adab 2005: suqut al-tanwir al-hukumiyy." ruwaq nasr abu zayd, April 11, 2009. https://rowaqnasrabuzaid.wordpress.com/2009/04/11/.

———. "qira'at al-turath fi kitabat ahmad sadiq sa'd." In *ishkaliyat al-takwin al-ijtima'iyy wa al-fikriyat al-sha'biyya fi misr*, 197–213. Damascus: dar kan'an li-al-dirasat wa al-nashr, 1992.

Achtar, Ahmad Sakhr. "Contact between Theology, Hermeneutics, and Literary Theory: The Role of Majaz in the Interpretation of the Anthropomorphic Verses in the Qurān from the 2nd AH/8th CE until the 7th AH/13th CE." PhD diss., SOAS, Univ. of London, 2012.

Adamson, Peter, and Alexander Key. "Philosophy of Language in Medieval Arabic Tradition." In *Linguistic Content: New Essays on the History of Philosophy of Language*, edited by Margaret Cameron and Robert J. Stainton, 75–108. Oxford: Oxford Univ. Press, 2015.

Albazei, Saad. *istiqbal al-akhar: al-gharb fi al-naqd al-'arabiyy al-hadith*. Beirut: al-markaz al-thaqafiyy al-'arabiyy, 2004.

Al-Hawari, Ahmad Ibrahim. *naqd al-mujtama' fi hadith 'isa ibn hisham li al-muwaylihi*. 2nd ed. Cairo: dar al-ma'arif, 1986.

Al-Husseini, Muhsin, and Hasan Muhsin Al-'Aamiliyy. *khitat jabal 'amel*. Beirut: matba'at al-insaf, 1961.

Al-Idrisi, Abu Ja'far. *kitab anwar 'ulwiyy al-ajram fi al-kashf 'an asrar al-ahram*. Edited by Ulrich Haarman. Beirut: Franz Steiner, 1991.

Al-Jabarti, 'Abd al-Rahman. *'aja'ib al-athar fi al-tarajim wa al-akhbar*. Edited by Hasan Muhamad Jawhar, 'Abd al-Fattah al-Sirinjawiyy, and Ibrahim Salim al-Sayyed. Cairo: lajnat al-bayan al-'arabiyy, 1958.

Al-Jabri, Mohammed Abed. *al-'aql al-siyasiyy al-'arabiyy: muhadidatuh wa tajaliyyatuh*. 4th ed. Beirut: markaz dirasat al-wihda al-'arabiyya, 2000.

———. *binyat al-'aql al-'arabiyy: dirasa tahliliyya naqdiyya li-nuzum al-ma'rifa fi al-thaqafa al-'arabiyya*. Beirut: markaz dirasat al-wihda al-'arabiyya, 2009.

———. *fikr ibn khaldun: al-'asabiyya wa al-dawla: ma'alim nazariyya khalduniyya fi al-tarikh al-islamiyy*. 6th ed. Beirut: markaz dirasat al-wihda al-'arabiyya, 1994.

———. *nahnu wa al-turath: qira'at mu'asira fi turathina al-falsafiyy*. 6th ed. Beirut: al-markaz al-thaqafiyy al-'arabiyy, 1993.

Allan, Michael. *In the Shadow of World Literature: Sites of Reading in Colonial Egypt*. Princeton, NJ: Princeton Univ. Press, 2016.

Allen, Roger. "The Beginnings of the Arabic Novel." In *The Cambridge History of Arabic Literature*, edited by M. M. Badawi, 180–92. Cambridge: Cambridge Univ. Press, 1997.

Allen, Roger, ed. and trans. *A Period of Time: A Study and Translation of* Hadith 'Isa Ibn Hisham *by Muhammad al-Muwaylihi*. Edited and translated by Roger Allen. 2nd ed. Reading: Ithaca, 1992.

Amin, Samir. *Eurocentrism: Modernity, Religion, and Democracy: A Critique of Eurocentrism and Culturalism*. Translated by Russell Moore and James Membrez. 2nd ed. Oxford: Pambazuka, 2011.

Apter, Emily. *Against World Literature: On the Politics of Untranslatability*. New York: Verso Books, 2013.

———. "Untranslatables: A World System." *New Literary History* 39 (June 1, 2008): 581–98.

Asfour, Gabir. *al-sura al-fanniyya fi al-turath al-naqdiyy wa al-balaghiyy 'ind al-'arab*. 3rd ed. Beirut: al-markaz al-thaqafiyy al-'arabiyy, 1992.

Al-'Askari, Abu Hilal. *al-furuq fi al-lugha*. Accessed January 24, 2022. http://www.alwaraq.net/Core/waraq/coverpage?bookid=3270.

Attar, Farid ud-Din. *The Conference of the Birds*. Translated by Afkham Darbandi and Dick Davies. London: Penguin, 1984.

Averroes. *Middle Commentary on Aristotle's "Poetics."* Translated by Charles Butterworth. 2nd ed. Chicago: St. Augustine, 1999.

Al-Azhari, Abu Mansur Muhammad ibn Ahmad. "a-n-s." In *tahdhib al-lugha*, 1827–29. Al-Warraq Online Classical Arabic books. Accessed January 24, 2022. http://www.alwaraq.net/Core/AlwaraqSrv/bookpage?book=3134&session=ABBBVFAGFGFHAAWER&fkey=2&page=1&option=1.

Al-'Azm, Sadiq Jalal. *al-istishraq wa al-istishraq al-ma'kus*. Beirut: dar al-hadatha lil tiba'a wa al-nashr, 1981.

———. *difa'an 'an al-madiyya wa al-tarikh: thalath muhawarat falsafiyya, mudakhala naqdiyya muqaraba fi tarikh al-falsafa al-haditha wa al-mu'asira*. Beirut: dar al-fikr al-jadid, 1990.

Al-'Azmeh, Aziz. *al-kitaba al-tarikhiyya wa al-ma'rifa al-tarikhiyya: muqaddima fi usul sina'at al-tarikh al-'arabiyy*. Beirut: dar al-tali'a, 1983.

———. *Muslim Kingship: Power and the Sacred in Muslim, Christian and Pagan Polities*. London: I. B. Tauris, 1997.

Badawi, M. M. *Early Arabic Drama*. Cambridge: Cambridge Univ. Press, 1988.

Badawi, Muhammad Mustafa, ed. *Modern Arabic Literature*. Cambridge: Cambridge Univ. Press, 1995.

Balibar, Etienne. "Althusser's Dramaturgy and the Critique of Ideology." *Differences* 26, no. 3 (2019): 1–22.

Bauer, Thomas. "Mamluk Literature: Misunderstandings and New Approaches." *Mamluk Studies Review* 9, no. 2 (2005): 104–32.

Benjamin, Walter. *The Origin of German Tragic Drama*. Translated by John Osborne. New York: Verso, 2009.

Bil'arj, Bilqasim. "zahirat tawwasu' al-ma'na fI al-lugha al-'arabiyya: namadhij min al-qur'an al-karim." *majallat al-'ulum al-insaniyya* 6, no. 9 (2006). https://www.asjp.cerist.dz/en/downArticle/97/8/16/37791 (accessed July 4, 2023).

Black, Deborah L. *Logic and Aristotle's Rhetoric and Poetics in Medieval Arabic Philosophy*. Leiden: E. J. Brill, 1990.

Blaut, James Morris. *The Colonizer's Model of the World: Geographical Diffusionism and Eurocentric History.* New York: Guilford, 1993.
Bleeker, Maaike. *Visuality in the Theatre: The Locus of Looking.* New York: Palgrave Macmillan, 2008.
Bou Ali, Nadia. *Psychoanalysis and the Love of Arabic: Hall of Mirrors.* Edinburgh: Edinburgh Univ. Press, 2020.
Bourdieu, Pierre. "The Force of Law: Toward a Sociology of the Juridical Field." Translated by Richard Terdiman. *Hastings Law Journal* 38, no. 5 (1987): 805–13.
Buck-Morss, Susan. *The Dialectics of Seeing: Walter Benjamin and the Arcades Project.* Cambridge, MA: MIT Press, 1989.
Campe, Rüdiger. "Shapes and Figures: Geometry and Rhetoric in the Age of Evidence." *Monatshefte* 102, no. 3 (Fall 2010): 285–99.
Cavus, Yeliz. "Between Ibn Khaldunism and Ottoman Exceptionalism: Abdurrahman Seref Efendi's 'Tarih-i Devlet-i Osmaniyye' ('History of the Ottoman State')." Presented at the MESA, Sheraton New Orleans Hotel, November 16, 2019.
Chakrabarty, Dipesh. "Labor History and the Politics of Theory: An Indian Angle on the Middle East." In *Workers and Working Classes in the Middle East: Struggles, Histories, Historiographies,* edited by Zachary Lockman, 321–34. New York: State Univ. of New York Press, 1994.
———. *Provincializing Europe: Post-Colonial Thought and Historical Difference.* 2nd ed. Princeton, NJ: Princeton Univ. Press, 2007.
Cole, Juan Ricardo. *Colonialism and Revolution in the Middle East.* Princeton, NJ: Princeton Univ. Press, 1992.
Colla, Elliott. *Conflicted Antiquities: Egyptology, Egyptomania, Egyptian Modernity.* Illustrated ed. Durham, NC: Duke Univ. Press, 2007.
Coller, Ian. *Arab France: Islam and the Making of Modern Europe, 1798–1831.* Berkeley: Univ. of California Press, 2011.
Comay, Rebecca. *Mourning Sickness: Hegel and the French Revolution.* Stanford, CA: Stanford Univ. Press, 2010.
Corbin, Henry. *Creative Imagination in the Sufism of Ibn Arabi.* Translated by Ralph Manheim. Princeton, NJ: Princeton Univ. Press, 1969.
Dawud, Nadwa. "mustalahat 'al-taswir' wa 'al-tamthil' wa al-'takhyil' 'ind al-Zamakhshari fi al-Kashshaf'." *Journal of Qur'anic Studies* 10, no. 2 (2008): 142–77.

Dayeh, Islam. "From Tashīh to Tahqīq: Toward a History of the Arabic Critical Edition." *Philological Encounter* 4 (2019): 245–99.

De Man, Paul. *Allegories of Reading: Figural Language in Rousseau, Nietzsche, Rilke, and Proust*. New Haven, CT: Yale Univ. Press, 1979.

Derrida, Jacques. "Force of Law: The 'Mystical Foundation of Authority.'" In *Deconstruction and the Possiblity of Justice*, edited by Drucilla Cornell, Michel Rosenfeld, and David Grey Carlson, 1–67. New York: Routledge, 1992.

El-Desouky, Ayman. "Beyond Spatiality: Theorising the Local and Untranslatability as Comparative Critical Method." In *Approaches to World Literature*, edited by Joachim Küpper, 1:59–86. Berlin: Akademie Verlag, 2013.

———. "Heterologies of Revolutionary Action: On Historical Consciousness and the Sacred in Mahfouz's *Children of the Alley*." *Journal of Postcolonial Writing* 47, no. 4 (September 1, 2011): 428–39.

———. *The Intellectual and the People in Egyptian Literature and Culture: Amara and the 2011 Revolution*. London: Palgrave Pivot, 2011.

Di-Capua, Yoav. *Gatekeepers of the Arab Past: Historians and History Writing in Twentieth-Century Egypt*. Berkeley: Univ. of California Press, 2009.

Dolar, Mladen. "The Endgame of Aesthetics: From Hegel to Beckett." *Problemi International* 3, no. 3 (2019): 185–214.

Dykstra, Darrell I. *A Biographical Study in Egyptian Modernization: 'Ali Mubarak (1823/24–1893)*. Ann Arbor: Univ. of Michigan Press, 1993.

El Shamsy, Ahmed. *Rediscovering the Islamic Classics: How Editors and Print Culture Transformed an Intellectual Tradition*. Princeton, NJ: Princeton Univ. Press, 2020.

Elshakry, Marwa. *Reading Darwin in Arabic, 1860-1950*. Chicago: Univ. of Chicago Press, 2013.

Erginbas, Vefa. "Ibn Khaldunism in the Seventeenth Century: Khaldunian Concepts in Katip Celebi's 'Fadhlaka.'" Presented at the MESA, Sheraton New Orleans Hotel, November 14–17, 2019.

Ernst, Kantorowicz. *The King's Two Bodies: A Study in Medieval Political Theology*. Princeton, NJ: Princeton Univ. Press, 2016.

Esmeir, Samera. *Juridical Humanity: A Colonial History*. Stanford, CA: Stanford Univ. Press, 2012.

EzzelArab, AbdelAziz. "The Experiment of Sharif Pasha's Cabinet (1879): An Inquiry Into the Historiography of Egypt's Elite Movement." *International Journal of Middle East Studies* 36, no. 4 (November 2004): 561–89.

Fahmy, Khaled. *In Quest of Justice: Islamic Law and Forensic Medicine in Modern Egypt*. Berkeley: Univ. of California Press, 2018.
———. "Prostitution in Nineteenth Century Egypt." In *Outside In: On the Margins of the Modern Middle East*, edited by Eugene Rogan, 77–103. London: I. B. Tauris, 2002.
Fahmy, Ziad. *Ordinary Egyptians: Creating the Modern Nation through Popular Culture*. Stanford, CA: Stanford Univ. Press, 2011.
Fawwaz, Zaynab. *al-durr al-manthur fi tabaqat rabat al-khudur*. Bulaq: al-matbaʻa al-amiriyya, 1895.
Fludernik, Monika. "The Diachronization of Narratology." *Narrative* 11, no. 3 (2003): 331–48.
———. *The Fictions of Language and the Languages of Fiction*. London: Routledge, 1993.
Frederic, Jameson. *Allegory and Ideology*. New York: Verso, 2019.
———. "Third-World Literature in the Era of Multinational Capitalism." *Social Text* 15 (Autumn 1986): 65–88.
Frye, Northrop. *Anatomy of Criticism: Four Essays*. Princeton, NJ: Princeton Univ. Press, 1957.
Gelder, Geert Jan Van, and Marle Hammond, eds. *Takhyil: The Imaginary in Classical Arabic Poetics*. 2 vols. Oxford: Oxbow, 2008.
Ghurab, Mahmud. *al-khayal: ʻalam al-barzakh wa al-mithal: min kalam al-shaykh al-akbar, muhyi al-din ibn al-ʻarabi*. 2nd ed. Damascus: dar al-kitab al-ʻarabiyy, 1993.
Gleave, Robert M. "Conceptions of the Literal Sense (*zahir, haqiqa*) in Muslim Interpretive Thought." In *Interpreting Scriptures in Judaism, Christianity and Islam: Overlapping Inquiries*, edited by Mordechai Z. Cohen and Adele Berlin, 183–203. Cambridge: Cambridge Univ. Press, 2016.
———. *Islam and Literalism: Literal Meaning and Interpretation in Islamic Legal Theory*. Edinburgh: Edinburgh Univ. Press, 2013.
Gould, Rebecca. "Book Review: *Takhyil: The Imaginary in Classical Arabic Poetics. Volume 1: Texts, Volume 2: Studies by Geert Jan van Gelder*; Marlé Hammond." *Journal of Arabic Literature* 41, no. 3 (2010): 327–30.
Greenblatt, Stephen, ed. *Allegory and Representation: Selected Papers from the English Institute, 1979–1980*. Baltimore, MD: Johns Hopkins Univ. Press, 1981.
Guo, Li. *Arabic Shadow Theatre, 1300–1900: A Handbook*. Leiden: E. J. Brill, 2020.

———. *The Performing Arts in Medieval Islam: Shadow Play and Popular Poetry in Ibn Daniyal's Mamluk Cairo*. Leiden: E. J. Brill, 2012.

Hafez, Sabry. *The Genesis of Arabic Narrative Discourse: A Study in the Sociology of Modern Arabic Literature*. London: Saqi, 1993.

Hafiz, Ibrahim Muhammad. *layali sitih*. Cairo: kalimat, 2011.

Halabi, Zeina. *The Unmaking of the Arab Intellectual: Prophecy, Exile, and the Nation*. Edinburgh: Edinburgh Univ. Press, 2017.

Hämeen-Anttila, Jaakko. *Maqama: A History of a Genre*. Wiesbaden: Harrassowitz Verlag, 2002.

Hanna, Nelly. *Artisan Entrepreneurs in Cairo and Early-Modern Capitalism*. Syracuse, NY: Syracuse Univ. Press, 2011.

———. *In Praise of Books: A Cultural History of Cairo's Middle Class, Sixteenth to the Eighteenth Century*. Syracuse, NY: Syracuse Univ. Press, 2003.

Hanna, Sameh. *Bourdieu in Translation Studies: The Socio-Cultural Dynamics of Shakespeare Translation in Egypt*. New York: Routledge, 2016.

Hansenn, Jens, and Max Weiss, eds. *Arabic Thought beyond the Liberal Age: Towards an Intellectual History of the Nahda*. Cambridge: Cambridge Univ. Press, 2016.

Harb, Lara. *Arabic Poetics: Aesthetic Experience in Classical Arabic Literature*. Cambridge: Cambridge Univ. Press, 2020.

Heath, Peter. "Allegory in Islamic Literatures." In *The Cambridge Companion to Allegory*, edited by Rita Copeland and Peter T. Struck, 83–100. Cambridge: Cambridge Univ. Press, 2010.

Heinrichs, Wolfhart. "The Classification of the Sciences and the Consolidation of Philology in Classical Islam." In *Centers of Learning: Learning and Location in Pre-Modern Europe and the Near East*, 119–39. Leiden: Brill, 1995.

———. "Contacts between Scriptural Hermeneutics and Literary Theory in Islam: The Case of Majaz." *Zeitschrift Fur Geschichte Der Arabisch-Islamischen Wissenschaften* 7 (92 1991): 253–84.

———. *The Hand of the Northwind: Opinions on Metaphor and the Early Meaning of Istiʻāra in Arabic Poetics*. Wiesbaden: Deutsche Morgenlandische Gesellschaft, Kommissions-verlag Franz Steiner GmbH, 1977.

———. "Istiʻarah and Badiʻ and Their Terminological Relationship in Early Arabic Literary Criticism." *Zeitschrift Für Geschichte Der Arabisch-Islamische Wissenschaften* 1 (1984): 180–211.

———. "On the Figurative (*Majaz*) in Muslim Interpretation and Legal Hermeneutics." In *Interpreting Scriptures in Judaism, Christianity, and Islam:*

Overlapping Inquiries, edited by Mordechai Z. Cohen and Adele Berlin, 249–65. Cambridge: Cambridge Univ. Press, 2016.

———. "On the Genesis of the Haqiqa-Majaz Dichotomy." *Studia Islamica*, no. 59 (1984): 111–40.

———. "Takhyil." In *Encyclopaedia of Islam*. Accessed January 20, 2022. https://referenceworks.brillonline.com/entries/encyclopaedia-of-islam-2/takhyil-COM_1156?s.num=157&s.start=140.

———. "'Takhyil' and Its Traditions." In *Gott Ist Schön und Er Liebt Die Schönheit Festschrift für Annemarie Schimmel*, edited by Alma Giese and J. Chr. Bürgel, 227–47. Berne: Peter Lang AG, 1994.

Hill, Peter. "Utopia and Civilisation in the Arab Nahda." PhD diss., Univ. of Oxford, 2015.

———. *Utopia and Civilization in the Arab Nahda*. Cambridge: Cambridge Univ. Press, 2019.

Hourani, Albert. *Arabic Thought in the Liberal Age, 1798–1939*. Cambridge: Cambridge Univ. Press, 1983.

Ibn Ahmad al-Farahidi, Al-Khalil. *al-ʿayn*. Accessed January 24, 2022. http://www.alwaraq.net/Core/waraq/coverpage?bookid=62.

Ibn al-ʿArabi, Muhyi al-Din. *The Bezels of Wisdom*. Translated by R. W. J. Austin. Mahwah, NJ: Paulist, 1980.

Ibn ʿAshur, Muhammad al-Tahir. *tafsir al-tahrir wa al-tanwir*. 19 vols. Beirut: muʾassasat al-tarikh, 2000.

Ibn Kathir, ʿImad al-Din Ismaʿil. *tafsir al-Qurʾan al-ʿazim*. 3 vols. Beirut: Dar al-Maʿrifa, 1987.

Ibn Khaldun. *The Muqaddimah: An Introduction to History*. Edited and translated by Franz Rosenthal. 3 vols. London & New York: Pantheon Books, 1958.

Ibn Khaldun, ʿAbd al-Rahman. *al-muqaddima*. Edited by ʿAbdallah Muhammad Darwish. Damascus: dar yaʿrib, 2004.

Ibn Manzur, Muhammad ibn Mukarram. "ʾ-n-s." In *lisan al-ʿarab*, 213–19. Al-Warraq Online Classical Arabic books. Accessed January 24, 2022. http://www.alwaraq.net/Core/waraq/coverpage?bookid=89&option=1.

Ibn Rushd. *talkhis kitab al-shiʿr*. Edited by Charles Butterworth and Ahmad ʿAbd Al-Majid Haridi. Cairo: al-hayʾa al-misriyya al-ʿamma li al-kitab, 1986.

Ibn Sina, Abu ʿAli. "fann al-shiʿr min kitab al-shifaʾ." In *aristutalis fann al-shiʿr*, edited by AbdulRahman Badawi, 161–98. Cairo: maktabat al-nahda al-misriyya, 1953.

———. *sharh kitab al-musiqa*. Edited by Ghattas 'Abd al-Malik Khashaba. Cairo: al-majlis al-a'la li al-thaqafa, 2004.
Ibn Syduh, Abu al-Hassan 'Ali. *al-mukhassas*. Accessed January 24, 2022. http://www.alwaraq.net/Core/waraq/coverpage?bookid=277.
Ibrahim, 'Abdullah. *mawsu'at al-sard al-'arabiyy*. 9 vols. Dubai: qindeel li al-tiba'a wa al-nashr wa al-tawzi', 2016.
"In Search for a Hidden Group: Where Are the Awlad al-Nas." Presented at the AnneMarie Schimmel Kolleg Conference, Bonn & Online, December 17, 2022. https://www.academia.edu/44668381/_In_search_for_a_hidden_group_Where_are_the_awlād_al_nās_.
Inan, Kenan. "Avrasya U–Tursun Bey's Tarih-i Ebü'l-Feth (1488) and Ibn-i Haldun's Mukaddime." Presented at the MESA, Sheraton New Orleans Hotel, November 16, 2019.
Jacobi, Renate. "Al-Khayalani A Variation of the Khayal Motif." *Journal of Arabic Literature* 27, no. 1 (1996): 2–12.
———. "The 'Khayal' Motif in Early Arabic Poetry." *Oriens* 32 (1990): 50–64.
Al-Jawhari, Abu Nasr. "'-n-s." In *taj al-lugha wa sihah al-'arabiyya*, 24–25. Al-Warraq Online Classical Arabic Books. Accessed January 24, 2022. http://www.alwaraq.net/Core/AlwaraqSrv/bookpage?book=273&session=ABBBVFAGFGFHAAWER&fkey=2&page=1&option=1.
Kahle, Paul. "The Arabic Shadow Play in Egypt." *Journal of the Royal Asiatic Society of Great Britain and Ireland*, no. 1 (1940): 21–34.
Kahle, Paul, ed. *Three Shadow Plays by Muhammad Ibn Daniyal*. Cambridge: Trustees of E. J. W. Gibb Memorial, 1992.
Kazmi, Yedullah. "Historical Consciousness and the Notion of the Authentic Self in the Qur'an: Towards an Islamic Critical Theory." *Islamic Studies* 39, no. 3 (2000): 375–98.
———. "The Notion of History in the Qur'an and Human Destiny." *Islamic Studies* 37, no. 2 (1998): 183–200.
Kesrouany, Maya. *Prophetic Translation: The Making of Modern Egyptian Literature*. Edinburgh: Edinburgh Univ. Press, 2019.
Key, Alexander. *Language between God and the Poets: Ma'na in the Eleventh Century*. Berkeley: Univ. of California Press, 2018.
Al-Khafaji, Isam. *Tormented Births: Passages to Modernity in Europe and the Middle East*. London: Bloomsbury, 2004.
Khalidi, Tarif. *Arabic Historical Thought in the Classical Period*. Cambridge: Cambridge Univ. Press, 1994.

Khoury, Elias. "For a Third Nahda." In *Arabic Thought against the Authoritarian Age towards an Intellectual History of the Present*, edited and translated by Jens Hansenn and Max Weiss, 357–69. Cambridge: Cambridge Univ. Press, 2018.

Kramnick, Jonathan. "Empiricism, Cognitive Science, and the Novel." *Eighteenth Century* 48, no. 3, special issue, "Empiricism, Substance, Narrative" (Fall 2007): 263–85.

———. "Presence of Mind: An Ecology of Perception in Eighteenth-Century England." In *Mind, Body, Motion, Matter: Eighteenth-Century Literary Perspectives*, edited by Mary Helen McMurran and Alison Conway, 47–71. Toronto: Univ. of Toronto Press, 2016.

Kramnick, Jonathan, and Anahid Nersessian. "Form and Explanation." *Critical Inquiry* 43 (Spring 2017): 650–69.

Kurd, Muhammad 'Ali. *khitat al-sham*. 2nd ed. Beirut: dar al-'ilm li al-malayin, 1969.

Larkin, Margaret. *The Theology of Meaning: 'Abd al-Qahir al-Jurjani's Theory of Discourse*. New Haven, CT: American Oriental Society, 1995.

Laroui, Abdallah. *mafhum al-'aql: maqala fi al-mufaraqat*. Beirut: al-markaz al-thaqafiyy al-'arabiyy, 1996.

———. *mafhum al-dawla*. Beirut: al-markaz al-thaqafiyy al-'arabiyy, 2011.

Levine, George. *Dying to Know: Scientific Epistemology and Narrative in Victorian England*. Chicago: Univ. of Chicago Press, 2002.

Likrari, 'Abd al-Basit. *dinamiyyat al-khayal: mafahim wa aliyyat al-ishtighal*. Rabat: ittihad kuttab al-maghrib, 2004.

Macherey, Pierre, and Etienne Balibar. "Literature as an Ideological Form: Some Marxist Propositions." *Oxford Literary Review* 3, no. 1 (1987): 4–12.

Mahdi, Amel. *azmat al-hadara al-'arabiyya am azmat al-burjuwaziyat al-'arabiyya?* Beirut: dar al-farabi, 1974.

———. *muqaddimat nazariyya li-dirasat athar al-fikr al-ishtirakiyy fi harakat al-taharrur al-watani*. Beirut: dar al-farabi, 1980.

Mahjub, Muhammad. *al-madina wa al-khayal: dirasat farabiyya*. Tunis: dar al-'ahd al-jadid, 1989.

Al-Maqrizi, Taqi al-Din. *igathat al-'umma bi kashf al-ghumma*. Edited by Karam Hilmi Farahat. Cairo: 'ayn li al-dirasat wa al-buhuth al-insaniyya wa al-ijtima'iyya, 2007.

———. *kitab al-mawa'idh wa al-i'tibar bi-dhikr al-khitat wa al-athar, al-ma'ruf bi al-khitat al-maqriziyya*. Edited by Muhammad Zinhum and Madiha al-Sharqawi. 3 vols. Cairo: maktabat madbuli, 1998.

Marrash, Francis bin Fathallah. *ghabat al-haqq*. 2nd ed. Beirut: matba'at al-qidis jawrijiyus li al-rum al-urthudhuks, 1881.

Marsot, Afaf Lutfi Al-Sayyid. *Egypt in the Reign of Muhammad Ali*. Cambridge: Cambridge Univ. Press, 1984.

Matar, Nabil. "Alfarabi on Imagination: With a Translation of His 'Treatise on Poetry.'" *College Literature* 23, no. 1 (1996): 100–110.

Matlub, Ahmad. *mu'jam al-mustalahat al-balaghiyya wa-tatawwuriha*. 2nd ed. vol. 2. Beirut: maktabat lubnan, 2006.

McKeon, Michael. "A Defense of Dialectical Method in Literary History." *Diacritics* 19, no. 1 (1989): 83–96.

———. *The Origins of the English Novel, 1600–1740*. Baltimore, MD: Johns Hopkins Univ. Press, 1987.

———. "Romance Transformation II: Bunyan and the Literalization of Allegory." In *The Origins of the English Novel, 1600–1740*, 295–314. Baltimore, MD: Johns Hopkins Univ. Press, 1987.

———. *The Secret History of Domesticity: Public, Private, and the Division of Knowledge*. Baltimore, MD: Johns Hopkins Univ. Press, 2005.

Mendola, Tara, and Jacques Lezra, eds. *The Year Book of Comparative Literature: Allegory and Political Representation*. Toronto: Univ. of Toronto Press, 2015.

Mestyan, Adam. "Arabic Lexicography and European Aesthetics: The Origin of Fann." *Muqarnas* 28 (2011): 69–100.

Misbahi, Muhammad. *jadaliyyit al-'aql wa al-madina fi al-falsafa al-'arabiyya al-mu'asira*. Beirut: muntada al-ma'arif, 2013.

Mitchell, Timothy. *Colonising Egypt*. Cambridge: Cambridge Univ. Press, 1988.

Modarressi, Hossein. "Some Recent Analyses of the Concept of Majaz in Islamic Jurisprudence." *Journal of the American Oriental Society* 106, no. 4 (1986): 787–91.

Modrak, Deborah K. W. *Aristotle's Theory of Language and Meaning*. New York: Cambridge Univ. Press, 2001.

Mondal, Anshuman A. "Between Turban and Tarbush: Modernity and the Anxieties of Transition in Hadith 'Isa Ibn Hisham." *Alif: Journal of Comparative Poetics*, no. 17 (1997): 201–21.

Monroe, James T. *The Art of Badi' Az-Zaman al-Hamadhani as Picaresque Narrative*. Beirut: American Univ. of Beirut, 1983.

Monroe, James T., and Mark F. Pettigrew. "The Decline of Courtly Patronage and the Appearance of New Genres in Arabic Literature: The Case of the

Zajal, the Maqama, and the Shadow Play." *Journal of Arabic Literature* 34, nos. 1–2 (2003): 138–77.

Montgomery, James E. *The Vagaries of the Qasidah: The Tradition and Practice of Early Arabic Poetry*. Oxford: E. J. W. Gibb Memorial Trust, 1997.

Moosa, Matti. *The Origins of Modern Arabic Fiction*. London: Lynne Rienner, 1997.

Moreh, Shmuel. "The Shadow Play ('Khayal al-Zill') in the Light of Arabic Literature." *Journal of Arabic Literature* 18 (1987): 46–61.

Moretti, Franco. "Conjectures on World Literature." *New Left Review*, no. 1 (February 1, 2000): 54–68.

Mubarak, Ali. *'alam al-din*. Alexandria: matba'at jaridat al-mahrusa, 1882.

———. *al-khitat al-tawfiqiyya al-jadida li misr al-qahira wa muduniha wa biladiha al-qadima wa al-shahira*. 20 vols. Cairo: Bulaq, 1889.

Muhanna, Elias. *The World in a Book: Al-Nuwayri and the Islamic Encyclopaedic Tradition*. Princeton, NJ: Princeton Univ. Press, 2017.

Al-Muwaylihi, Muhammad. *hadith 'isa ibn hisham*. Edited by Roger Allen. Cairo: al-majlis al-a'la li al-thaqafa, 2002.

Al-Naqib, Khaldun. "bina' al-mujtama' al-'arabiyy: ba'd al-furud al-bahthiyya." *al-mustaqbal al-'arabiyy* 79 (September 1985): 4–41.

Newman, Daniel L. *An Imam in Paris: Account of a Stay in France by an Egyptian Cleric (1826–1831)*, by Rifa'a Rafi' Al-Tahtawi, 114–16. Edited and translated by Daniel L Newman, New York: Saqi, 2012.

Al-Nisaburi, Farid al-Din al-'Attar. *mantiq al-tayr*. Translated by Badi' Muhammad Jum'a. Beirut: Dar al-Andalus, 1984.

Omri, Mohamed-Salah. "Local Narrative Form and Constructions of the Arabic Novel." *Novel: A Forum on Fiction* 41, nos. 2–3 (2008): 244–63.

Orfali, Bilal W., and Maurice Pomerantz. *The Maqamat of Badi' Al-Zaman al-Hamadhani: Authorship, Texts, Contexts*. Berlin: Reichert Verlag, 2022.

Ouyang, Wen-chin. "Fictive Mode, 'Journey to the West,' and Transformation of Space: 'Ali Mubarak's Discourses of Modernization." *Comparative Critical Studies* 4, no. 3 (2007): 331–58.

Patel, Abdulrazzak. "Language Reform and Controversy in the Nahda: Al-Shartuni's Position as a Grammarian in Sahm." *Journal of Semitic Studies* 55, no. 2 (2010): 509–38.

Powell, Eve Trout. *A Different Shade of Colonialism: Egypt, Great Britain, and the Mastery of the Sudan*. Los Angeles: Univ. of California Press, 2003.

Ramadan, 'Abd al-'Azim, and 'Abd al-Mun'im Ibrahim al-Jumay'iyy, eds. *al-tankit wa al-tabkit*. Cairo: al-hay'a al-misriyya al-'amma li al-kitab, 1994.
Rastegar, Kamran. *Literary Modernity between the Middle East and Europe: Textual Transactions in Nineteenth-Century Arabic, English, and Persian Literatures*. New York: Routledge, 2007.
Reid, Donald Malcolm. *Whose Pharaohs?: Archaeology, Museums, and Egyptian National Identity from Napoleon to World War I*. Berkeley: Univ. of California Press, 2002.
Rosenthal, Franz. *The Muqaddimah: An Introduction to History*. Abridged ed. Princeton, NJ: Princeton Univ. Press, 2005.
El-Rouayheb, Khaled. *The Development of Arabic Logic (1200–1800)*. Berlin: Schwab Verlag, 2019.
Sacks, Jeffrey. "Futures of Literature: Inhitat, Adab, Naqd." *Diacritics* 37 (December 1, 2007): 32–55.
———. *Iterations of Loss: Mutilation and Aesthetic Form, al-Shidyaq to Darwish*. New York: Fordham Univ. Press, 2015.
Al-Saghani, Rida al-Din. "'-n-s." In *al-'abab al-zakhir*, 60–62. Al-Warraq Online Classical Arabic Books. Accessed January 24, 2022. http://www.alwaraq.net/Core/waraq/coverpage?bookid=3133.
Said, Edward. *Orientalism*. London: Penguin, 1978.
Salim, Latifa Muhammad. *al-quwwa al-ijtima'iyya fi al-thawra al-'urabiyya*. Cairo: dar el-shuuk, 2009.
Santner, Eric L. *The Royal Remains: The People's Two Bodies and the Endgames of Sovereignty*. Chicago: Univ. of Chicago Press, 2011.
Sariyannis, Marinos. "Ottoman Ibn Khaldun Revisited: The Pre-Tanzimat Reception of the Muqaddima from Kinalizade to Sanizade." In *Political Thought and Practice in the Ottoman Empire*, edited by Marinos Sariyannis, 251–86. Heraklion: Crete Univ. Press, 2019.
Sartain, E. M., ed. *Jalal Al-Din al-Suyuti, Volume 2, Al-Tahadduth Binimat Allah*. Cambridge: Cambridge Univ. Press, 1975.
Schwarz, Roberto. *A Master on the Periphery of Capitalism: Machado de Assis*. Translated by John Gledson. Durham, NC: Duke Univ. Press Books, 2001.
Selim, Samah. "Languages of Civilization: Nation, Translation, and the Politics of Race in Colonial Egypt." *Translator* 16 (April 2009): 139–56.
———. *Popular Fiction, Translation and the Nahda in Egypt*. London: Palgrave Macmillan, 2019.

———. *The Novel and the Rural Imaginary in Egypt, 1880–1985*. London: Routledge Curzon, 2004.

Shah, Mustafa. "Classical Islamic Discourse on the Origins of Language: Cultural Memory and the Defense of Orthodoxy." *Numen* 58 (2011): 314–44.

———. "The Philological Endeavours of the Early Arabic Linguists: Theological Implications of the Tawqif-Istilaḥ Antithesis and the Majaz Controversy- Part I." *Journal of Qur'anic Studies* 1, no. 1 (1999): 27–46.

———. "The Philological Endeavours of the Early Arabic Linguists: Theological Implications of the Tawqif-Istilah Antithesis and the Majaz Controversy (Part II)." *Journal of Qur'anic Studies* 2, no. 1 (April 1, 2000): 43–66.

El-Shakry, Omnia. *The Great Social Laboratory: Subjects of Knowledge in Colonial and Post-Colonial Egypt*. Stanford, CA: Stanford Univ. Press, 2007.

Sheehi, Stephen. *Foundations of Modern Arab Identity*. Gainesville: Univ. of Florida Press, 2004.

Sheppard, Anne. "Preface." In *Takhyil: The Imaginary in Classical Arabic Poetics*, edited by Marle Hammond and Geert Jan Van Gelder, ix–xv. Oxford: Oxbow, 2008.

Al-Shidyaq, Ahmad Faris. "fi al-mukhayyila wa al-takhayyul." In *kanz al-ragha'ib fi muntakhabat al-jawa'ib*, by Ahmad Faris Al-Shidyaq, edited by Salim Faris, 10–13. Istanbul: matba'at al-jawa'ib, 1871.

Shukri, Ghali. "min al-ishkaliyyat al-manhajiyya fi al-tariq al-'arabiyy ila 'ilm ijtima' al-ma'rifa." *al-mustaqbal al-'arabiyy* 77 (July 1985): 126–36.

Spivak, Gayatri Chakravorty. "Can the Subaltern Speak?" In *Marxism and the Interpretation of Culture*, edited by Cary Nelson and Lawrence Grossberg, 271–313. Chicago: Univ. of Illinois Press, 1988.

Starkey, Paul. *Modern Arabic Literature*. Edinbrugh: Edinburgh Univ. Press, 2006.

Al-Tabari, Abu Ja'far. *tarikh al-rusul wa al-muluk*. Edited by M. J. de Goeje. 15 vols. Leiden: Brill, 1879.

Tageldin, Shaden M. *Disarming Words: Empire and the Seductions of Translation in Egypt*. Berkeley: Univ. of California Press, 2011.

Al-Tahtawi, Rifa'a Rafi'. *al-diwan al-nafis fi iwan baris aw takhlis al-ibriz fi talkhis bariz*. Edited by 'Ali Ahmad Kan'an. Beirut: al-markaz al-'arabiyy li al-dirasat wa al-nashr, 1977.

———. *al-kanz al-mukhtar fi kashf al-aradi wa al-bihar*. 2nd ed. Torah: matba'at al-tubajiya, 1835.

———. *takhlis al-ibriz fi talkhis bariz*. Edited by 'Alam Mahdi, Ahmed Ahmed Badawi, and Anwar Loqa. Cairo: sharikat maktabat wa matba'at mustafa al-babi al-halabi wa awladih bi misr, 1958.

Tanoukhi, Nirvana. "The Scale of World Literature." *New Literary History* 39, no. 3 (2008): 599–617.

Al-Tawhidi, Abu Hayyan. *al-imta' wa al-mu'anasa*. Accessed January 28, 2022. www.alwaraq.net/Core/waraq/coverpage?bookid=11.

Al-Tuwayrani, Hasan. *al-nashr al-zahriyy fi rasa'il al-nisr al-dahriyy*. dar al-khilafa: matba'at mahmud bek, 1889.

Taymur Pasha, Ahmed. *tarajim a'yan al-qarn al-thalith 'ashar aa 'awa'il al-qarn al-rabi' 'ashar*. Cairo: dar al-'afaq al-'arabiyya, 2001.

Tekin, Kenan. "Reforming Categories of Science and Religion in the Late Ottoman Empire." PhD diss., Columbia Univ., 2016.

Turner, Colin. "Wealth as an Immortality Symbol in the Qur'an: A Reconsideration of the Mal/Amwal Verses." *Journal of Qur'anic Studies* 8, no. 2 (2006): 58–83.

Vrolijk, Arnoud, ed. *Bringing a Laugh to a Scowling Face: A Study and Critical Edition of the "Nuzhat al-Nufus Wa-Mudhik al-'abus" by 'Ali Ibn Sudun al-Basbugawi (Cairo 810/1407–Damascus 868/1464)*. Leiden: Research School CNWS, School of Asian, African, and Amerindian Studies, 1998.

Wang, Qin. "Fredric Jameson's 'Third World Literature' and 'National Allegory': A Defense." *Frontiers of Literary Study in China* 7, no. 4 (2013): 654–71.

Weiss, Bernard G. "Medieval Muslim Discussions of the Origins of Language." *Zeitschrift Der Deutschen Morgenlandischen Gesellschaft* 124, no. 1 (1974): 33–41.

———. "Text and Application: Hermeneutical Reflections on Islamic Legal Interpretation." In *The Law Applied: Contextualizing the Islamic Shari'a. A Volume in Honor of Frank E. Vogel*, edited by Peri Bearman and Wolfhart Heinrichs, 374–96. New York: I. B. Tauris, 2008.

Young, Terri de. *Mahmud Sami Al-Barudi: Reconfiguring Society and the Self*. Syracuse, NY: Syracuse Univ. Press, 2015.

Zamir, Syed Rizwan. "'Tafsir Al-Qur'an Bi-l-Qur'an': The Hermeneutics of Imitation and 'Adab' in Ibn 'Arabi's Interpretation of the Qur'an." *Islamic Studies* 50, no. 1 (2011): 5–23.

Zaydan, Jurji. *tarikh 'adab al-lugha al-'arabiyya*. Windsor: Hindawi, 2017.

'Urabi, Ahmad. *mudhakkirat ahmad 'urabi: kashf al-sitar 'an sirr al-asrar fi al-nahda al-misriyya al-mashhura bi al-thawra al-'urabiyya*. Edited by 'Abd al-Mun'im Ibrahim al-Jumay'iyy. Cairo: dar al-kutub wa al-watha'iq al-qawmiyya, 2005.

Al-Zamakhshari, Abu al-Qasim. *al-kashshaf 'an haqa'iq al-tanzil wa 'uyun al-'aqawil fi wujuh al-ta'wil*. 3 vols. Cairo: al-maktaba al-tijariyya al-kubra, 1953.

Index

'Abduh, Muhammad, 31, 198, 215
Abdulhamid (Sultan), 198
Abul Su'ud Effendi, 236
Abu Zayd, Nasr Hamid, 204–5, 210n4, 211n11, 212n20, 219n31, 237n10
actor, 60, 89, 133, 140–41, 189–90
'Ad, people of, 113, 245n26
adab, 91, 95, 114, 129, 138, 149, 151–52, 160–61, 166, 197, 200–201, 243n14, 253n4; commitment, 253n4; ethical dispositions/*akhlaq* 23, 56, 146–51, 160–61, 165, 193–200, 202, 253n4; *'ibra*/moral, 57, 116, 118, 136, 166, 194, 195–99, 238n15, 253n4; virtue and vices, 53, 56–57, 116, 197, 199, 238n20
Addison, Joseph, 65
al-Afghani, Jamal al-Din, 31, 198, 215n17
aggression, 147–49, 154–56, 161
Agoub, Joseph 233n34
al-ahali. See al-nas
ahqaf, 235n2, 245n26. *See also athar*
akhbar, 150, 166
'alam al-din. See Mubarak, 'Ali
'Ali, Muhammad (Pasha), 15, 30, 70–71, 172, 176, 215n13, 226n64
allegory, 26, 39–41, 51, 75, 79–90, 98–120, 128, 130, 178, 183, 188, 232n28, 246; *tamthil*, 79–80
America: civil war, 15; New World, 83–85, 125; slavery, 15, 83, 85, 90, 92, 102, 178

'Amil, Mahdi, 204, 211n11, 212n20
'amma/khassa, 54–57, 138, 164, 180, 199–200. *See also* class
Antun, Farah 216n18
archaeology, 110–12, 120, 124, 138–39
architecture, 108–14, 120–22, 127, 134, 139, 153, 251n69
Aristotle, 65, 217–18nn20–21, 219n28
artifact, 107–12, 120, 126–27
'asabiyya, 150, 152–55. *See also al-nas*
al-'Askari, Abu Hilal, 248n42
Ashanti Empire, 93
Assyrians, 25, 27, 82
athar, 106–38, 142–43, 150–62, 168, 183–90, 204, 236n6, 236n8, 236–37n9, 249–50n49; *'idha'at al-athar*, 109; *iqtifa' al-athar*, 108, 141; monumental trace, 110, 114, 120, 126–28, 131–34, 137, 152–53; Quranic, 113–18, 121–31, 136–37; *rasm*, 153; ruin, 16, 28–29, 36, 38, 71, 107–10, 128, 130–32, 134, 214n7, 236n8; *talal*, 108; true/false, 123, 127–28, 137–38
'Attar, Farid ud-Din, 235n1
audience, 26–27, 29–30, 38–41, 48–52, 60–61, 70, 77, 105, 170; reader, 29–30, 70, 99–102, 133, 144, 148, 165–66, 170, 177–79, 186–91, 194–96, 241n7; spectator, 26

author/authorship, 61, 103, 165, 171–72, 202, 234n43; authorial voice, 103, 171–72; authority, 117; voice, 8, 89, 103, 148, 171–72, 178, 202, 243n12
'ayan. *See* sensory
al-Azhar, 15, 31, 61, 93, 223n54
al-'Azm, Sadiq Jalal, 219n31

badi' poetry, 48–52
al-bahima, 246n36
balagha, 217–18n20
Baroque period, 236n8
al-Barudi, Mahmud Sami, 31, 215n17
benefit, 109, 119, 127, 166–67, 196–97; *naf'*, 167, 197
binaries, 147; dichotomy, 95, 113–14, 127, 131, 137, 142, 147, 159, 164, 205–6; dyad, 44–45, 55, 152

Cairo, 15, 30, 38, 93–94, 97, 100, 120, 123, 136–37, 153, 157, 189
canon, 12–14, 17–18, 21–23, 26–28, 34, 44, 57, 63, 69–72, 74, 78, 82, 99, 102–3, 109, 140–43, 156, 161–62, 165–69, 176, 182–87, 192–95, 201–6, 211n15; poetic canon, 49–52, 222n39; canonizing, 11; canonicity, 13–16
Canterbury Tales, The, 20
cemetery, 30, 71, 116–19, 132
character/ization, 14, 17, 20, 25–29, 38–39, 69–70, 88, 99–100, 104–5, 123–25, 133, 141–44, 148, 161, 166–79, 183–91, 212n19. *See also al-nas*
Chaucer, Geoffrey, 20
Circle of Eight Words, 149–55, 160, 194–95
civilization, 15–16, 25, 61, 82–90, 96–97, 108–10, 126–31, 142–43, 146–48, 150–55, 157, 178–81, 186, 191, 204, 244n18; *al-tamaddun*, 178; *al-madaniyya*, 151, 157, 242n9, 244n18; *'umran*, 148, 150–53, 244n18, 251–52n69; *'imara*, 179, 244n18, 251–52n69; polis, 55, 57, 149, 157, 180, 242n9, 244n17
civil war, 15, 100, 102
class, 200, 221n36, 246n36; bourgeoisie. 204; *effendiyya* 205; land-owning, 201; middle, 197, 205; ruling, 127, 134–37, 176
classical Arabic ode, 28, 36, 71, 107–8, 111, 145; eulogy/*madih*/panegyric, 56, 165–66, 218n23; *hija'*/lampoon, 56, 165; *nasib*, 36, 111, 218n23; *qasida*, 36–37; *rahil*, 218n23
collective. *See al-nas*
colonialism, 2, 197–98, 252–53n2
commoners. *See 'amma/khassa*
corporeal/incorporeal, 22, 67, 222n46
cosmology, 44–46, 53, 57, 63–64, 253n4
court, 38, 123–24, 177, 186
crossing, 39, 43–46, 51–57, 64, 69–70, 79, 86, 99–102, 161–65, 177–81, 86, 218n24, 222–23n46, 23228; *majaz*, 39, 42, 47, 56, 64, 79, 173, 219n28, 221n34, 246–47n36; *'ubur*, 57
culturalism, 181–82, 252n1
cycle/cyclical, 82, 113–14, 118–19, 124, 128, 131–32, 137, 150–51, 201; rise and fall, 70–71, 82, 113, 124, 128, 131–32, 159–60, 201

dahr, 105, 107, 237–38n14
Dalloz, Victor, 53
death, 30, 71, 110, 116–18, 132–36
deed(s), 105–8, 111–15, 129, 131–33, 138, 166, 226n67

Index   273

al-Desuqi, Ibrahim, 179
development, 80
discourse, 33–34, 40, 43, 45, 62, 90–91, 107, 109–10, 112–13, 116–17, 133, 160–61, 175, 203; direct, 170; knowledge-producing, 23, 107, 113, 150–52; literary, 197–200; poetic, 68–69, 169; Sufi, 56
divine, the, 35, 39, 44–46, 54–56, 112–15, 121, 127–31, 142, 164, 221n34
dream, 15–17, 24–26, 29–30, 33, 36–39, 42, 70–73, 83–86, 115–16, 145
dynasty, 117, 119, 130, 135, 150–56, 172; Islamic, 128, 195

Earth, 104, 125, 146
East/West, 6, 9, 25, 82, 126, 166, 187, 205
education, 16, 92, 101, 134, 189, 197, 200, 224n60, 241n7; degrees, 158; institutions, 15, 93; journey, 93; *tarbiya*, 160–61, 197, 200, 246n36
effacement 111, 134, 153. *See also* athar
Egypt, 15, 31, 32, 37, 40, 90, 93–94, 109, 127–30, 143–44, 178, 188, 198–99; Alexandria, 61, 93–94, 97, 100; Ancient, 25–27, 97, 127; bankruptcy, 197–98, 215n17; Egyptians, 95, 130, 132–33, 172; occupation, 2, 198, 215n17; Pharaoh, 113, 122, 127–31, 134; plague, 100; revolution, 205; Tanta, 93
Eiffel Tower, 120–27, 186
elision, 5–12, 81, 131, 205–6; French Revolution, 95, 159; names, 171–75
elite/masses. *See ʿamma/khassa*
embodiment, 50, 56, 79, 97, 158, 222n46; disembodiment, 167; sensory, 22, 168

emotions, 27–29, 37, 83–84, 89, 105, 145; affective, 23, 28, 33–36, 41–43, 49–52, 56, 69, 75, 165, 169
empiricism, 21–22, 33, 51, 64, 97, 168; cognition/cognitive, 45–52, 64, 66–67; epistemology, 43, 143, 173, 185–203; evidence, 21, 64, 79, 90; mind, 21–22, 33–34, 42–45, 49–50, 60–62; science/scientific, 51, 62, 82, 123, 128–29, 145–46, 181, 192
encyclopedia, 78, 92, 95
England, 15, 61, 93, 96, 196; London, 143
episode: episodic structure, 4, 17, 19, 57, 71–72, 91–92, 97–98, 140, 169, 186–89
epistemology, 80, 90, 96, 112, 115, 143, 162, 173, 185–86, 190–203; hierarchy, 75
estrangement technique, 135, 140
ethics, 56, 60, 199, 202
Eurocentrism. *See* trope of the encounter
Europe, 1, 3–13, 17, 61, 106, 130, 203; creditors, 198
externalization, 29, 54, 61, 84–85, 144, 229n4

al-Farabi, Abu Nasr, 54–55, 179–80
Fawwaz, Zaynab, 109
fiction: fictionality, 17, 49, 218n22, 250n52; metafiction, 250n55
"Forest." *See* al-Marrash, Francis
form, 1–4, 8–13, 16–22, 29, 43–44, 61, 91–92, 100, 106–10, 114–17, 144–46, 154–55, 159, 161–62, 183–86, 203–6, 242n9; episodic, 19, 72; formal cohesion, 18, 20; ideological, 81, 92; *lafz* (vocal form), 45, 64; literary, 29, 62, 69, 71–72, 92, 95–96, 193–94, 198–200; narrative, 1, 51, 80, 103,

form (*cont.*)
106, 187; *sura*, 152; theatrical, 37–38, 58–60, 88
frame tale/narrative/episode, 20, 33, 70
France, 15, 30, 32, 58–59, 61, 77–78, 93–95, 122, 143, 157; civilization, 157; dual control, 198; French Revolution, 94–95, 100, 124, 159–60, 190, 206; literature, 3, 8, 53; Marseilles, 93–94, 97, 143; Palace of Versailles, 123–25, 186–90; Paris, 32, 58, 120–23, 143, 156–58, 189, 239n24
freedom (*al-hurriya/al-hurriyyin*), 87, 156–59, 178, 186–87, 246–47n36

Garraud, René, 53
general/particular, 165–75, 177–79, 183. See also *al-nas*
genre, 12, 23, 30, 37–40, 72, 79, 90–92, 105–9, 151, 153, 187; hybridity, 10, 90; novel, 4–8; romance, 212n19
geography, 95, 144–46
ghabat al-haqq. See al-Marrash, Francis
governance, 123–25
Greater Syria, 2, 6, 85–86, 90, 92, 100, 102, 109, 125, 178; sectarian strife, 100, 102

hadith (narrative), 105, 107; *'ilm al-hadith*, 111; *'isa ibn hisham*, 29–31, 70–71, 99–100, 116–20, 124–31, 132–33, 157–59, 164–77, 188–89, 245n26, 246n36; *'isnad*, 103; *khabar*, 107, 150; *riwaya*, 107, 150. See also *athar*; history
al-Hamadhani, Badi' al-Zaman, 30
haqiqa, 31, 39, 42, 64, 170, 221n34. See also *khayal*; *majaz*

al-Hariri, 171
Heinrichs, Wolfhart, 34, 216–17n20, 219–20n32
hermeneutic, 39, 42–57, 63–64, 161–80. See also *khayal*; *al-nas*
history, 21–22, 24–32, 58–72, 76–77, 105–7, 125–42, 153–56; ahistoricity, 10, 203; historical truth, 33, 73, 85–86, 89–92, 98, 101; historicism, 181; historicity, 21, 182, 204–5; *tarikh*, 106–7, 150, 198; *waqa'i'*, 57–58, 60–62, 69, 107, 166–69, 225. See also *athar*; *al-nas*
hizb. See nation
Homer, 60, 65
horama (diorama, panorama), 58–60
human nature, 22, 44–46, 97, 113, 141–62, 167–68, 181. See also *athar*; *al-nas*

Ibn al-'Arabi, 53–55, 165, 179–80, 216–17n20, 221n38, 222n44, 222n46, 223nn49–50
Ibn al-Haytham, 38
Ibn al-Mu'taz, 49
Ibn 'Ashur, Muhammad al-Tahir, 174–75
Ibn Daniyal, 38–40, 42, 219n25; *'ajib wa gharib*, 38; *al-mutayyam wa al-da'i' al-yutayyim*, 39; *tayf al-khayal*, 38–39;
Ibn Khaldun, 'Abd al-Rahman, 142–55, 159–64, 225n63. See also *athar*
Ibn Manzur, Muhammad ibn Mukarram, 15, 93, 162, 163
Ibn Rushd, 214n7
Ibn Sina, Abu 'Ali, 56, 68, 166
Ibrahim, Hafiz, 171, 174, 240n39
ideology, 18, 80–81, 212n19
al-Idrissi, Sharif, 229n4; *anwar 'ulwi al-ajram*, 229

iham, 216–18n20
imagination. *See* Addison, Joseph; *khayal*
immanence, 107–23
al-Insan newspaper, 14. *See also* al-Tuwayrani, Hassan Husni
intellect, 25–27, 54–55, 83–84, 123, 128–29, 226–27n69
interiority, 17, 142, 229n4. *See also* character/ization; externalization
interpretation. *See tafsir*
invisibility, 112, 141–42, 167–84. *See also khayal; al-nas*
Iraq, 40, 225; Basra, 38; Mosul 38
Istanbul, 198–99, 215n17
isti'ara, 47, 49 216–17n20
istilah wa tawqif, 22134. *See also* cosmology; *majaz*

al-Jabarti, Abdulrahman, 108, 233–34n39, 247–48n39
al-Jabri, Muhammad 'Abid, 225n63
al-Jahiz, Abu 'Uthman, 176, 249n48; *Kitab al-Bukhala'*, 176, 249n48
al-Jawa'ib, 198
jidd/hazl, 58
judgment, 43, 139–41, 161–62, 181–82, 189–95, 199–202. *See also* history; human nature
jurisprudence (*fiqh*), 109, 150
al-Jurjani, 'Abd al-Qahir, 48–52, 216–17n20
justice/injustice, 66–67, 113–14, 127–28, 153–55, 194–97. *See also* Circle of Eight Words

kalam. *See* discourse
khayal, 17–18, 22–28, 31–58, 60–69, 73–76, 157, 165–68, 179–84, 221n36, 227; fancy, 40–41; image, 17, 22–24, 33, 35–36, 40–44, 65–68, 75, 165–69, 179–80, 202; imagination, 8, 17, 31, 65; *khayal al-ma'ata*, 40; phantasma, 40, 65; specter, 17, 32, 37–41, 88, 183–84; *tayf al-khayal*, 36–42. *See also* dream; sensory
khitat, 108–9, 153–55, 187; *al-khitat al-sultaniyya*, 154–55
kinaya, 47, 169–79, 183, 188, 251n63

lafz/ma'na, 44, 45, 59, 64, 68, 168, 171
Lane, Edward William, 61, 93, 179
Laroui, 'Abdullah, 223n49, 225n63, 243–44n16, 251n65
Layali Sitih, 171, 240
lexicography, 36, 40, 45, 48, 163–64, 175
Lisan al-'Arab, 15, 61, 93, 162
literary: history, 188, 192, 202; object, 19, 73, 186; optic, 69–72, 99–102, 139–40; perception, 83, 183, 219n26; staging, 74–82, 97–101; truth, 20–22, 33–34, 57, 73. *See also* form

Macedonia, 82, 97
madih/hija'. *See* classical Arabic ode
majaz, 39, 42, 47, 56, 64, 79, 173, 219n28, 221n34, 246–47n36. *See also* crossing
al-malik, 32, 40, 157. *See also* sovereignty
al-manar, 215n17
al-Manikli, Ahmed Pasha, 15, 30, 70, 171, 215n13
al-Maqrizi, Taqi al-Din, 229n4; *ighathat al-'umma bi-kashf al-ghumma*, 229n4
al-Marrash, Francis, 15, 24, 26–29, 69–72, 86–92, 98–103, 123–29, 177–80, 246–47n36

mediation, 43–44, 55, 63, 66, 71, 78–88, 92, 226–27n69. *See also khayal*; sensory
memory, 56–57, 67–68, 108, 113–14, 121, 128–32, 135–37, 147. *See also athar; khayal*
metaphor. *See isti'ara*
metonymy. *See kinaya*
middle class. *See* class
mimesis. *See muhakah*
mirrors for princes, 151
"modernist" poets. *See muhdathun*
modernity, 1–12, 16–17, 20, 80–81, 203–5
modernization paradigm, 1, 16. *See also* trope of the encounter
Molière, 176, 249n48
monarchy, 149–50
morality plays, 91
mortality/immortality. *See athar*
motif, 36–37, 39
Mu'tazalite, 52
Mubarak, Ali, 14–15, 57–63, 70, 75–82, 92–95, 97–103, 107, 109, 122–24, 128–29, 143–54, 159–60, 179, 190, 206, 213n2, 226n64, 229n4, 233n33, 244n18; *'alam al-din*, 15, 60–61, 74, 78–82, 92–103, 123–25, 128–29, 143–48, 159–61, 179, 190
muhakah, 56, 217–18n20
muhdathun, 48–50
al-Muqaddima, 143–44, 147, 150–53. *See also* Ibn Khaldun, 'Abd al-Rahman
museum, 124–25, 190
music, 36, 44, 56–57, 221n33
al-Muwaylihi, Ibrahim, 15, 31, 198
al-Muwaylihi, Muhammad. *See hadith*

al-Nadim, 'Abdullah, 129–30, 171, 197–202, 246n36; *kitab al-masamir*, 198; "Medical Council," 14, 16, 115, 130–32; *al-tankit wa al-tabkit*, 129–30, 198, 246–47. *See also* 'Urabi Revolt
nahda, 2–13, 75, 80–81, 94, 98, 106, 111, 204–5. *See also* trope of the encounter
Napoleon, 2, 94–95, 127, 131, 160, 233n34
al-Naqib, Khaldun, 252n2
al-Naqqash, Marun, 171
narrative/narrativization. *See* form; *hadith*
narratological: description, 91; practice, 33–34, 71–74, 79, 140–41, 168–71; problems, 115, 154, 190–91, 197; structure, 94, 96–102, 144, 193, 202. *See also* literary
narrator, 25–30, 70–71, 82–86, 88–89, 99–100, 104–5, 133, 170–71, 178–79, 231n17, 243n12; *al-rawi*, 243n12. *See also* character/ization
al-nas, 18, 40, 42, 62, 107, 116, 124–27, 131–32, 137–42, 149, 156–203, 247n38, 247–48n39, 248n40, 248–49n42, 249n49; *al-ahali*, 157, 247n38; *al-insan*, 55–56, 95, 144, 152, 162–64, 223n49, 246n36; public, 58–60, 133, 138, 165–66, 168, 173–77, 200. *See also* character/ization
al-nashr al-zahri ("Floral Publishing"). *See* al-Tuwayrani, Hassan Husni
Nasib. *See* classical Arabic ode
nation, 61–62, 112, 155, 164; *hizb*, 252n2; *hubb al-watan*, 155; nationalism, 4, 197, 252–53n2; national literature, 5, 8; *watan (al)*, 130, 186, 199; *'umma*, 166
nature, 22, 71, 94–97, 102, 186, 195; *theatrum* of nature, 91, 100. *See also* human nature

Neoplatonic and Aristotelian traditions, 65, 150, 216–18n20
New World. *See* America
novel. *See* genre
Nubar Pasha, 172

object: archaeological, 110, 120–25; architectural, 110; empirical, 21, 101, 168; of knowledge, 1–11, 44–45; literary, 19, 186, 189; 73–88, 97–101, 107, 139–42; political, 156–57, 181–84, 200–201, 231n17; props, 91–92, 102, 128; sensory, 18, 21–29, 39–43, 46–47, 62–64, 118, 165, 177, 182–83, 189, 218n24
One Thousand and One Nights, 20
ontology, 43–44, 51–53, 165, 180. *See also* epistemology
optical devices, 17, 25–29, 33–34, 70–71, 99–100, 104, 161, 189; optical mime, 38
order/chaos, 93, 95–97, 147
Ottoman Empire, 2, 37, 71, 104, 125

pedagogy, 18, 23, 33, 50, 60–61, 92, 99, 138–45, 165–66, 174, 192–200. *See also* education
people, the. *See al-nas*
perceivability. *See* sensory
periphrasis. *See kinaya*
permanence. *See athar*
Persia, 82, 97
personification, 14–15, 83–84, 177–80. *See also* character/ization
phantasma. *See khayal*
philosophy, 177–78; of history, 90–92, 95, 107, 123; philosophers, 48–56, 150, 242n9

plot, 17, 20, 30, 33, 38–40, 72, 87–92, 142, 158–59, 179, 187–88; emplotment, 7, 21, 74–75, 106, 115. *See also* form; history
poetics, 45–56, 216–18n20. *See also khayal*
poets/poetry, 48–50, 145, 242–43n11
politics, 16–18, 32, 44, 47, 55–56, 66, 90–91, 129–80, 194–205, 216–18n20, 242n11, 246n36, 252–53n2; *'ilm al-siyasa al-madaniyya*, 151; polis, 55–57, 149, 157, 179–80, 242n9, 244n17; representational, 32, 242n9; *siyasa*, 246n36; treatises, 91. *See also al-nas*
poststructuralism, 16, 79–81
power. *See* sovereignty
protagonist. *See* character/ization; narrator
public, the. *See al-nas*

qawl, 53
al-Qays, Imru', 28, 71

racism, 181–82, 252n1
al-Rafi'i, Mustafa Sadiq, 253n4
rationality, 21, 129. *See also* empiricism
al-Razi, 216–18n20
realism, 48, 79–82, 98–103; hyperrealism, 51, 75, 169, 183; protorealism, 120. *See also* allegory; history
reference: referentiality, 174–91, 250n53. *See also athar; al-nas*
reform, 23, 33, 50–51, 87, 129, 138, 174, 187, 192, 198, 253n4; *islah*, 149. *See also* pedagogy
relationality. *See al-nas*
republic, republican mode of rule, 150, 156–57

rhetoric (*al-khataba*), 54–55, 150–51, 216–18n20
Rida, Rashid, 31, 215–16n17
Roman Empire, 25, 27, 82
Romanticism, 65, 236n8
Rosenthal, Franz, 242n9, 243–44n16

Said Pasha, 215n13
saj', 30
al-Sakkaki, 216–18n20
Sannu', Ya'qub, 171
al-saq 'ala al-saq. See al-Shidyaq, Ahmed Faris
science, 21-27, 62-64, 82, 181, 192, 213, 233-34; scientific experiment, 192-94; scientific method, 21, 26-27, 61
secularization, 236-37
self-rule, 32, 149-51, 156-57, 161-62, 216
Senegambia, 93
sensory: direct perception, 65, 75, 183; indirect perception, 40; and nonsensory, 57; perception, 27, 46, 51–52, 55, 57, 110–15, 121–23, 183–84, 219–20n32
al-Shanqiti, Muhammad Mahmoud Amin, 31, 215–16n17
al-Shartuni, 234n43
Shawqi, Ahmed, 109
al-Sheikh Abu al-Huda al-Sayyadi, 198
al-Shidyaq, Ahmed Faris, 64–69, 168–69, 171–72, 198, 215, 227, 234
Shukrallah, Hani, 205
Shukri, Ghali, 252n1
simile. See *tashbih*
slavery, 15, 83, 92, 102, 155, 178
social totality. See *al-nas*
soul, 50–55, 216–18n20
sovereignty, 139–205. See also *al-nas*
spectator. See audience

specter. See *khayal*
stage, 25–27, 58–64, 82–91; directions, 88; lights, 82, 92, 102; object, 92, 97–102, 126–28; prop, 88, 91, 97, 102; staging, 75–78. See also *athar*; *khayal*; *al-nas*
al-sunna. See *hadith*

al-Tabari, Abu Ja'far, 108
tafsir, 36, 163, 174, 204–5
al-Tahtawi, Rifa'a, 58–64, 75–78, 109, 155–57, 223n54, 224n60, 229n4, 233n34
tashbih, 216–18n20, 246–47n36
al-Tawhidi, Abu Hayyan, 20, 248–49n42
tawkil, 157
tawriya, 216n20
textuality, 103, 202–4, 237n10
theater. See stage
time. See *athar*; *al-nas*
topography. See *khitat*
tradition: critical, 59; philosophic, 150–51; poetic, 145; traditional form, 1–18; *turath*, 35, 204–5, 234n43
transcendent(al). See divine, the; immanence
trial, 25–27, 61–62, 87–96, 148–49, 176, 196–97, 199–202, 250n55. See also stage
trope of the encounter, 1–10, 203–6
turath. See tradition
al-Tuwayrani, Hassan Husni, 14–15, 28–29, 32, 35–37, 42, 63, 69–71, 99, 104–6, 114–15, 119–20, 125, 127–31, 195, 198, 233n38, 235n1, 245n26

'Ukasha, Usama Anwar, 251n69
union, 129, 154–55; university, 240n39

universal, the, 21–27, 51, 70, 85–91, 96–97, 107, 113–14, 125–26, 181–85, 190–94. *See also athar*; civilization
'Urabi, Ahmed, 197–201
'Urabi Revolt, 100, 215, 252n2
'Uthman, Jalal, 171
utopia, 120, 128, 151

virtues, 14, 15, 38, 50, 56, 60, 62, 65–66, 76, 79, 142, 165–67, 169, 177–78, 182, 187, 196, 201–2, 218n23, 224n60, 238n20; and vices, 165–67
visuality. *See khayal, al-nas*

voice, 8, 89, 103, 148, 171–72, 178, 202, 243n12. *See also* narrator
Voltaire, 53

Wajdi, Muhammad Farid, 252n1
waqf/endowment, 134–36, 189
world literature, 4, 8–9
al-Wujud, 55, 249; *al-madini*, 55

al-Zamakhshari, Abu al-Qasim, 52, 53, 55
Zaydan, Jurji, 253n4

Maha AbdelMegeed is assistant professor of Arabic Literature at the American University of Beirut.

www.ingramcontent.com/pod-product-compliance
Lightning Source LLC
Chambersburg PA
CBHW030527230426
43665CB00010B/790